EXPLORING THE WO

Wines and Spirits

EXPLORING THE WORLD OF
Wines and Spirits

CHRISTOPHER FIELDEN
in association with the
Wine & Spirit Education Trust

with a foreword by
JANCIS ROBINSON

WINE & SPIRIT EDUCATION TRUST ®

Wine & Spirit Education Trust
39-45 Bermondsey Street, London SE1 3XF
e-mail wset@wset.co.uk
internet www.wset.co.uk

A CIP catalogue record for this book is available from the British Library

ISBN 0 9517936 6 7

PHOTOGRAPHIC CREDITS
CEPHAS: 3, 4, 19B, 61, 71, 93, 95, 98, 105, 118, 126B, 156, 182, 193
(Mick Rock), 11B (Dario Fusaro), 20 (R and K Muschenetz), 21L, 21R
(Kevin Judd), 28 (Ian Shaw), 56 (Kjell Karlsson), 103, 114 (Herbert
Lehrmann), 135T (Wink Lorch), 159 (Kevin Argue)

46, 47, 48, 50, 51, 52, 53 (CIVB), 14B, 49B, 54, 73, 76 (Sopexa); 10
(Eugenio Hughes/Wines of Chile); 49T (Richard Bampfield/Château
Preuillac); 171T, 171B (CIVC), 99, 100, 101 (Austrian Wine Marketing
Board); 147B (Martin Forsyth/The Faldo Press Office); 187 (The Sherry
Istitute of Spain); 203T, 203B, 208, 209 (Diageo); 206L (Bacardi-Martini)

WSET: 7, 11T, 15, 18, 22, 25B, 29, 32, 64, 65, 67, 69, 70, 112T, 112B,
131T, 131B, 132, 133, 139T, 140, 141, 144, 147T, 149, 151T, 151B,
152, 155, 157T, 157B, 158, 162, 163, 164, 165, 166, 167, 179, 181,
201 (Michael Buriak), 5, 25T, 63 (Nicolla Greaves), 38 (Caxton Wines),
81 (David Wrigley MW), 125 (Erica Dent), 6, 8, 13, 14, 17, 19T, 21T, 23,
24, 33T, 33B, 34, 39T, 39B, 40, 57, 63, 73T, 74, 75, 78, 79, 80, 84, 88,
89, 90, 91, 92, 104T, 104B, 107, 110T, 110B, 111, 116, 122, 123, 124,
126, 128, 130, 135L, 135R, 136, 137, 139B, 173T, 173B, 177, 184,
186, 188, 189, 196, 199, 205, 206R, 214, 215 (WSET collection)

COVER PICTURES
Background picture: Victoria Clare
Top: Sopexa
Middle: Michael Buriak
Bottom: Diageo

Designed by Peter Dolton
Production services by Book Production Consultants plc
Printed and bound in Italy by Lego Spa

Contents

SECTION 4: CENTRAL AND SOUTH-EASTERN EUROPE

SECTION 5: SOUTHERN EUROPE AND THE MEDITERRANEAN

SECTION 6: NEW WORLD REGIONS

SECTION 7: SPARKLING AND FORTIFIED WINES

SECTION 8: SPIRITS AND LIQUEURS

APPENDICES

Foreword

As someone responsible for two of the meatier wine reference books, *The Oxford Companion to Wine* and *The World Atlas of Wine*, I am only too aware of how rapidly the world of wine is now changing. Updating the Oxford book for example generally involves some change to at least half the entries, and the addition of an extraordinary number of new ones.

This is why the WSET sees the need to update *Exploring the World of Wines and Spirits* regularly. Britain's (increasingly the world's) premier source of wine education has to be up to date and seen to be up to date with the myriad developments in wine production and consumption the world over. I am sure that the teaching and courses now offered by the WSET are unrecognisably different from those I benefited from as I began my wine writing career in the 1970s. I seem to remember that we spent a great deal of time studying the minutiae of sherry production, something that is – quite unjustifiably in my view – not exactly in the most sought-after aspect of wine education nowadays. And even when I did my Master of Wine exams in 1984, Australian wine was still regarded as at best a novelty, at worst a joke. (Who's laughing now?)

I was thrilled when in 1978 I learnt that I had won the top prize for Diploma students, the Rouyer Guillet cup. Until then I was not at all sure what standard my wine knowledge was, but I was sure that the WSET courses gave me a great deal of confidence in my newfound work. I knew, because an eminent third party overseeing the syllabus had seen to it, that I really had covered the ground in its entirety, not just those little byways that interested me most.

I know that the courses have been constantly adapted, particularly in recent years, to reflect the sort of wines most often made and drunk now. When people tell me they want to get into the wine trade, or simply advance their wine knowledge for their personal enjoyment, I always draw their attention to the WSET courses, whether in the UK or further afield.

I'm sure that you will find this book as useful as I found my WSET courses.

Jancis Robinson

Introduction

Welcome to *Exploring the World of Wines and Spirits*.

Since the Wine & Spirit Education Trust was founded in 1969, the interest in knowing more about wines and spirits has grown immensely. This is the case for people involved in making, distributing, retailing and serving wine, but also amongst enthusiastic consumers who are discovering more and more the fascinations of the world of wines and spirits.

Whilst this book is the prescribed text for the Wine & Spirit Education Trust's Advanced Certificate Course, it also gives a fascinating insight into the world of wines and spirits for those who are reading it purely for pleasure and to enhance their personal knowledge.

As more and more countries start producing quality wines – and more and more spirits companies diversify their offerings – it is very easy to lose track of exciting new developments within the wine and spirits market and *Exploring the World of Wines and Spirits* is aimed at ensuring that it provides the most up-to-date information in a readable, yet informative, manner.

I very much hope that you enjoy this book and if you feel that you would like to take a formal qualification in wines and spirits, or indeed attend one of our more informal courses, please do not hesitate to contact us or visit our website at www.wset.co.uk for further details.

Ian Harris
Chief Executive, Wine & Spirit Education Trust

Acknowledgements

The creation of a book is rarely an easy process and this is no exception. Starting with what could be described as a mis-conception, the pregnancy was at times painful, but we hope that we have now produced a bouncing baby book. In the first place thanks are due to staff at the Wine & Spirit Education Trust. The midwife in chief might be said to be Tony Moss, who has edited and reshaped the material, with the help of Karen Douglas, who has acted as project manager and Erica Dent and Sandra Clement reading the proofs to ensure the book matches its specification.

At the beginning, a number of consultant specialists were called in. These included: Nicholas Belfrage MW, David Bird MW, Kerry Brady, Michael Brajkovich MW, Javier Hidalgo, Robin Kinahan MW, Richard Mayson, Jasper Morris MW, John Radford and Tom Stevenson. They have contributed much in seeing that this book is as up to date and relevant as possible.

We are grateful to the various wine promotional bodies and commercial offices, who have always been willing to help, in particular Jean-Pierre Platel and Vincent Dumot at the BNIC; Anne Marbot at the CIVB; Richard Bampfield MW; Chris Skyrme and Catherine Manac'h at Sopexa; Laurence Wipff and Séverine Lelièvre at the CIVA; Iris Kovács at the Austrian Wine Marketing Board; Margarita Perez at Wines from Spain; Mari A. Kirrane at the Alcohol and Tobacco Tax and Trade Bureau; and John Stoyles and Anita Jackson at Wines of Chile.

A debt of gratitude is owed to Sue Gray and Roz Williams at Book Production Consultants plc for guiding us through the process of converting raw text into the book you now hold. We would particularly like to thank Peter Dolton at BPC for his exceptional work on the design of the book, and Chris Groom at Design Study for his work on the maps. We would also like to thank Gavin Williams at Direct Wines for supplying examples of their labels.

Christopher Fielden
September 2004

1 Grape Varieties

The grape variety used accounts for a large part of the style and quality of many wines, which is why it is common for wines to be labelled by variety. But what exactly is a grape variety? The grape is the fruit of a vine, a member of the *Ampelidaceae* family. Winemakers are concerned only with the *Vitis* genus of that family, which is divided into a number of species. Of these, just one, *Vitis vinifera*, is our major concern, for more than 99 per cent of all wines are made from this species. All the familiar grape variety names, like Chardonnay, Cabernet Sauvignon and Merlot, are varieties of *V. vinifera*.

Other members of the *Vitis* genus may, however, have smaller parts to play in the wine story. *V. labrusca* grapes are grown for wine in the eastern states of the United States. As you will see later in this chapter, hybrids of *V. riparia*, *V. berlandieri* and *V. rupestris* often provide the rootstock on which *V. vinifera* scions are grafted. These species are of American origin, having been imported to Europe initially in the nineteenth century. Wine produced from their fruit generally has a distinctive flavour, which is often described as foxy.

WHAT IS A GRAPE VARIETY?

The reproductive organs of the grape are contained in the flowers. The grape has evolved as a wind-pollinated, animal-dispersed species. So, while the flowers are small and insignificant, the fruit is brightly coloured, sweet and attractive. The flowers of nearly all commercial grape varieties are hermaphrodite, that is, they contain both male and female organs within the same flower. Sexual reproduction commences when the anthers (equivalent to testes) mature and release pollen (equivalent to spermatozoa). The pollen is transported by the wind, and lands on the stigmas of other grape flowers. This is the process of pollination. The pollen transfers its genetic material via a tube to the ovary, where it combines with the genetic material contained in the ovules (eggs), in the process of fertilisation. The fertilised ovules will develop into seeds, and the ovary develops into the surrounding flesh and skin of the grape. Just as with human reproduction, the seed will have a selection of genetic material from both parents. Also, as with humans, the expressed characteristics of the resulting 'offspring' are not simply a combination of the expressed characteristics of the parents. They may favour one parent over the other, and the offspring will exhibit some characteristics that are to be found in neither parent. The expressed characteristics that interest the wine producer are aspects such

as yields, hardiness, disease-resistance, fruit character and levels of tannin, acidity and sugars within the grape. Sexual reproduction results in the natural evolution of species and creates the possibility of adaptation through natural selection.

Hybrids

A scientist or nursery is capable of effecting artificial evolution by 'marrying' two separate species, in order to gain the benefits of both (a bit like crossing a lion with a tiger to produce something with stripes and a mane – this would never happen in the wild, but has been done in zoos). In the world of wine this 'marriage' is between two different vine species such as the European *V. vinifera* vine, the American *V. labrusca*, *V. riparia*, *V. rupestris* or *V. berlandieri*, or the Asiatic *V. amurensis*. The resultant plant is described as a hybrid. Generally speaking, such plants are forbidden for the production of quality wine in the European Union (EU). However, they are widely grown in a number of countries as they may be particularly resistant to heavy frosts or excessive humidity. Their most important use in viticulture is as rootstock. Here, one might combine the low vigour and phylloxera tolerance of *V. riparia* with the deep roots and phylloxera resistance of *V. rupestris*. The resulting hybrid might then be fertilised with another hybrid that has gained some tolerance of alkaline soils from a phylloxera-resistant *V. berlandieri* parent. Commercial rootstocks are generally the result of an elaborate series of hybrid fertilisations, followed by trials to see if the desired characteristics have emerged. When the relations between genes and expressed characteristics are more fully understood, direct genetic modification may allow suitable material to be developed in a much less laborious way.

Crossings

Crossings occur when reproduction takes place the natural way, when the parents are different varieties of the same species. Just as it is possible for two dark-haired human parents to have a child with red hair, there is no reason to expect that the crossing will inherit all of its characteristics from the parent varieties. Morio-Muskat, which gives overwhelmingly floral wines, has Sylvaner and Pinot Blanc as its parents, both of which are quite neutral in character. Once created, the crossing is a new variety and can be propagated only through cuttings, like all other varieties; it cannot be recreated. (Riesling has been crossed with Sylvaner on countless occasions, giving different results every time.) Some crossings, such as Pinotage (Pinot Noir × Cinsault) in South Africa and Müller-Thurgau in Germany, are long established in the vineyards of the world. Among the centres that specialise in the development of new varieties in this way are the Davis Campus of the University of California and the Research Institute at Geisenheim in Germany. The former focuses on creating high-yielding quality varieties, such as Ruby Cabernet (Cabernet Sauvignon × Carignan), that cope well with the high temperatures of the Californian Central Valley. The latter has created many aromatic varieties that achieve high sugar levels in cool climates, such as Morio-Muskat.

Varieties and Asexual Propagation

While hybridisation and crossing are sexual operations, cloning is an asexual process. Cuttings are taken from individual vines that show desirable traits. It is important to realise that a seed taken for example from a Riesling grape will not grow into a Riesling vine, as the genetic instructions in the seed will be as different from the vine as the genes of a baby are from its mother. The only way to ensure that one vine has the same characteristics as another is to take a cutting and allow it to grow into a new vine. The human equivalent would be to take a tissue sample and attempt to grow a human clone from it. While we may not

do this yet with people, plants have been cloned for hundreds of years. Over the centuries, unsuitable vines died or were removed and cuttings from the better vines replaced them in the classic vineyards. Whole regions came to be planted with cuttings that could theoretically trace their roots back to one chosen vine. This is how classic varieties originally developed.

Clones

Growing a plant from a cutting requires the genetic instructions to be copied every time a new cell is created. Although the copying is very accurate, occasionally mistakes, known as mutations, occur. These tiny changes mean that plants propagated using cuttings may show small differences. Propagating a species using cuttings is a form of cloning. The slightly different versions of a variety that arise due to mutations during the cloning process are said to be different clones of the same variety. Within a variety, some of the clones may show outstanding natural traits, such as particular flavour characteristics, high yields or disease resistance. A vinegrower or a plant nursery may then select the clones with the desired qualities for further propagation. The development of a single desirable clone may take many generations. Clonal selection is particularly important with ancient varieties such as Pinot Noir, whose immediate family includes members with widely varying capabilities. Strictly speaking, Pinot Blanc and Pinot Gris are not grape varieties in their own right. They are clones (mutations) of Pinot Noir.

Phylloxera and Grafting

The turning point for the development of modern viticulture was the wholesale destruction of European vineyards by the phylloxera louse in the second half of the nineteenth century. The louse is

Patch of phylloxera-affected vines within an otherwise healthy-looking vineyard. Oregon, USA.

Cabernet Sauvignon head-grafted on to less profitable Sauvignon Blanc rootstocks, St Helena, Napa Co., California.

easily transported on plant material, and the few wine-producing regions that remain unaffected now have to maintain strict quarantine procedures. The wounds that the louse makes while feeding on the vine roots allow bacteria and fungi to enter, leading to decay and disease and the eventual death of *vinifera* vines over a period of years. American vines form protective layers beneath the feeding wounds, thus preventing further damage. As the louse killed off the existing *vinifera* vines, growers rapidly had to find a solution to their problems. The first recourse was to treat the vineyards, but this proved to be ineffectual. The next solution was to plant American *V. labrusca* vines, which were known to tolerate phylloxera. Unfortunately, the wine that these gave proved to be of an unacceptable quality. The next step was to try breeding in the American vines' tolerance by crossing *V. vinifera* and American species, but this was only partially successful. Eventually it was discovered that European varieties could resist phylloxera if they were grafted on to American rootstock. The task of creating suitable rootstocks to match soil types and grape varieties was not simple, and research continues in this area. For some varieties, such as Folle Blanche (in Cognac), no truly suitable rootstocks have been found; as a result these varieties have largely disappeared in their traditional regions.

There are many regions of the world where phylloxera is not a problem, including Chile, South Australia, much of Argentina and Hungary. This could be due to the geographical isolation of the region and strict quarantine procedures. Sandy soils are known to restrict the life-cycle of phylloxera. In such places vines do not have to be grafted but can be grown on their own **rootstock**, which means that planting is much cheaper. However, there are other reasons for grafting – the increasing use of drip-irrigation has led to increasing problems with nematodes and many growers are now using resistant rootstock as a defence. Ungrafted vines are now the exception rather than the rule.

With grafting, each vine consists of two parts: the American rootstock and the European scion. Just as one selects the variety, so one selects the rootstock, for it can offer a variety of benefits and must be suitable for the soil into which it will be planted. Grafting traditionally was a labour-intensive craft; today it is generally done with a simple bench-mounted machine. Major wineries will have their own nurseries; others will buy from commercial nurseries. Grafting is generally carried out with young vines, though mention should also be made of head-grafting. This is

particularly prevalent in New World vineyards. Consumption of wine is increasingly becoming a matter of fashion. For example, promotion of the benefits of the Mediterranean diet quickly led to a demand for red wine, particularly soft red wine. As it normally takes a minimum of three years for a vine to come into production, it can be difficult to cater for such rapid changes in the market. One answer is head-grafting. By this system the top of an existing vine, say a Sauvignon Blanc, is removed and, a cutting of Merlot is grafted on to the plant. This should produce the required fruit at the next vintage.

Selection of Grape Variety

It is almost impossible to calculate how many different grape varieties are grown, but the figure will be in the thousands. Many will have only local relevance, but some have a global reputation, either because they are grown around the world or because they are responsible for giving one or more of the world's great wines. The most important of these are listed below. In most of the wine-producing areas of Western Europe, the grapes that are grown are there by tradition, often backed by law. In the New World there is much more pragmatism and experimentation, and a host of varieties can be seen growing side by side.

MAJOR GRAPE VARIETIES
White Grapes

Chardonnay takes its name from a village in the Mâconnais, but has expanded widely from its Burgundian roots and is planted around the world. It can produce quality wines in a wide range of climates, though the style varies considerably. Cool climates, such as Champagne and Chablis, give very steely wines, medium to light in body, with high acidity and apple or green plum fruit notes. More favourable sites, and slightly warmer regions, result in more citrus-flavoured wines. In hotter regions, the fruit character tends towards melon and peach, and even exotic flavours such as banana, mango and fig. Chardonnay from very hot regions can be very full-bodied, high in alcohol and low in acidity. The fruit character of Chardonnay is rarely very pronounced; it could be described as non-aromatic. This means that other characteristics such as vineyard character and winemaking techniques can contribute much to the flavour of a Chardonnay wine. It is common to use malolactic fermentation, which softens the fruit and acidity and gives flavours of butter and hazelnut. Chardonnay also takes well to oak, and many are fermented and/or aged in French or American oak. This gives some tannin and rich, toasty, nutty flavours to the wine. Lees stirring is also used to give complexity and body to Chardonnay wines. Classic regions include Burgundy, Champagne, California, Australia and New Zealand, but high-quality Chardonnay wines are made in many other regions. In the vineyard it is liable to suffer from powdery mildew.

Sauvignon Blanc is planted widely in Bordeaux, in the Loire Valley and the New World, particularly New Zealand. If planted in cool regions on poor soils, it has the classic green, herbaceous flavours, often reminiscent of gooseberries, green pepper, grass, passion fruit or elderflower. In warmer regions, it can fail to develop much aromatic character and just have hints of peach. Oak is sometimes used to give the wines more body, particularly in the United States, where the oak-aged wines are frequently labelled as *Fumé Blanc*. Most Sauvignons are best consumed while young and fruity. Those that do not simply fade can develop vegetal aromas of asparagus and peas as they age, which some people enjoy. Classic regions include Sancerre, Pouilly-Fumé and Marlborough. Good examples can also be found from other parts of the Loire and New Zealand, as well as South Africa, Chile, Bordeaux, the Midi and California.

Riesling is widely planted around the world. For many years it seems to have been about to become fashionable again, though this is probably wishful thinking by those who love Riesling wines and

Ripening Chardonnay bunch.

cannot believe that they will continue to be unappreciated by the public for much longer. It is a fruity, aromatic grape variety that retains its acidity. It ripens late, but is very hardy, making it an ideal source for late-harvest wines. It can produce great wines in a range of styles, in a range of climates. In cool climates, such as the Mosel, it can have a very fresh grape and apple fruit character, and the high natural acidity is often balanced with some sugar. Late-harvested grapes from these regions, and vines grown in warmer regions such as Alsace, Austria and the Clare Valley, result in more citrus and peach fruit notes. Some Australian Rieslings have a distinct lime fruit character. Like Chardonnay, Riesling produces wines that vary with and reflect their location. Unlike Chardonnay, Riesling does not benefit from techniques such as oak-ageing. One might almost argue that with its distinctive fruit, it does not need any added flavours. The exceptions to this are the extremely fine dessert wines made with botrytis-affected Riesling grapes. Due to their high acidity, even quite modest Riesling wines can age very well, developing notes of honey, smoke and sometimes something like petrol. Classic regions are the Mosel, Nahe, Rheingau and Pfalz in Germany; the Wachau in Austria; Alsace in France; the Clare and Eden Valleys in Australia; and Marlborough and Nelson in New Zealand.

Because of its status, **Riesling**'s name has been widely borrowed, particularly in newer vineyard areas, by a range of varieties that are no way

Botrytis affecting a bunch of Riesling grapes at Geisenheim.

Pinot Gris produces its finest wines in Alsace, though this style is copied in other regions, including Tasmania and parts of New Zealand and the Pacific north-west USA. Even the dry wines tend to be almost oily, rather high in alcohol and low in acidity. There can be rich, aromatic, exotic fruit, such a melon, ripe banana and mango, and sometimes botrytis flavours can appear in the dry wines. Botrytis-affected dessert wines are also made. In north-east Italy a different approach is taken with **Pinot Grigio**. The grapes tend to be harvested early to retain acidity and avoid the development of too much fruit. The resulting wines are generally light and more neutral in character, with crisp acidity. This popular light, crisp, style is increasingly being copied in many New World regions. The variety is also grown in Germany, where it is known as Rülander or Grauburgunder.

Viognier is becoming increasingly fashionable. In simple terms, it may be thought of as a variety that offers some of the soft, full-bodied texture of Chardonnay, but with more aromatic fruit character. The great difficulty with Viognier, apart from its tendency to give low yields, is that it rapidly builds up very high sugar levels, often before its delicate peach, pear and violet aromas have had a chance to develop. This can result in some unbalanced, high-alcohol wines. Once the flavours have appeared in the grapes, careful handling is needed to retain them in the wine. Oak-ageing is sometimes used, but it is easy for the resulting contact with air to destroy the fruit. The finest Viogniers come from the tiny regions of Condrieu and Château Grillet in the northern Rhône. These express all the delicate perfume, silky texture and mineral flavours that the grape can show. There are many fine examples of this variety being made in the south of France, Australia and California. Generally, these are wines to drink young, though a small number can age.

related. The true Riesling is sometimes labelled as *Rhine Riesling*, *Johannisberg Riesling* or *Weisser Riesling* in New World countries, to distinguish it from Hunter Valley Riesling (Semillon) or Cape Riesling (Crouchen Blanc). These latter names are not permitted for wines imported into the EU however, so within the EU any wine labelled as Riesling will be Riesling. The exception is **Welschriesling**, which is a totally unrelated variety. To avoid any confusion, therefore, Welschriesling must always appear under its full name or one of its synonyms:

Welsch Riesling in Austria, Hungary and Bulgaria
Laski Rizling in Slovenia, Croatia and Serbia
Olasz Rizling in Hungary.

Compared to the Rhine Riesling, it is an easy vine to cultivate, producing a less delicate wine with lower acidity. It suffers widely from over-cropping, but when treated well it can produce crisp, refreshing, dry white wines, and some sensational botrytis-affected dessert wines.

Muscat is not one variety, but a prolific family that is represented around the world. The wines, which are often sparkling or fortified, have one thing in common: an intense grapey flavour. The aristocrat is the Muscat Blanc à Petits Grains. This is used for Asti, certain Vins Doux Naturels, the sweet Muscats of Samos, and a version of this is used for Rutherglen Muscats. It gives the most complex, full spectrum of aromatic notes. Unaged wines are full of grape, peach, rose and citrus aromas. Those that see oxidative oak-ageing become very dark in colour, and develop aromas of raisins, fruit cake, toffee and coffee, yet always seem to retain their characteristic Muscat perfume. More commonly found is the Muscat of Alexandria, which is used for other French Vins Doux Naturels, Spanish Moscatels and as a component in some mainly medium-dry wines in California, Australia and South Africa. This is a less aromatically complex variety, and the wines tend to smell simply of grapes. A third kind of Muscat, **Muscat Ottonel**, is used for attractively perfumed dry white wines in Alsace and Central Europe. With the exceptions of the oak-aged fortified wines, none of these lasts long once bottled, and all are best consumed while they are youthful, fruity and fresh.

Chenin Blanc is capable of producing a broad range of wines from the bone-dry to the great sweet Loire wines of Bonnezeaux and Quarts de Chaume. It is also widely planted in South Africa (where it is known as Steen) and California. The great difficulty with Chenin Blanc is that it ripens very unevenly. If grapes are not harvested very selectively, perhaps in tris, there is a danger that a portion of unripe grapes will result in vegetal, leafy flavours in the wine. Wines made from Chenin Blanc tend to be high in acidity and can have some rather unusual fruit characteristics. There may be vegetal notes, aromas of green apples and flavours of citrus pith in young, dry Chenin Blancs. Late-harvested sweet versions can have powerful aromas of botrytis, and exotic fruit, such as pineapple; their intense sweetness will be balanced by high acidity. The finest Chenin Blancs age extremely well, developing flavours of honey and toast. Much of the wine made in South Africa and California is simple, fruity and often slightly off-dry, though there are some high-quality wines made in these regions. The classic region for Chenin Blanc is the Loire, particularly appellations such as Vouvray, Savennières and Côteaux du Layon.

Black Grapes

Cabernet Sauvignon is the grape with perhaps the widest reputation for the production of red wines. It is the classic grape of the Médoc in Bordeaux and is widely planted throughout the New World. It buds late, reducing the possibility of damage from spring frosts. The bunches are loosely formed and the grapes are thick-skinned, have a high skin-to-pulp ratio and are resistant to rot and insects. It gives low yields of full-bodied, high-acid, tannic wines, which age well. The classic flavours are of blackcurrants. In cooler regions, this can be accompanied by notes of green capsicum and cedarwood, which become more accentuated as the wine ages. Warm climate Cabernet Sauvignon can have more of a black

Lyre-trained Cabernet Sauvignon vineyards in Oakville, California.

cherry, and even black olive, fruit character. Many Australian Cabernet Sauvignons, particularly those from Coonawarra, also have distinctive hints of mint, eucalyptus or menthol. Classic regions include the Médoc, Coonawarra, Hawkes Bay, Napa and Colchagua.

Merlot is the other of the two great grapes of Bordeaux and is frequently blended with Cabernet Sauvignon. It is dominant in Saint-Emilion and Pomerol. With the increasing demand for red wine as part of a healthy diet, it has become very much in demand, leading to extensive plantings, particularly in California, Chile and the south of France. Unblended, it can give soft, undemanding, easy-to-drink wines with soft tannins. The best quality Merlots tend to follow one of two styles. Some are made from grapes that are harvested as late as possible to generate the maximum possible degree of intense purple colour, blackberry and plum fruit, and soft, velvet-textured tannins, combined with a rich, full body due to high alcohol and concentrated fruit. All this may be supported by toasty flavours of new oak. This is the 'international style', and is made with great success in many New World countries, the south of France and some Bordeaux estates. The other approach is to harvest earlier and make a wine with lighter body and alcohol, but with higher acidity and more of a red fruit character (raspberries, ripe strawberries), and maybe even some vegetal, leafy aromas. The second approach is rarely found outside Bordeaux.

Syrah/Shiraz is thought to be one of the oldest varieties. It is responsible for the great reds of the northern Rhône, and plantings are being increased in the south of France to improve blends. It is the most widely planted variety in Australia, where it is often blended with Cabernet Sauvignon. It is also becoming increasingly important in South America. Typical Syrah/Shiraz is very deep in colour and has blackberry fruit flavours. In cooler climates, the acidity and tannin levels can be very high, and the blackberry fruit can be accompanied by notes of black pepper and sometimes mint. Hot climate Syrah/Shiraz is more full-bodied, with soft tannins and earthy, leathery flavours and spice notes that are more like liquorice and anise. Shiraz wines can age extremely well.

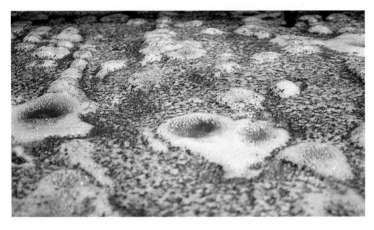

Fermenting Shiraz grapes, McLaren Vale.

Grenache/Garnacha is the most widely planted red wine grape in Spain, from where it originates. It is the main grape of Navarra and is an important grape in Rioja, particularly in the Rioja Baja. In France it is grown in the southern Rhône and the Midi. It is also found in California and South Australia, particularly McLaren Vale. It is responsible for many of the world's greatest rosé wines and is a vital constituent of many great blended wines, including Châteauneuf-du-Pape. In this guise, it benefits from oak-ageing. The sweet, thin-skinned grapes give wines that are high in alcohol and are full-bodied, but light in colour and tannins. The wines can oxidise easily, and often show a clear browning at the rim, even when quite young. Classic Grenache has red fruit flavours, such as strawberry and raspberry, and hints of white pepper, which develop into flavours of leather, tar and toffee as the wine ages.

Pinot Noir was originally planted in Burgundy, where it has created the reputation of that region's red wines. It ripens early, and is well suited to the climate there. It has very tight bunches of small berries, which give a very sweet juice. Because of the tightness of the bunches, it is prone to rot, though due to systemic sprays this is now much less of a problem than it used to be. Young Pinot Noir wine typically displays a fruity perfume of raspberries, strawberries or red cherries, and because the grape is thin-skinned it usually has soft light tannins and is seldom deep in colour. Pinot Noirs tend to age unpredictably, leading some to claim that they are at their best for a very short period only. This is true if you like your Pinot Noir in one style only, but many Pinot Noirs can be enjoyed at all stages of their life, without having to battle with mouth-puckering tannins or raw acidity. With age, vegetal and farmyard aromas develop that can be off-putting or exciting, depending on your tastes. Outside of Burgundy, Classic Pinot Noir wines can be found in Carneros and Sonoma (California), Walker Bay (South Africa), the Yarra Valley (Australia) and Martinborough, Marlborough and Central Otago (New Zealand). It is also an important constituent of Champagne, and many New World sparkling wines.

Sangiovese at its best produces the greatest Chianti, Brunello di Montalcino and Vino Nobile di Montepulciano, as well as many other non-DOC Tuscan wines. It may also be blended with other international varieties, particularly Cabernet Sauvignon, to produce 'Super-Tuscans'. Typical Sangiovese is not aromatic in the manner of Cabernet, Syrah or Pinot Noir. Its wines are high in acidity, with a sour red cherry fruit character, sometimes rather astringent tannins and earthy, dusty aromas that are reminiscent of tea leaves. It is widely grown throughout central and southern Italy, but, with the exception of Argentina, it is only recently being grown in other countries.

Tempranillo is widely planted throughout northern Spain and is considered to be the country's leading quality red grape variety. It appears under a wide range of names: **Ull de Llebre**, **Cencibel** and **Tinto del País**, as well as **Tinta Roriz** and **Aragonez** in Portugal. It is the major constituent of the best Riojas, as well as the wines of Ribera del Duero. It ripens early and grows best on chalky soil. It is light on tannins, so is often best when blended with other varieties. It has a nose of soft leather and can taste of ripe strawberries. Outside Iberia, it is well established in Argentina, and producers in other New World countries are beginning to experiment with it.

Further information about these varieties can be found in the sections covering the regions where they are grown.

Climate and Weather

2

To achieve optimal ripeness, a grape needs approximately a minimum of 1500 hours of sunshine during the ripening season. Red grapes generally need more than white. This is one reason why, in vineyard areas with a cool climate, white wines are more widely produced than red. A vine also needs approximately 700 mm of rainfall in a year, though less may suffice in a cooler climate. In many regions rainfall may be supplemented by irrigation, but until recently this was generally forbidden in the vineyards of the European Union.

Although wild vines grow widely throughout the world, commercial plantings of V. *vinifera* for winemaking are largely concentrated into two broad bands in the northern and southern hemispheres, roughly between 30° and 50° latitude. Here there is the ideal balance of warmth and coldness, sunshine and rainfall. There are however plantings outside these bands, for example in Britain and in the subtropical north-west of Argentina, and advances in viticultural techniques have allowed plantings in such diverse countries as Cuba, Venezuela, India and Thailand.

CLIMATE CLASSIFICATION

Climate can be understood as an indication of what weather to expect in a typical year. The most important aspects of climate for the vine are temperature and rainfall. These depend on many factors, including latitude, altitude, topography and proximity to bodies of water.

Because water heats up and cools down much more slowly than land, it has a moderating effect on temperature fluctuations. Regions close to large bodies of water have a **Maritime climate** characterised by warm summers and mild winters. A maritime climate where most of the rainfall occurs in winter is known as a **Mediterranean climate**. This climate, with dry summers, is particularly suited to viticulture and is found in California, Chile, South Africa and much of south and south-west Australia, as well as the shores of the Mediterranean. If a vineyard is in the middle of a substantial landmass, say in La Mancha in the centre of Spain, it will probably have a **Continental climate** with extreme temperatures in both winter and summer.

Cold currents such as the Alaska Current (western USA), the Humboldt Current (Chile) and the Benguela Current (South Africa) have a marked cooling effect on the climate of the local vineyards. Conversely, the Gulf Stream has a significant warming effect on the climates of north-west Europe. Vineyards close to rivers are less likely to suffer from frost damage, because the movement of the water encourages air currents. Where warm air and cold bodies of water meet (as in Tokaji or Sauternes), mists are created which can encourage the onset of noble rot, enabling the production of sweet wines. **Shallow lakes**, like the Neusiedlersee in Austria can have a similar effect.

Mountains have many effects. They can cast a 'rain shadow': the Vosges mountains for example protect the vineyards of Alsace as the rain falls on the western slopes in Lorraine, making Alsace one of the driest regions in France or they can be a source of cold winds such as the Mistral in the Rhône valley. Temperatures drop with increased altitude, so in regions that may otherwise be too hot for viticulture, suitable sites can be found at high altitudes (Salta in Argentina; Orange in Australia). Higher altitudes also give greater differences in temperature between day and night. Cool nights can help some varieties ripen without losing acidity or fresh fruit aromas.

There are a number of ways to classify climatic conditions. As far as European wine law is concerned, regions are divided into Zones A, B, CIa, CIb, CII, CIIIa and CIIIb. Legislation concerning permission to enrich or de-acidify varies according to the zone in which the vineyard is located. For example in the coldest zone, A, the alcoholic strength of a wine may, in the poorest years, be increased by up to 4.5 per cent by enrichment and the wine can be de-acidified. In the hottest zone, tartaric acid may be added, but enrichment and de-acidification are forbidden. In California, climates are generally classified using degree-days, working on the principle of heat summation. The amount that the temperature exceeds 50° F (10° C) is added for each day of

THE WORLD WINE PRODUCING AREAS

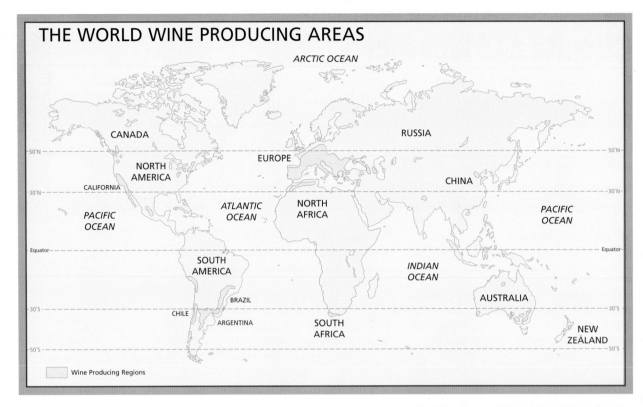

ARCTIC OCEAN

CANADA

RUSSIA

50°N

EUROPE

NORTH
AMERICA

CHINA

CALIFORNIA

30°N

*PACIFIC
OCEAN*

*ATLANTIC
OCEAN*

NORTH
AFRICA

*PACIFIC
OCEAN*

Equator

SOUTH
AMERICA

INDIAN
OCEAN

BRAZIL

AUSTRALIA

30°S

CHILE

ARGENTINA

SOUTH
AFRICA

NEW
ZEALAND

50°S

Wine Producing Regions

the growing season, giving a measure of total usable heat for the year. In Australia, a similar system operates using the Mean Temperature of the Warmest Month, with adjustments made to take account of other factors such as hours of sunlight, humidity, rainfall and evaporation, and continentality (the difference between mean summer and winter temperatures). No system is perfect, as other factors can have an effect on the development of the vine.

A region will have an overall climate, but individual vineyard plots may differ climatically from their neighbour. It is on factors such as these, and the soil, that the hierarchies of vineyard classification in Burgundy, Alsace and Germany are based. Particularly in regions with a more marginal climate, maximum exposure to the sun is essential. **Site climate** is the climate of an individual vineyard site, or part of a vineyard. It is sometimes referred to as 'micro-climate', but specialists reserve this last term for the climate *within* the vine leaf canopy. A skilled vinegrower can affect the climate of an individual vine by **canopy management**. Extra shady leaf cover can simulate the conditions of a region that is a few degrees cooler. Alternatively, leaf plucking can maximise exposure of grapes to the sun, and make the maximum use of sunlight in cooler regions.

The Valle del Elqui, 528 kilometres north of Santiago, Chile, is classified as a desert, yet has a cool climate due to cooling Pacific breezes.

WEATHER

Some regions have very stable climates, and the weather varies very little from one year to the next. In other regions, vintages become important, as the quality of the wine produced may vary widely between different years. This is particularly true for regions that have climates that are only just suitable for viticulture (for example Champagne and Tasmania), regions with the risk of heavy rainfall at harvest time (Bordeaux) and regions that are liable to frost or hail damage (Burgundy).

Both winter and spring **frosts** can cause problems. A very severe winter frost may damage the grafts and lead to the death of the vine. The normal protection against this is earthing up. In more temperate regions late spring frosts, particularly after prolonged mild weather, can cause severe damage to the nascent buds. There are three main forms of protection against frost. The first is smudge pots. These create smoke which acts like a blanket to keep heat in. More sophisticated are wind-machines, generally established in vineyards notoriously prone to frost. They draw in warm air from above to keep the temperature at ground level above freezing point.

Alternatively, many vineyards now employ the aspersion system of frost protection. Sprinklers are installed in the vineyards and, when frost is forecast, the vines are sprayed with water so that an insulating coat of ice protects the shoots.

Oil-burning smudge pots in Oakville, Napa. These create convection currents to circulate air and avoid frost pockets developing.

Nebbiolo vines damaged by harvest time hail storm in 2002. La Morra, Barolo, Piemonte, Italy.

Grapevines like dry conditions, and a certain level of water stress is considered to contribute to the quality of the harvest, but water is needed for photosynthesis to take place. In **drought** conditions, high temperatures and insufficient rainfall can cause the leaves to shut down, with the result that sugar is not produced and the grapes do not ripen properly. Within the EU irrigation has generally been banned except for young vines and experimental vineyards. However, it is beginning to be permitted more widely. In the New World it is generally permitted, though it is not always needed. It can take the form of drip-irrigation, sprinklers or, more particularly in Chile and Argentina, flood irrigation. Many growers will have computer-controlled drip-irrigation to ensure that each vine gets no more than the optimum amount of water.

Conversely, excessive **rain** close to harvest time can result in dilution of sugars and flavours in the grapes, and can lead to damp conditions that allow rot. Summer **hail** can also be very destructive. In Argentina it is estimated that it potentially will destroy 5 per cent of any harvest. There, protective netting is widely used to counter the problem. Elsewhere, planes are used to seed potential storm-clouds with chemicals to ensure that it is rain that falls, rather than hail.

The vine is self-pollinating but needs warm, dry and breezy weather for the flowers to set and pollinate successfully. **Coulure** is the term used when the flower does not set, and **millerandage** when the fruit fails to set, usually as a result of unsatisfactory pollination. There are certain grape varieties that are particularly prone to this problem. It is most frequently caused by cold, rainy weather at the crucial time.

Soils and Topography

3

The importance that soils play in the ultimate quality of a wine is widely discussed. Soil affects the vine physically, through its ability to absorb and drain away water and its heat-retention properties; and through its chemical characteristics, such as the availability of nutrients and minerals.

SOILS

Just as canopy management can be used to create a better micro-climate, in many regions sophisticated irrigation regimes are used to simulate the **water-retention** characteristics of ideal vineyard sites. Because of concerns about excessive yields and loss of 'authenticity', irrigation is permitted in very few regions in the EU. There is no doubt that extreme water shortages have an adverse effect on grape quality, and in some circumstances irrigation can improve quality. However, irrigation stops vines developing deep root systems, and for those that believe that wines should express the conditions in which the vines are grown, irrigation is seen as something that distorts *terroir* (see below). Soil can contribute in other ways, For example the 'pudding-stones', or *galets*, that cover the vineyards of Châteauneuf-du-Pape act as storage heaters and contribute to the high alcohol content that characterises that wine. The dark slate in some German vineyards and the gravel in Bordeaux act in a similar way.

Like lack of water, a soil that is poor in **nutrients** can stress a vine. It is generally accepted that better grapes come from a vine that is slightly stressed, since stress causes the vine to focus its energies on producing fruit, allowing the species to be propagated away from the stressful site. Many vineyards are planted on land that would support few other crops. Excessively fertile soils, such as those found in Chile, can result in lush, leafy vines that yield poor quality, unripe fruit. Unless the vigour of the vine is severely restricted, a lush leaf canopy can cause too much shade and create ideal conditions for rot.

As well as food, the vine needs many **minerals** if it is to grow healthily. Excess of certain minerals can cause problems. Although lime-rich soils often have good drainage properties, and the balance of minerals can help preserve acids in the ripening grapes, these soils can make the vine susceptible to **chlorosis**. This is a symptom of the vine that can have many causes (excess heat, transpiration, lack of water or lack of free iron in the soil). It causes the leaves to turn yellow and yields fall as a result of reduced photosynthesis. The best solution is careful selection of rootstock, but in an established vineyard the soil can be treated with ferrous sulphate. Other mineral deficiencies in the soil can be countered by restricted use of specialist fertilisers. Occasionally, a wine may seem to smell or taste of minerals or stones such as slate or flint, as if the minerals from the vineyard have managed to find a way into the wine. Vine physiology is not well enough understood to know how this transport of minerals from the soil to the grape occurs, or even if it happens at all.

TOPOGRAPHY: ASPECT AND SLOPE

These are important aspects affecting wine quality and style. Slopes can be used to expose vines to the sun for maximum ripeness in marginal climates. East-facing vineyards benefit from the gentle warmth of a rising sun, sometimes veiled by morning mists. West-facing vineyards experience fiercer afternoon warmth. Those angled at a slope of 30° towards the equator may receive twice the solar radiation of a vineyard angled at 30° towards the poles. Vineyards on slopes are generally better drained, and have more air circulation, than vineyards on flat sites, though steeper vineyards are more difficult and expensive to work.

Stones in Châteauneuf-du-Pape store heat during the day and reflect it back at night, encouraging the development of high sugar levels in the grapes.

Vines in Madeira, affected
by chlorosis.

TERROIR

This word refers to the ensemble of natural
influences that give a wine a sense of place. In
its most narrow usage, it refers only to the effects
of different soil structures within an area of
unvarying climate and topography. More usefully,
it can be taken to cover the combined effects of
aspect, slope, climate and site climate on raw
grape material. These effects are usually subtle,
but are sometimes dramatic, and with careful
winemaking, they can be transposed into
recognisable flavours and other aspects (such
as tannins or acids) in a wine. Many wine
characteristics that would once have been a clue
as to the region of origin are strictly speaking
aspects of viticulture of winemaking. These
include choice of grape variety, use of oak,

Amphitheatres, such as
this one near Sancerre,
act as heat traps and
encourage ripening in
marginal climates.

malolactic fermentation and lees stirring (see
Chapter 5). The limits of how the wine style of
one region can be copied in another, using an
array of viticultural and winemaking techniques
that includes canopy management, irrigation and
must adjustments (see Chapters 4 and 5), are still
being explored. It would be unreasonable to
require all wines to express their geographical
origins, if by doing so some were of poor quality
or unpleasant. However, there is a danger that as

techniques and expertise are shared throughout
the world, international styles emerge and
diversity is lost. Countering this trend, many wine
producers are realising that the sense of place is
a unique aspect of their wine that can be used
to market it, and help it achieve higher prices.
Cabernet Sauvignon and Chardonnay can be
made almost everywhere. Coonawarra Cabernet
and Chablis cannot.

Viticulture
Winemaking falls into two stages: the growing of the grapes, or viticulture, and the processing of them into wine, or vinification. Traditionally, it has been the winemaker who has gained the glory, but now one regularly hears the expression, 'The wine is made in the vineyard.' Great wine needs great grapes, which in turn require suitable soils, climate, weather and expert viticulture. However, it is possible for poor weather or bad farming to result in poor grapes from sites with great potential, and great grapes can also be turned into bad wine.

4

ESTABLISHING A VINEYARD
Planting

A vine may be planted for two reasons: to create a new vineyard or to replace an existing one. The life of a vine can be long; there are century-old vines in production around the world. Some old vines produce fruit of exceptional quality, though the older it is, the less fruit a vine produces. A balance has to be struck, therefore, between quality and profitability. Normally, a vine will be grubbed up when it is between 35 and 50 years old. A vineyard owner will normally have a replanting cycle that ensures that as little as possible of their vineyard is out of production at any one time. Normally, vineyard land is left fallow for three years or more after grubbing up

so that it can recover. This also has to be taken into consideration.

Before the young vines are planted, where possible, the soil should be prepared to a fine tilth. The young vines may be protected against weeds by covering the land around the vine with black plastic or against animals by an individual plastic sleeve. The first yield normally comes in the third year from planting and in the European Union the first fruit may not be used in the production of quality wine.

How a vineyard is planted depends on a number of factors, which may, or may not, include legislation, the yield that you want and the degree of mechanisation used, not just during the growing season but also at harvest-time. The

Irrigation used to establish vines in a new vineyard in Sonoma, California.

density of planting might be anything from 3 000 to 15 000 vines per hectare. The more dense the planting, the more the stress on the vine and, hopefully, the better the fruit.

Once established, the form that the vine takes will be governed by the way that the grower prunes and trains it. Every vine has distinct parts:

roots
trunk
cane/spur
shoots
flowers/fruit
leaves

As was mentioned in Chapter 1 most vines consist of American rootstock, on to which has been grafted a *V. vinifera* scion. It is the latter that will form the trunk of the vine. The graft can normally be seen just above soil level. Shoots bearing tendrils and leaves grow from the scion. Over the course of the following winter these shoots mature and turn brown. They are then called **canes**. Buds form where the previous season's leaves joined the cane, and from these eventually new shoots grow. A cane will have between eight and 15 buds. The vine's flowers,

and ultimately fruit, develop on shoots formed in the spring of the same year. If a cane is pruned short, leaving only two or three buds, it is known as a **spur**. By the end of the following year the canes and spurs are old wood and are normally removed at pruning, when new replacement spurs and canes will have been allowed to grow.

Pruning

In traditional vineyard areas within the EU, the pruning method and the way that the vine is trained are controlled by legislation. The object of the main winter pruning is twofold: to select the buds that will form shoots for the production of fruit in the coming harvest and to prepare the vine for fruiting in future harvests. Pruning may also be used to control the number of buds – just one factor that will ultimately affect the yield of the vine and the quality of the fruit.

Summer pruning may be carried out:
- to restrict the vegetation to concentrate the vigour of the vine into production of fruit;
- to control the leaf canopy so that the bunches of grapes have the optimum exposure to, or shade from, the sun, and aeration to minimise fungal infection;
- to keep the vineyard tidy to ease work during the growing season and vintage.

Basically, there are two types of pruning: spur, in which a number of short, two- or three-bud spurs are left on the vine; and cane, when one or two longer canes, each of 8–15 buds are left (see illustrations).

Training

Once the vine has been pruned, any remaining canes will then be trained. The object is to display the foliage and the fruit. The training system will depend on the type of pruning employed. In some areas, the vines will be free-standing, and in others they will be trained along wires or pergolas. The training of the vine will also vary according to such factors as the climate, the vineyard and the yield required. Vines may be trained low to benefit from reflected heat or to avoid wind damage or high to minimise reflected heat or maximise exposure to wind and sun.

There are four main systems for training vines:

1. B**ush training** or **gobelet**. This spur-pruned system is used in warmer vineyard regions such as Beaujolais, the Rhône Valley, Rioja and the older vineyards of Australia. The vines are free-standing and normally four or five spurs are left around the head of the vine trunk. In Beaujolais these spurs are tied together at their tips. As the

Bush (spur) pruning

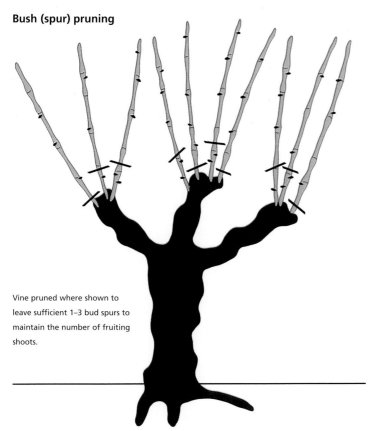

Vine pruned where shown to leave sufficient 1–3 bud spurs to maintain the number of fruiting shoots.

new producing canes being used each year, one in the case of single Guyot and two in double Guyot.

3. The **cordon spur** system. The trunk of the vine is developed horizontally, with a number of spurs left along its length. This may be a low cordon, as in the Cordon de Royat system used in Champagne, or high, as in the Geneva Double Curtain.

4. The **parral** or **pergola**. In this the vines are trained high on pergolas, with bunches of grapes being generally head-high. This gives plenty of leaf cover in hot climates.

Guyot pruning, before and after, showing the amount of wood removed.

Guyot training sequence

A mature double Guyot vine before pruning.

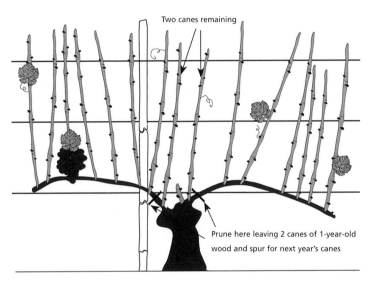

Two canes remaining

Prune here leaving 2 canes of 1-year-old wood and spur for next year's canes

The same vine after pruning, double Guyot-trained.

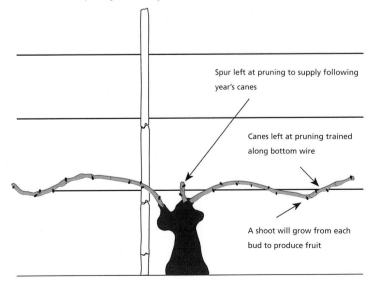

Spur left at pruning to supply following year's canes

Canes left at pruning trained along bottom wire

A shoot will grow from each bud to produce fruit

resulting air circulation is poor, this is not suitable for damp regions where there might be rot. As the vines are left close to the ground, they should not be trained in this fashion if there is a risk of spring frosts.

2. The **replacement cane system**, which includes the **Guyot**, as used in Burgundy and Bordeaux. Here canes are trained along lateral wires, with

YIELD MANAGEMENT

Excessive yields may result in the grapes failing to ripen properly as the sugars produced in the leaves are shared between too many grapes. High rainfall or excessive irrigation can give large crops of bloated, flavourless grapes and any wine made from these will lack character.

Under the European Quality Wine systems, yields are generally controlled in an effort to guarantee quality. However, there may be considerable variations. For example, the grower of Pinot Noir in Alsace will be permitted yields more than double those of the grower in a Burgundy *Grand Cru* such as Romanée-Conti.

Similar legal controls may not be in place in the New World, but someone who is seeking to make quality wine there will restrict their yields, as yield is an important factor in the price that they ultimately ask for their wine. Yields may be expressed in weight, such as tons of grapes per acre or hectare, or volume, such as hectolitres to the hectare.

Here are some of the factors that are involved in the ultimate yield:
- Number of vines to the hectare, determined at time of planting.
- Number of buds to the vine, determined at time of pruning.
- Number of shoots, dependent on bud-burst, soil and climatic conditions, especially frosts, and on the number of buds to the vine.
- Number of clusters to the shoot. This is the fruitfulness, determined the previous spring when the bud was formed.
- Number of berries to the cluster, determined by the flowering, which is dependent on the weather at flowering. This is the most variable and no one can predict with any accuracy the size of a potential crop until flowering has taken place.
- Weight of the berries. This depends on the grape variety, the berry number, the amount of water through rain or irrigation during the growing season and the nutrient supply.
- Green harvesting. This is increasingly being used to reduce yields. The grower will go through their vineyards before the grapes ripen and pick out excess bunches.

VINEYARD PESTS

As well as hazards arising due to poor weather or unsuitable soil, vinegrowing can be adversely affected by a number of pests and diseases.

Phylloxera

This has been discussed above in the section on grafting.

Grape Moths (Cochylis, Pyralis and Eudemis)

Caterpillars attack the buds in the spring and the grapes themselves later in the year. Treatment is by spraying the vines with insecticides.

Red spider mite and yellow spider mite

These are most prevalent in hot, dry weather. They have become increasingly common because insecticides have killed off their natural predators. They infest the leaves and thus lessen the vegetative growth. Specialist sprays have been developed to deal with them. In organic vineyards natural predators are used.

Nematodes

These are microscopic worms that attack the roots of vines. Treatment is very difficult, so prevention is the best cure. This involves totally sanitising the soil before replanting and using resistant rootstocks. Increasing use of drip-irrigation in Argentina and Chile has led to a dramatic increase in the number of nematodes there. Now many vineyards are being planted with grafted vines, not as a protection against phylloxera, but rather against nematodes.

Birds and Animals

In many vineyard regions birds will consume large quantities of ripe grapes. They often learn to ignore bird-scarers. Netting is probably the most effective solution but is expensive. Many animals

Netted vines to protect ripe grapes from birds, Auckland, New Zealand. Roses give an early warning of mildew.

such as deer, wild boar and badgers will also eat ripe grapes. Young vines all make attractive food. If necessary, protective fencing will have to be installed.

DISEASES

In order to minimise disease in the vineyards, protective spraying will be carried out during the growing season. Generally this is done by tractor, though in an emergency, and for inaccessible sites, helicopters or light planes may be called in. In most temperate vineyard areas, where there is rainfall during the growing season, between eight and twelve sprayings will be necessary each year. In more generous climates, it may be no more than four.

Mildew

There are two main kinds of this fungal disease. **Powdery mildew** (*Oidium*) develops on all green parts of the vine as a white powdery growth of spores. If buds or grapes are attacked, they do not develop properly and eventually split. It does not need damp conditions, but likes a warm, shady environment. The solution is to spray or dust with sulphur. **Downy mildew** (*Peronospera*) was the third major disease to be brought over from America to European vineyards in the nineteenth century after *Oidium* and phylloxera. Like *Oidium*, it can attack all green parts of the vine, leaving a downy growth of fungus. Bad cases will cause leaves to drop, stopping photosynthesis and preventing sugars being generated for the fruit. It likes damp conditions. Originally the only treatment was with Bordeaux mixture (copper sulphate and lime in solution). Now systemic fungicides have been developed and the disease is less widespread.

Rot

Depending on the circumstances, *Botrytis cinerea* (grey rot, or noble rot) is either welcomed or dreaded by the grower. This fungal disease is spread by damp, humid conditions, and presents a bigger problem for black grapes than white as it causes loss of colour in the wine and because maceration on the rotten skins can lead to off-flavours. As **grey rot**, it tends to affect mostly immature berries. Early treatment by spraying is advised, though this has to be completed before the grapes begin to ripen. It can seriously affect both yield and quality. In the right conditions – damp mornings and dry afternoons – this is the **noble rot** that facilitates the production of the great sweet wines of Bordeaux, Germany and elsewhere. In its benevolent form, the botrytis will

affect ripe grapes, consuming water from the berry by way of microscopic filaments through the pores of the grape-skin. This concentrates the sugars, reducing the grape to a shrivelled raisin and adding its own unique flavours. The fact that it is never uniform in its development means that, ideally, there should be several pickings to complete the harvest. **Black rot** is a second common rot fungus, brought on by heavy rain and affecting both the leaves and the grapes. It is treated by spraying with Bordeaux mixture.

Long-Term Diseases

While rot and mildew will affect the quality and quantity of grapes of one harvest, other diseases attack the vine itself, with long-term effects.

Long-term **fungal diseases** of the vine include Eutypa dieback (Eutypiose, Dead-Arm). This has been present in New World vineyards for a long time, and has been spreading in Europe since the 1980s. It attacks the vine wood through pruning cuts, causing part of the vine to rot and die, and greatly reducing yields, though it does not adversely affect quality. No successful treatment has yet been discovered.

Oidium causes the grapes to split.

Helicopter spraying vines on the hill of Corton, Pernand-Vergelesses, Côte d'Or, France.

Glassy-winged sharpshooter, the insect responsible for the spreading of Pierce's Disease in the vineyards of California.

The most serious **bacterial disease** is Pierce's Disease, which is spread by small insects called sharpshooters. It was first recognised as long ago as 1892, but there is still no effective cure for it. An infected vine will die within five years. Prevention by surrounding vineyards with a *cordon sanitaire* appears the most effective way of combating it. It has recently caused extensive damage in the vineyards of Mexico and southern California.

Numerous **viruses** can infect vines. Most do not kill the vine, but reduce yield and quality. They are highly contagious and persistent, and are usually spread via cuttings or nematodes. Once established they cannot be eradicated except by grubbing up and sanitising the land. Ideally, this land should not be replanted with vines. The only way to avoid viruses is to plant virus- and nematode-free land with virus-free cuttings.

THE VINEYARD CALENDAR

Each grower will have their own calendar and this might change as new techniques and machinery become available. As an example, below is the year of a typical grower in Burgundy, with a vineyard planted in the single Guyot system. Note that some of the activities here may take place a month earlier or a month later in other regions, depending on the grape variety and the climate. In an average year in the Midi, for example, the grower's year will begin towards the end of August and in Alsace it will finish in November.

In the Southern Hemisphere, the picking may begin in January and finish in April or even May. Wherever they are, the year for the grower starts immediately after the harvest.

October

After the vintage, apart from work in the cellar, the main priority is to clear the land where vines are going to be planted. Any unproductive vines in the vineyards should be uprooted and the ground prepared for their replacement. The vine leaves begin to change colour and will fall with the first frosts.

November

Autumn ploughing breaks up the soil. Autumn pruning: this year's producing branch is cut off, as are any non-productive canes. The base of the vine is earthed up to protect the graft against winter frost damage. Any soil that might have been washed down the slopes during the previous season should be carried back up. The sap falls and the vine is dormant until the spring. Shoots lignify to form canes, with embryonic buds at the point where leaves and tendrils grew.

December

Continuation of November's work.

January

The beginning of the main pruning starts, though tradition has it that this should not begin before the feast-day of the patron saint of vine-growers, Saint Vincent, on 22 January. Pruning is the most specialised work in the vineyard and cannot be done mechanically. Each vine has to be treated as an individual and the person who is pruning will see to its individual needs.

February

Continuation of pruning.

March

Pruning is completed, fertiliser is spread, the vine sap begins to rise and the first signs of new growth can be seen. Grafting of any new vines is performed in March.

April

The earth is taken away from the base of the vines and hoeing should take place to loosen up the earth around the vines. The coming year's productive cane should be tied down to the lower wire. Spreading of herbicide. The new season's buds, which will develop into shoots, burst. These buds are very prone to frost damage so they should be protected against spring frosts.

Planting of young vines from the nursery, which were grafted the previous year takes place in

April. These will be either new plantings or replacements within the rows.

May

The first spraying against insects and fungal diseases is done. Suckers must be removed and spreading shoots brought within the horizontal wires. This enables sunlight to reach the nascent bunches and clears the row for the passage of tractors. There is a distinct growth of shoots. The first leaves form on the vine and the cane matures to form old wood.

Planting of newly grafted vines in the nursery occurs in May.

June

The positioning of the shoots continues, and branches are tied to the horizontal wires. The first crucial stage in the cycle of the grape is flowering. This should take place in early summer and traditionally, in France, the harvest takes place

LEFT CENTRE
Vines at the moment of flowering.

LEFT
Once pollinated, the grapes begin to form. These are embryonic Chardonnay grapes.

BELOW
Véraison of Pinot Noir grapes.

approximately 100 days later, though in Chile, for example, it may be as much as 130 days. After the vine flowers, the fruit sets on the shoots. In ideal conditions this can take place quite rapidly, within a week, but in poor weather it can take as long as three weeks, with a knock-on effect on the harvest date. Fruit set is the first moment at which an estimate can be made as to the potential size of a harvest. Spraying continues.

July

Tying of branches continues. The tips of the vine shoots are trimmed to ensure that the maximum amount of nutrient is diverted to the grape bunches. Excess bunches are removed to restrict yield (green harvest). Vigorous growth of vegetation occurs, though berries are still small.

Spraying continues.

August

This is the quietest month of the year in the vineyard as spraying should be discontinued at least a month before the harvest. Some trimming is done, but the main task is preparation for the vintage: cleaning of press-house and all equipment. Early in the month the grapes begin to change colour (*véraison*). Berries swell as they reach maturity.

Machine harvesters at work. The forks shake the vines, causing ripe grapes to fall. Unripe grapes are left behind.

September

Final preparations for the vintage continue; the winery equipment will be cleaned and serviced. Grapes will be tested regularly for sugar and acidity; they may also be tasted to follow the development of flavours and the character of acids and tannins. The harvest will take place when the grapes have achieved maximum ripeness, not just as far as the sugar content is concerned, but also phenolic ripeness of the pips. Ideally, this should happen at approximately the same time.

The Vintage

The vintage ideally begins when the grower perceives that they have the ideal balance between sugar and acidity in their grapes. This will vary from variety to variety and also from plot of land to plot of land. On occasion, threatening weather conditions may cause a grower to bring forward their harvest to save their crop.

Harvesting can be by hand or machine. In an ideal world a good team of hand-pickers cannot be bettered, but there are a number of factors that have to be taken into consideration. These may include how the vineyard is planted, labour availability and cost, the topography of the vineyard, weather conditions and grape varieties.

The principal advantage of the machine harvester is speed. This may be essential if the vintage is threatened by bad weather, or with certain grape varieties, such as Sauvignon Blanc, that mature from ripe to over-ripe very quickly. They can also work through the night, which allows cool grapes to be brought to the winery. This saves money and energy that would be spent on lowering the temperature of the grapes before fermentation, and it retards the dissipation of aromas that would occur while they are waiting to be fermented. Machine harvesters work by shaking the vine and collecting the ripe berries as they fall off, leaving the stalks behind. They are not selective, taking all the ripe berries from the vines whether they are healthy or not, as well as shaking off 'matter other than grapes' (bits of leaf, insects, other contaminants). They can only be used on dry flat, or gently sloping land.

Manual harvesting is slower and more labour-intensive. It does, however, permit selection of the grapes – rotten or unripe grapes can be left on the vine. For botrytised grapes hand-picking and the selection it implies are essential. Less damage occurs when grapes are harvested by the bunch and the stalks, or at least some of them, can be left to add tannin for red wines. With broken grapes oxidation is a constant problem and with those white wines made from black grapes, such as Champagne, hand-picking is essential in order to minimise colouring of the juice. Hand-picking can be done in all terrains and in all weathers. In those regions with steep, hillside vineyards, such as the Mosel, the Douro and the Rhône valleys, there is no alternative.

From here the work moves from the vineyard to the cellar.

Winemaking

Once the work in the vineyards has been finished and the grapes have been harvested, it is the responsibility of the winemaker to turn the grapes into wine. This task is called vinification. Viticulture and vinification are complementary; neither is more important than the other. Indeed, they each rely on the other as both parts can dramatically affect the nature of the wine. It is the job of the grower, or viticulturalist, to produce the best grapes from their vineyards and that of the winemaker to make the best wine from those grapes. In both cases, a number of external factors have to be taken into consideration, some of them natural, like the climate, some of them not, like financial pressures and the profit motive. In some cases, the two roles may be carried out by the same person but, in all cases, good grapes are needed. Good wine cannot be made from poor grapes, but it is easy to make poor wine from good grapes.

5

The date of the vintage will not be established by the vineyard manager alone; they must liaise with the winemaker as to what the latter requires and both will test the grapes on the vine regularly for the degree of maturity that is required. They must then plan together the order in which the grapes will be picked and delivered to the winery. Where a property consists of a number of parcels of vines, there may well be a spread of dates for harvesting; this might run over three months or more. Large wineries that buy in grapes, or co-operative cellars with a number of members, will also have to plan the reception of grapes in detail in order to spread the workload and operate their winery in the most efficient fashion.

CONSTITUENTS OF THE GRAPE

A grape is made up of many different parts. The winemaker's job is to perform the alchemy that changes these parts into wine. By far the largest constituent of most grapes is water, and this in turn, forms by far the largest part of wine. It is the sugar in the grapes that is turned into the alcohol that distinguishes wine from common grape juice. The juice of the grape will also contain acids, flavours and small amounts of natural compounds such as pectins. The skins, pips and, sometimes, the stalks will also have a part to play in the final style of the wine. While there are a few black wine grapes that have a coloured pulp, in the vast majority of cases the pulp is colourless. All the colouring material is in the skin, which also contains some flavouring compounds and tannins.

There are two factors that are considered when the ripeness of a harvest is assessed. One of these is the **phenolic ripeness**, which includes the skins and pips; the other is sugar ripeness. Generally, the two occur at approximately the same time, but in marginal climates, climatic pressures may mean that picking takes place before optimum ripeness is achieved in both cases. Where the climate is more benign at harvest-time, grapes may be left longer before picking so that full phenolic ripeness is achieved.

The **sugar ripeness** of the harvest is judged by the amount of sugar in the grapes. As they ripen the density of the juice increases, so a rough idea of the potential alcohol content of the wine can be estimated by measuring the juice's density, or **must weight**. A number of scales have been devised, of

The ripeness of the grapes is assessed by measuring the density of the juice: here a refractometer is being used in the vineyard.

which the most common are Baumé (used mainly in France) and Oechsle and KMW (in Germany and Austria). In California and Australia, a third method of measuring sugar content is used. This is called **Brix**, or **Balling**. There are other constituents in a grape apart from sugar that help to make up the must weight; this means that the final alcoholic strength of a wine may not be the same as that indicated by the must weight. In addition, certain processes in winemaking affect the ultimate alcoholic degree. For example, when red wine is fermented at high temperatures, some alcohol will be lost. Different yeasts may be more or less efficient at converting sugar to alcohol (it takes approximately 16.5 g/l of sugar to generate 1% abv). Rather less grape sugar is needed for the same strength of white wine than for red. Because of these factors, and because the different scales measure sugar levels by different indirect methods (density, percentage of solids and so on), the scales are not fully equivalent to each other. However, an approximate comparison can be made.

The waxy bloom on the outside of a grape skin may contain wild yeasts that can start the fermenting process, as well as bacteria. The most important bacteria present are acetobacter, which will, in the presence of oxygen, turn the wine into vinegar. If uncontrolled, the more abundant wild yeasts will start fermentation, but die off at about 4% abv, when the *Saccharomyces cerevisiae* yeast kicks in, converting the remaining sugar to alcohol. The winemaker may use these wild yeasts as part of the fermentation process, but most use cultured yeasts because the results are more predictable.

CRUSHING, PRESSING AND MUST ADJUSTMENTS

When they arrive at the winery all grapes will be checked for their potential degree of alcohol. Then, for better wines, they will pass along a short conveyor belt, known as a selection table. Here all unripe and diseased grapes will be rejected, as well as any other 'foreign' material such as leaves.

Chardonnay grapes arriving at the winery. From the reception hopper they will be transferred directly to the press.

Baumé	Brix/Balling	Oechsle (KMW)	Potential Alcohol (% abv)
8	14.4	57 (11.4)	7.4
9	16.2	66 (13.2)	8.4
10	18.0	75 (15.0)	9.4
11	19.8	84 (16.8)	10.3
12	21.7	93 (18.6)	11.3
13	23.5	101 (20.2)	12.3
14	25.3	110 (22.0)	13.3
15	27.1	119 (23.8)	14.3
16	28.9	128 (25.6)	15.3

Crushing breaks the skins of the grapes and allows the juice to run out. Stalks are generally removed from the grapes before they are pressed, often by a combined crusher/destemmer. In certain regions, some growers will leave a certain proportion of stems to add tannin to their red wines. Removing stalks damages the structure of the grape, so where white wine is being made from black grapes, the bunches will be left intact.

At a later stage in the making of every wine, separation of the liquid and solid constituents of the grape occurs. This is usually achieved by **pressing**, though a small number of wines are made purely from the free-run juice that is

Cross-section of a grape berry

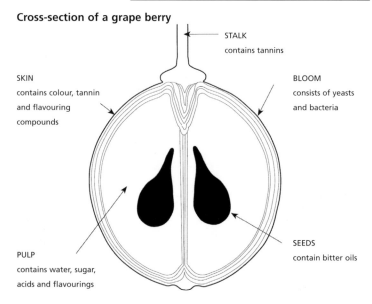

STALK
contains tannins

SKIN
contains colour, tannin and flavouring compounds

BLOOM
consists of yeasts and bacteria

SEEDS
contain bitter oils

PULP
contains water, sugar, acids and flavourings

Pneumatic press

Pneumatic presses use compressed air to achieve a gentle pressing of the grapes.

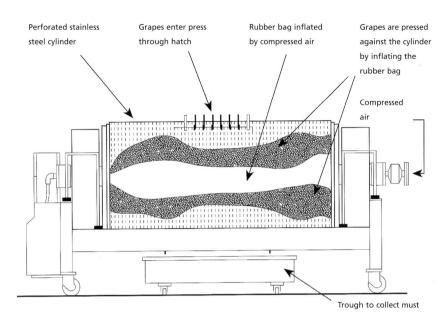

Perforated stainless steel cylinder

Grapes enter press through hatch

Rubber bag inflated by compressed air

Grapes are pressed against the cylinder by inflating the rubber bag

Compressed air

Trough to collect must

released during the more gentle crushing process. In the case of white wines, pressing occurs before the start of fermentation, while for red and rosé wines it will be after a period of contact between juice and skins.

Traditionally, all wine-presses were vertical, with the pressure on the grapes coming from above through a screw. Indeed, the basket press is still used by many wineries for making their top-class red wines. It is still widely used in Champagne. More recently, there has been a move to horizontal presses. With some models, the pressure comes from the ends, again applied by means of a screw, but the degree of pressure can be controlled more accurately than with a vertical press. The latest models consist of an inflatable rubber tube within a perforated, horizontal, stainless steel cylinder. Here the pressure is gentle and gradual. The amount of juice that can be extracted from a grape varies according to variety and is dependent on the pressure exerted in the pressing. As a rough guide, however, 1 kg of grapes will give enough juice for one 75 cl bottle of wine. Pips are high in bitter tannins which can give an unpleasant stringency to the wine if released. The modern techniques make for a gentle pressing of the grapes, so this is now generally avoided.

The winemaker may make a number of **adjustments** before and during fermentation, either to improve the must or to control the winemaking process in order to produce better wine.

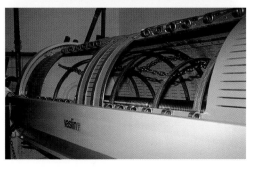

Early presses were vertical but most regions now use horizontal presses.

Enrichment

In cooler climates, there may be insufficient natural sugar in the grapes to give the wine a satisfactory degree of alcohol. In such circumstances must enrichment (generally called **chaptalisation**, after the Comte Chaptal, the Napoleonic minister who proposed its use in order to support the French sugar beet industry) may be carried out. This is the addition of sugar to the must, either before or during fermentation, to increase the end degree of alcohol to the desired level. This process is forbidden in many parts of the world and is strictly controlled where it is permitted. If carried out with care, chaptalisation may give a better wine. If abused, it can ruin it by creating a wine that tastes hard and thin, because there is insufficient fruit to balance the artificially elevated alcohol.

Sulphur Dioxide (SO₂)

Sulphur dioxide (SO_2) is almost indispensable in the winery. It acts as an anti-oxidant and an antiseptic. It is now widespread practice to kill off the wild yeasts and the bacteria that the grapes bring with them on their skins with sulphur dioxide before fermentation is started with cultivated yeasts. This minimises the risk of off-flavours. Traditionally, cellarworkers sanitise their empty casks by burning a sulphur candle in them. This gives off antiseptic sulphur dioxide gas as it burns. Sulphur dioxide may be used in the making of cheaper sweet wines. It may be added to the wine to kill off the yeasts before they have consumed all the sugars.

Sulphur dioxide is also useful after fermentation. Almost all wines will have sulphur dioxide added to prevent oxidation. It will also kill any remaining yeasts or bacteria that might adversely affect the quality of the wine. Care must be taken not to use too much as this can give an unpleasant smell and flavours to the wine. For this reason European legislation restricts the amount of sulphur dioxide that may be added to a wine.

Other Adjustments

Given the broad range of climates in which wine is produced, it is not surprising that there is a broad range of excesses and deficiencies that might need to be treated. What is permitted will vary from region to region. Such treatments may include the adding of acid where wines lack it, and the countering of it where it is excessive. **Acidification** is normally carried out by the addition of tartaric acid in powder form. In Europe, this treatment is permitted in warmer regions only, but it is common in the New World. **De-acidification** is more common in cooler climate regions. Here neutralising excess acid may be achieved by the addition of potassium bicarbonate. If there is insufficient **tannin**, this too may be increased by the addition of powder or by adding some stalks to the vat. It may also be imparted by maturation in oak casks. Legal controls exist for all treatments that involve the addition of some substance to the wine.

FERMENTATION

Yeasts are naturally present on the skins of the grapes and around the winery, so, once the grapes are crushed, fermentation will start naturally. However, in New World wineries it is almost the automatic practice, and it is becoming more common in the Old World, for the winemaker to select cultivated yeasts that are the best adapted for the wine that is to be made. Cultured yeasts, normally added in the form of powder, reduce the need to add sulphur dioxide and may be selected to give a particular character to a wine. Specially cultivated yeasts are essential for the production of certain wines. For example, the secondary fermentation of Champagne, requires a yeast that is capable of operating under extreme pressure. The main yeast that is responsible for alcoholic fermentation is *Saccharomyces cerevisiae*, which can act in the presence of oxygen (aerobic) or without it (anaerobic). However, a number of other yeasts can contribute, either beneficially (adding complexity) or harmfully (adding off-flavours). When the yeasts die at the end of the fermentation, they sink to the bottom of the fermentation vessel and form a sediment, which is called lees. Often white wines may be left 'on their lees' while ageing, as this can impart extra body and character to the wine.

Fermentation is the conversion of sugar, by the interaction of yeasts, into alcohol, with carbon dioxide gas and heat as by-products. In theory, the higher the sugar content of the grape, the higher the ultimate alcohol content of the wine will be. However, yeasts generally die when there is about 15 per cent alcohol in a wine, even if unfermented sugar remains. High levels of sugar and/or alcohol are toxic to yeast, and so are some of the compounds found in rotten grapes, particularly those affected by botrytis, so for sweet wines fermentation may cease naturally at quite low alcohol levels. Alternatively, a winemaker may seek to stop the fermentation before total conversion of the sugar has been achieved in order to produce a medium or even sweet wine. This may be done by filtration or by adding sulphur dioxide. The fermentation may also stop if the temperature becomes too high or too low, or if the yeasts run out of essential nutrients. Any unfermented sugar remaining in the wine is called residual sugar. Even dry wines may have a small quantity of sugar which cannot be fermented, but which may not be detected on the palate. When discussing the alcoholic strength of a wine, the amount of ethanol in the wine is measured as a percentage by volume and is called the 'actual alcohol'. The residual sugar is referred to as the 'potential alcohol' and the sum of the two is the 'total alcohol'.

Heat is also generated during fermentation, and this will need to be controlled, especially for white wines. During the fermentation, the temperature of the must in each vat will be monitored and recorded on a graph. Modern vinification techniques generally call for white wines to be fermented slowly at a low temperature to impart extra fruitiness. Red wines, however, have to be fermented at higher temperatures so that the maximum amount of colour is extracted from the skins. Modern fermentation vats will have sleeves through which cold or hot water can be circulated to control the must temperature. Alternatively, the wine can be passed through a heat exchanger, or simply pumped over. Sophisticated temperature control during fermentation is perhaps the most important advance that has been made in modern winemaking. In hotter climates, and particularly with the greater availability of grape-picking machines, the harvest takes place at night so that the grapes arrive at the press-house as cool as possible. In marginal climates, however, such as Burgundy, it might be necessary to heat the grapes when they arrive, or the must in the vat, to activate the yeasts.

Red, white and rosé wines are vinified in different ways, using similar equipment, but in a different sequence.

Red Wine Vinification

Red wines are generally made solely from black grapes, though in a few regions it is traditional to vinify the red grapes with a small proportion of white grapes, for example the Viognier grapes that may join the Syrah in Côte-Rôtie, and increasingly in other regions. It is particularly important that black grapes are picked in perfect condition and that they are not affected by rot, as this might affect the ultimate colour and taste of the wine. The classic treatment is for them to be destalked and crushed. The resultant mass, which includes the skins and pips, is then put into a vat where it is allowed to ferment. Some winemakers, however,

The winemaking process

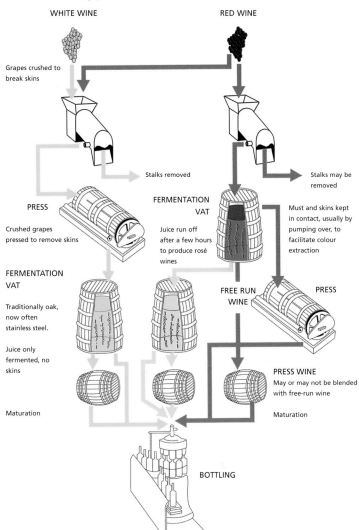

WHITE WINE

RED WINE

Grapes crushed to break skins

Stalks removed

Stalks may be removed

PRESS

Crushed grapes pressed to remove skins

FERMENTATION VAT

Juice run off after a few hours to produce rosé wines

FERMENTATION VAT

Must and skins kept in contact, usually by pumping over, to facilitate colour extraction

FERMENTATION VAT

Traditionally oak, now often stainless steel.

Juice only fermented, no skins

FREE RUN WINE

PRESS

PRESS WINE

May or may not be blended with free-run wine

Maturation

Maturation

BOTTLING

prefer to leave the grapes to macerate for a period at a low temperature before setting off the fermentation.

With red wines the fermentation should begin at about 20° C, but will cease to continue if the temperature reaches about 35° C. It is essential, therefore, to control the temperature of fermentation. The ideal temperature may vary from grape variety to grape variety, and from region to region. Sometimes grapes are heated before fermentation. This encourages the skins to release their colouring matter to the maximum, giving deeply coloured wines. The potential danger of this thermo-vinification is that, unless carefully controlled, it can give a 'soupy' taste to the wine.

Pumping over

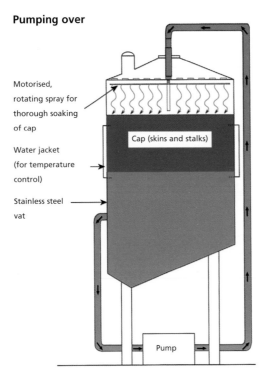

Motorised, rotating spray for thorough soaking of cap

Cap (skins and stalks)

Water jacket (for temperature control)

Stainless steel vat

Pump

If left to itself, a fermenting vat of red wine will soon have a thick mass of pulp and skins on the surface. If nothing is done about this, the juice will take on little colour. The objective is to extract as much colour as possible and this can be achieved in a number of ways. Most red wine is now produced by **pumping over** (*remontage*). This involves drawing off wine from the bottom of the vat and pumping it up on to the top, thus breaking up the crust. When practised, this is normally done twice a day. Some are produced by breaking up and **punching down** the cap (*foulage* and *pigeage*). Traditionally, this meant getting into the vat and trampling the crust down. This posed certain dangers, as there was always the possibility of someone being overcome by carbon dioxide released by the fermentation process. Now the same effect can be achieved with paddles or rakes, or even mechanical *pigeurs*, which look like sophisticated road drills. **Rotary fermenters** are modern devices where red wines are fermented in horizontal tanks, which rotate, bringing the juice regularly back into contact with the skins. The presence of the skins makes fermentation in oak *barriques* impractical for red wines. Vessels used range from large, inert, stainless steel vessels to smaller, wooden, open-top fermenters.

To concentrate the colour and tannin in a wine it is possible to draw off some of the fermenting juice, thus increasing the proportion of solids to

Punching-down the grape-skin cap of Pinot Noir fermenting in oak cuves in Beaune, Côte d'Or, France.

the juice in the vat. This also leaves the producer with a quantity of rosé wine. Ideas about the length of vatting have changed. It used to be thought that the longer the wines and skins were left together (maceration), the more colour, tannin and flavour would be extracted. Colour extraction occurs most rapidly at the beginning of maceration and slows as fermentation continues. Initially, tannin is released more slowly, so longer maceration is needed for wines that are expected to be aged long in bottle. Current thinking suggests that nothing is gained by leaving the wine in contact with the skins once the sugars have been fermented out. Typical maceration times may be six days for a wine with good colour and moderate tannins and 12 or more days for a tannic wine destined for bottle ageing. If the maceration time is limited to one or two days and the juice then drawn off to ferment without the skins, the result will be a rosé wine with low tannins.

The length of time required to complete the fermentation will vary from area to area and grower to grower. It might be anything from one to three weeks. The objective with almost all red wines is to convert all the sugar into alcohol.

Apart from the traditional way of fermenting red wines, there are a number of other techniques. Of these, one of the most widely practised is **carbonic maceration**. In this, complete bunches of uncrushed grapes, together with their stalks, are placed in a vat under a blanket of carbon dioxide. The fermentation begins within the grapes themselves using the grapes' own enzymes and in the absence of yeast. They ultimately burst and a normal fermentation then takes place. This extracts colour, but not tannin, and the resultant wines are soft and full of fruit, with distinctive

notes of kirsch, banana, bubblegum and cinnamon-like spice. They generally do not age well. This is the way that Beaujolais Nouveau and much other wine of the region is made. There are half-way houses between the traditional and carbonic maceration methods and often wines made in the two different ways are blended before bottling.

Whichever vinification method is used, when the vatting has finished the free-run wine is drawn off. The remaining grape skins, gorged with juice, are then pressed. This gives the press wine, most of which will be blended in with the rest and then put back into vats or barrels, to undergo the secondary, or malolactic, fermentation, and ageing. The final pressing of the skins often releases wines which are too tannic and coarse to be used for blending and these will be distilled.

Rosé Wine Vinification

There are essentially three ways of making rosé wine. In the first, the black grapes are pressed directly and the juice is then fermented, as in white wines. Technically this produces a **vin gris**. Most traditional rosés produced in the EU are made by an **abbreviated red wine vinification,** with crushed grapes being macerated for one to three days before the pale-coloured juice is run off to continue its fermentation without the skins. The third, or **saignée, method** requires the grapes to be destalked, but not crushed, and vatted for 12–24 hours; the lesser the contact, the paler the colour. The juice is then run off and fermented

without skin contact. Sometimes only a portion of the juice will be bled off; the remainder will be used to make a more concentrated red wine. Rosé wines are usually fermented in tank rather than cask and bottled young. In the EU, with the exception of Champagne, it is forbidden to make quality rosé wines by blending red and white wine.

White Wine Vinification

White wines have to be treated with more care than reds, as the danger of oxidation of the grapes is more real. The grapes are pressed on arrival at the press-house as colour and tannin are not required, though there may be two or three hours' skin contact at low temperature to impart more flavour and fruit. The juice is drawn off from the press, either into vats or casks, where it is allowed to ferment.

Normally, fermentation will take place at a lower temperature (usually between 15° C and 20° C, sometimes even as low as 9° C) and over a longer period than red wine. This is to enhance the fruit flavours of the wine and avoid loss of freshness. Given that the fermentation reaction itself creates heat, this may well mean that the must will need cooling. In a modern winery, this is a straightforward process, for each vat will have its individual heating/refrigeration system. Fermentation at too low a temperature results in the creation of peardrop aromas and the failure to extract varietal fruit from the skins of the grapes. Fermentation at higher temperatures can encourage more complex aromas to evolve, but the risk is that varietal fruit characteristics will be dissipated.

If the wine is fermented in barrel, the lees may be stirred up on a regular basis to impart further flavour and richness to the wine. Many winemakers produce white wine fermented in new oak. Once the fermentation is over, the wine will be racked (transferred into clean casks) to avoid spoilage from over-long contact with the lees.

Sweet Wine Vinification

Sweet wines can be created in a number of ways. The best wines come from grapes that are extremely rich in sugar because of concentration by botrytis; or drying processes such as *passito* or grapes shrivelling on the vine; or grapes freezing on the vine so that the water can be removed. The fermentation then stops naturally when the yeasts have converted as much sugar into alcohol as they can. This happens in wines such as Sauternes and Tokaji Aszu, which have an actual alcohol content of 13–14% abv, and for wines such as German *Trockenbeerenausleses* and *Eisweins* which can be as low as 7% abv. If a fermenting must is filtered using a membrane filter that is so fine that it removes all the yeasts, before the sugar has been totally consumed, a sweet wine will result. As not all the sugar has been converted, it will be light in alcohol. This method is used for Asti and Moscato d'Asti. For lesser quality wines, sulphur dioxide can be used to kill off the yeasts before they have finished their work.

In some countries, particularly Germany, medium sweet wines can be created by the addition of unfermented grape juice, or *Süssreserve*. This is a sterile product made by membrane-filtering must before fermentation starts, or by dosing it with sulphur dioxide. *Süssreserve* is added to dry wines after fermentation. This sweetens them and balances their acidity. A cheaper method, also carried out once the fermentation has been finished, is the addition of concentrated must. This process is not used for better quality wines as it can impart off-flavours to the wine.

Yeast can also be killed off by the addition of alcohol as in the production of Port and the Vins Doux Naturels of France. This is covered in more detail in Chapters 33–6 fortified wines.

MALOLACTIC FERMENTATION

During **malolactic (or secondary) fermentation**, lactic bacteria convert the tart malic acids (as in apples) into the softer lactic acids (as in milk). For red wines this fermentation is considered to be necessary and may be encouraged by raising the temperature of the wine and by not adding sulphur dioxide. With white wines, a choice must be made. Malolactic fermentation softens and reduces acidity, and can be a source of new flavours such as butter and hazelnut. On the other hand, some of the pure fruit aromas may be lost, and the richer, rounder, softer white wine will be less refreshing to drink. Malolactic fermentation may be avoided through scrupulous hygiene, storage at cool temperatures and the use of sulphur dioxide.

Maturation and Bottling

It should be recognised that most of the wine that is produced in the world is made for early, if not immediate, consumption. Such wine does not need maturation. However, many finer wines will benefit from further ageing in cask and/or in bottle. This particularly applies to red wines, which may initially have harsh flavours and tannins that need to soften. Some quality wines have a minimum ageing period included in the laws that control their production.

6

MATURATION

To survive medium- or long-term ageing, wines need high levels of tannin, acidity or alcohol, but more importantly, they must have fruit that will develop into interesting flavours in order to make such ageing worthwhile. The changes that occur to a wine during maturation can be divided into three categories. Firstly, the maturation vessel may add components to the wine, for example the tannins and toasty flavours of a new oak barrel. Secondly, some chemical reactions require the presence of oxygen; these include those that lead to the caramel, coffee and nut flavours in liqueur muscats and tawny Ports. These flavours will also contribute in a subtle way to the complexity of wines such as *barrique*-aged Chardonnays and Bordeaux reds. The question of cask-ageing is one for the winemaker to decide. Generally, the better the wine, the greater the need for barrels, and especially for new barrels. The third category covers flavour developments that can occur only in an inert, oxygen-free environment such as a glass bottle. The first two kinds of ageing are discussed next; bottle-ageing is discussed at the end of this chapter.

Vessels used for Maturation

Factors to consider when selecting new barrels are the source of the oak; whether it has been sawn or split; how it has been dried, whether it has been 'toasted' or not; and, if it has, to what extent. Most wine casks are made from French or American oak. French barrels are considerably more expensive than American barrels, as the production process, which involves splitting the trunk of the tree, is labour-intensive and more wasteful of wood than the more efficient sawing that is used for American oak staves. Whereas American barrels tend to give sweet, vanilla and coconut flavours, and a little, rather sappy, tannin, French oak barrels tend to give a broader spectrum of flavours and tannins that help a wine age better once bottled.

Small casks have a more marked effect on the wine than large ones because they present a larger ratio of wood surface to the wine. The standard cask, or *barrique*, holds 225 litres, the equivalent of 300 bottles, or 25 twelve-bottle cases. It has now been adopted by wineries in most parts of the world. New wood adds an aroma and flavour of oak to the wine, usually identified by a vanilla or smoky character, as well as wood tannins. This effect diminishes as the cask gets older, so a one-year-old cask gives less flavour than a new one and, by the time a cask is four years old, it imparts little flavour or tannin. A declining scale of the contribution that the ageing vessel imparts to the wine might read:

> small new oak barrels;
> second-hand oak barrels (one or two years old);
> large old casks and vats;
> neutral vats: stainless steel, epoxy, glass-lined.

Normally, a cask-aged red wine will spend a maximum of 18 months to two years in cask before bottling, though there are some, such as Barolo, which might spend considerably more. During this time the casks will be topped up regularly and racked every six months or so. Before the final racking, the wine will usually be fined (see below) to remove any unstable proteins.

While most white wines have been fermented in vat, some will then be aged in wood for a short time. This is to give extra complexity to the wine.

Short-Cuts

Casks are not the only means by which oak flavours can be added to a wine. Oak chips are often added to the grapes as an economical alternative to casks. Recent developments include inner-stave treatment, by which a vertical pole is put into a fermentation vat with staves sticking out from it like signposts. By this method oak and wine come into contact effectively at a much lower cost than by a cask.

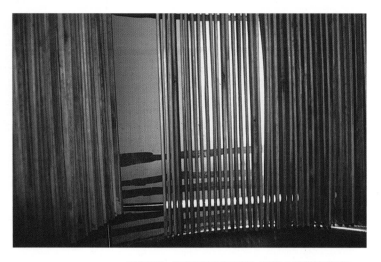

Inner-staves, one short-cut by which oak flavours can be added to wine.

FINING, STABILISATION AND FILTRATION

The key to understanding the various treatments that occur before bottling, including the differences between fining and filtration, is to ask what sorts of thing might be unacceptable in a bottled wine, how these things might occur, and how they might be prevented.

Fining

If we decide that a bottled wine must be clear and bright (and many growers pride themselves on bottling wines unfiltered), then any particles that are large enough to cause cloudiness must be removed. This is done by filtration. Some particles are too small to cause cloudiness at the moment of bottling, but their molecules may, through chemical reactions that occur slowly after bottling, result in the formation of new, larger particles that do cause cloudiness. It may be impossible to use filtration to remove the particles that cause this to happen because they are so small that they cannot be removed without stripping the wine of other components that contribute to its character. **Fining** is a method that stimulates these tiny, problematic molecules to coagulate into larger lumps which either sink to the bottom of the wine, or can be removed by filtration. Substances used for this include egg white (albumen), bentonite (diatomaceous earth) and isinglass, as well as many proprietary products. The process may take place on one or several occasions during a wine's existence in bulk. **Casse** is the term used to describe a number of chemical faults in a wine that give rise to haziness or a deposit, accompanied often by off-smells or flavours. It may be the result of unstable proteins in the wine. In this case there is generally a grey haze, but no off-flavours. Fining with bentonite should prevent and may cure this. Fining can also be used to

change the character of a wine: many Classed-Growth Bordeaux estates use egg whites to remove astringent tannins from the wine, without taking away flavour components. To summarise, suspension of particles that are too small to be seen is called a colloid. If these particles may change to become visible, then the suspension is called an unstable colloid. The key difference between fining and filtration is that fining removes unstable colloids, whereas filtration removes solid particles, some which may have been formed during the fining process.

Chemical Stabilisation

Throughout its life, wine is likely to precipitate certain deposits. In white wines these may be tartrates, and in red, the tartrates, may be deeply stained and joined by other colour components. The deposits are harmless, but can spoil the clarity and flavour of a wine, which is one reason why wines are sometimes decanted before being served. If we wish to prevent deposits of any kind from forming, then the wine must be stabilised. The most common chemical instability leads to the formation of crystals of calcium or potassium **tartrate**. These look like sugar or, perhaps, fine shards of glass. White wines are particularly prone, with cold weather often the cause. However, because certain markets, particularly the United States and Japan, insist on star-bright wines, many wines will be chilled in bulk when they are young so that the precipitation of tartrates, takes place before bottling. Fining is also used to remove **tannins** from many large-volume red wines to prevent deposits forming. **Oxidation** occurs when a wine is attacked by oxygen. White wines become dark in colour, rosé wines turn orange and red wines take on an orange, or even brown, tinge. This effect can be countered by the correct use of sulphur dioxide before bottling and by ensuring that the wine is not exposed to air. Other cases result from over-high levels of **metals**, particularly iron and copper, probably acquired by the wine coming in contact with old-fashioned cellar equipment. This is now rarely a problem. Iron produces a grey deposit and a smell of bad eggs; copper an orange-brown colour and a musty smell. The most common cure for both copper and iron *casse* is by using **blue fining**. This is based on potassium ferrocyanide, which is a poisonous substance, and so may be carried out by a qualified chemist only.

Microbiological Stabilisation

Micro-organisms, such as yeasts and bacteria, as well as playing an essential role in the creation of wine, can also be the cause of a number of problems. Among these is the possibility of fermentation starting up again after a wine has been bottled. It might include acetic spoilage, caused by aerobic acetobacter converting the ethanol in the wine into acetic acid. This can spread from one cask to another so needs to be prevented by the addition of suitable doses of **sulphur dioxide**, which combines with oxygen to render the acetobacter inoperative. One way to reduce unwanted problems is by killing the micro-organisms using sulphur dioxide or heat. **Pasteurisation**, used mainly for red wines, is an example of the latter. This is generally achieved by a 'flash' system, which heats the wine to 95° C for a second or so. This is widely used by large producers in areas such as the Beaujolais, where large volumes of wine of consistent quality are needed. A more gentle method of eliminating unwanted micro-organisms, and one where there is less risk of harming the wine, is by physically removing them by **filtration**, generally at the time of bottling. This can be carried out at room temperatures.

Filtration

In order to prepare the wine for bottling, the last positive action that a winemaker takes in the life of a wine, they will do their best to see that it is perfectly bright. Modern technology enables the winemaker to remove even the finest invisible matter from wine. There is, however, the danger that, as filters are not selective, some of the character of the wine may be removed with the particles. The finer the quality of the wine, the more gentle the filtration should be, as long as stability can be assured. Indeed, some winemakers proudly proclaim that their wines are unfiltered. This is more often the case with red wines, where a deposit in a bottle of fine wine is more acceptable. If the wine is anything but dry, it is

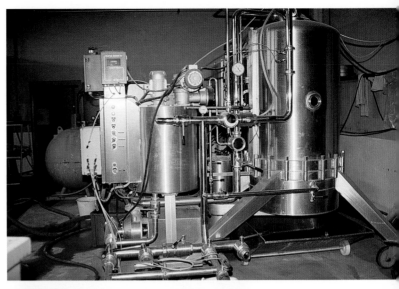

Kieselguhr machine.

Waste Kieselguhr after use.

much less stable and should go through some form of treatment, either by heat or filtration, before bottling. The most common type of filter is a **plate filter**, which will remove all unwanted particles: however, wines which are low in alcohol, or have some residual sugar, should be sterile-filtered, using a **membrane filter**. This will remove both yeasts and bacteria. Because they are so fine, the membranes are easily blocked, so the wine will previously have passed through a plate

Plate filter

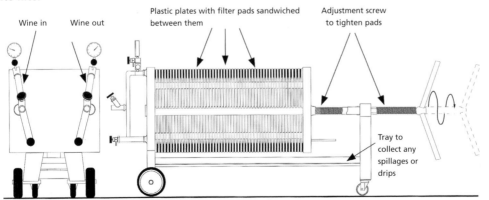

Wine in   Wine out   Plastic plates with filter pads sandwiched between them   Adjustment screw to tighten pads

Tray to collect any spillages or drips

The plate filter consists of a number of plastic plates interspersed with filter pads, which are available in various grades. The pipe-work is arranged so that wine will pass through one filter pad only, so increasing the number of pads will increase the maximum throughput of wine.

filter to remove the larger particles. Because sterilising-grade membrane filters leave a wine totally free of micro-organisms, it is essential to avoid later contamination through the bottling-line, corks or bottles.

BOTTLING

White wines are generally bottled much younger than reds. Such wines are specifically made for drinking young. Up to the time of bottling, they will have spent all their life in a temperature-controlled stainless steel vat.

Wines that are low in alcohol or have some residual sugar are potentially unstable, and should undergo **cold, sterile bottling**. This implies

Stripped cork waiting for collection.

complete sterilisation not just of the wine, but also of the filling equipment, bottles and closures. Cold in this case means normal winery temperature. By contrast, certain cheaper wines may be 'hot'-bottled; this is a cheaper, but less gentle, kind of pasteurisation.

There is currently much discussion as to which is the most effective closure for a bottle of wine. **Cork** has long been the favourite, but it seems generally accepted that about 5 per cent of bottles with a cork closure suffer from taint or other effects due to the varying properties of a natural product. Cork producers have invested considerable sums in developing treatments that will eradicate these problems. **Artificial corks**, generally made from some form of plastic, have been developed as a replacement and give an acceptable result for wines that are not to be aged. For longer periods of storage, artificial corks offer insufficient protection against oxygen, though research is being undertaken to remedy

this. The third alternative, which initially found most of its support in white wines from Australia and New Zealand, but which is now becoming increasingly used worldwide, even for red wines, is closure with some form of **screw-cap**. In such a case, there will be a protective blanket of inert gas between the wine and the closure.

Bottle Ageing

For a short period after a wine has been bottled, it can suffer from what is known as 'bottle sickness', which means that it may not smell of much, or taste as it should. The majority of wines are bottled for immediate consumption, and ageing them results in a loss of fresh fruit flavours. However, there are many which improve after many months', or even years', ageing in bottle. The most notable examples of this include Vintage Port, the finest German Rieslings, Classed-Growth Bordeaux and the best red and white Burgundies, which may not reach their peaks for 20 years or more after bottling. The wine legislation of countries such as Italy and Spain insist that certain wines may not be released until they have aged for a minimum number of years in bottle. It is essential that any ageing time should be spent undisturbed in a cool dark place, with a constant temperature, ideally around 12–13° C. There should also be constant humidity. The bottles should be stored lying on their side, so that the corks remain moist to provide the optimum seal.

Alternatives to Bottles

Glass bottles are inert, impermeable, portable, cheap to produce and quite strong (although they tend to shatter). Their main disadvantages are that they are heavy and rigid. Weight adds to transport costs, and their rigidity means that they cannot be packed to make the best use of the available space. It also means that once opened, an ullaged (part-filled) bottle will contain a space for air, which will attack the wine unless it is sucked out or replaced by an inert gas such as nitrogen.

Plastic bottles and bags are much lighter than glass, and bag-in-box packs collapse as the wine is consumed, avoiding the ingress of air. Unfortunately, the plastics used for these are not as inert as glass, and are slightly permeable, so the wines will degrade over a period of months. This is fine for most wines, since they are intended for immediate consumption, but for long-term storage and ageing, glass bottles are currently the best vessel.

A glossary appears at the end of this book.

Factors that Affect the Price of a Wine

The costs that contribute to the retail price of a bottle of wine can be divided into the cost of production of the liquid and costs involved in packaging and distribution. At each stage, the individuals or organisations involved must make sufficient profit for their activity to be worthwhile. Finally, it must be remarked that, no matter how cheap or expensive the production and distribution costs may be, a wine can only sell at a price that the market will support.

7

PRODUCTION COSTS

These are discussed in more detail in Chapter 4 on Viticulture and Chapter 5 on Winemaking and the specific regional chapters, but it is useful to bring together here the factors that account for differences in the price of the finished wine.

Costs that can affect the price of the raw grape material include:
- The labour demands of the vineyard. Isolated, steep, small, hand-tended plots are very labour-intensive; vast flat mechanised sites are less so.
- The cost and availability of labour and/or equipment.
- Economies of scale.
- The degree of selection of the grape material. This has a labour cost, and the discarded material also means less wine will be made.
- Yields. High yields allow all the other fixed costs to be divided between a larger quantity of grapes. Lower yields may result in higher quality, and higher prices may be demanded.
- Supply and demand. Certain varieties and regions will be able to command a higher price, irrespective of the costs of production, simply because there is a particular demand and limited supply. Equally, where there is overproduction, there is a danger that the price paid for the grapes may fail to cover the production costs.

Where the cost of land is very high (as, for example, in Champagne, and in some regions where there is competition for other kinds of land use, such as the expanding suburbs of Adelaide), the cost of grapes must be high enough to make the investment in the land worthwhile. Conversely, where high prices can be demanded for the grapes, land prices are pushed upwards.

Factors that can affect the winemaking costs include:

- Equipment (presses, fermentation and storage vessels, and so on). These costs are considerable, and much of this equipment lies idle for most of the year. The more use that can be made of them at vintage time, the wider the costs can be spread.
- Barrels, where used. The cost will depend on the type of oak, how it has been coopered, whether it is new or second-hand. There is also the labour cost involved in ensuring that barrels are always topped up.
- Ageing (whether in vat, cask or bottle) requires expensive storage facilities, and ties up capital.

Equipment is often shared. A **co-operative** (*cave co-opérative, cantina sociale, Winzergenossenschaft*) is an institution that is jointly owned by a number of members. It enables winemaking facilities, and sometimes marketing costs, to be shared. The wine made may be blended from the product of several members and marketed under the name of the co-operative, or individual growers' wines may be returned to the growers to be bottled and sold under their own name. Co-operatives exist almost everywhere wine is made. A **merchant** (*négociant*) buys in grapes and/or finished wine from growers and/or co-operatives. The grape grower then has less need to invest in winemaking, ageing, bottling and marketing. Merchants can take advantage of economies of scale because they will often be able to source and supply larger quantities of any given wine than any individual estate. The large-volume New World brands follow this model. Because of the shared costs, co-operative and merchant wines are generally lower in price than **estate** (domaine) wines from the same region. However, the smaller-scale production at estates can allow greater care to be taken at each stage, though with resultant extra labour costs. In most regions, estates make the best wines, but because they cost more to make, and are usually available in smaller quantities, prices will be higher than for merchant and co-operative wines. Whether they still represent value for money is a matter for the consumer to decide. It should be recognised that the best merchant and co-operatives produce wines that are of extremely high quality, and can sell them at high prices. It might also be admitted that estate wines have fewer options for blending to fill out any deficiencies, and their quality depends on the skill of a smaller team of vinegrowers and winemakers. Consequently, the quality of estate wines can be less reliable, and the style less predictable, than those of merchant and co-operative wines.

PACKAGING, DISTRIBUTION AND SALE

The **ex-cellars price** includes not only the cost of the liquid, but also of the packaging, bottle, closure, label and carton. Before the bottle reaches the consumer, it must be transported to a distribution point in the country of sale. This may be done by an agent or by the retailer. It must then be transported to the final location of sale. Factors that can affect the costs of packaging and distribution include:

- Price of packaging. Unusually shaped and extra-heavy bottles cost extra.
- Transport. Shipping in bulk and bottling in the country of consumption may save costs, though some wines must, by law, be bottled in the region of production. Distance is a factor, though shipping over large distances can be much cheaper than road transport over smaller distances.
- Labour costs and overheads. A small-scale retailer will have to cover higher costs per bottle than large-volume outlets. As the consumer may choose to go to either, the small-scale retailer must find ways to compete (such as service and advice, convenience, a wider range, or great care in the selection of wines in order to offer competitive prices).
- Storage of the wine. Most wine is bought and sold on a 'just-in-time' basis, but in order to maintain a full range, and (for a retailer) full shelves, stock needs to be held. This ties up capital, and the storage facilities also cost money, particularly if they are to be a cool, humid, constant-temperature environment suitable for long-term storage. These costs may account for a significant part of the selling price of older wines, though part of the higher price may be due to their rarity and reputation.
- The selling environment. Wines will generally cost more in restaurants than in shops, partly because a higher degree of profit is expected, but also because the price takes account of the occasion, the environment, and the level of service.

TAXES AND LEVIES

In most countries there will be an excise tax as well as one or more lots of value-added or sales tax. In some cases, the excise is charged on the volume, in others on a value basis. Often the level of tax will vary too, depending on the style of wine – still or sparkling, light or liqueur, imported or domestic.

We can include under this category the contributions, both voluntary and compulsory, that producers make in order to fund regulatory and promotional organisations.

THE MARKET

Irrespective of the costs of production, ultimately the price that a wine sells for is the price that the market will support. In a totally free market, if someone is able to make large profits, other producers will enter the market and will, by providing extra supply and competitively undercutting prices, cause a lowering of the price so that it more closely reflects production costs. Wine does not fit this model, because nature and legislation limit the degree to which production can be increased to match demand.

There may be many classic wine regions still to be found. However, the style of wine that can be produced depends on the soils, the topography and the climate. This means that if a certain style is wanted, the extent of the suitable regions may be so small that they struggle to meet world demand, once again pushing prices upwards. For many wines, the maximum production is legally limited by the size of a defined production area, and the maximum permitted yields within that area. If demand for Champagne, for example, continues to increase, it cannot be matched by an increase in supply, so there is an upward pressure on price, unless consumers can be persuaded that other sparkling wines offer a suitable substitute.

This brings us on to the question of **branding**. The first wine brands were, literally, symbols branded onto casks to indicate their origin. In the Middle Ages, just as now, certain regions had reputations for their wines which allowed them to be sold at higher prices. The brands on the casks helped identify those wines, and acted as a deterrent to fraud.

The most helpful way to treat a brand is to think of it as something that gives a consumer some guarantee of quality and/or style. This treatment would embrace the large-volume New

World brands as well as some merchants and co-operatives, and even famous estates, such as Domaine de la Romanée Conti and Château Haut Brion (the latter was perhaps the first wine to be marketed as a brand, in seventeenth-century London). It would also allow us to include many appellations, such as Chablis or Chianti. It would even include certain countries that have established reputations for reliability, such as Australia, Chile or New Zealand. Certain grape varieties, such as Chardonnay, Sauvignon Blanc and Cabernet Sauvignon, undoubtedly are perceived to be like brands by the consumer, as they enable them to select a wine they may not have tried, with an idea of what to expect.

The consumer may be prepared to pay a little extra, as a kind of 'insurance', to gain this guarantee. In order for the brand reassurance to exist in the first place, the consumer must be familiar with the brand, and the expectations it creates. This can be achieved through a combination of media promotion and encouraging the consumer to sample the product (either by organising tasting events or through price promotions). Such promotions may be funded by trade organisations, the producer companies, or distribution agents and retailers.

Throughout this book, there are summary tables that give an indication of the retail price of the wines. The actual price will vary with the market, but relative prices will be approximately the same (though in wine producing countries far from the EU, local wines may be relatively cheaper compared to imported EU wines). As a guideline, the symbols indicate:

PRICE	MEANING	EXAMPLES
●	Low-priced, generally wines produced in large quantities.	Liebfraumilch
●●	Medium-priced.	Mâcon Villages, Côtes du Rhône Villages
●●●	High-priced.	Chablis Premier Cru
●●●●	Premium-priced.	Hermitage
●●●●+	Prices can be extremely high for these wines.	Grand Cru Burgundy

Example   ■ Red   Where there is a range of
□ White   prices within one type,
■ Rosé   say Low to High, it will
be shown as ●○○

Anjou-Saumur			
KEY AC WINES		**MAIN GRAPE VARIETIES**	**PRICE**
Saumur AC	□	Chenin Blanc	●●
	■	Cabernet Franc	●●
Anjou AC	□	Chenin Blanc	●●
	■	Cabernet Franc	●●
	■	Grolleau, Cabernet Franc, Gamay	●
Côteaux du Layon	□	Chenin Blanc	●●○○
Savennières	□	Chenin Blanc	●●○○

8   Tasting and Evaluating

Wine is there to be consumed, but the pleasure that is derived from it is enhanced if while we drink it, we take the time to taste it. Tasting has a very important role to play not only within the wine trade, but also for the consumer. A winemaker will taste wine regularly during the production process to monitor how it is developing, while blending, and as part of the final quality control checks before release. Later down the line, the buyer will taste a range of similar wines before selecting which to list. Journalists and wine advisers need to be able to recognise quality and describe wines in order to make recommendations. Finally, as wine is increasingly sold in outlets such as supermarkets where detailed advice may not be available, it is increasingly important that the consumer is able to make informed choices. Experience and understanding can enhance our experience of wine and many other aspects of life. By learning to understand something, we learn not only to appreciate it, but to enjoy it. It is by regular tasting that the individual can build up a memory-bank of wines that will enable them to make qualitative judgements in the future. Experience is the major factor in the ability to taste wine, but a systematic approach backs this up.

PREPARATION FOR TASTING

In tasting, three of the senses play a primary role: sight (to evaluate the appearance of the wine), smell (to evaluate the flavours of the wine on the nose) and taste (to evaluate the sweetness, acidity and bitterness of the wine on the palate). The sense of touch plays a secondary role when assessing the texture of a wine, especially sparkling wines.

It is important that the major senses should be given a free rein to operate to best effect; thus the environment in which the tasting takes place should be as neutral as possible. The location should not be influenced by outside smells and the lighting should be as natural as possible. If the tasting cannot take place in daylight, then daylight fluorescent strip-lighting is the best alternative. There should be a white background against which the wines can be studied. This might be the surface of the tasting-bench, or a sheet of plain white paper.

The taster must approach the tasting with a clean palate, unaffected by food or cigarettes, for example. Chewing a piece of bread or drinking water may help to cleanse the palate. Such problems as a cold or hayfever quite naturally affect the ability to smell and taste well.

It is imperative that there should be no outside odours to confuse the power of smell. Again, tobacco, perfume and aftershave should be avoided. There should be no food smells coming from a nearby kitchen or canteen. A tasting glass, too, might have residual smells, of cardboard from the box in which it was stored or of detergent with which it was washed or the cloth with which it was dried. All these can invalidate a tasting. Smell the glass before you use it and look to see if it is star-bright.

Equipment

What is the ideal tasting glass? It should be large enough to allow a tasting measure of wine to be

The ideal tasting room, with plenty of natural light, neutral colour scheme and white surfaces. Spittoons and sinks are available for tasters to use.

swirled about. The sides should slope inwards, in a tulip shape, so that the wines can move freely to release the flavours, to be concentrated at the top for smelling. There should also be a stem so that the glass can be held without the temperature of the wine being affected, and so that the colour can be assessed. All of these features have been incorporated in the standard, or ISO (International Standards Organisation), glass illustrated.

For a serious tasting, a separate glass should be provided for each wine to be tasted. This enables comparisons more easily and gives the possibility to return to the wine to see how it is developing in the glass in contact with the air.

The taster should also have a notebook in which to record their judgement of the wine. Tasting is very personal, but a systematic approach will enable fair comparisons to be made over a long period, either with the development of the same

wine or with similar wines. Although memory plays an important role in tasting, detailed notes provide the essential support.

Preparation of the Wines

This is of great importance. To be fairly judged, each wine has its ideal temperature. White wines should be served cool, but not cold. Red wines should be served at room temperature, provided the tasting room is not too warm, so might be brought there the evening before the tasting. Wines may be decanted before tasting. There could be a number of reasons for this: to separate them from any deposit in the bottle, to enable them to breathe, or, in some cases, to avoid pre-judgement by seeing the label or bottle shape.

The order in which wines are tasted is also important, for the palate should not be influenced by what has gone before. For white wines, dry should come before sweet. With red wines it is rather more difficult. Some think that older wines should be tasted before younger ones because they are likely to be more delicate. There are others who will always start with the young wines and work back in age. White wines are generally tasted before reds. What is best is the order with which the taster is most comfortable.

It is also worth remembering, in the context of serious analytical tasting, that most wines are made to be consumed with food. As an example of this, many Spanish and Italian red wines in isolation taste harsh, but when married with the local cuisine, which is heavily dependent on olive oil, seem more appealing.

THE STAGES OF TASTING
Appearance

There is a logical order in which the senses should be brought into play when a wine is tasted. Naturally, sight is the first to play a role and most people find it easiest to say what a wine looks like.

Clarity is of vital importance to a wine. Cloudiness is the first indication that there might be a problem. There are two major causes for this. Particularly with an old red wine, it might have come about because the wine has been decanted clumsily and the sediment disturbed. Of more concern would be cloudiness caused by re-fermentation in the bottle, or bacterial problems. This would subsequently be confirmed both on the nose and the palate.

The **colour**, both the **intensity** and the **hue**, of a wine can suggest much about it. To get the true colour of a wine in a glass, hold it away from you at an angle of 45° against a plain white background. This should reveal two distinct

Glasses of red and white wine, illustrating the spectrum of intensities and hues that may be found: pale to deep, purple to tawny, water-white to golden.

Rim vs Core

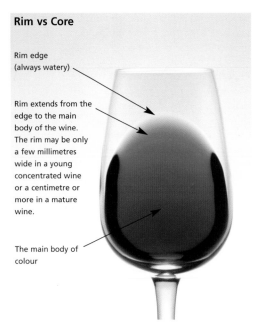

Rim edge (always watery)

Rim extends from the edge to the main body of the wine. The rim may be only a few millimetres wide in a young concentrated wine or a centimetre or more in a mature wine.

The main body of colour

colours, one at the rim of the wine and the other in its body, or core

Red wines get paler as they age, and the first sign of this ageing will be at the rim, which may change from purple, to ruby, to russet and then, with extreme age, to brown. Most wines are made for drinking young, so may never reach the second stage in this process. It should also be understood that each grape variety has its individual depth and hue, with some grapes being grown specifically to add colour. The degree of colour extraction during vinification affects the appearance of the final wine. A pale red wine with a tawny rim could be a mature wine from a range of varieties, or it could be a youthful wine if made from Pinot Noir or Nebbiolo for example. An opaque purple wine could be a mighty Shiraz or it could be a lighter wine made from a variety that releases colour easily, such as Dornfelder. In both cases, smell and taste will reveal more.

White wines have a broad watery rim and may have a greenish tinge when young. Their colour will deepen with age, becoming deep yellow-gold, with a greater graduation of colour towards the rim. Ageing in cask will also alter the colour of a white wine; even quite young wines may gain a golden tint through being put in new wood.

A simple word like red or yellow implies little. These should be qualified as much as possible. Red, for instance, might be anything from tawny, through garnet and brick-red to ruby and purple. Yellow could be lemon or gold. When describing the colour of a wine, it is essential to have a precise vocabulary.

There may be **other observations** to note. 'Legs' or 'tears' are the traces that are left on the side of a glass once you have swirled the wine round. These normally suggest either high alcoholic content or residual sugar. Similarly, very sweet white wines can sometimes appear 'oily' in the glass. Occasionally in white wines there is a deposit of crystals, looking rather like sugar. These are tartrates which have been deposited in cold weather; they do not affect the quality of the wine. Indeed, one German wine producer calls them 'wine diamonds' – something precious in the wine as it shows that it is natural! On occasion, small bubbles may appear in what is supposed to be a still, not a sparkling, wine. With some white wines designed to be drunk young, a little CO_2 may be left in the wine to help preserve its freshness. Indeed, in Portuguese *vinho verde*, it might be introduced artificially at the time of bottling. On the other hand, it may indicate that secondary fermentation has started in the bottle. This would be a fault and should be confirmed on the nose and palate.

The **bubbles** are one aspect of the quality of sparkling wines. Generally speaking, long, slow bottle fermentation produces the smallest, finest bubbles. When examining the bubbles in the glass, however, a great deal can depend on how the glass has been washed. Even small amounts of detergent or grease can stop the bubbles forming, and variations in the texture of the glass can lead to big differences in bubble size, evenness and speed. Definitive assessment of the quality of bubbles can only be made on the palate.

Nose

Since appearance is affected by grape material and winemaking as well as age, it is seldom possible to draw a definitive conclusion about a wine from sight alone. While one might reject a wine at that stage, it is unlikely that you would accept it without further confirmation of merit by the other senses. There are many tasters who consider the sense of smell to be the most important when judgement is to be made. To liberate the full odours of a wine, it should be swirled about in the glass. In order to release them effectively, it may be necessary to warm the glass by cupping the bowl in the palm of your hand.

The first thing to consider when you smell a wine is its **condition**. Is it clean? Unclean? Experienced tasters will often approach a wine with caution, first giving it no more than a gentle sniff. Then, if all is well, swirling the glass around and having a more positive sniff. A bad smell inhaled too deeply can spoil your tasting for the rest of the day. The most common fault that can be picked up at this stage is **cork taint**. It is estimated that 5 per cent of all wines are affected by this, though what in some cases what is considered to be corkiness may be the result of a dirty barrel. The tell-tale signs are hints of mustiness, or sometimes a smell of damp rags. Even if faint on the nose, it is generally more pronounced on the palate. It has nothing to do with particles of cork you might find in your glass. These can be picked out with your finger, or the glass rejected! **Excessive sulphur dioxide** is perhaps the most aggressive of all smells and is found most often in cheap white wines. It is used as a preservative and to kill off yeasts in wines with residual sugar. If used to excess, it can give the wine an acrid smell of burnt matches. Those who suffer from asthma and other respiratory complaints can find it particularly offensive. A wine suffering from **oxidation** is sometimes described as being 'maderised', having a burnt smell like the wines of Madeira, or of caramel. It can generally be recognised visually as well, as the wines have an unnatural brownish tinge and a dull appearance. **Volatile acidity** causes aromas like nail polish and vinegar, and is caused by the presence of acetic bacteria and oxygen together. Any wine with such a smell should be immediately rejected.

The next step is to decide on the **intensity** of the aroma, for this can give a hint as to the quality of the wine. A weak smell may indicate a weak, insipid wine; fine wines will normally have a more intense nose, though they can appear 'closed' or 'dumb' when young. A healthy, outgoing nose is always a good sign.

Wines change over time, and their state of **development** can be assessed on the nose. A youthful wine smells of the primary aromas of the grapes used in its production. With ageing, they soften and harmonise better. Thus a wine that is subtle and complex on the nose is likely to be more mature and of better quality. There is a profound difference between age and maturity. A five-year-old classified growth from Bordeaux will still be in its infancy, while a five-year-old Beaujolais may well be long past its best. Thus, whilst some wines might seem tired on the nose when they are three years old, others may still seem youthful at thirty. In the technical vocabulary of tasting, aromas are generally used for describing young wines and are derived from the fruit itself, whilst the term bouquet applies to the assembled assortment of smells that come with a wine's ageing, particularly in bottle.

The final stage is to describe the **character** of the aromas. Little is more personal than one's perceptions of smells and flavours. Each person has in their memory a limited number of tastes and smells and their range will depend upon the individual's experiences. Smells and tastes can be classified in a number of ways. At the end of this chapter, we include the WSET Systematic Approach to Tasting Wine, which includes suggestions of words we might use to describe aromas, and how those aromas might be classified. With practice, we can learn to associate certain combinations of aromas with specific grape varieties, regions and sometimes even individual vineyards. Note that although many sweet wines have a distinctive nose, sugar is not volatile and therefore cannot be detected by the sense of smell. There are some wines, such as many *trocken* wines of Germany, which may appear sweet on the nose, but are in fact dry.

Palate: Taste, Texture and Smell (again)

The last of the major senses to be used in the whole process is that of taste. For the experienced taster this may do no more than confirm impressions that have already been made. In order to liberate the full flavours of a wine in the mouth, a taster will purse their lips, lean forward and draw air in through the wine. It is surprising how a wine opens up in this way as the volatile components are released. A number of elements in a wine are detected by the physiological reactions of the wine on the taste buds in the mouth. Different aspects of a wine's taste can be noted by the reaction of different parts of the mouth, tongue and gums. This is another reason for swirling the wine round in your mouth when you taste it.

Sweetness is often the first sensation that you get when you taste a wine; this is because sweetness makes itself known on the tip of the tongue.

Acidity is recognised at the sides of the tongue, towards the back, so this is often the second sensation after sweetness, which it tends to dominate. (All the greatest sweet wines have high acidity to balance the sweetness.) High acidity in a wine may make your mouth water. Wines lacking acidity will be flabby and unappealing.

Tannin is an important constituent of a red wine that is to be aged. It has a drying effect on the gums and teeth, in contrast to the salivating effect of acidity. It is most pronounced in young red wines. It should not be confused with a similar sensation sometimes given by red wines that are just past their best and beginning to 'dry out'. Bitterness may be the result of excessive tannin in a wine due to over-extraction. It can be recognised in the middle of the tongue towards the back.

Body is sometimes called mouth-feel; it is the impression of a wine's weight in the mouth. Some wines give the impression of being light; these are referred to as 'light-bodied'. Others, which feel heavy, are described as being 'full-bodied'. Alcohol, tannin, concentration of fruit, sugar and glycerol all contribute to the mouth-feel of a wine.

Alcohol is often difficult to detect on the palate, but is generally a constituent of the 'body'. When a wine is high in alcohol, it may give warming sensation at the back of the mouth. (In the UK, 'low alcohol' is a specific legal definition of a type of wine, so it is better to say that a wine is 'light' in alcohol.) Alcohol is an essential ingredient of wine, generally representing about 12 per cent of the total volume. The taste of a wine comes from the grapes that have been used and the way that they

Sensitive areas of the tongue

Bitter

Sour (Acids)

Salt

Sweetness

Tannin is mainly detected on the gums

have been treated. Alcohol is what binds these flavours together and rounds them off. It is part of the body of the wine, but not the body itself. The level of the alcohol in the wine must be in balance with the flavours; thus a full-bodied wine, such as a Californian Zinfandel, needs a higher level of alcohol than a delicate Riesling from the Mosel.

Generally, the **flavour characteristics** found on the palate will confirm those already recognised on the nose, but this is not always the case. They will, however, be more complex, as there are three distinct stages in the taste of a fine wine and each of these might vary not just in its flavours but also in its intensity. The first stage is what might be called the immediate impression; this may last for only a short time. Then comes the mid-palate, when the full flavour of the wine becomes apparent

in the mouth. Finally, there is the aftertaste or **finish**, the time when the flavours of the wine linger on the palate after the wine has been swallowed, or spat out. The complexity and the length of all these stages are to be taken in consideration when assessing quality.

For sparkling wines, the **bubbles** should also be considered. Gentle bubbles are an indication of age and high quality. In the best wines the bubbles will be long-lasting. Aggressive bubbles that dissipate quickly in the glass indicate an inferior wine.

Conclusions

The most important conclusion to be drawn is an assessment of the **quality** of the wine. You may be assessing it against a group of other wines, perhaps from the same grape variety or region, perhaps selling at the same price. To decide whether a wine is a poor, mediocre, good or great example of a Mâcon, for example, we must first have an idea of what a Mâcon should be like. The same applies when we are deciding whether a wine offers good value for money: we should each develop a clear idea of what we are entitled to expect across a range of prices. This is where a wide-ranging tasting experience becomes very important.

One danger with judging wines against their class is that it is very difficult to know how to assess wines that are not typical. To return to the example of Mâcon, if we are presented with two wines, both of which are crisp, with clean, citrus aromas, but one of which has more intensity of flavour, longer length and more character, it is quite easy to judge which one is better. But suppose one year a producer decided to make a sweet wine? What would we compare it to? Is there such a thing as an absolute set of criteria for judging quality in wines? How do you compare the qualities of a medium-price red Burgundy and a medium-price Australian Shiraz, or Chardonnay, or a premium-price Vintage Madeira? The characteristics of these wines may seem so different that comparisons are meaningless. Yet, consumers make decisions based on such comparisons whenever they buy a bottle of wine. Although there is little agreement as to what constitutes quality in a wine, apart from that it should be free of defects, a number of criteria recur when critics are justifying their assessments. These include the balance of components; the length of the finish; the intensity of the aromas and flavours (in the sense that a dilute wine is a poor wine, though a super-concentrated wine isn't necessarily a good one); the complexity of the aromas and flavours; how expressive it is of its region of origin or its grape variety; how well the wine will last; and

WSET® Systematic Approach to Tasting Wine

WSET® LEVEL 3 ADVANCED SYSTEMATIC APPROACH TO TASTING©

APPEARANCE

Clarity	clear - dull
Intensity	water-white - pale - medium - deep - opaque
Colour white	colourless - lemon green - lemon - gold - amber
rosé	pink - salmon - orange
red	purple - ruby - garnet - mahogany - tawny
Other observations	rim vs. core, legs, bubbles

NOSE

Condition	clean - unclean (faults?)
Intensity	light - medium - pronounced
Development	youthful - developing - aged
Aroma characteristics	fruit - floral - spice - vegetal - nut - oak - other

PALATE

Sweetness	dry - off-dry - medium-dry - medium - medium-sweet - sweet
Acidity	low - low-medium - medium - medium-high - high
Tannin	low - low-medium - medium - medium-high - high
Body	light - light-medium - medium - medium-full - full
Intensity	light - medium - pronounced
Bubbles size	small - medium - large (sparkling wine only)
texture	delicate - creamy - aggressive
Flavour characteristics	fruit - floral - spice - vegetal - nut - oak - other
Alcohol level	low - medium - high - fortified
Length	short - medium - long

CONCLUSIONS

Quality	poor - acceptable - good - excellent
Maturity	immature - ready to drink, but could age - ready to drink - tired
Value category	inexpensive - mid-priced - high-priced - premium

WSET® Systematic Approach to Tasting Wine

AROMA AND FLAVOUR CHARACTERISTICS

FRUIT

Citrus	grapefruit, lemon, lime
Green Fruit	apple (green/ripe?) gooseberry, pear
Stone Fruit	apricot, peach
Red Fruit	raspberry, red cherry, plum, redcurrant, strawberry
Black Fruit	blackberry, black cherry, blackcurrant
Tropical Fruit	banana, kiwi, lychee, mango, melon, passion fruit, pineapple
Dried Fruit	fig, prune, raisin, sultana

FLORAL

| Blossom | elderflower, orange |
| Flowers | perfume, rose, violet |

SPICE

| Sweet | cinnamon, cloves, ginger, nutmeg, vanilla |
| Pungent | black/white pepper, liquorice, juniper |

VEGETAL

Fresh	asparagus, green bell pepper, mushroom
Cooked	cabbage, tinned vegetables (asparagus, artichoke, pea etc.), black olive
Herbaceous	eucalyptus, grass, hay, mint, blackcurrant leaf, wet leaves
Kernel	almond, coconut, hazelnut, walnut, chocolate, coffee
Oak	cedar, medicinal, resinous, smoke, vanilla, tobacco

OTHER

Animal	leather, wet wool, meaty
Autolytic	yeast, biscuit, bread, toast
Dairy	butter, cheese, cream, yoghurt
Mineral	earth, petrol, rubber, tar, stony/steely
Ripeness	caramel, candy, honey, jam, marmalade, treacle, cooked, baked, stewed

what potential it has to improve in the bottle. It is also important never to forget that a great wine should be enjoyable to drink!

The other aspect we should note when drawing our conclusions is the **state of evolution** of the wine. If it is not past its best or ready to drink, how much longer should we keep it? A wine that is past its best will appear dull. Both red and white wines develop a brown hue as they become out-of-condition. Their flavour may fade, or they may develop unpleasant sherry-like notes. Assessing whether a wine has a future is more difficult. High levels of tannin or acidity may make a wine difficult to enjoy. If there is sufficient fruit concentration, then it may be possible for the wine to mellow and increase in complexity over time, enabling it to offer pleasure at some point in the future. We would say it is not ready to drink. As we gain experience of following how wines age, it becomes possible to guess how many months or years will be needed for the wine to become enjoyable, and then for it to attain the desired degree of bottle-development. Tannins, alcohol and sugar help preserve a wine while the constituent components evolve and integrate. Taken together, the tannin, acid, alcohol, sugar and fruit extract are said to constitute a wine's **structure**. Wines that are high in acidity or tannin, but lacking fruit, do not get any better as they age: they simply dry out and fade. We would conclude that these wines are out of balance and will not improve. Similarly, if one, usually unpleasant, flavour dominates the wine, we may say that it is out of balance. The **balance** between the constituent components (tannin, acid, alcohol, sugar and the flavour components) is an important aspect to consider when assessing a wine's quality.

In addition to assessing the quality and state of evolution of the wine, we should also consider how the wine might be used. Who might buy it? What occasions might it be used for? What sorts of food might it accompany?

TASTING NOTES

In order to assist students in their tasting and note-taking, the Wine & Spirit Education Trust has developed progressive guides to tasting at each of the course levels. A copy of the Advanced Certificate Systematic Approach to Tasting Wine is shown above. The left-hand column lists the aspects that should be considered for each wine that you taste. The right-hand column offers a number of examples of terms that may be used, but is not an exclusive list.

FRENCH WINE LAWS

The production of wine today is tightly controlled by two organisations, which can be likened to the carrot and the stick. The carrot is the *Institut National des Appellations d'Origine* (INAO). This took over the role of the *Comité National des Appellations d'Origine* after the Second World War and controls the hierarchy of French quality wines. The stick is the *Service de Repression des Fraudes*, which is responsible for the application of the very complicated laws on wine production. From the moment that the grapes are picked, they must be covered by some form of documentation, until, in France, the wine is purchased by the final consumer. (On the French domestic market, every bottle of wine carries a capsule with the French government seal on it, showing that the tax has been paid.) In addition to the above organisation, there is the *Office National Interprofessionel des Vins de Table* (ONIVINS), which controls all French table wine. In 1963 the French laws were absorbed into, and indeed, provided much of the framework for, the European Community wine regime.

QUALITY WINE

France has two levels of QWPSR (Quality Wine Produced in a Specified Region).

Appellation d'Origine Contrôlée (AC or AOC)

This is the highest level that a French wine can attain. Though the requirements may vary widely from one region to another, they are the most tightly defined and the following points will always feature:

1. Areas of production – the boundaries of which are based on the composition of the soil. Some ACs may include a number of different soil types within the area.

2. Permitted grape varieties – the principle being that they 'should be hallowed by local, loyal and established custom'.

3. Viticultural practices – including planting distances and pruning methods.

4. The maximum permitted yield per hectare.

5. Vinification methods, including ageing.

6. The minimum alcoholic degree, which must be achieved without chaptalisation.

Within most regions there is a well-established hierarchy of appellations, which, in general, are geographically based. The more specific the geographic description, the higher the appellation and the tighter the regulations. There may be the possibility to declassify a wine to a lesser appellation. In some areas an individual vineyard, therefore, may be eligible for a number of ACs at different levels of quality.

Some regional and district appellations have the right to the additional qualification *supérieur*, e.g. Mâcon Supérieur, Bordeaux Supérieur. These wines have an extra half or full degree of alcohol compared to the basic appellation.

Vins Délimités de Qualité Supérieure (VDQS)

This classification was established in 1949 as a stepping-stone to AC status; many wines that were VDQS have now been promoted to AC. Such examples include Minervois and Corbières. On the other hand, there are some, such as Vins du Bugey, which appear to have no aspirations to promotion. The laws cover the same ground as for AC wines but are generally less stringent on yields and grape varieties. In one aspect, however, the VDQS laws were initially stricter. The right to the VDQS label was granted only after tasting. Now the requirement has been extended to AC wines as well. Overall, this is now a minor category, as it represents less than 1 per cent of French wine production.

TABLE WINE

France also has two classes of table wine.

Vins de Pays

This classification was finally confirmed by a decree in 1979 and came about partly as the result of an initiative of the wine trade, which wanted to give added value to certain *Vins de Table*. At the same time, a broader objective was to upgrade the quality of the wine of the Midi. At present there are approximately 150 different *Vins de Pays*, spread throughout viticultural France from the Belgian to the Spanish and Italian frontiers. They represent something over 20 per cent of France's total production. There are three levels of *Vins de Pays*.

First, there are four **major multi-departmental**

Vins de Pays. These are: Vin de Pays d'Oc, by far the most important, covering all of Languedoc and Roussillon; Vin de Pays des Comtés Rhodaniens, which includes the vineyards of the Rhône valley and the Alps; Vin de Pays du Jardin de la France, basically the vineyards of the Loire valley and its tributaries; and the Vin de Pays du Comté Tolosan, which covers the vineyards of south-west France, excluding the Bordeaux region. Secondly, there are 54 **departmental** *Vins de Pays*, such as Vin de Pays des Pyrenées-Orientales. Specifically excluded from this level are the fine wine regions of Alsace, Champagne, the Côte d'Or, Beaujolais and Bordeaux (though this may change). And thirdly, there is a myriad of **regional** *Vins de Pays* of various sizes. A wine must qualify under four separate headings for this category:

1. Area of production. As we have seen, this can vary considerably, and a single vineyard may be eligible for three different *Vins de Pays* names.

2. Grape varieties. For each V*in de Pays* there is a recommended list of the varieties which may be planted. Generally, this will be much broader than for a local AC or VDQS wine, enabling the grower to plant classic varieties from other regions. This has led to much interesting experimentation.

3. Yields. This is normally 90 hl/ha, though for some *Vins de Pays* this has been reduced to 80 hl/ha.

4. Analytical standards. Among other things this includes a minimum alcoholic strength of 9% vol. in the north and 10% vol. in the south, and maximum tolerance levels for sulphur and volatile acidity.

Two Sauvignon Blancs from France. The one on the left is a Vin de Pays from the south, the one on the right is Appellation Contrôlée wine from a region where Sauvignon Blanc is an established, traditional variety.

Vins de Table

Thirty per cent of the wine produced in France falls into this category. *Vins de Table* can be produced anywhere in the country with no restriction as to grape variety, though chaptalisation is forbidden. No maximum yield is stipulated, but a proportion of production over 100 hl/ha must be sent for distillation and the greater the over-production, the lower the price per litre for distilling wine. This measure was introduced to act as a stimulus to producers to reduce yields and plant finer grape varieties in order to improve quality. There are signs that this has had a positive effect. No region, grape variety or vintage may be stated. The wines may not be chaptalised and the price is usually based on alcoholic strength.

9   Bordeaux and South-West France

Bordeaux was an important town under the Romans and, in the Middle Ages, was, with Libourne on the Dordogne, a trading centre for the wines of the 'high country' upriver. Many of these 'high country' wines, such as Bergerac, Cahors and Madiran, are only recently regaining the reputation that they had in the Middle Ages. It was not until the beginning of the eighteenth century that Bordeaux wines, as we now know them, were first shipped to England, often as contraband through Ireland, Scotland and the Channel Islands. In those days they were known as New French Clarets. Even at that time certain châteaux were beginning to create an individual reputation: Samuel Pepys kept a stock of Haut-Brion in his cellar. From this time there began to evolve a clear hierarchy among the vineyards, particularly among those of the recently drained district of the Médoc.

In some ways Bordeaux is in a state of crisis, for there is polarisation in the marketplace. Prestigious châteaux that have created a reputation for their wines can, generally speaking, sell them every year without difficulty, though the price that they fetch may vary considerably from year to year. However, they account for no more than a small proportion of the total market and this leaves a vast amount of wine to be sold. Many merchants feel that the future lies in brands, but few of them have the resources to launch them and compete on world markets. A further complication is that Bordeaux wines generally need ageing to show at their best; they do not have the immediate appealing fruitiness of their New World competition. Few consumers have the patience or the means to store wines for several years before they are ready. Unfortunately, most producers and retailers either do not want to trouble themselves with the complications of careful storage, or cannot afford to finance a long period between purchase and sale.

THE CHATEAU CONCEPT

Most vineyards in Bordeaux are not known by names attached to specific plots of land, as is the case in Burgundy, but rather to estates under single ownership, generally attached to a substantial house. These are known as châteaux. Over the years the estate may vary in size by the purchase or sale of vineyard plots. For example, the very highly rated Château Pétrus in Pomerol has increased in size by approximately 50 per cent since 1969. Thus a château name is more of a brand than a designation of a specific vineyard. There are more than 3000 individual château names in the Bordeaux vineyards, though until recently it was only a very small proportion of these that appeared on wine labels. Those that did were mainly the prestigious and long-established names; the rest were blended by the Bordeaux merchants, for sale under their own labels.

CLIMATE

Bordeaux lies at 45° latitude and therefore is quite northerly in the winemaking context. In the ripening season it has long hours of sunshine, but these are moderated by the maritime climate. This means that frost is not a problem though it can occasionally cause severe damage – a notable example being in April 1991. Humidity is high, not only because of the proximity of the sea, but

Early autumn in Bordeaux.

also because of the major rivers that flow through the region. This encourages both noble rot and grey rot, a particular problem for red wines. Strong winds blowing in from the Atlantic are to some extent broken up by the pine forests and the mountainous coastal sand-dunes. Being in a temperate zone, the vintages of Bordeaux wines can vary considerably from year to year. A sound knowledge of the differences between the individual vintages is therefore important, though for the finest wines, strict selection of grapes and barrels, and the use of second wines, greatly reduce the differences in style and quality between the vintages.

SOILS AND TOPOGRAPHY

On the borders of the rivers there is a band of rich alluvial soil. Here only the lowest appellation wines may be produced. The finest vineyards are found on well-draining gravel, where quartz and flint pebbles lie over a subsoil of marl. This occurs particularly in the commune villages of the Haut-Médoc, to the north of Bordeaux and in the northern Graves. In parts of Saint-Emilion, the gravel lies on a limestone base. Hillside vineyards in Bordeaux are comparatively rare; where they do occur, they are generally of limestone and clay.

GRAPE VARIETIES

All the red wines of Bordeaux and almost all the whites are produced from a blend of grape varieties. This is no accident of history. The varying climates that are found and the wide annual variations in weather patterns make vinegrowing in Bordeaux unpredictable. Different grape varieties respond differently to the weather. Thick-skinned grapes resist rot better, others ripen later or flower earlier, some resist frost and damp soil better than others, and so on. By mixing the varieties planted, the growers can hedge their bets as to variations in the weather, thus enabling the production of reasonable wine even when the conditions have been unfavourable. This practice has been perfected in Bordeaux over the generations.

Fourteen grape varieties are permitted under the AC regulations, but in practice no more than five black grapes and three white are used.

Bordeaux – gravel soils close-up.

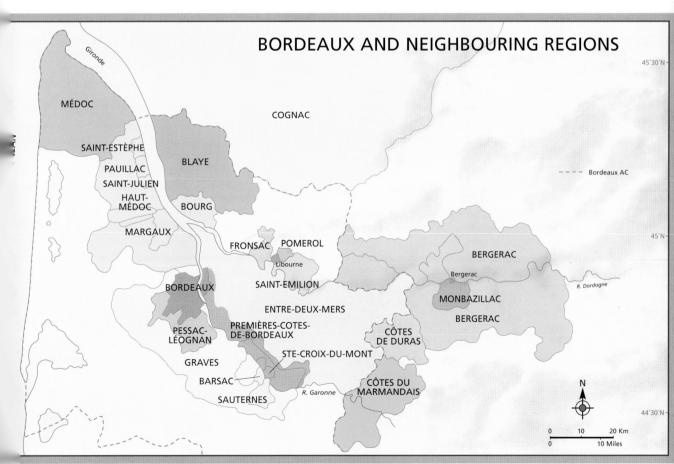

BORDEAUX AND NEIGHBOURING REGIONS

Cabernet Sauvignon is widely recognised as the classic black variety of Bordeaux, though now there are wider plantings of Merlot. It accounts for three-quarters of the blend in the finest wines of the Médoc, where it is mainly found. Across the region as a whole it accounts for no more than 29 per cent of the plantings of black grapes. It gives only moderate yields and produces quality, tannic wines with a characteristic blackcurrant aroma when fully ripe, though it is difficult to ripen and can produce some very tough, vegetal wines which are usable only if softened with Merlot.

Cabernet Franc is mainly grown in Saint-Emilion and, to a lesser extent, in the Médoc and Graves. It gives bigger yields than the Cabernet Sauvignon, but the wine has rather less body and finesse. Its flavours can be herbaceous or stalky, and the wine matures more rapidly.

Both Cabernets prefer to be grown on well-drained, warm, gravel soils.

Merlot produces a medium yield of full-bodied, moderately tannic wine, which also matures earlier than the Cabernet Sauvignon. It adds softness, richness and body when added to the austere Cabernet Sauvignon. This grape is particularly important in Saint-Emilion and Pomerol, where it benefits from the limestone soils. On its own, it can lack character unless yields are very low. Even at estates that can produce world-class Merlot, a proportion of Cabernet Franc or Cabernet Sauvignon is usually added to provide aromatic fruit, colour and tannin.

Malbec is mainly used for early drinking red wines such as those of Bourg and Blaye. It suffers particularly from *coulure*. Its importance is small and declining.

Petit Verdot ripens fully only in very hot years, giving a very deep-coloured, tannic wine which ages slowly. It never plays more than a minor role in a blend, where it is used mainly to add tannin, colour and some exotic spicy notes to great wines.

Sémillon is the most widely planted white variety in Bordeaux and, given its thin skin and its attraction for noble rot, is used widely for sweet wines. It gives wines with a golden colour and plenty of body.

Sauvignon Blanc produces wines with distinctively vegetal, grass and elderflower aromas. In Bordeaux it is used increasingly for single varietal, dry white wines – the one exception to the generalisation that all Bordeaux wines are blends. When blended, its high acidity acts as a counterbalance to the potential flabbiness of the Sémillon. This is particularly true of the great sweet wines.

Hand-harvesting grapes in Bordeaux.

Muscadelle has a distinctive grapey Muscat flavour and is therefore used as a minor constituent in sweet wines.

VITICULTURE

The vineyards of Bordeaux are generally densely planted with vines trained along low wires to benefit from reflected heat from the ground. The best châteaux maintain a high average age among their vines by carefully planning their replanting cycle.

Machine harvesting is widely practised in all but a few of the top growths of the Médoc. It gives lower costs and greater flexibility at vintage, particularly if bad weather threatens. Hand-picking is, of course, necessary for the finest sweet wines as the pickers have to select the individual bunches as they pass through the vineyards on a number of separate occasions.

VINIFICATION

Red wine vinification in Bordeaux can be said to be classical in that it is the system on which so many other regions model themselves. However, there is a broad variation in prices and qualities within the Bordeaux hierarchy and this reflects the different ways in which the winemakers approach their task. The finest clarets are among the most expensive wines in the world, so the top producers can afford to spend more than the owners of more humble properties, when they make their wines. They are also better placed to insist on lower yields in order to have better fruit.

Selection of Grapes

Let us look at where some of those differences might occur. If we assume that abnormal weather conditions have not forced our hand, the first choice concerns the proportions of the various grape varieties that go into the blend. If you are making a wine for early maturity, sale and consumption, the tendency will be to have a higher proportion of Merlot; if the intention is to produce a longer-lasting, later-maturing wine, then it will be dominated by the lower-yielding Cabernet. The next step is in the selection of the grapes. Ideally, there should be selection at various stages. The first might be a green harvest (*vendange verte*) to lower yields and ensure that the sugars produced by the leaves are concentrated in a smaller number of grapes; then, at the time of picking, only the ripest and healthiest bunches should be taken; and finally at the press-house, where the grapes will pass along one or two selection tables, when individual grapes will be rejected. Each stage of this process adds to the costs.

Fermentation

At the press-house, if the wine is to be long-lasting, a proportion of stalks may be put in the fermentation vat to increase the tannins. This may depend on the nature of the vintage and now occurs less frequently. The majority of winemakers destalk their whole crop. The traditional fermentation vat in Bordeaux is made of oak. This has now been widely replaced by stainless steel, or epoxy-lined concrete vats. The individual grape varieties are vinified separately.

Ageing and Blending

Top-quality red Bordeaux is aged in small oak *barriques* or *pièces* of 225 litres. Traditionally, though, production figures have been quoted in *tonneaux* (1 *tonneau* = 4 *pièces* = 900 litres). In the finest châteaux, all the wine may be put into new casks. As these cost approximately €700 each, this represents a considerable investment. Lesser properties may use a smaller proportion of new casks; some may even age only in second-hand casks. For some of the lesser wines, there may be no cask-ageing at all. How much time the wine will spend in cask varies from property to property. For the finest wines, this may be anything up to 24 months. In the early part of the year following the vintage, they will be assembled together to create the desired style and quality of wine. Most of the leading châteaux now have second, and even third, wines produced from wines rejected at this stage, including wine from young vines. Some wine may even be sold off in bulk under the communal or regional appellation.

White Wines

The vinification of **dry whites** has improved considerably with the general use of stainless steel vats and the ability to control fermentation temperatures. Top white Graves properties continue to age their wine in often new oak barrels. This is also becoming more common for lesser wines. As for the finest **sweet white** wines, the major problem is often to ferment out as much sugar as the yeast can absorb. In order to

Selection table at Château Preuillac, ensures only healthy, ripe grapes are used.

Cru Classé claret commencing its maturation in new oak in the first year chais of Château Mouton-Rothschild, Premier Cru Classé.

Médoc vineyards with the River Gironde in the background.

encourage this generally lengthy process, the greatest wines of ACs like Sauternes and Barsac will be aged in oak.

THE PRINCIPAL AREAS OF BORDEAUX

The Dordogne and Garonne rivers combine to form the Gironde Estuary and divide the Bordeaux vineyards into three broad areas. West and south of the Gironde/Garonne lie the districts of Médoc, Graves and Sauternes. Most of the area between the Dordogne and the Garonne is covered by the Entre-Deux-Mers AC (literally 'between two seas'). Finally, the principal districts to the north and east of the Gironde and Dordogne are Saint-Emilion and Pomerol. The AC hierarchy in Bordeaux consists of three levels: generic, district and commune.

Generic Appellations are names that are applied to AC wines produced anywhere in the Gironde. Examples include Bordeaux and Bordeaux Supérieur.

District Appellations may be the highest appellation attainable in a particular locality, as, for example, Entre-Deux-Mers, or they might embrace a number of superior commune appellations, as in the Haut-Médoc.

Commune Appellations are the highest appellations in Bordeaux, except in the particular case of the Saint-Emilion Grand Cru AC.

Château names themselves form no part of any AC. For example, Château Latour has the AC Pauillac and Château Climens the AC Barsac. Because of the large number of châteaux, classification systems of qualitative grading grew up over the years and, in some cases, long before the advent of Appellation Contrôlée. Sadly, these classifications vary considerably within the different regions of Bordeaux. They are described at the end of this chapter.

Generic Appellations

In terms of *Appellation Contrôlée* wine, Bordeaux has by far the largest production of any region of France, accounting for almost a quarter of the total output, with approximately five million litres of red wine each vintage and one million litres of white. The single largest appellation, accounting

for almost two million hectolitres, is **Bordeaux AC**. The average standard of these basic Bordeaux wines has improved considerably as producers have responded to criticism, and have benefited from a series of good-to-excellent vintages. At their best, the medium-bodied dry reds display some of the black berry and cedar notes of the more prestigious wines. Many, unfortunately, are rather thin and have astringent tannins and unripe flavours from overcropped vines. White Bordeaux can be a rather plain dry wine, but some show a little fresh grassiness from the Sauvignon component or toasty notes from some oak-ageing. Varietal wines from Merlot or Sauvignon Blanc are becoming more common, and the latter can be very crisp, with elderflower aromas.

The Left Bank: West and South of the Gironde and Garonne

The long stretch of vineyards between the Gironde and the sea is divided into two. At its apex, north of the village of Saint-Estèphe, lies the **Médoc AC**. Here, the soil is predominantly clay, but there are significant outcrops of gravel. The 1855 Classification (see the section at the end of this chapter) included no properties from this area. From Saint-Estèphe southwards lie the more highly rated vineyards of the **Haut-Médoc AC**. With one exception, all the red wines in the 1855 Classification come from here. Maximum permitted yields are slightly lower than those of the Médoc and there are a number of commune appellations within which most of the higher classified vineyards can be found. From north to south, the four with the highest reputation are **Saint-Estèphe AC, Pauillac AC, Saint-Julien AC** and **Margaux AC**. These commune ACs generally have even lower maximum yields and each has a widely recognised distinctive style. Here, Cabernet Sauvignon will dominate the blend with most wines being made to age.

Generic Appellations			
KEY AC WINES		MAIN GRAPE VARIETIES	PRICE
Bordeaux, Bordeaux Supérieur	■	Merlot, Cabernet Sauvignon, Cabernet Franc	●○
Bordeaux	□	Sémillon, Sauvignon Blanc	●○

In the **Graves AC** both red and white wines are produced, with the reds generally coming from the gravel soils to the north and the whites from sandier soils further south. Cabernet Sauvignon dominates the red wines. In general, these are a little lighter in body and more fragrant in style than the red wines of the Haut-Médoc. They tend to mature more quickly, though not as quickly as the Merlot-dominated wines of Saint-Emilion or Pomerol. The white wines are normally dry, though some sweeter examples are produced. In 1987, the **Pessac-Léognan AC** was created for the finest vineyards in the north of the Graves, where all of the *Cru Classé* châteaux are situated. White wine may be made, as well as red, but it must be dry. Wines from the top chateaux are made with as much care as any in Bordeaux, with prices to match.

Sauternes AC lies on the west bank of the Garonne, upstream from Graves. The appellation is only given for sweet white wines; if the wine is dry, it has the right to no higher appellation than Bordeaux AC. Wines from the village of **Barsac AC** have the right to call themselves under their own village name or that of Sauternes. Here, Sémillon dominates because of its thin skins and susceptibility to botrytis. Sauvignon Blanc supplies refreshing acidity and fruity aromas, and the Muscadelle, where used, adds exotic perfume. In some years, cool local streams create the ideal misty autumn conditions for botrytis to develop

West and South of the Gironde and Garonne			
KEY DISTRICT ACs		**MAIN GRAPE VARIETIES**	**PRICE**
Médoc	■	Cabernet Sauvignon, Merlot, Cabernet Franc	●●○
Haut-Médoc	■	Cabernet Sauvignon, Merlot, Cabernet Franc	●●●○
Graves	■	Cabernet Sauvignon, Merlot, Cabernet Franc	●●○
	□	Sémillon, Sauvignon Blanc	●●○
KEY COMMUNE ACs			
Saint-Estèphe	■	Cabernet Sauvignon, Merlot, Cabernet Franc	●●●○+
Pauillac	■	Cabernet Sauvignon, Merlot, Cabernet Franc	●●●○+
Saint-Julien	■	Cabernet Sauvignon, Merlot, Cabernet Franc	●●●○+
Margaux	■	Cabernet Sauvignon, Merlot, Cabernet Franc	●●●○+
Pessac-Léognan	■	Cabernet Sauvignon, Merlot, Cabernet Franc	●●●○+
	□	Sémillon, Sauvignon Blanc	●●●○+
Barsac	□	Sémillon, Sauvignon Blanc	●●●○+
Sauternes	□	Sémillon, Sauvignon Blanc	●●●○+

on fully ripened grapes. The harvest may be spread over several weeks, with the pickers passing through the vines, picking on each occasion only those bunches or individual grapes that are sufficiently shrivelled. Yields are necessarily low and production costs high. The most expensive wines are made with the most carefully selected grapes and are usually fermented and aged in new oak. They are high in alcohol, lusciously sweet, yet balanced by crisp acidity, and have the unique aromas of botrytis, along with notes of apricot, honey and vanilla. Wines that are not used by the top châteaux are sold off and blended to make wines that may show little of the characteristics of great Sauternes, but are still, nevertheless, highly priced.

Between the Garonne and the Dordogne

The largest appellation here is **Entre-Deux-Mers**. This is a dry white wine, historically made from Sémillon. Now it is more likely to be a Sémillon–Sauvignon blend or, increasingly frequently, a straight Sauvignon Blanc. Red wine is also made in this part of Bordeaux, but it must be labelled AC Bordeaux.

Sainte-Croix-du-Mont AC is a sweet wine made in the Sauternes style. The vineyards face those of Sauternes across the Garonne and experience similar misty autumns, but because they generally have lower levels of botrytis, the wines tend to have less concentration and complexity. The prices are lower than those of Sauternes and rarely compensate the effort and costs of ensuring

The botrytis-affected Sémillon grapes used for Sauternes cannot be harvested by machine, and must be selectively picked by hand.

Between the Garonne and the Dordogne

KEY DISTRICT ACs		MAIN GRAPE VARIETIES	PRICE
Entre-Deux-Mers	☐	Sémillon, Sauvignon Blanc	●○
Premières Côtes de Bordeaux	■	Merlot, Cabernet Sauvignon, Cabernet Franc	●○
KEY COMMUNE ACs			
Sainte-Croix-du-Mont	☐	Sémillon, Sauvignon Blanc	●●○

North and East of the Gironde and Dordogne

KEY DISTRICT ACs		MAIN GRAPE VARIETIES	PRICE
Côtes de Bourg	■	Merlot, Cabernet Franc, Malbec	●●
Premières Côtes de Blaye	■	Merlot, Cabernet Franc, Malbec	●●
KEY COMMUNE ACs			
Saint-Emilion satellites	■	Merlot, Cabernet Franc	●●○
Saint-Emilion	■	Merlot, Cabernet Franc	●●●○
Saint-Emilion Grand Cru	■	Merlot, Cabernet Franc	●●●○+
Pomerol	■	Merlot, Cabernet Franc	●●●●+
Fronsac/Canon-Fronsac	■	Merlot, Cabernet Franc	●●●

that each grape is picked at a stage of optimal botrytis influence.

Premières Côtes de Bordeaux is usually a dry red wine similar in style to Bordeaux AC, though medium-sweet whites are also made.

The Right Bank: North and East of the Gironde and Dordogne

This is predominantly an area for red wines, with the Cabernet Sauvignon playing a lesser role to Merlot and Cabernet Franc.

The most important appellation is that of **Saint-Emilion AC**, which covers nine communes, with three distinct groups of vineyards on differing soils. First are the vineyards on a plateau to the north and west of the town of Saint-Emilion. Here the warm, well-drained gravel and limestone soils encourage the inclusion of Cabernet Franc and, occasionally (unusual for Saint-Emilion), some Cabernet Sauvignon. Secondly, there are vineyards on the limestone escarpment to the south and east. The most prestigious wines of Saint-Emilion, including the *Grand Cru Classé* wines, and most of the wines that gain the appellation **Saint-Emilion Grand Cru AC** come from these two regions. They are made with great care from low-yielding vineyards and are usually aged in expensive new French oak. The wines have rich tannins and complex red berry fruit aromas, developing tobacco and cedar nuances as they evolve. Finally, there are many vineyards on the sandy soils at the foot of the escarpment. The style of wines from here is distinctly lighter and the prices lower (though still high to premium).

View across Saint-Emilion.

Along the River Dordogne, Bordeaux vineyards in Fronsac.

The **Saint-Emilion satellite** villages of Lussac, Montagne, Puissegin and Saint-Georges can add their name before that of Saint-Emilion, and thus gain some reflected glory at lower price points.

The reputation of nearby **Pomerol AC** is as high as that of Saint-Emilion – and the prices higher, as most of the estates are tiny, so the wines gain added value because of their rarity. The wines tend to be richer, with a spicier, blackberry fruit character. Among the vineyards with the highest reputations are Pétrus and Le Pin, whose prices are always among the highest in Bordeaux. There is no formal classification of the vineyards in Pomerol.

For those looking for excellent value in the red wines of Bordeaux, **Fronsac AC** and **Canon-Fronsac AC** are two places to start the search. Here hillside vineyards, planted largely in Merlot, produce full-bodied, surprisingly tannic wines. For those looking for something rather softer, **Bourg** and **Blaye**, on the opposite bank of the Gironde from the Haut-Médoc, make early drinking red and white wines, often sold under château names. The best appellations here are Côtes de Bourg AC and Premières Côtes de Blaye AC.

THE BORDEAUX TRADE

There has been a substantial change over the past few years in the nature of the wine trade in France and this has particularly been true in Bordeaux.

When the city was a great port, the merchants, or *négociants*, had cellars along the quays that fronted the river. Here they would bottle a broad range of wines mainly under a generic or village name.

The role of the merchant has declined dramatically as the owners of the individual châteaux have become stronger and insisted on selling their wine in bottle. (In order to make this easier for the owners of the smaller properties, mobile bottling-lines are now commonplace.) In addition, outside France, Bordeaux is no longer perceived to be the centre of the wine world, whose wines demand to be bought. Competition, particularly from the New World, has been fierce on export markets and Bordeaux has been slow to react. As the sales of generic wines fell, that of *petits châteaux* rose. Now they are in decline. Is branded wine the answer?

Many of the traditional merchants have either disappeared or been taken over. Those that remain have, for the most part, moved their cellars out of the city and now mainly hold stocks of bottled wine, perhaps from *petits châteaux* with whom they have an exclusive arrangement. Some are little more than brokers, relying on access to stocks held at the châteaux or bought *en primeur* by speculators. Many also, for the bulk of their trade, sell wines from other regions, particularly the Languedoc.

En Primeur Sales

The capital demands made upon the more prestigious properties in Bordeaux are considerable. Cash flow management may well be an additional problem, because of money tied up in stock. In order to lessen their exposure, most producers release quantities of their crop for sale in the year following the harvest, generally after the quality of the individual wines has been rated by the critics. The price will include all costs up to and including bottling. This is known as a sale *en primeur*. The wines are released in a number of *tranches* (or limited quantities). As questions such as pride and prestige go to create the price asked, the first *tranche* is often very limited, to test the market. What happens if one opens more cheaply, or more expensively, than one's neighbour? Generally, but not always, the price increases with each *tranche*. Because much top-quality Bordeaux wine is bought for speculative purposes, buying *en primeur* can be a lottery.

Wine bought in this way will be kept at the château for maturation until it is bottled and released when it is approximately two years old. This system depends for its success on the availability of surplus money and therefore works best in periods of boom. For the private individual, independent professional advice should be sought before investing in the young wines of Bordeaux!

BORDEAUX CLASSIFICATIONS
The Médoc and Sauternes

In 1855, on the occasion of the Paris Universal Exhibition, the Bordeaux Chamber of Commerce was approached to produce an official list of their best wines. They delegated the task to a panel of brokers and a list was drawn up which classified the red wines of the Médoc and the white wines of Sauternes. The list was based on existing, unofficial classifications and the prices that the various wines had been fetching on the market. This is now known as the 1855 **Classification**. Over the intervening years, there have been numerous changes in the number and size of the various estates, in ownership and in the quality of the wine made. Nevertheless, the 1855 Classification still stands virtually intact. There are 61 *Crus Classés*, in the Médoc, divided into five ranks.

The first growths (*Premiers Crus*) are:

Château Haut-Brion
Château Latour
Château Lafite
Château Mouton-Rothschild
Château Margaux

In Bordeaux the concept of a château is perhaps more important than anywhere else. This is Château Giscours, in Margaux, classified as Troisième Cru Classé in 1855.

Château Haut-Brion was the one wine from outside the Médoc to be included in the 1855 Classification. Château Mouton-Rothschild was a second growth until 1973. This was the only time that a château has been reclassified.

Below this there are:

14 châteaux classified as Second Growths (*Deuxièmes Crus,* or *Seconds Crus*)

14 châteaux classified as Third Growths (*Troisièmes Crus*)

10 châteaux classified as Fourth Growths (*Quatrièmes Crus*)

18 châteaux classified as Fifth Growths (*Cinquièmes Crus*)

The 1855 Classification accounted for only a very small number of the estates of the Médoc. In 1932, a further classification of *Cru Bourgeois* was introduced and this was updated in 1978 and again in 2003, with the idea that this should then be revisited every ten years. It includes something over 200 properties and is divided into three levels:

Grand Cru Bourgeois Exceptionnel

Grand Cru Bourgeois

Cru Bourgeois

Also classified in 1855 were the sweet white wines of Sauternes. Here Château d'Yquem was classed by itself as a *Premier Grand Cru Classé* with, beneath it:

11 châteaux classified as First Growths (*Premiers Crus*)

14 châteaux classified as Second Growths (*Deuxième Crus,* or *Seconds Crus*)

Graves (including Pessac-Léognan)

The wines of the Graves were classified in 1959 with parallel, but separate, lists for red and white wines. There is no ranking; all listed wines may simply call themselves *Cru Classé*. Château Haut-Brion is included, though it retains its 1855 Classification as of right.

Saint-Emilion

The classifications for the Saint-Emilion appellation work on a rather different basis and, uniquely in Bordeaux, are integrated into the AC system. There is a separate AC, Saint-Emilion Grand Cru, which has two subdivisions: Saint-Emilion Grand Cru Classé and Saint-Emilion

Premier Grand Cru Classé (itself divided into Grand Cru Classé A and Grand Cru Classé B). The original classification was in 1955 and there are reclassifications, with the possibility of promotion and demotion, every ten years. Individual châteaux that are not classified as Cru Classé may submit their wines to be considered for the appellation Saint-Emilion Grand Cru on an annual basis, in this relatively democratic system.

Garage Wines

One recent movement, particularly associated with the Right-Bank Appellations, is the appearance of wines made in tiny quantities from small plots of land, but with no expense spared in the vineyard or the winery. Because these are new ventures, they usually fall outside the various classifications. The vineyard sites may be quite ordinary, or they may be sites of enormous potential that happen to have been overlooked, or fall outside the current ownership of the Classed Growths. Carefully selected, super-ripe grapes from low-yielding vines (usually Merlot) are used to create full-bodied, concentrated wines, often with high alcohol, moderate acidity and soft, velvet-textured tannins. These will then be aged in new French oak *barriques*, which give meaty, toasty flavours to the wine, and add complexity to the rich dark berry fruit and spice. With the right marketing, these wines can gain very high reputations. As the quantities produced are tiny, the price they can command is very high, and can exceed the prices of the top Classed Growths.

SOUTH-WEST FRANCE

These wines may be divided into two groups: first, products that come from vineyards from regions that adjoin those of Bordeaux and have, in the main, the same grape varieties – for convenience we shall call these 'Bordeaux clones'; second, there are a number of regions which make individual wines from varieties often never seen in Bordeaux, with styles that differ considerably – these we shall call 'south-west wines'.

Bordeaux Clones

To the east of the vineyards of the Entre-Deux-Mers lie the vineyards of the Dordogne. Here the

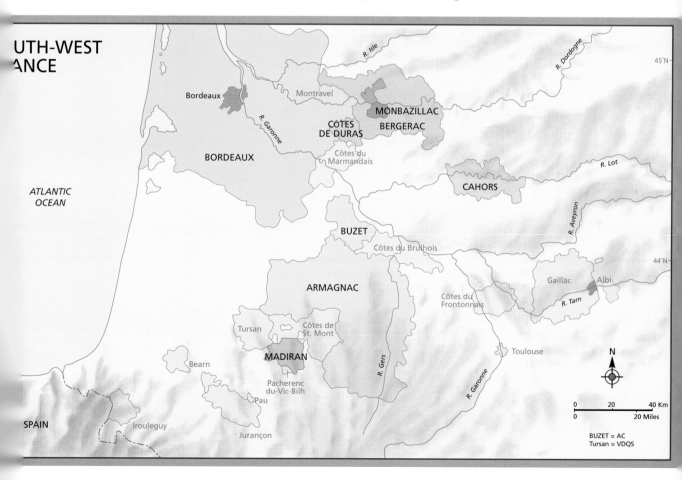

Bordeaux Clones

KEY AC WINES		MAIN GRAPE VARIETIES	PRICE
Bergerac	■	Cabernet Sauvignon, Cabernet Franc, Merlot	●●
Monbazillac	☐	Sémillon, Sauvignon Blanc	●●○
Côtes de Duras	■	Cabernet Sauvignon, Cabernet Franc, Merlot	●●
Buzet	■	Merlot, Cabernet Sauvignon, Cabernet Franc	●●

South-West Wines

KEY WINES		MAIN GRAPE VARIETIES	PRICE
Cahors AC	■	Malbec, Merlot, Tannat	●●○
Madiran AC	■	Tannat	●●○
Vin de Pays des Côtes de Gascogne, Vin de Pays du Gers	☐	Various, including Ugni Blanc	●

Leaf thinning in order to achieve maximum exposure of Tannat grapes to the sun in Madiran.

climate is similar to that of Bordeaux, though with less moderating maritime influence where the major AC is **Bergerac** which may be used for both red and white wines made from the same varieties as in Bordeaux. However, there is a number of smaller ACs within the region, some of which enjoy a worldwide reputation and others that have a problem to make themselves known in their own country. Great botrytised sweet wines come from **Monbazillac AC** (and Saussignac AC and Haut-Montravel AC); and the best dry whites are Bergerac AC (and Montravel AC and Rosette AC). Pécharmant AC has its own red wine appellation.

South of the Bergerac region, but again adjoining the Bordeaux vineyards, lie **Côtes de Duras** and Côtes du Marmandais AC. Here lighter Bordeaux-style wines are being produced, though local grape varieties also occasionally appear: in Duras, white wines may include Mauzac and Ondenc and in the Marmandais the rarer Abouriou may be found in red wine blends.

Higher up the valley of the Garonne are the vineyards of **Buzet AC**, which are predominantly red, though some rosé and white wines are also made. Here the local co-operative cellar is the most important producer.

South-West Wines

From the upper valley of the Lot, a tributary of the Garonne, come the wines of **Cahors AC**. Historically, these were described as 'black' wines, and were very tannic and long-lasting. Now a broad range of styles is produced depending on whether the vineyards are in the fertile valley bottom, on the poorer soils of the slopes or on the plateau above. The most important grape variety is Malbec (here known as Auxerrois), which must account for at least 70 per cent in any blend. The other varieties planted are Merlot and Tannat. At their best, the wines are aged in oak, deeply coloured, high in tannin, with intense, dark berry fruits that mature slowly to reveal notes of cedar and earth.

Further south, a group of vineyards roughly overlaps those that also produce base wine for distillation into Armagnac. Here **Madiran AC**, a full-bodied, rustic brambly red, is produced from the Tannat grape. There is also considerable production locally of **Vin de Pays des Côtes de Gascogne** and **Vin de Pays du Gers**. These are generally aromatic, crisp light white wines made from Armagnac varieties, with aromas and flavours of sour green apples.

Burgundy

With its myriad appellations and vineyards split between numerous owners of varying competence and experience, Burgundy can appear complicated and infuriating, to both the wine student and the consumer. There was a time when the only way to find a great Burgundy was to recognise the most reliable, skilful producers. Fortunately, many co-operatives, négociants and domaines now produce large quantities of good quality, expressive wines which gain wide distribution, and it is easy to select an enjoyable bottle of Burgundy with little more than the most basic knowledge. Many who believe Burgundy to be the source of the world's most exhilarating wines (both red and white) would struggle to explain the differences in style between the different villages or the individual vineyards. Yet, for those with an interest in the effects of soils and topography, Burgundy offers opportunities to explore that are matched by few other regions.

10

The historic popularity of the wines of the region has meant that its names have commonly been abused around the world and it is only now that names such as Burgundy and Chablis are being accepted as being specifically Burgundian. It has been a long, hard battle, but final victory is in sight.

CLIMATE AND SOILS

Burgundy enjoys a northern continental climate, with winters that can be severe (much more severe than in Bordeaux, where the ocean plays a moderating role) and hot summers. These are hotter than in Bordeaux for the same reasons. The autumns are cool and rainfall is frequent at vintage time. The annual rainfall, however, is distinctly lower, with 650 mm of rain falling in an average year in Dijon and 890 mm in Bordeaux. Among the natural climatic hazards that the grower may face are spring frosts, particularly in the Chablis region, where they can appear as late as May, summer rains causing grey rot and localised summer hailstorms. However, the main vineyards of the region lie on the eastern fringe of the Massif Central, which acts as a protective barrier.

Burgundy, and the Côte d'Or in particular, provide a good example of the way that grape varieties are planted according to the composition of the soil. Where limestone soils predominate, Chardonnay is found; where there is more marl and clay, Pinot Noir is found. As an extreme example, take the Beaune *Premier Cru* vineyard of Clos des Mouches. Beaune is a centre for red wine production, but, in part of this vineyard, there is a limestone outcrop; here Chardonnay is grown, while in the rest of the same vineyard Pinot Noir is grown.

Over centuries of tasting, enjoying and evaluating, certain vineyards have been recognised as the source of wines of particularly high quality or particularly recognisable character. Burgundy is a region where features such as the steepness or direction of the slopes, as well as depth, drainage, heat retention and mineral content of the soils can vary dramatically within small areas. Although we are only just beginning to gain a detailed picture of all of these aspects, and how they affect wine quality, both Pinot Noir and Chardonnay are very sensitive to the subtle variations in *terroir*. An understanding of the different styles of wine that come from the various individually named sites can enhance your appreciation and enjoyment of the wine.

Summer pruning of low-trained Pinot Noir growing in marl soil in Charmes Chambertin.

GRAPE VARIETIES AND VITICULTURE

The vast majority of wines in Burgundy are produced from one of four grape varieties, and it should be pointed out that Burgundies are almost exclusively mono-varietal wines. These are, for red wines, Pinot Noir and Gamay, and for white wines, Chardonnay and Aligoté.

Pinot Noir is the classic black grape variety of Burgundy and it succeeds here better than anywhere else in the world. It is grown throughout the region (with the exception of Beaujolais). Pinot Noir is a very old variety that mutates very easily, with the result that over the centuries many subtly different versions of this variety, called clones, have evolved. These clones may have different yields, different ripening times, different flavours and different quality potentials. Selection of the correct clone (or clones) is important and is thought to account for some of the differences between wines from the different vineyard sites in Burgundy. Classic Burgundian Pinot Noir has red fruit flavours (cherry, raspberry, strawberry) in youth that evolve into vegetal and savoury, gamey notes as the wine matures. Levels of tannins and acidity vary according to the vineyard, the producer and the vintage, but tannins are rarely too astringent, and the wines are usually quite full-bodied, due to natural ripeness or chaptalisation.

Historically, **Gamay** was cultivated throughout Burgundy, because it is easy to grow and gives a high yield of early-maturing wines. It now thrives in the Beaujolais, especially in regions with granitic soils, where it gives its best: young, fruity wines with light tannins. In the rest of Burgundy, it contributes only to the humble Bourgogne Grand Ordinaire and Bourgogne Passetoutgrains AC wines.

Chardonnay provides all the great white wines of Burgundy. The bunches are similar in size to those of Pinot Noir, but longer and less compact, so less prone to rot. With its rich, ripe, creamy-buttery fruit, Chardonnay is now widely planted around the world. It gives a wine that can benefit from restrained barrel treatment and ageing in contact with the lees. The character of Chardonnay varies dramatically as we move from the lean, steely, high-acid wines of Chablis, via the often fabulously complex, expressive wines of the Côte d'Or, south to the more full-bodied, riper-fruited wines of Mâcon.

Aligoté is grown for making Bourgogne Aligoté and for sparkling wines. In the past it tended to produce thin, high-acid wines. Quality has recently improved and some good wines are now being made, though even the best Aligoté tends to have no more than a two-dimensional flavour to it.

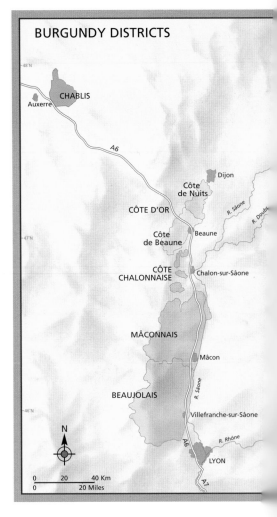

Vines in Burgundy are among the most densely planted in the world, at up to 12 000 plants to the hectare. Most are trained low along wires according to the single Guyot system; the exceptions are some higher-trained vines in the Hautes-Côtes, and the *gobelet*-trained Gamay in the Beaujolais.

VINIFICATION

Climate is an important factor for the Burgundian winemaker. Because of the cool autumns and the cold winters, fermentation may cease if the musts are not warmed. Superficially, this may seem to be a threat for red musts only, but, particularly in Chablis, the temperature can fall low enough to cause a problem even for cool-fermented white wines. The cellars are therefore heated if necessary.

Vinification techniques for red wines vary as you move south. On the Côte d'Or, there has been a vogue for cold-soaking musts before starting the fermentation. Traditional, open vat fermentation with pumping over of the juice, or, in some cellars, punching down of the cap, is normal for the Côte d'Or and the Côte Chalonnaise. Destemming may occur, but many winemakers retain a portion of the stems for the fermentation to provide a source of tannins and to ease the drainage of the juice through the cap. The use of carbonic maceration for red wines is slight in the Mâconnais, but widespread in Beaujolais.

For top-quality red and white wines, barrel ageing is normal; 16–18 months for red wines and 6–9 months for whites. Generally speaking, the better wines will be aged in only a proportion of new oak, though this varies from property to property. Burgundy is an important cooperage centre, being conveniently placed for the oak forests of the Vosges, Nevers and Allier, and its barrels are exported around the world.

Largely because of the Napoleonic laws of inheritance, the vineyards in Burgundy are very fragmented and this has had important repercussions on both the AC laws and the nature of the trade. Generally, the grower will make the wine themselves, as well as growing the grapes. In certain regions, particularly Chablis, Mâcon and Beaujolais, the **co-operative cellars** play a major role, vinifying a large proportion of the total crop. In a small but growing number of cases, the grower might sell their grapes to a merchant, who will vinify the wine. If the grower has made the wine, there are two options open to them. They can bottle the wine and sell it under their own label: such wines are known as **domaine**-bottled, and account for approaching 40 per cent of the total production. Alternatively, a grower might sell their wine in bulk to a *négociant* (merchant) or a co-operative. When considering the percentage figures for domain-bottling, it must be borne in mind that the merchants own many of the most substantial domains. The Burgundy *négociant* has to produce wines in sufficient quantities to meet the demands of their customers around the world. Say they have sales each year of 10 000 cases of Beaune. There will be few, if any, individual growers who will produce such a quantity of that wine, so the *négociant* buys smaller quantities from a number of growers and then blends the various wines, giving them a sufficient quantity of that vintage. To help them in this work they rely on a number of *courtiers*, or brokers. These are in close contact with the growers in their specific area, knowing always what is available for sale and at what price. With one exception, all major Côte d'Or merchants work through brokers.

The merchants in Burgundy have recently been going through a difficult period, and there has been a great deal of consolidation of ownership. With the increase in domain-bottling, less wine has been available in bulk; this in turn has meant higher prices with further demands on capital. For this reason, many of those merchants without vineyard holdings have found it difficult to survive and have either closed their doors, or, more generally, been taken over by a rival. Despite this, the total number of merchants has not fallen, for, at the other end of the scale, many growers with rising reputations have faced increasing demand for their wines. Buying and vinifying grapes from their neighbours is much easier than buying vineyards in Burgundy, as land is terrifyingly expensive. The number of small and often very specialist *négocants* is increasing steadily. There is also a distinct trend towards the merchants buying grapes from the growers, rather than wine. This enables them to have greater control over the ultimate product.

THE HIERARCHY OF BURGUNDY APPELLATIONS
Regional ACs
At the base of the hierarchy are the regional and district appellations. They account for almost two-thirds of the production of the region.

Regional ACs will always have the word Bourgogne in their title (for example Bourgogne Aligoté). Most will come from vineyards which do not have the right to a superior appellation, though they may be wines which have been declassified from a superior appellation. Such declassification may be due to excessive yields or because a quality-minded producer wants to preserve the prestige of the superior appellation by not including lower-quality wines, especially wines from young vines. The majority may be produced anywhere in Burgundy, and in certain parts of the Beaujolais, but there is an increasing number of more localised names deemed to be of equal status (for example Bourgogne Hautes-Côtes de Nuits).

For those wines that can come from anywhere in Burgundy, there is an ascending hierarchy:

Bourgogne Grand Ordinaire AC – mainly red wine made from the Gamay grape. If white it is likely to be made from Melon de Bourgogne (Muscadet), blended with Aligoté.

Burgundy Appellations (Regional ACs)			
KEY AC WINES		**MAIN GRAPE VARIETIES**	**PRICE**
Bourgogne Aligoté	☐	Aligoté	●●
Bourgogne Rouge	■	Pinot Noir	●●○
Bourgogne Blanc	☐	Chardonnay	●●○

Bourgogne Aligoté AC is high in acidity and comparatively low in alcohol. It is largely produced in the Chablis region, in certain villages on the Côte d'Or (such as Pernand-Vergelesses and Puligny-Montrachet) and on the Côte Chalonnaise. In this last region, the village of Bouzeron has its own appellation for its Aligoté.

Bourgogne Passetoutgrains AC – literally, Burgundy 'chuck all the grapes in together'. In practice, it is a red wine made from a mixture of both Pinot Noir and Gamay grapes, with the former accounting for at least 30 per cent of the blend.

Bourgogne Rouge AC, Bourgogne Blanc AC wines must be made from the best grape varieties in the area in which it is grown. This usually means Pinot Noir for red wine and Chardonnay for white. There must also be a higher minimum level of alcohol than for other regional wines.

There are also a number of restricted area regional appellations. These include:

- **Côte d'Or** – Bourgogne – Hautes-Côtes de Nuits, Hautes-Côtes de Beaune
- **Saône et Loire** – Bourgogne Côte Chalonnaise

District ACs
District appellations are a step up the hierarchy and do not include the word Bourgogne (for example Mâcon).

Commune ACs
The next step in the hierarchy is that of communal or village appellations such as Givry or Gevrey-Chambertin. These account for just under a quarter of the total production. Usually, just the name of the commune will be given on the label. Occasionally, if the wine comes entirely from one vineyard that is not recognised as a *Premier Cru*, the vineyard name may appear, but it must be in smaller print than that of the village. Thus:

BEAUNE Lulune
Appellation Beaune Contrôlée

Single Vineyard ACs: *Premier and Grand Crus*
There are fundamental differences between the AC structures in Bordeaux and Burgundy. In Bordeaux, a château name is largely a trademark. The owner can increase the size of the property by purchasing vineyard plots anywhere within the same appellation as they become available and still sell the wine under the name of the château. With the exception of Saint-Emilion, the designations *Grand Cru* (and *Premier Cru* etc.)

are not part of the AC system, so for example even a *Premier Grand Cru Classé* such as Château Lafite is still simply Pauillac AC. In Burgundy, however, a vineyard name is attached to a specific plot of land, which is registered in each town hall. Its size rarely alters. Each *Premier Cru* and *Grand Cru* vineyard has its own AC. Because of this, while Bordeaux has approximately 60 names protected under the AC system, Burgundy has more than ten times as many, even though the area it has under vines and its total production of wine are less than half that of its illustrious rival. Also in Bordeaux, the same team of workers will tend all the vines of a given château, and one winemaking team in the one winery will make its wine. While this team might produce more than one quality of wine from the vineyard, there will be consistency of style. On the other hand, in Burgundy, the vineyard with just one owner (*monopole*) is the exception; most will have a number of different owners, each with an individual parcel of vines, making wines in their individual style. This appears very complicated, but the key is that, in general, *Premier Cru* sites have more potential to produce great wine than ordinary village-level sites do, and *Grand Cru* sites have the greatest potential of all for long-lasting, expressive, complex wines, though they will have prices to match.

In all, there are more than 560 **Premiers Crus** spread between Chablis, the Côte d'Or and the Côte Châlonnaise. Together, they provide approximately 11 per cent of Burgundy's production. *Premier Cru* wines usually state their *Premier Cru* status on the label, but occasionally this status is indicated by the village and the vineyard sharing the same size of print:

BEAUNE GRÈVES
Appellation Beaune Grèves Contrôlée

Or,

BEAUNE GRÈVES
Appellation Beaune Premier Cru Contrôlée

There is also the possibility of wines being blended together from various *Premier Cru* vineyards within a village and being sold as, for example:

BEAUNE 1er Cru
Appellation Beaune Premier Cru Contrôlée

At the peak of the pyramid come the **Grand Cru** vineyards accounting for no more than 1 per cent of the total production. There are 30 of these on the Côte d'Or and they can be recognised by the fact that the vineyard name stands alone on the label and is not attached to that of the commune.

The reputations of these wines are so established that it is considered unnecessary to state from which village they come.

MONTRACHET
Appellation Montrachet Contrôlée

It is important not to confuse the vineyard name and the commune name (for example Chambertin and Gevrey-Chambertin). At the start of the twentieth century, the mayors of certain villages on the Côte d'Or thought that it would help the sale of their simple village wines if they were to add the name of their finest vineyard to that of the village. Thus Aloxe took le Corton and became Aloxe-Corton; Nuits took les Saint-Georges to become Nuits-Saint-Georges, and so on. This accounts for the multiplicity of double-barrelled names on the Côtes!

In Chablis, the *Grand Cru* status is similar, except that there is one *Grand Cru* site, which is spread over seven adjoining plots of land, or *climats*. Thus you have on the label:

CHABLIS LES CLOS
Appellation Chablis Grand Cru Contrôlée

BURGUNDY APPELLATIONS (DISTRICTS, COMMUNES AND VINEYARDS)
Chablis

The vineyard area is centred on the town of Chablis, which lies in the valley of the River Serein, surrounded by hills. Here the soil has an important effect on the wine. In the best sites it is limestone overlaid with a layer of Kimmeridgian clay, which is very rich in marine fossils. Originally, for a vineyard to qualify for the appellation Chablis, it had to lie on this soil. Recently, however, the appellation has been extended to vineyards on similar Portlandian clay. Some of these lesser vineyards may still bear the appellation **Petit Chablis AC**. Vineyards are generally planted following the contours of the slopes. The major climatic problem of the region is frost. Most of the better vineyards now have

View over the River Serein to the Grand Cru vineyards of Chablis.

Chablis			
KEY AC WINES		**GRAPE VARIETY**	**PRICE**
Chablis	☐	Chardonnay	●●○
Chablis Premier Cru	☐	Chardonnay	●●●○
Chablis Grand Cru	☐	Chardonnay	●●●●+

aspersion sprinkler systems installed as a protective measure, though heaters and even helicopters can be used to circulate air and dissipate frost pockets. The only grape permitted is the Chardonnay.

Basic **Chablis AC** can be very austere, with mean, green-plum fruit and high acidity. Better examples show a hint of the stony or smoky minerality that is a more marked characteristic of the *Premier Cru* and *Grand Cru* wines. Forty vineyards have the right to **Chablis Premier Cru AC**. Among the best-known names are Montée de Tonnerre, Vaillons and Fourchaume. These are generally on the well-exposed slopes that fan out from the *Grand Cru* site. Compared to basic Chablis, Chablis Premier Cru generally shows riper fruit (lemon citrus, rather than apple or greengage), more body and perhaps a slightly softer, creamier texture as well as greater concentration and more mineral aromas and acidity. At the highest level, seven vineyards together form **Chablis Grand Cru AC**. They are all on one hillside across the river from the town of Chablis. These are *Les Clos, Vaudésir, Valmur, Les Preuses, Bougros, Blanchot* and *Grenouilles*. The brand name *La Moutonne* also has *Grand Cru* status. A Chablis Grand Cru is more likely to have some oak flavours, though these become integrated into the wine as it ages. Chablis Grand Cru and the best Premiers Crus, need bottle age to show their best. They can develop extraordinary smoky complex aromas, with a long, mouthwatering finish due to the refreshingly high acidity. Although some producers ferment or age a portion of their best wines in oak, oak is rarely a major flavour component.

The Côte d'Or

The vineyards of the Côte d'Or form the viticultural heartland of Burgundy, for it is here that the greatest wines are made. The vineyards lie in a narrow band on the slopes facing predominantly east or south-east, thereby gaining

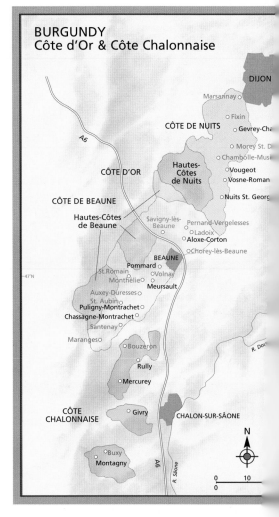

the maximum benefit from the rising sun, and, at the same time, enjoying the protection of the hills of the Morvan behind them. They take their name from the colour of the vineyards after the vintage, as the leaves turn to russet-gold.

The soil is mainly limestone mixed with marl. Where the limestone predominates, Chardonnay is grown; elsewhere it is Pinot Noir. The pruning method is predominantly Guyot.

Viticulturally the Côte is split into two. The northern part is the Côte de Nuits, and it is here that the fullest-bodied, longest-lived red wines are produced. The southern part is the Côte de Beaune; here slightly lighter red wines are made, but also, perhaps more importantly, what many people would consider to be the finest dry white wines in the world. All the red *Grands Crus*, save one (Corton), are produced on the Côte de Nuits, while all the white *Grands Crus*, save one (the exceptionally rare Musigny Blanc) come from the Côte de Beaune. This is mainly as a result of the soils.

The Côte d'Or

KEY AC WINES		GRAPE VARIETIES	PRICE
Village wines	■	Pinot Noir	●●●○
	□	Chardonnay	●●●○
Premier Cru wines	■	Pinot Noir	●●●●+
	□	Chardonnay	●●●●+
Grand Cru wines	■	Pinot Noir	●●●●+
	□	Chardonnay	●●●●+
Côte de Nuits Villages/ Côte de Beaune Villages	■	Pinot Noir	●●○
Bourgogne Hautes-Côtes de Nuits/ Hautes-Côtes de Beaune	■	Pinot Noir	●●
	□	Chardonnay	●●

The hill at Corton with woods on the summit, *Grand Cru* vineyards on the slopes and *commune appellation* vineyards in the foreground.

From north to south, the key villages of the Côte de Nuits (with their most famous *Grand Cru* sites) are **Gevrey Chambertin AC** (*Chambertin AC, Chambertin Clos de Bèze AC*), **Vougeot AC** (*Clos du Vougeot AC*), **Vosne-Romanée AC** (*Romanée-Conti AC, La Tâche AC* and *La Romanée AC*), and **Nuits-Saint-Georges AC**.

Côte de Nuits Villages AC can be a red or a white wine and is produced from those vineyards that lie on the Côte, but do not have right to one of the village appellations listed above.

In the hills behind the vineyards of the Côte, 18 villages produce wine that can be labelled by the regional appellation **Bourgogne Hautes-Côtes de Nuits AC**. The vintage normally takes place approximately a week later than on the main Côte and many of the wines are made in a co-operative cellar in Beaune. They are both red and white. These are generally lighter in body and less concentrated than wines from the main villages of the Côte de Nuits.

On the Côte de Beaune, the important villages (and their *Grand Crus*) are **Aloxe-Corton AC** (*Corton AC, Corton-Charlemagne AC*), **Beaune AC, Pommard AC, Volnay AC, Meursault AC, Puligny-Montrachet AC** (*Le Montrachet AC*), and **Chassagne-Montrachet AC** (*Le Montrachet AC*). All, with the exception of Volnay, produce white wine as well as red. The three villages with the highest reputation for their white wines are Meursault, Puligny-Montrachet and Chassagne-Montrachet, with the last two villages sharing the exceptional *Grand Cru* of Le Montrachet. The Aloxe-Corton vineyard, Corton-Charlemagne, also produces white wine of *Grand Cru* status. The wines from these villages are the finest, and

most expensive, wines made anywhere with the Chardonnay grape. Low yields and perfect conditions of soil, drainage and exposure result in intensely flavoured wines. Fermentation and ageing in new French oak supplies further body, tannins and toasty flavours; lees stirring can add viscosity and complex flavours. These wines can take a decade to reach their peak, but when they do, they are arguably the most complex dry white wines in the world.

Côte de Beaune Villages AC is an important wine for the *négociants* as it can be blended in large quantities. It must be red and it can come from any one, or a combination, of the villages on the Côte de Beaune, except Aloxe-Corton, Beaune, Pommard and Volnay. Thus, the finesse of a wine from Monthélie may be blended with the earthiness of a wine from Chorey, to produce a larger quantity of wine that may also be better than its components. By its nature, it is generally a blended wine.

Bourgogne Hautes-Côtes de Beaune AC is a regional appellation that directly parallels Hautes-Côtes de Nuits.

The Côte Chalonnaise

This area is a continuation of the vineyards of the Côte d'Or. The soils are similar and the grape varieties are the same; however, this is not a region of monoculture as there are gaps between the wine villages, with woods and pastureland. The wines are also similar, though they tend to mature rather more quickly. Because these wines carry less prestige than the wines of the Côte d'Or, prices are generally lower and many offer good value for money.

The walled vineyard of Chevaliers-Montrachet, a *Grand Cru* of the Côte de Beaune.

The Côte Chalonnaise

KEY AC WINES		GRAPE VARIETIES	PRICE
Bourgogne Côte Chalonnaise	■	Pinot Noir	●●
	☐	Chardonnay	●●
Rully, Mercurey, Givry	■	Pinot Noir	●●○
	☐	Chardonnay	●●○
Montagny	☐	Chardonnay	●●○

Bourgogne Côte Chalonnaise AC applies to all wines made on the Côte from Pinot Noir for red, and Chardonnay for white. It is classified as a regional appellation.

Rully AC produces more white wine than red. It is also an important centre for the production of sparkling wine. **Mercurey AC** is the village on Côte Chalonnaise whose red wines enjoy the highest reputation – and prices. **Givry AC** is the smallest of the four village appellations. Its reds are particularly admired. **Montagny AC** produces only white wines.

Mâcon

It is in the Mâconnais that one first becomes aware of moving to the south of France. It is not just the climate; it is also the attitude to life. Here dairy farming is as important to the local economy as winemaking. (Limestone-rich soils are ideal for Chardonnay, but they are also ideal for grazing dairy cattle.) Once this was an area of red wines made from Gamay; now red wines account for no more than a third of the production and quarter of that is made from Pinot Noir. Co-operative cellars play a vital role in wine production.

Mâcon AC can be made from anywhere within the region, from Chardonnay for white wines and from Gamay or Pinot Noir for red. To call the wine Mâcon Supérieur AC, the minimum level of alcohol is 0.5% abv higher than Mâcon; most wines qualify. Although some wines from this

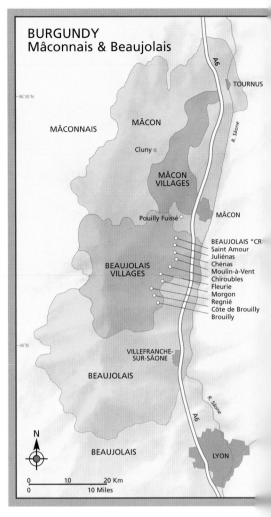

The rock at Solutré, Mâcon.

large region can be rather lacking in flavour, most show a good balance of fresh apple or citrus fruit, crisp acidity and medium-to-full body. There may be a hint of creaminess from malolactic fermentation.

Mâcon Villages AC or **Mâcon + village name AC** may be applied to a white wine from one of 43 different villages and the wines generally represent excellent value for money, particularly for those who like soft Chardonnays. Certain individual villages, such as Lugny, have built up a considerable following for their wines. Another village in the group is Chardonnay, from which the grape takes its name. A wine called Mâcon Villages may come from any one, or a combination, of the villages. The wines are generally similar in style to white Mâcon, but tend to display more ripeness, body and character.

Pouilly-Fuissé AC is the most distinctive wine of the Mâconnais, being produced in a series of amphitheatre-like slopes, which act as natural

suntraps. The wines are among the richest in Burgundy, achieving up to 13.5% abv. Of all the wines of the Mâconnais, these benefit most from barrel-ageing. The location and exposure results in wines that taste very ripe and full-bodied. Peach and melon fruit can combine with savoury, nutty flavours of new oak. Some wines can even taste quite 'New World' in style. **Viré-Clessé AC, Saint-Véran AC** and **Pouilly-Vinzelles AC** also have their own appellations.

BEAUJOLAIS

The first thing to be realised about the Beaujolais is that it is red wine country; red wine made from the Gamay grape (only 1 per cent of the wine is white, made from Chardonnay). Gamay gives fragrant wines that are full of raspberry and cherry fruit, and is very light in tannins. These characteristics are often further enhanced by the vinification technique, a variation on carbonic maceration that extracts colours and fruit flavours and very little tannin, giving the wine a character that can suggest kirsch, bananas, bubblegum and cinnamon-like spices.

Beaujolais accounts for approximately half the production of greater viticultural Burgundy. It can be split into two distinct parts.

Mâcon			
KEY AC WINES		**GRAPE VARIETY**	**PRICE**
Mâcon	☐	Chardonnay	●○
Mâcon Villages	☐	Chardonnay	●●
Pouilly-Fuissé	☐	Chardonnay	●●○○

Beaujolais			
KEY AC WINES		**GRAPE VARIETY**	**PRICE**
Beaujolais	■	Gamay	●
Beaujolais Villages	■	Gamay	●○
The ten *cru* villages (listed below)	■	Gamay	●●○

Beaujolais and Beaujolais Noveau

To the south and east, the vineyards lie in the alluvial plain of the River Saône. Here the soil is sandy and the vines are trained along wires. It is here that plain **Beaujolais AC** is produced, mainly by carbonic maceration. This is also the major source of *Beaujolais Nouveau*, a wine that is specifically made for early drinking and now accounts for up to half the total annual crop of Beaujolais. Its fashion seems to have largely passed in Britain, though it is now a commercially successful novelty in countries such as Japan. It cannot be released to the consumer until after

Gamay vines growing in Brouilly, with Côte de Brouilly in the background.

midnight of the third Wednesday in November after the vintage, that is the morning of the third Thursday, and cannot be sold by growers or merchants after the following 31 August. (*Beaujolais Primeur* may be the same wine as *Beaujolais Nouveau*, but may not be sold to the trade after the 31 January following the vintage.) *Nouveau* and *Primeur* can be only of Beaujolais or Beaujolais Villages quality; the ten *crus* cannot be sold in this way.

Beaujolais Villages and the Beaujolais *Crus*

To the north and west of the region, the vineyards are planted on a series of rolling hills, where the soils are predominantly granitic schist. Gamay has a particular affinity to granite, giving wines of greater character here than on the sandy soils further south. Thirty-nine villages here have the right to call their wine **Beaujolais Villages** and

they account for about a quarter of the total production of the region. The wines are usually blended between the villages, but occasionally one can find a wine with an individual named village. The vines are free-standing and trained *en gobelet*.

Within the rolling granitic hills, ten villages are recognised to produce wines of particular distinction and identifiable character. These are the Beaujolais *crus*. From north to south, they are: **Saint-Amour AC, Juliénas AC, Chénas AC, Moulin à Vent AC, Chiroubles AC, Fleurie AC, Morgon AC, Régnié AC, Côte de Brouilly AC** and **Brouilly AC**. Moulin à Vent and Morgon are the most powerful and full-bodied, and will improve in the bottle; Brouilly is the most widely available as it has the largest production. Most of these wines will be vinified in a traditional style and many will receive some ageing in oak, often in large vats rather than casks.

Alsace

11

Geographically, Alsace stands apart from the rest of France, separated by the Vosges mountains, which form its western frontier. On the east, the boundary is the River Rhine. For much of its life it was part of Germany, and its vinous role was to produce vast quantities of common wine, thus protecting the position of the traditional great wine estates of the Rhine and the Mosel. When Alsace finally became part of France, at the end of the First World War, it chose a path as a producer of quality wines. The first step was the banning of hybrid vines in 1925. *Appellation Contrôlée* was finally introduced in 1962. Further steps have included legislation that insists on bottling in the region of production (1972) and the compulsory use of the Alsace flute bottle (except for Pinot Noir and sparkling wines).

In some ways the appellation system in Alsace is very simple for there are only two ACs for still wine. However this simplicity can cause problems as producers seek to distinguish between the different qualities of wine that they produce. Because of this, it is common to find on labels such statements as *Réserve Personnelle* and *Cuvée Spéciale*; these, however, have no legal status.

Alsace AC (or **Vin d'Alsace AC**) accounts for over 80 per cent of the wine production of the region. Normally, the main feature on the label will be the mention of an individual grape variety, though there are many blends that appear under brand names.

Alsace Grand Cru AC. Since 1975, a number of individual vineyards have been recognised as having traditionally produced the finest wines. There are currently 50 with *Grand Cru* status. For an Alsace wine to describe itself as *Grand Cru*, not only must it come from one of these vineyards; it must be produced from noble grape varieties (Riesling, Muscat, Gewurztraminer or Pinot Gris) and the maximum yield is considerably lower than that of Alsace AC. Each *Grand Cru* has its own committee and has the power to tighten the controls by, for example, forbidding chaptalisation. A *Grand Cru* label will have the name of the vineyard and the grape:

Schlossberg Riesling
Appellation Alsace Grand Cru Contrôlée

There are two other classifications for Alsace wines; these depend upon the ripeness of the grapes. These are *Vendange Tardive* and *Sélection de Grains Nobles*. The requirements for these two levels have been progressively increased since they were first introduced.

Vendange Tardive (**VT**) = 'Late Harvest'. These wines can be made from only the four 'noble' varieties and must have a natural potential alcohol (chaptalisation is forbidden) of 13.1% abv for Riesling and Muscat grapes and 14.4% abv for Pinot Gris and Gewurztraminer. Originally, this classification of wine might be either dry, if the winemaker chose to ferment out all the sugar, or sweet. Now, all should have some residual sugar.

Sélection de Grains Nobles (**SGN**) = 'Selection of Nobly Rotten Grapes'. This wine is produced in outstanding vintages only and is always sweet. Generally, at least some of the grapes will be affected by noble rot. The minimum natural potential alcohol must be, for Riesling and Muscat grapes, 15.2% abv and, for Pinot Gris and Gewurztraminer, 16.6% abv.

View of Riquewihr from the *Grand Cru* Schoenenbourg vineyard.

Alsace			
KEY WINES		**MAIN GRAPE VARIETIES**	**PRICE**
Alsace	☐	Riesling, Gewurztraminer, Pinot Gris, Muscat, Pinot Blanc, Sylvaner	●●○
	■■	Pinot Noir	●●○
Vendange Tardive, Sélection de Grains Nobles	☐	Riesling, Muscat, Gewurztraminer, Pinot Gris	●●●○+
Alsace Grand Cru	☐	Riesling, Muscat, Gewurztraminer, Pinot Gris	●●●○+

CLIMATE, SOIL AND TOPOGRAPHY

The Rhine flows through a vast rift valley, where, 25 million years ago, what was the Alsace Plain collapsed leaving on the west the Vosges mountains and, on the east, those of the Black Forest, with the river flowing down the middle of the valley. The vineyards of Alsace lie mainly on the exposed foothills of the Vosges, where there is a great variety of soils. The slopes include granitic, limestone, sandstone, clay, loam and even volcanic soils, whilst on the plain they are largely alluvial. This geological complexity is one factor that contributes to the broad range of styles of wines the region produces.

Another important factor is the climate. Although this is basically continental, Alsace enjoys almost perfect conditions for wine production. This is due primarily to the influence of the Vosges; these shelter the vineyards from the prevailing westerly, rain-bearing winds. Lorraine, which lies to the west of the Vosges, is one of France's wettest regions; Alsace to the east is the driest, together with Roussillon, immediately north of the Pyrenées. Rainfall is as little as 500 mm per year and coupled with over 1800 hours of sunshine, with hot summers and long, dry autumns. These all go to create ideal conditions for making great wine.

The wine villages lie in a narrow band 140 kilometres long, at the foot of the Vosges, across two *départements*, with the Haut-Rhin to the south and the Bas-Rhin to the north. The better vineyards are situated on the lower slopes, which face due east and capture the maximum benefit of the morning sun. The slopes may be as steep as 40°. The lesser vineyards lie on the plain. Here the grapes are often used for the production of Crémant d'Alsace, the local AC sparkling wine. The best wines come from vineyards in the Haut-Rhin in a number of villages around the town of Colmar, where the Vosges are at their highest and exert their strongest influence on the climate. It is here, where there is less rainfall than in southern Spain, that the majority of the *Grand Cru* vineyard sites are located.

GRAPE VARIETIES

Alsace differs from most other vineyard areas of France in that it is generally the grape variety that is the dominant feature on the label. Here, if a grape is named, the wine has to be made 100 per cent from that variety. Over the years, in an effort to improve the quality of the wines, the range of varieties planted has decreased considerably. Only Riesling, Gewurztraminer, Pinot Gris and Muscat are considered to be the 'noble' varieties, suitable for making *Vendange Tardive, Sélection de Grains Nobles* and *Grand Cru* wines. Because of the way in which they are made, Alsatian wines clearly reflect the character of the grape used to make them. In general, they are drier and more full-bodied than their German equivalents, though it is quite common to find some residual sugar even in non-*Vendange Tardive* wines, particularly in those made from Pinot Gris or Gewurztraminer. Although this should now be indicated on the label, it is not always easy to tell whether a wine is bone-dry, off-dry or medium-sweet until it has been tasted.

Riesling. With its steely clarity of flavour, the Riesling is the variety of which Alsatian growers are proudest. This is the same variety that is found in Germany with the same combination of fine fruit and high acidity. The last of all varieties to ripen, it is ideal for late harvest wines because of its hardiness. At its best on granite or schist, it is responsible for nearly a quarter of all plantings.

Gewurztraminer. *Gewürz* is the German word for spice. It aptly describes this wine with its pungent aromatic spicy nose, reminiscent of lychees, roses and cashews. The skin of the grape has a light pink tinge, giving colour to the wine. Gewurztraminer tends to be low in acidity and high in alcohol with wines of 14% abv not being uncommon. It is a good complement to smoked fish or strong cheese. At its best on deep marl soils, it accounts for a fifth of all plantings.

Pinot Gris. In Alsace this has long been known as Tokay d'Alsace. Because Pinot Gris has never been used in the production of Tokaji, the EU objected to this name, but agreed to the temporary compromise 'Tokay Pinot Gris', though the word Tokay is scheduled to be abandoned by the year 2006. Pinot Gris gives wine that is rich and high in alcohol. It has a similar colour to Gewurztraminer, but is less aromatic. On the palate it can be luscious and full of flavour. Its yield varies considerably and it is best planted on deep clay soils. It now accounts for an eighth of the area under vines.

Muscat. This is becoming a rare grape in Alsace, with no more than 3 per cent of the vineyard area. One of the problems is that it is prone to rot. It ripens early, likes sandy soil and gives a lowish yield. The best wines come from the Muscat à Petits Grains, but the Muscat Ottonel is more widely planted because it can be relied on to crop more regularly. The wine has the classic grapey Muscat flavour, whilst remaining dry.

Pinot Blanc (*Auxerrois, Klevner*). A fairly early ripening grape, grown on light, fertile soils. Plantings are increasing, because it is widely used for the production of sparkling wines, but as a still wine, it is light and refreshing. It now accounts for over a fifth of all the vineyard area.

Sylvaner. Once the most widely planted variety in Alsace, this now mainly occurs in the Bas-Rhin where it gives large yields of usually undistinguished wine. It likes deep, sandy or chalky soils. Now less than an eighth of the vineyard area is planted with this variety.

Pinot Noir. This grape is of increasing importance as it satisfies the demand of the local consumer who seeks something other than white wine. It now accounts for nearly a tenth of plantings. Two different styles of wine are made: the traditional is a fruity rosé, while the modern reds will have been aged in small barrels and have much more colour and body. These are the only Alsatian wines, apart from the sparkling wines, that are not required to be bottled in tall flutes. Burgundy-style bottles may be used.

Spring frost damage is a hazard faced by the vinegrower in Alsace.

VITICULTURE AND VINIFICATION

The vines are trained high in rows, which follow the contours of the hillside slopes. This maximises exposure to the sun and minimises the risk of damage from spring frosts. On the steepest slopes the vineyards will be terraced and the planting of the vines is denser than on the plain, where machinery can be used. Double Guyot is the common pruning system.

The area under vines in Alsace has increased by more than a quarter since the mid-1980s, and production by a third. At the same time the number of growers has decreased by a quarter. It is a region of small vineyard holdings; the average being less than 3 hectares. Much of the wine is sold directly at the 'farm gate', but four-fifths of all growers are just that: they just grow grapes, which they sell either to the co-operative cellars (which have an important role in Alsace) or to merchants. Many growers will have a number of small plots of vines, planted with different varieties. As these ripen at different times, the vintage may be spread over quite a long period. This normally starts towards the middle of October and may last until the end of November or even the beginning of December.

There is a saying in Alsace to the effect that the best wine is the one that has received the minimum of treatment. The grapes are pressed, generally in pneumatic presses, and despite the climate, chaptalisation is widely practised. The juice ferments in large oak casks, many 100 years or more old. On the inside of these there is a thick tartrate deposit, which prevents the wood from having any influence on the wine. In modern cellars, stainless steel vats are now more commonly used, facilitating the control of temperatures at the time of fermentation. This is often stopped before all the sugar has been converted to alcohol, and even non-late-harvested wines may have some residual sugar. With the exception of Pinot Blanc, malolactic fermentation is normally not allowed to take place since this would mask the pure fruit flavours. Bottling usually takes place in the spring following the vintage, while the wine is young and fresh. Most wines are then ready to drink, but many are capable of further evolution in the bottle.

Old oak casks are traditionally used to ferment Alsace wines.

The Loire Valley

The Loire is France's longest river. It rises in the mountains of central France in the Ardèche *département* and flows north for almost 400 kilometres, before turning west near Orléans and finally reaching the Atlantic near the city of Nantes. It is the last 600 kilometres of its course that are of viticultural interest. Here the vineyards can be loosely grouped into four subregions. Going downstream, these are the Centre, Touraine, Anjou-Saumur and the Nantais.

12

Unlike other areas there is no regional generic appellation for the Loire such as AC Bordeaux or AC Bourgogne. There is, however, a *Vin de Pays*, Jardin de la France, which covers the whole region, over 13 *départements*. Much of the *Vin de Pays* is Chardonnay, a grape otherwise used only for the production of sparkling wine. Just two AC wines include the name of the region in their title – Rosé de Loire and Crémant de Loire – though production of these is focused in Anjou and Saumur respectively. Over half the total production of the four Loire regions is of white wine and a quarter red; nearly 12 per cent is rosé; the balance is sparkling.

Because of the length of the river, there are considerable climatic differences between the different regions. In the Nantais and Anjou, the dominant influence is the Atlantic Ocean. Further upstream the climate becomes increasingly continental. However, the Loire and its many tributaries play a moderating role. Because the vineyards lie in the marginal zone, there can be significant variations in the weather patterns from year to year, and vintages can differ widely.

THE CENTRAL VINEYARDS

At the eastern end of the viticultural Loire, before the river turns west towards the Atlantic, lies the area known as the vineyards of the Centre. In terms of production it is by far the smallest of the four regions, though it contains two of the most famous Loire vineyards, Sancerre and Pouilly-Fumé. Indeed, the two towns of Sancerre and Pouilly-sur-Loire almost face each other across the river. Geographically and climatically they are more linked to Burgundy, for the climate is distinctly continental, with severe winters and hot summers. Here summer hails and spring frosts are recurrent problems.

For many wine-lovers **Sancerre AC** makes the finest dry white wines of the Loire Valley. The vineyards are spread over 15 villages on very chalky stony soil, much of it, like that of the not too distant Chablis, rich in marine fossils, which drains well. They lie mainly on the slopes of low hills that face south-east and south-west. The vineyard holdings are small and generally divided into minute parcels of vines.

Most Sancerre is white, high in acidity and made from Sauvignon Blanc. Traditionally, it used to be fermented slowly in 600-litre wooden casks, but now much never sees wood at all, spending its life in stainless steel. It shares with Marlborough Sauvignon Blanc a distinctive herbaceous character, known to those who dislike the style as 'cat's pee', and to the less antagonistic as elderflower or gooseberry. Certain individual villages such as Chavignol, and vineyards such as Les Monts Damnés, have created high reputations for wines that display a smoky minerality and are able to evolve in the bottle, though in most cases

The River Loire viewed over a vineyard at Les Loges, Pouilly-Fumé, with the hilltop town of Sancerre in the distance.

The Central Vineyards

KEY AC WINES		MAIN GRAPE VARIETIES	PRICE
Sancerre	☐	Sauvignon Blanc	●●○
	■ ■	Pinot Noir	●●●
Pouilly-Fumé	☐	Sauvignon Blanc	●●○○
Menetou-Salon	☐	Sauvignon Blanc	●●
	■ ■	Pinot Noir	●●

Sancerre is not a wine for ageing. A good accompaniment for the best wines of Sancerre is the local goat cheese, *crottin de Chavignol*. Due to its huge popularity and the limited area of the vineyards, there is pressure for the (already high) prices to rise or for the wine not to be available all year round in all markets.

About 20 per cent of the production is red or rosé wine made from the Pinot Noir grape. This is a vestige of a period, pre-phylloxera, when there were much closer links with Burgundy; a period when most wine from Sancerre was in fact red! Because the best sites are usually now reserved for Sauvignon Blanc, the red and rosé wines are generally light in style, though their rarity and novelty ensure high prices.

On the opposite side of the Loire, **Pouilly-Fumé AC** is produced on soils much the same as those in Sancerre, but with more flint. These are dry and very similar to Sancerre, but perhaps because they are more often cask-aged, appear to lack some of the aggressive herbaceousness of their neighbour. Unlike Sancerre and Menetou-Salon, there are no red wines made under this appellation. Prices are similar to Sancerre, with a small number of producers able to charge super-premium prices.

To the west and south of Sancerre, wine is produced from vineyards lying on the tributaries of the Cher. Here the most important appellation is **Menetou-Salon AC**. This has Kimmeridgian clay soils similar to those of Chablis, but makes white wines from Sauvignon Blanc and small quantities of red and rosé wines from Pinot Noir. It is growing in importance as a source of more moderately priced alternatives to Sancerre and Pouilly-Fumé.

TOURAINE

As Touraine is 200 kilometres from the sea, its climate is still distinctly continental. The vineyards of Touraine fall into two main groups; to the west is the red wine area of Chinon and Bourgueil, to the east the white wine vineyards of Vouvray. **Touraine AC** covers the whole subregion, with the red wines being made largely from Cabernet Franc or Gamay grapes and the dry, white wines from Chenin Blanc or Sauvignon Blanc. These

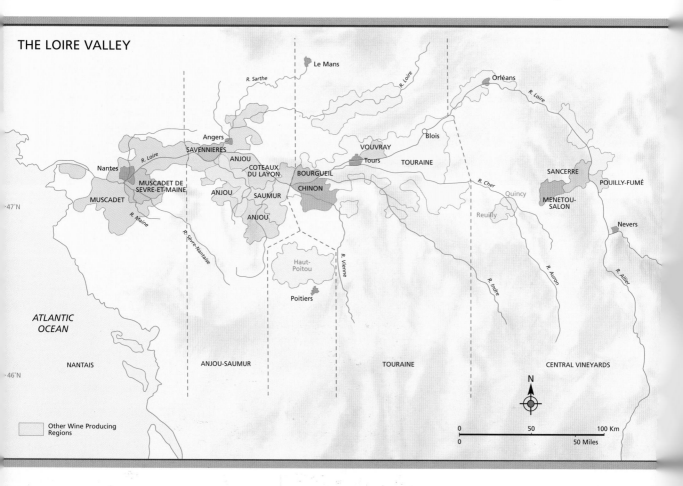

THE LOIRE VALLEY

ften appear under a varietal label, for example
auvignon de Touraine or Gamay de Touraine.

Vouvray AC wine is always white and is made
rom the Chenin Blanc grape, though it can
ppear in a full range of styles – still, *pétillant*
nd sparkling – from dry to, in the finest years,
usciously sweet. When there is noble rot in the
ineyards, the vintage here can be among the
atest in France. Many growers have their cellars
ut into the cliffs of soft *tuffeau* that are a feature
f both banks of the river here. This kind of
halky limestone is full of marine creatures and is
ery porous, allowing the vines to develop large
oot systems. Good drainage allows the vines'
vater needs to be met without flooding the roots
r bloating the grapes. The high calcium content
nables the grapes to retain their acidity as they
ipen.

Chenin Blanc is the grape responsible for the
reatest white wines of both Touraine and Anjou-
aumur, dry or sweet, still or sparkling. The
ariety of styles that this grape produces here is
lirectly related to the degree of ripeness that it
has achieved at the time of picking, and the
esultant amount of sugar in the grape. One
lifficulty with this variety is that even within
one bunch it is common for grapes to reach
lifferent levels of ripeness. This can result in leafy
romas if care is not taken during the harvest to

Touraine			
KEY AC WINES		**MAIN GRAPE VARIETIES**	**PRICE**
Touraine	☐	Sauvignon Blanc, Chenin Blanc	●○
	■	Gamay, Cabernet Franc	●○
Vouvray	☐	Chenin Blanc	●●○○
Chinon	■	Cabernet Franc	●●○
Bourgueil	■	Cabernet Franc	●●○

Yellow *tuffeau*: the soft
soil on which Vouvray's
vineyards are planted.

exclude unripe grapes. Barely ripe fruit is used for
sparkling wines, while the dry, medium and sweet
styles of still wine reflect the use of increasingly
ripe berries, including those shrivelled in the sun
or affected by noble rot. Chenin Blanc grows best
on limestone soils and, because of its natural
acidity, ages well. Young wines can have flavours
that vary from fresh apple through to exotic fruit,
depending on the ripeness of the grapes, and can

Barrels in a cellar cut out
of the soft yellow *tuffeau*,
Touraine.

Anjou-Saumur

KEY AC WINES		MAIN GRAPE VARIETIES	PRICE
Saumur AC	☐	Chenin Blanc	●●
	■	Cabernet Franc	●●
Anjou AC	☐	Chenin Blanc	●●
	■	Cabernet Franc	●●
	■	Grolleau, Cabernet Franc, Gamay	●
Côteaux du Layon	☐	Chenin Blanc	●●○○
Savennières	☐	Chenin Blanc	●●○○

Chenin Blanc finds ideal conditions for sweet wines on these sites near Rablay, Côteaux du Layon.

Cabernet Franc gives the wines of all these three appellations a certain rusticity and many of them need some bottle-ageing before they can be appreciated fully. Cabernet Franc is the main red wine grape of the Loire. It is similar to Cabernet Sauvignon, with which it is often blended, but is more suited to the cooler Loire climate and appears greener and stalkier on the nose and palate. Wines can be fragrant and juicy with light tannins and crisp acidity, suitable for drinking lightly chilled. More ambitious wines that can age well in the bottle are also made, with more grippy tannins and the use of oak. Cabernet Franc is also used for rosé wines.

ANJOU-SAUMUR

This is the heartland of the Loire. The vineyards to the west border those of Muscadet, to the east they stretch some 10 kilometres beyond the town of Saumur. It is here that the continental climate begins to change to a maritime one. The dampness of the climate increases further to the west, towards the Atlantic. There are no extremes of temperature in winter or summer. The soil also changes from limestone-chalk and *tuffeau* in the east to a schist subsoil in the west. Of the subregions of the Loire valley, this is the most productive, with red, white and rosé wines being produced in almost equal proportions. Most of the greatest wines are produced south of the river.

At the eastern frontier of Anjou, around the pretty town of Saumur, are the vineyards of **Saumur AC**. Here, just as in Anjou, the white wines made from Chenin Blanc range from dry to, in the best years, sweet. The best of the local red wines, made from the Cabernet Franc, is the fashionable **Saumur-Champigny AC**. Many of the cellars are cut into the steep banks of *tuffeau* on both banks of the river. Saumur is also an important centre for the production of sparkling wine.

The broad appellation **Anjou AC** covers red, white and rosé wines. Just as in Touraine, a broad range of grapes is grown. Chenin Blanc and Cabernet Franc, in particular, are important varieties. Grolleau (Groslot) is found only in Anjou where it is the workhorse red grape, giving large yields of rather thin, acidic wines. These often form the base of Rosé d'Anjou or sparkling wine. There are three appellations for rosé wines of which the highest quality is **Cabernet d'Anjou AC**. This is always medium-sweet in style and is made from a blend of Cabernet Franc and Cabernet Sauvignon grapes. **Rosé d'Anjou AC** is also slightly sweet, but is of declining importance. It is made from a blend of Grolleau, Cabernet

also express smoky mineral notes or the influence of botrytis. They become richer, rounder and more honeyed with age. Quite high levels of sugar can become so fully integrated into the wines that the sweetness becomes almost undetectable.

The most prestigious red wine of the Loire Valley is **Chinon AC**, produced around the town of the same name. The production is almost totally red, though a little rosé is also made from the Cabernet Franc grape (a little Cabernet Sauvignon may also be found). The appellation has three distinct styles of wine, depending on where the grapes have been grown. The lightest wines come from the sandy soils of the vineyards in the valley of the River Vienne. This joins the Loire from the south some 15 kilometres to the west of Chinon. On the plateau to the north, the soil has more clay and gravel, giving firmer-bodied wines. The finest wines, however, come from hillside slopes where the soil is predominantly limestone. These are wines for keeping. One other factor that can affect the quality of the wine is whether or not the wine has been aged in oak; if it is used, it is generally in the form of old casks.

North of Chinon, on the far bank of the Loire, are the vineyards of **Bourgueil AC** and **Saint-Nicholas de Bourgueil AC**. These are protected from the cold north winds by a wooded plateau and have an individual favourable site climate.

Franc and/or Gamay. Finally, there is **Rosé de Loire AC**, which is always dry and must have a minimum of 30 per cent Cabernet grapes in the blend.

The best wines of Anjou-Saumur are white and made from Chenin Blanc. Most of these will have high acidity balanced by some residual sweetness, as botrytis develops well in the sheltered valleys. This is especially true of the deeper valley of the Layon, which flows into the Loire from the south, west of Angers. This valley gives the sweet wines of the **Côteaux du Layon AC**. In style, these combine the fresh fruit character and mouthwatering acidity of the sweet wines of Germany with some of the body and alcohol of Sauternes. The pickers may pass through the vines on a number of occasions to pick all the grapes, which become sweeter the later they are picked. The two most favoured sites, Quarts de Chaume and Bonnezeaux, have their own appellations and rank among the world's greatest sweet wines.

Savennières lies on the north bank of the Loire. Air circulation around the well-exposed vineyards impedes the development of noble rot, but enables late-harvested Chenin Blanc Grapes to be used for full-bodied, dry wines of exceptional complexity. These wines are rather austere when they are young due to their high acidity, but as with fine Vouvray they can build layers of honey and smoky-mineral flavours as they evolve over decades in the bottle.

THE NANTAIS

Brittany's only vineyards lie on both banks of the River Loire close to its mouth, with the important city of Nantes at their centre. The main wine of the region is **Muscadet**, whose vineyards sprawl over a series of rolling slopes. The better vineyards are in the Sèvre et Maine subregion south and east of Nantes. These are planted on well-draining soils of shale and gneiss, over a bedrock of granite. Traditionally, vines were pruned in the *gobelet* system, but in order to facilitate machine-picking, vines trained on wires are becoming more common. The climate is moist and temperate, with mild summers and winter. Frost damage is rare.

View from the Roche aux Moines towards the Clos de la Coulée de Serrant, two of the *crus* within Savennieres.

The Nantais			
KEY AC WINES		**MAIN GRAPE VARIETY**	**PRICE**
Muscadet	☐	Melon de Bourgogne	●
Muscadet de Sèvre et Maine	☐	Melon de Bourgogne	●
Muscadet de Sèvre et Maine sur Lie	☐	Melon de Bourgogne	●○

Vineyards in Muscadet
showing the gently rolling
slopes.

Only one grape is permitted for the production of Muscadet and this is variously known as the Melon de Bourgogne or Muscadet. The former name is now more generally used than the latter. Regarded as a neutral variety, its best wines display attractive green apple or grassy aromas. It ripens early and its frost-resistance suits it to this marginal climate.

All wines from Muscadet should be dry. Indeed, until recently, they had a reputation for their austerity. Sadly, perhaps, now they are generally vinified in a softer, more commercial style. Chaptalisation is generally used, but the *maximum* permitted strength for the wine is 12.3% abv. Traditionally, the wines were fermented in cask but now concrete or stainless steel vats are more common. The wine should be drunk young and is a traditional accompaniment for seafood, particularly shellfish.

Muscadet de Sèvre et Maine sur Lie AC is a speciality with increasing commercial importance. The wine is bottled direct from the cask or tank in the spring following the vintage, having spent the winter on its lees (*lie* is the French for lees). Because of its nature it is largely domain-bottled and in the spring, mobile bottling-lines go from cellar to cellar. Because the wine is handled very little, it should retain its delicacy and freshness, and may have lazy bubbles beading the rim of the glass. Contact with its lees gives it more body and a slightly yeasty character.

The Rhône Valley

The Rhône is one of the great wine rivers of the world. With its source in the Alps, south of the Swiss city of Lucerne, it flows west through the vineyards of the Valais, and then north-west into Lake Geneva. It then passes through the vineyards of Savoie, and joins the River Saône at Lyons. There it turns south for some 400 kilometres, before it flows into the Mediterranean west of Marseilles. It is the stretch between the old Roman city of Vienne in the north and Avignon in the south that is responsible for producing the finest Rhône wines. This is the second largest quality vineyard region in the world, with approximately 80 000 hectares of vineyards. These produce overwhelmingly red and rosé wines, though there are many interesting white wines to be found.

13

Though the Rhône is considered as one vineyard region, it falls naturally into two distinct parts, with different climates and largely different grape varieties. The northern Rhône vineyards lie between Vienne and Valence, a distance of about 70 kilometres. There is then a gap of about 60 kilometres before the vineyards begin again at the village of Donzère, just south of the town of Montélimar, perhaps best known for its production of nougat. In the northern Rhône, the trade is dominated by *négociants* (merchants who buy grapes or finished wine to assemble and sell under their own name). In the south, the co-operative cellars have a dominant role, though there is a trend for grape-growers that previously supplied co-operatives to set up estates to make and bottle their own wine.

As in other parts of France, there is a distinct hierarchy within the wines of the Rhône. At its foot lies the generic-level appellation Côtes du Rhône, which comes almost entirely from the south, though in theory it may be produced anywhere within the region. Above this comes Côtes du Rhône Villages from a small number of villages, all of which are in the south. Then, at the commune level, there are 13 individual *crus*, villages that have their own AC status. Eight of these are in the north and five in the south.

THE NORTHERN RHÔNE

Many of the wines from the Rhône with the highest reputations, and the highest prices, come from the northern Rhône, though it is responsible for only approximately 5 per cent of the total production. Individual growers with cult status around the world have done much to create the quality image for Rhône wines, though this would

have been impossible to sustain if the wines had failed to match their reputation.

Topography, Climate and Viticulture

Here the valley is quite narrow and steep, with the vineyards mainly planted on the western slopes, close to the river. The soil is basically granitic and often has to be carried back up into the vineyards after being washed down in heavy rains. There are a number of lateral valleys, which give optimal exposure for the vines to the sun and also protect them from the dominant climatic feature of the region, the **Mistral**. This is a strong, cold, north wind, which creates a noticeable chill factor, but inhibits diseases by improving air circulation and can reduce grape sizes and thus concentrate flavours. Because of its strength, vines are generally staked; even bush-trained vines will have individual posts. The climate is similar to that of the Beaujolais: southern continental, with summers that are hot, but not oppressive.

Winemaking and Grape Varieties

This part of the valley has long been a bastion of traditional winemaking, with wines being

The Northern Rhône			
KEY AC WINES		**MAIN GRAPE VARIETIES**	**PRICE**
Côte-Rôtie	■	Syrah	●●●●+
Condrieu	☐	Viognier	●●●●+
Saint-Joseph	■	Syrah	●●○
	☐	Marsanne, Roussanne	
Crozes-Hermitage	■	Syrah	●●○
	☐	Marsanne, Roussanne	●●
Hermitage	■	Syrah	●●●●+
	☐	Marsanne, Roussanne	
Cornas	■	Syrah	●●●

fermented in open vats and aged in old oak for up to two years. New oak is, however, becoming more widely used, bringing extra depth to the wines.

For red wine production here, **Syrah** is the dominant grape. It gives deeply coloured, tannic wines, with good ageing potential. These typically have soft black fruit flavours (blackberries and blueberries), with spicy hints of black pepper when young, and gamey aromas when mature.

For white wines, the most interesting grape is the **Viognier**. This gives a low, irregular yield of opulently fruity wines with exotic aromas. Until recently, this variety survived in only a few locations in the northern Rhône. Since then it has taken on cult status and is increasingly widely planted in the Languedoc, Australia, California, South Africa and South America.

The **Roussanne** is another quality grape, though again its plantings have declined, largely because it is susceptible to rot and resists wind poorly. It often adds finesse, fruit and crisp acidity to a blend with **Marsanne**, which has higher yields and is high in alcohol. Whilst Roussanne and Marsanne often appear in harness together, Viognier is never blended with them in the northern Rhône.

Regions and Wines

Let us look at the northern Rhône *crus* in order, from north to south.

Côte-Rôtie AC. The most northerly vineyards of the Rhône valley, around the town of Ampuis. The name, which translates as 'roasted slope', gives some idea of their exposure to the sun. The vines are grown on precipitous, narrow terraces which are hard to work (machine access is impossible, though some spraying can be done by helicopter). They are generally trained into a tepee shape to stabilise the vine against the strong, hot, southerly winds. Only red wines are produced, from the

NORTHERN RHÔNE

Vienne
CÔTE-RÔTIE
CONDRIEU

SAINT-JOSEPH

HERMITAGE

Tournon
CROZES-HERMITAGE
R. Isère

CORNAS
Valence

R. Drôme
Die

R. Rhône

Tying vines on to stakes with raffia in steep Côte-Rôtie vineyards to form the traditional taille en archet *or 'wigwam' shape.*

Syrah grape. Up to 20 per cent Viognier can be added, inspiring the increasingly fashionable Shiraz-Viognier blends in the New World, though it is unusual to include more than 5 per cent. The extremely elegant wines are deeply coloured, full-bodied, spicy and complex. They are as sought-after and expensive as those of Hermitage.

Condrieu AC is a dry white wine made solely from the Viognier grape. It has a unique, floral perfume, at its best when consumed young. **Château Grillet AC** is a single vineyard enclave within Condrieu, producing similar barrel-aged wines. The best wines come from low-yielding old vines, and great skill is required to extract the delicate perfumes from the grape skins. The effort involved in tending the steep vineyards, and the tiny quantities of wine produced, require premium prices.

Saint-Joseph AC is also produced from vineyards lying on the west bank of the river. Although some white is made from Marsanne and

Roussanne grapes, most of the wine is red, and made from Syrah. These are generally the lightest-bodied northern Rhône red wines, expressing the raspberry and pepper-perfumed aspects of the Syrah grape. The very best wines come from the terraced vineyards near Tournon. Large volumes of less characterful wines come from the more fertile, flatter sites at the top and bottom of the slopes. Prices are similar to, or slightly higher than, those of Crozes-Hermitage.

The most important appellation in terms of volume is **Crozes-Hermitage AC**, whose vineyards lie on mixed terrain around the hill of Hermitage. The red wines are made from Syrah (with the option of adding up to 15 per cent Marsanne or Roussanne). Their quality and style varies considerably (as does price). Lighter wines are made to a budget from high-yielding machine-harvested flatter sites, while more concentrated, complex wines come from hand-tended vines growing on the steeper slopes. Some of the more expensive wines may be aged in oak. The less prestigious reputation of this region (compared to Hermitage and Côte-Rôtie), and the relatively large volumes produced, mean that most Crozes-Hermitage is medium-priced. Some white wines are also produced, mainly from Marsanne grapes. These are medium-bodied and fruity, and are best consumed young.

Hermitage AC, in the nineteenth century, had the reputation of producing two of the greatest wines in the world, for both the red and the white were highly appreciated. After a period in decline, their reputation has regained much of its former lustre, pushing prices up to premium levels. The vineyards lie on the eastern bank of the river, on a steeply rising, south-facing hillside, behind the town of Tain-l'Hermitage.

Red Hermitage is one of the fullest-bodied of French wines and ages well. The greatest wines may last for 50 years or more. Though up to 15 per cent of white grapes may be fermented with Syrah, this is now rarely done.

Approximately a fifth of the production is white Hermitage. Marsanne predominates in the blend, providing body. Roussanne, when used, contributes fragrance and crisp acidity. These are full-bodied, long-lived wines, which can develop very complex honey and hazelnut flavours as they age.

Many consider **Cornas AC** to be the most undervalued wine of the Rhône valley, though they are still high-priced wines. The sheltered, sun-baked bowl containing the vineyards enables the production of deeply coloured, full-bodied red wines, which often rival those of Hermitage. Other northern Rhône red appellations permit a percentage of white grapes as a vestige of the days

Exposed vineyards on the hill of Hermitage, above Tain.

when a vineyard would contain several varieties
that would be picked and fermented together. As
vineyards are becoming more regimented, the
trend is for the red wines to become closer to 100
per cent Syrah. Cornas is the exception and *must*
be made from Syrah only.

THE SOUTHERN RHÔNE
Climate and Topography
Here the climate changes from continental to
Mediterranean, with milder winters and hotter
summers. The valley of the Rhône opens out,
with pockets of sandy soil amongst the rough,
rocky scrubland, the *garrigues*. With no slopes to
protect the vines from the power of the Mistral,
windbreaks have to be planted.

Grape Varieties and Viticulture
Instead of the wines being made from just one or
two different varieties, here Grenache leads for
the red wines, but may be blended with a dozen

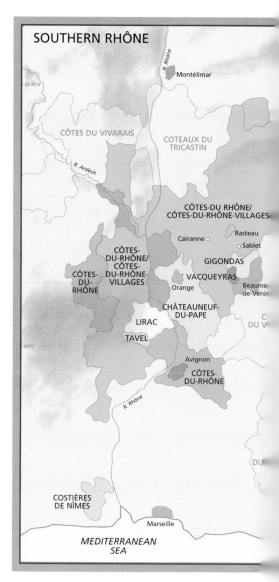

Vineyards in the southern
Rhône, with the Dentelles
de Montmirail in the
background.

or more different varieties, of which the most
important are Syrah, Mourvèdre and Cinsault.
Grenache gives high-alcohol wines that are usually
low in tannin and colour, with flavours of spiced
red berries (especially strawberry; the fruit
character can be quite baked, jammy or even
burnt). **Syrah** provides colour and tannins,
Cinsault is low in tannin, but high in fruit and
acidity, whilst **Mourvèdre** is deep-coloured and
tannic. By marrying them together, the sum is
much better than the individual parts.

For white wines, Clairette and Grenache Blanc,
Bourboulenc and other varieties join the northern
Rhône trio of Viognier, Marsanne and Roussanne.
The whites are usually fat and full-bodied, high in
alcohol, with light acidity. New oak is rarely used.

All of these varieties are pruned low to aid

ripening from reflected heat. Syrah is generally
wire-trained in the single Guyot system, whilst
the others are spur-pruned to give a free-standing
bush. Many of the vineyards, especially in parts
of Châteauneuf-du-Pape, are covered with
substantial rounded 'pudding-stones' which are
particularly effective in storing heat and keeping
the vineyards warm throughout the night. These
help the grapes gain added ripeness.

Winemaking
It is not only the range of soils and of grape
varieties used that varies, but also the methods of
vinification, so it is almost impossible to describe
a typical southern Rhône red. It might be fresh
and fruity if made by carbonic maceration, a
technique that is used even by some estates in

Châteauneuf-du-Pape, to make wines that are lighter in tannins and suitable for drinking while still young. Wines that are traditionally fermented and aged in oak can be very full-bodied and meaty.

Regions and Wines

Côtes du Rhône AC accounts for more than 80 per cent of the production of the region. Much of this is light, fruity, simple wine made by co-operative cellars. While there is a move towards using carbonic maceration, this is used less than in the Beaujolais or the Midi.

Within the southern Côtes du Rhône, a number of villages are entitled to call their red and, on occasion, white and rosé wines **Côtes du Rhône Villages AC**. To qualify, more stringent requirements on grape varieties, minimum alcohol levels and maximum yields must be satisfied. If the wine is a blend from a number of the relevant villages it can be sold as Côtes du Rhône Villages, but there are 16 individual villages which can add their name if the wine is not blended, for example Côtes du Rhône Villages Cairanne. Of these villages, there are two, Beaumes de Venise and Rasteau, that also have separate ACs for their Vins Doux Naturels (see Chapter 36).

Two villages have gained promotion from this classification to have their own appellations; thus we have **Vacqueyras AC** and **Gigondas AC,** with their own specifications for grape varieties, alcohol levels and yield.

Perhaps the best-known wine of the Rhône valley is **Châteauneuf-du-Pape AC**. This has a particular place in French wine history, because it was here that the very concept of *Appellation Contrôlée* was founded. Indeed, in a bid to improve quality, machine-harvesting is forbidden and hand-sorting of grapes is obligatory. Although the variety of grapes permitted in the blend is broad (up to 13), Grenache dominates as elsewhere in the southern Rhône. Some very successful Châteauneufs are 100 per cent Grenache, which can generate very intense wines when low-yielding old vines are used.

A small quantity of quality white Chateauneuf is made from Clairette, Roussanne, Bourboulenc and Grenache Blanc (Viognier is not permitted).

To the west of Châteauneuf-du-Pape on the other bank of the Rhône, where limestone in the soil helps grapes to ripen without losing their acidity, the production of rosé and even white wines is encouraged. **Tavel AC** produces rosés only some of which are reputed to be the best in France. They are full-bodied, intensely flavoured

The Southern Rhône			
KEY AC WINES		**MAIN GRAPE VARIETIES**	**PRICE**
Côtes du Rhône	■	Grenache, Syrah, Mourvèdre and others	●○
	□	Clairette, Grenache Blanc and others	●○
	▣	Cinsault, Grenache and others	●○
Côtes du Rhône Villages	■	Grenache, Syrah, Mourvèdre and others	●●
	□	Clairette, Grenache Blanc and others	●●
	▣	Cinsault, Grenache and others	●●
Vacqueyras	■	Grenache (+ Syrah, Mourvèdre and others)	●●○
Gigondas	■	Grenache (+ Syrah, Mourvèdre and others)	●●○
Châteauneuf-du-Pape	■	Grenache (+ Syrah, Mourvèdre and others)	●●●○+
	□	Clairette, Roussanne and others	●●●○+
Lirac	■	Grenache (+ Syrah, Mourvèdre and others)	●●
	▣	Cinsault, Grenache and others	●●
Tavel	▣	Cinsault, Grenache and others	●●
Rhône satellites	■	Grenache (+ Syrah, Mourvèdre and others)	●

and capable of developing savoury complexity when aged in bottle. **Lirac AC** and Tavel rosés are both made mainly from Grenache and Cinsault grapes. Lirac also produces red and white wines.

Around the boundary of the southern Rhône are a number of 'satellite' appellations producing wines in a similar but lighter style, from the same mix of grapes. They are **Côtes du Vivarais AC** and **Côteaux du Tricastin AC** in the north, **Côtes du Ventoux AC** and **Côtes du Luberon AC** in the east, and **Côstières de Nîmes** in the south.

Pudding stones in Châteauneuf-du-Pape in the flat southern Rhône.

14 Southern France

The vineyards of southern France lie along the Mediterranean coast from Italy in the east to the Spanish border in the west. They are split into three groups, Provence, Languedoc and Roussillon, though the last two are often considered together. It is here, more than anywhere else in France's wine world, that things have changed recently. Historically, much of its production was for blending with wines from elsewhere to produce the ubiquitous *Vin de Table*, which slaked the thirst of every French wine consumer. However, sales collapsed, leading local growers to realise that their future lies in producing less, but better, wine. Fortunately, vast sums of money have been made available through the EU funding to help them in this modernisation.

There is a natural progression from the vineyards of the Rhône valley to those of the south. From the east of the river delta come the wines of Provence and from the west those of Languedoc-Roussillon. For the most part, the grapes that are grown are the same, plus Carignan, which, when its yields are restricted, produces robust, fruity wines. As we shall see, the development of the *Vin de Pays* category, particularly in Languedoc-Roussillon, has led to vast plantings of classical varieties more often associated with other regions of France, such as Cabernet Sauvignon, Merlot and Chardonnay.

Unsurprisingly the climate is Mediterranean and there is a vast range of differing soils: rich in the river valleys, alluvial sand in the Rhône delta, and clay and gravel in the plains. The common factor of many areas is the incidence of limestone. This, with a reliable climate, provides a firm basis for the production of excellent wines. Often the problem for the winegrower is balancing the income they can hope to make from producing smaller quantities of better wine as opposed to their traditional high yield of inferior wine. Here the policies of the individual co-operative cellars often have a major part to play. Some are very progressive, working hard to gain the necessary higher prices for their best wines. Others lack the means, or the will, to improve.

PROVENCE

Côtes de Provence AC. This is by far the largest AC in Provence, the wine being produced from vineyards to the east of the naval port of Toulon. The inland vineyards lie to the north of the Massif des Maures, while others lie along the coast. Traditionally, much of the wine was rosé, appeared in a traditional, distinctive bottle and was consumed by holidaymakers in the resorts of the Riviera. Any faults that it might have were disguised by the ice bucket. Now many producers are making more serious wines, often red, taking advantage of the right to add up to 30 per cent Cabernet Sauvignon to the blend. Such wines generally appear in Bordeaux-style bottles. To the west of the region, close to the town of Aix en Provence, are the vineyards of **Côteaux d'Aix en Provence AC.** A range of red, white and rosé wines is produced and some individual vineyards have established reputations for themselves. Insatiable local demand for rosé wines drives prices upwards in both these regions, and the ambitious local reds and whites also command

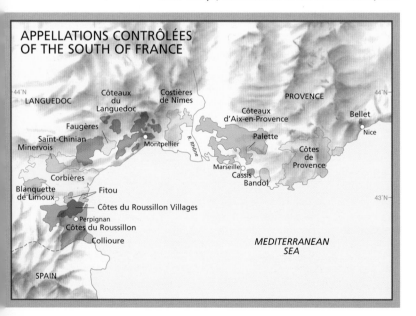

APPELLATIONS CONTRÔLÉES
OF THE SOUTH OF FRANCE

LANGUEDOC

Côteaux du Languedoc

Costières de Nîmes

PROVENCE

Côteaux d'Aix-en-Provence

Bellet

Nice

Faugères

Saint-Chinian

Minervois

Montpellier

Palette

Côtes de Provence

Marseille

Cassis

Bandol

Corbières

Blanquette de Limoux

Fitou

Côtes du Roussillon Villages

Perpignan

Côtes du Roussillon

Collioure

MEDITERRANEAN SEA

SPAIN

high, premium and occasionally superpremium prices.

Along the coast there are three isolated pockets of vineyards, each with its individual *Appellation Contrôlée*. The most important appellation of the three is **Bandol AC**, which is produced near Toulon, producing reds based on the Mourvèdre grape. These are dark, full-bodied wines with powerful tannins, and they require bottle age before they show their full spectrum of bramble, meat and licorice-spice flavours. Production is small, and those that know them are prepared to pay high prices for wines they regard as being of very high quality.

Vin de Pays des Bouches du Rhône and **Vin de Pays de Vaucluse** both generally offer southern-Rhône-style wines at lower prices.

LANGUEDOC-ROUSSILLON

These vineyards lie mainly in the plains that stretch between the southern limits of the Massif Central and the Mediterranean. It was the coming of the railways in the second half of the nineteenth century that enabled this region to be the wine-well for French consumers with their thirst for wine of any quality. In the warehouses of ports such as Sète, the heady coloured wines of the French colonies in North Africa were blended with the low-strength wines of Languedoc. The loss of these colonies and the entry of France into the Common Market with the competition of wines from Italy led to the collapse of the local economy based on vineyard monoculture. However, it is EU funds that have enabled the renaissance. Many vineyards have been grubbed up and orchards planted. High-yielding grape varieties, such as Aramon, are now all but forgotten. To satisfy worldwide markets that are drinking less but better, more appealing wines have to be produced.

Here, two developments have occurred in parallel, since the collapse of the basic table wine market: the promotion of several former VDQS wines to full AC status, and the rise in the importance of **Vins de Pays**.

Appellation Wines

In wine terms the region of Roussillon consists of the single *département* of Pyrénées-Orientales, whose main town is Perpignan. This is the driest region in France and the centre of the production of much fortified wine. The **Côtes du Roussillon AC** covers almost the whole plain between the Pyrénées and the sea, with the northern half, in the valley of the River Agly, having the right to the superior appellation

Provence		
KEY WINES	**MAIN GRAPE VARIETIES**	**PRICE**
Côtes de Provence AC ◼	Cinsault, Grenache, Tibouren	●●○
Côteaux d'Aix en Provence AC ◼	Grenache, Cinsault, Mourvèdre	●●○
Bandol AC ◼	Mourvèdre	●●●○
Vin de Pays des Bouches du Rhône ◼	Grenache, Syrah, Mourvèdre	●
Vin de Pays de Vaucluse ◼	Grenache, Syrah, Mourvèdre	●

Languedoc-Roussillon		
KEY WINES	**MAIN GRAPE VARIETIES**	**PRICE**
Côteaux du Languedoc AC ◼	Carignan, Grenache	●○
Minervois AC ◼	Grenache, Syrah, Mourvèdre	●●
Corbières AC ◼	Carignan, Grenache, Cinsault	●○
Fitou AC ◼	Carignan, Grenache, Syrah	●○
Côtes du Roussillon AC, Côtes du Roussillon Villages AC ◼	Blend (mainly Carignan, Grenache)	●
Vin de Pays d'Oc Vin de Pays de l'Hérault Vin de Pays de l'Aude Vin de Pays du Gard ◼	Various international, including Cabernet Sauvignon, Merlot Syrah	●○
☐	Various international, including Chardonnay, Sauvignon Blanc, Viognier	●○

Côtes du Roussillon Villages AC. The base grape for all these wines is Carignan, though it may not comprise more than 60 per cent of the blend. This variety is high in acidity and tannins, and gives deeply coloured, rather bitter wines. The style is sometimes quite rustic and simple, and sold at low prices. Frequently, carbonic maceration is used to extract softer tannins and more juicy fruit character for an easy-to-drink style, still sold at low prices. Further north, the Languedoc consists

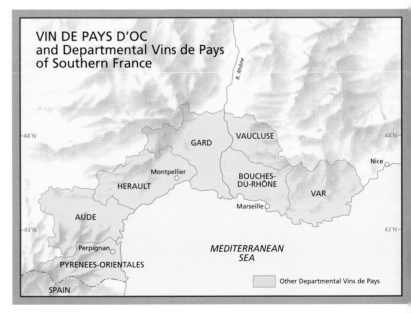

VIN DE PAYS D'OC and Departmental Vins de Pays of Southern France

Limestone outcrops behind vineyards of Syrah trained on wires in Corbières, just prior to harvesting.

of the Aude, Hérault and Gard départements. Here the **Fitou, Corbieres, Minervois** and **Côteaux du Languedoc** appellations are sources of large quantities of spicy, full-bodied reds. These are, with few exceptions, blends, consisting mainly of Carignan and various proportions of 'improving' varieties such as Grenache, Syrah and Mourvèdre. We can see the beginning of a move towards giving recognition to superior regions within some appellations, such as La Clape and Montpeyroux within the Côteaux du Languedoc and La Livinière within Minervois. **Faugères** and **Saint Chinian** are now well-established sources of powerful, full-bodied wines, often with meaty, savoury flavours of new oak. Some can command high and even premium prices. The AC status does impose restrictions however, for the regulations insist on the importance of tradition, particularly with regard to the grape varies that are used. Thus, despite the fact that a small proportion of Cabernet Sauvignon in the blend might improve the quality of, say, a Minervois, it is forbidden. This brings us to the second development; the rapid rise in the production of **Vins de Pays**.

Vins de Pays

Here, while yields are controlled, there is much more flexibility as to which grapes can be planted and the styles of the wines. Consequently, there have been considerable plantings of such 'foreign' varieties as Cabernet Sauvignon, Merlot, Chardonnay and Viognier. Initially, sales of Vins de Pays concentrated on using a host of small regional names, such as Vin de Pays des Côteaux de Peyriac, but these meant little or nothing to the consumer. Also the departmental names, such as Vin de Pays de l'Aude, were deemed to be too anonymous. This led to the creation of the regional Vin de Pays d'Oc covering all the vineyards of Roussillon as well as Languedoc, Gard, Hérault, Aude and Pyrenées-Orientales. To have this status, the wines have to pass tasting panels.

The concept of Vin de Pays has been particularly popular in such export markets as Germany and Britain. The system leaves plenty of scope for the artist to paint the picture they want, and it has led to a major influx of flying winemakers, as well as capital, from abroad. Because the scope is so broad, so is the range of prices that can be charged for the wines and they are frequently more expensive than their allegedly better AC neighbours.

Germany

15

One problem from which historically German wines have suffered is that, almost alone in the world, they were made not for drinking with food, but for social occasions. They were low in alcohol and, almost without exception, had residual sugar. If a German wanted to drink wine with a meal, in preference to the more habitual beer, they would choose a French wine. To counter this, in the early 1980s, many growers decided to make dry wine. Now, more than half the national consumption is of dry (*trocken*) or medium-dry (*halbtrocken*) style. For consumers brought up on traditional German wines, these come as something of a shock. Another historical problem has been the extreme fragmentation within the country of agricultural holdings, as in Burgundy, the result of the breaking up of the vast church estates and the imposition of Napoleonic inheritance laws. In order to counter this, successive German governments have carried out a redistribution of land to make it easier to work. One regrettable result of this has been that there has been much planting of vineyards on land not suited for the production of quality wine.

German wines are often misunderstood and under-appreciated, and it is not difficult to see why. Germany produces some of the finest wines in the world, but the reputation of the large quantities of bland, sugary wines that are produced for sale at very low prices discourages many wine lovers from trying the better wines.

CLIMATE

It is worthwhile remarking that German vineyards are much further north than the most southerly vineyards in the southern hemisphere are south. With the exception of Baden in southern Germany, all vineyards are in EU Climatic Zone A. In spite of the low average temperatures, Germany's continental climate gives warm summers, though these are followed by cold winters. Rain falls throughout the year, the two wettest months being July and August. Late spring frosts are a regular hazard, as are heavy rain and hailstorms during the summer. Within this broad framework, patterns vary considerably from year to year, leading to large differences in quality and quantity between vintages. The combination of heat and rainfall during the summer encourages high yields, which must be controlled. In contrast, the long dry autumns facilitate the production of high quality late-harvested wines. Grapes are able to ripen slowly and develop rich, complex flavours. In good years, the climate also

encourages, the development of noble rot (*Edelfäule*). In such marginal conditions, there can be vast differences in quality from wines from different vineyards. The best sites are planted on steep slopes to make the best possible use of the available sun. Largely because of the climate, the production of German wine has been predominantly white, though there is an increasing proportion of fine red wine being made.

GERMAN WINE LAWS

In 1971, Germany began the revision of its wine laws in a bid to bring them closer into line with those of the other members of the EC. As elsewhere, wines are divided into two classes: Table Wine and Quality Wine. At the level of Table Wine, the new laws were quite simple. However, with regard to Quality Wine, the picture is extremely confusing.

The two categories of German Table Wine are:

1. **Deutscher Tafelwein**. This is the lowest classification and accounts for less than 5 per cent of the wine produced in Germany. A geographical region of production may be shown, but it must be one of four designated regions. (It is essential that *Deutscher Tafelwein* is not confused with *Euro Tafelwein*, as much of the latter is bottled and sold by

German wine companies, generally with very Germanic labels. This is blended from wines from various countries within the EU.)

2. **Landwein.** This classification was introduced in 1982 and is the equivalent of French *Vin de Pays*. There are 17 specified areas of production and the relevant one must be shown on the label. One important restriction is that the wines must be either *trocken* or *halbtrocken*. Again, approximately 5 per cent of the German production falls under this classification.

Quality Wines also have two categories:

1. **Qualitätswein bestimmter Anbaugebiet (QbA)**, or wine from a designated Quality region. This has to be produced from one of the 13 *Anbaugebiete* (see below); blending with wines from other regions is forbidden. The label must show the region from which the wine comes and gives some indication of the style of the wine. These wines will generally be chaptalised and thus may have a higher alcoholic degree and/or level of sweetness than some Quality Wines with a higher classification.

2. **Qualitätswein mit Prädikat (QmP)**. This is a wine with special attributes of quality wine.

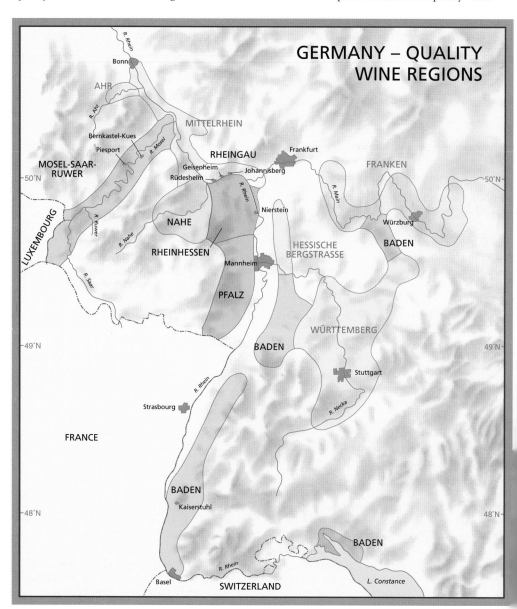

Again, the grapes must come from a single *Anbaugebiet*, whose name must appear on the label and from a single *Bereich* (see below). Wines with this classification may not have their musts enriched, though they may be sweetened using *Süssreserve*. The proportion of wines produced at this level varies considerably from vintage to vintage.

There are two parallel systems of classification for Quality Wines, one based upon geographical location and the other upon the style of the wine, particularly on the amount of sugar that the must (not the wine) contains. This second classification applies solely to QmP wines.

Geographical Classification
Let us look at the various geographical classifications in ascending order of size.

Einzellage (an individual vineyard). This is the most important geographical classification for quality German wines. It is the equivalent of the individual vineyard site (*Premier Cru* or *Grand Cru*) that is named on the very finest bottles of Burgundy. As we will see, however, the problem is that the label will not tell you whether the wine comes from an *Einzellage* or a *Grosslage* (group of vineyards). For the average consumer, who has not memorised the names of the hundreds of *Einzellagen* and *Grosslagen,* how is it possible to tell which is which? Price is an indication, but many single vineyard wines of good quality sell for absurdly low prices. Producers can be a guide, as many of the top producers refuse to use the *Grosslage* names. The only certain method is to become familiar with the names of individual vineyards. The quality of the wines that comes from these is usually very high, and the nuances of vineyard expression between different sites growing the same Riesling grape can be fascinating, so gaining this familiarity is not as arduous as it might sound.

Grosslage (a group of adjoining vineyards). The 1971 wine law created this unnecessary classification. These groupings of vineyards are particularly misleading, as most of the names chosen were those of previously existing individual sites within the grouping. Thus, Bernkasteler Badstube once had a good reputation as a single vineyard in the Mosel; now the name is used for a much larger area, some producing wine as good as the original Badstube, most not. A Piesporter Michelsberg (*Grosslage*) may be a cheap, rather bland, sugary wine from grapes grown in high-yielding, gently sloped vineyards that could be up

to 8 kilometres from Piesport. Piesporter Goldtröpchen (*Einzellage*) comes from a steep, south-facing amphitheatre of vines immediately above the village of Piesport, and with a reputation for some of the finest Rieslings in Germany. The latter might sell for 3–4 times the price of the former. The difference between *Grosslage* and *Einzellage* is therefore far more than a technicality.

Gemeind (a commune). In Burgundy, the equivalent would be a village name such as Gevrey-Chambertin or Volnay. If the name of the commune stands alone, this means that the wine comes from vineyards surrounding the village itself. On the label, the name of the commune is usually attached to the name of either a *Grosslage* or an *Einzellage*. Thus, the label would rarely say simply 'Bernkastel' or 'Brauneberg'; rather it would say 'Bernkasteler Badstube' or 'Bernkasteler Kurfurstlay' (*Grosslagen*), or 'Bernkasteler Lay' or 'Brauneberger Juffer-Sonnenuhr' (if it came from the Lay or Juffer-Sonnenuhr individual vineyards). (The 'er' added to the village name is a German grammatical ending that indicates 'belonging to'. Thus, the Juffer-Sonnenuhr vineyard 'belongs to' the village of Brauneberg. This also applies to vintages, so you may see for example '2002er', which simply means the wine 'belongs to' the 2002 vintage.)

Bereich (a district within a Quality Region, consisting of several communes). There may be one or more of these within a region. If matters are not confusing enough, a village that is a commune (whose name appears attached to *Einzellagen* and *Grosslagen*) may also give its name to a *Bereich*. In a similar way, the town of Beaune gives its name to the commune of Beaune (and is then attached to individual vineyard names such as Beaune-Grèves) and also gives its name to the much larger Côte de Beaune. Thus a wine called *Bereich Bernkastel* may, or may not, come from the village of Bernkastel. It could come from a number of other villages, including Erden, Wehlen, Graach and Brauneberg.

Anbaugebiet (Designated Quality Region). The vineyards of Germany are divided into 13 such regions, some of which will be dealt with later in the chapter.

By law a minimum of 85 per cent of the wine must come from the specified source if a *Bereich, Grosslage* or *Einzellage* is mentioned on the label.

Styles of QmP Wine
Here are the various styles of wine (**Prädikat**),

depending on their initial must weights in ascending order:

Kabinett wines are the most delicate QmP wines and often make ideal aperitifs. Rieslings made in this style will be light in body, with very crisp acidity and flavours of green apple or citrus fruit.

Spätlese indicates (literally) a 'late-harvest' wine. These will have more concentrated flavours. Riesling in this style will have a little more body than a *Kabinett* wine, and usually a little more sweetness. The fruit flavours will be riper, with usually no green apple notes and more firmly citrus aromas, perhaps with a hint of exotic fruit (pineapple or mango).

Auslese wines are made from individually selected extra-ripe bunches of grapes. This category encompasses the greatest range of styles for Riesling. Some producers treat this as a slightly richer, sweeter, riper *Spätlese*. Others will make wines that are very sweet, even showing enough botrytis character and sugar to be classed as a *Beerenauslese*. This is also the highest *Prädikat* category to appear commonly as a dry wine. The bunches of grapes for *Auslese* wines, and the individual grapes that are selected for the *Beerenauslese* and *Trockenbeerenauslese* wines, are usually harvested at the same time as the *Kabinett* or the *Spätlese* grapes, but are separated for special treatment either in the vineyard or at the winery.

Beerenauslese (BA) indicates a rare, expensive wine that will have been made from individually selected grapes, ideally those suffering from noble rot. Some varieties have been developed to achieve *Beerenauslese* must weights without the aid of botrytis, but the resulting wines never have the exhilarating complexity and refreshing acidity of a true Riesling *Beerenauslese*.

Eiswein (literally 'ice-wine'). This is a wine made from grapes that have been left on the vine and have the equivalent sugar levels of a *Beerenauslese* wine, but which are not suffering from noble rot. They are picked when the temperature is below −8° C. The water in the grapes freezes, but not the sugars. At pressing, the frozen water, in the form of ice, is removed with the grapes, leaving just the hyper-sweet juice for fermentation. This gives an expensive wine with an intriguing contrast of richness, acidity and great fruit purity.

Trockenbeerenauslese (TBA) wines are produced in minute quantities, in only the finest vintages, from individual grapes that have undergone noble rot to such a degree that they have shrivelled to

tiny raisins. The sugars in the grapes will give a minimal *potential* strength of 21.5% abv, but will be matched with high levels of acidity. After fermentation, the wines rarely have more than 8% abv of *actual* alcohol. Top-quality TBAs are among the world's most expensive wines.

There is some variation in the minimum must weights for the various classes of wine, depending on the region of production; thus what might be classified as an *Auslese* wine in the Mosel-Saar-Ruwer, might be only a *Kabinett* wine in Baden.

Other Terms

There are certain other terms that might appear on a label to describe its character. These include:

- **Trocken:** Dry.
- **Halbtrocken:** Off-dry.
- **Classic:** 'Harmoniously dry' with a minimum alcohol level of 12% (11.5% in Mosel-Saar-Ruwer). These must be made from a single grape variety from a single vintage in a single region, all of which must be stated on the label.
- **Selection:** As Classic, but these must have at least *Auslese* ripeness levels (or minimum 12.2% potential alcohol) and must come from an individual vineyard site (*Einzellage*), that will be named on the label.
- **Erstes Gewächs** (Rheingau only): A Riesling or Pinot Noir wine from one of the recognised top-quality (first growth or *Premier Cru*) *Einzellagen*. These are subject to a number of requirements, including a stringent taste test. **Erste Lage** and **Grosses Gewächs** have a similar meaning in the Mosel-Saar-Ruwer and in the other Anbaugebiete respectively.
- **Liebfraumilch**, primarily for the British market: This must have at least 18 g/l residual sugar, and must be produced exclusively in one of the four regions of Rheinhessen, Pfalz, Rheingau or Nahe. Of these four, the first two are the more important sources. Liebfraumilch cannot be blended from more than one region. The region, but no further geographical information, will be on the label. The grape varieties will not be named and the wine will be of QbA standard.

As has already been noted, there is much fragmentation in the German vineyards and a single *Einzellage* might belong to a number of different owners. In addition, each owner may, in the best of vintages, produce a broad range of styles of wines from the same parcel of vines. Thus someone who owns, say, a hectare of vines split between three different plots might produce approaching 20 different wines in a single vintage.

Severely botrytised grapes, destined for *Beerenauslese (BA)* or *Trockenbeerenauslese (TBA)* wine.

GRAPE VARIETIES

Because of its marginal climate, Germany has developed a number of varieties over the years which are best suited to its needs. The research station at Geisenheim in the Rheingau has played a major part in this programme.

White Grapes

These account for approximately four-fifths of the plantings in Germany and this proportion is declining slowly. The major varieties are as follows.

Riesling. This is the noble grape of Germany and accounts for just under a quarter of all plantings. This makes it the most widely planted variety. It is particularly important in the production of the best wines of the Mosel-Saar-Ruwer and the Rheingau. It ripens late, generally between October and November, but because of its hardiness is ideal for late-harvest wines. Its naturally high levels of acidity help the wines age well. When young they have a crisp floral character, but with age show hints on the nose and palate of petrol. Riesling has played a major role as a parent of many of the new crossings that have been developed.

Müller-Thurgau (Rivaner). Depending on whom you talk to, this grape is either the saviour or the bane of the German wine industry. Developed in the early 1880s, it is a variety of uncertain parentage; one is believed to be a Riesling, the other is unknown. It ripens early and gives big yields. It is prone to rot and damage from frosts. It is the backbone of most branded Liebfraumilch, giving a flavour that its friends describe as flowery and its enemies as mousy.

Silvaner. Yesterday's grape; plantings have declined dramatically in the face of competition of the new crossings that have been developed. Now it is mainly found in those regions where it has traditionally been strong, such as Franconia. It ripens in early October, it gives wines low in acidity and with rather neutral fruit.

Other white grape varieties include Scheurebe (Silvaner × Riesling), which has strong grapefruit aromas when fully ripe and is particularly suitable for sweet wines, as well as Kerner, Pinot Gris, Gewürztraminer, and many more.

Black Grapes

Spätburgunder (Pinot Noir) is a late-ripening variety that gives full-bodied, fruity wines in Germany. It is particularly grown in the more southerly vineyards of the Pfalz and Baden. Germans are now having some success with the production of barrel-aged Pinot Noirs of international quality. As a result, the grape is being more widely planted.

Dornfelder, which was developed as recently as 1956, has the distinction of having a red flesh. This means that the wines that it produces are particularly deep in colour, especially for Germany. Mainly because of this it is perceived to be a grape with a great potential.

Most other German red wines are light, rather pale and off-dry; they are consumed locally.

VITICULTURE

Because of the widely differing styles of the vineyards, there are widely differing styles of viticulture. The finest vineyards, which produce most of the higher quality QmP wines, are grown on the steep slopes in the river valleys. Here the vineyards may be terraced, but all the work will have to be done by hand and access for equipment is often only by cableway. In such vineyards the vines are generally planted 1.3 metres apart and

attached to an individual stake. It has been calculated that 8 per cent of German vines are planted in this way. Naturally, the costs of production in such vineyards are extremely high and must be recovered in the price for which the wine is sold. The increasing numbers of abandoned vineyards that can be seen, for example in the lower Mosel, bear witness to the marginal existence of many growers.

The majority of vineyards are now planted in the valley bottoms and on the plains. Here the vines are generally trained along wires and the rows planted up to 3 metres apart to facilitate the use of mechanical equipment. Here the emphasis

Post-trained Riesling vines on slate soils.

is on maximising yields and producing easy-to-drink wines at challenging prices. These vineyards have some of the highest yields achieved anywhere in the world.

In the final days before the harvest, the vineyards are closed to all, even the owners. At this time, many vineyards will be netted as a protection against birds. No grapes may be picked before the official starting date for the vintage, which is normally announced by the local trade association. It is up to the individual growers to decide when they want to pick after that date. Depending on the weather prospects, they may choose to leave the grapes on the vine so as to achieve higher possibilities within the QmP hierarchy. Picking may be by hand or by machine, according to the nature of the vineyard and the quality of wine to be made.

VINIFICATION

Because of the low degree of natural sugar occurring in most German wines, chaptalisation or must enrichment (*Anreicherung*) is generally carried out for all wines up to and including QbA – but it is forbidden for those of QmP status. In the more northern regions, the equivalent of up to 4.5% abv may be added. Because of the wines' natural high acidity, de-acidification, by means of the addition of calcium carbonate, or a similar proprietary product, is sometimes carried out. An official permit is needed to perform de-acidification or chaptalisation. While chaptalisation is used to raise the potential alcohol of a wine before fermentation, unfermented grape juice (**Süssreserve**) may be added to a fermented wine in order to sweeten it. Chaptalisation and the addition of *Süssreserve* should not be confused. *Süssreserve* is permitted even for QmP wines and regularly occurs, even up to Auslese level. The grape juice has to be from the same site, grape variety and at least the same quality as the wine to which it is added.

In the winery the grapes are first weighed and then graded by sugar content, before they are pressed. In a co-operative cellar, payment will be assessed not only on the weight, but also on the variety and the sugar content of the grapes. After pressing, the must will be enriched for the lower quality wines. A proportion of the individual musts should be held back for use as *Süssreserve*. The remaining must is then fermented out to as dry a wine as possible. This makes it more stable for storage than a wine low in alcohol, which contains residual sugar. The unfermented must is micro-filtered to remove yeasts, and stored, either at a low temperature or under pressure to prevent fermentation. Immediately before bottling, the

Schloss Johannisberg vineyard in the Rheingau: the best vineyards are on the steepest slopes, with flatter land down towards the river.

necessary *Süssreserve* is added to the wine, which then must be bottled in totally sterile conditions.

Only a quarter of those who grow grapes in Germany make wine themselves; the others may send their grapes to a co-operative cellar. If the wine has been made and bottled by the grower or the co-operative cellar, the label may say **Erzeugerabfüllung**, effectively 'estate-bottled'. An alternative term used by growers is *Gutsabfüllung*. The term *Weingut* is used for a wine estate.

QUALITY WINE REGIONS (*ANBAUGEBIETE*)
Mosel-Saar-Ruwer

This important region comprises the valley of the River Mosel, from where it joins the Rhine at Koblenz, to the Luxembourg frontier and its two small tributaries, the Saar and the Ruwer. The best wines come from the steep, slatey, mineral-rich slopes and are made from Riesling, which overall accounts for just over half of the plantings in the region. These are among Germany's greatest wines. Mosel Riesling *Kabinetts* should show a perfect balance of grapey sweetness and acidity which makes the wine seem crisp and never cloying. These are the lightest in body of the great German Rieslings, and their liveliness may be enhanced with a hint of residual CO_2. The very finest, for all QmP levels, come from *Einzellages* surrounding the villages of Piesport, Brauneberg, Bernkastel, Graach, Wehlen and Erden in the Mittel-Mosel. The wines are bottled in green bottles, unlike the more general brown.

Steep slopes above the Mosel. On the most exposed sites, Riesling grapes can gain an extra 2% abv potential alcohol.

The Saar and Ruwer wines often show a steely acidity and tend to be more robust than those of the Mosel.

Nahe

The valley of the Nahe, to the west of the Rhine and the south of the Mosel, protected by the Hunsrück Mountains to the north, comprises a variety of soils. In the north it is predominantly sandy loam, where Müller-Thurgau and Silvaner give agreeable uncomplicated wines. On the slopes of the valley around the towns of Schlossböckelheim and Bad Kreuznach, on porphyry, quartz and coloured sandstone soils, Riesling produces wines of delicacy and distinction, often with distinctive aromas of pineapple.

Rheingau

The Rhine flows west at this point so that the Rheingau vineyards, on its north bank, face south and are protected by the Taunus Mountains from the cold northerly winds. This gives ideal conditions for the optimal ripening of grapes. The soil is a combination of weathered slate, loess and loam on the slopes and gravel and sandy loam in the valley. Riesling is particularly suited to slatey soils and seems to thrive on its high mineral content. Furthermore, slate gives a dark soil which absorbs the heat of the sun by day and provides warmth to the vines by night. This is

Mosel-Saar-Ruwer			
KEY WINES		**GRAPE VARIETIES**	**PRICE**
QbA and QmP wines from *Einzellagen* of the following *Gemeinden*: Piesport, Brauneberg, Bernkastel, Wehlen, Graach, Erden	☐	Riesling	●●○○+
Grosslage wines: Piesporter Michelsberg, Bernkasteler Badstube	☐	Various	●

Nahe			
KEY WINES		**GRAPE VARIETIES**	**PRICE**
QbA and QmP wines from *Einzellagen* of the following *Gemeinden*: Schlossböckelheim	☐	Riesling	●●○○+
Grosslage wines: Bad Kreuznacher Kronenberg	☐	Various	●

Rheingau			
KEY WINES		**GRAPE VARIETY**	**PRICE**
QbA and QmP wines from *Einzellagen* of the following *Gemeinden*: Rüdesheim, Geisenheim, Johannisberg, Winkel, Oestrich, Erbach, Eltville, Hochheim	☐	Riesling	●●○○+

of particular assistance to late-ripening varieties such as the Riesling, which account for more than 80 per cent of the plantings. Many of Germany's best-known estates and finest wines are produced in the villages of Rüdesheim, Geisenheim, Johannisberg, Winkel, Oestrich and Eltville. The hillside vineyards give spicy wines with an elegant, balanced, fruity acidity, while those coming from vineyards in the valley have more body, richness and guts.

In 1984, a number of the more prominent producers of Riesling wines combined to form the Charta Group for the promotion of drinking wine with food. They have been protagonists in the campaign to produce drier wines.

Beyond Rüdesheim, where the Rhine turns north again, is the town of Assmannshausen, which is more famous for its red wines than its whites. These once claimed to be the finest in Germany, but have now given way to those of the Pfalz and Baden.

Whilst the very best German vineyards are planted on steep slopes, there are many on flatter land, especially in Rheinhessen, where mechanical harvesting is possible.

Rheinhessen

KEY WINES		GRAPE VARIETIES	PRICE
QbA and QmP wines from *Einzellagen* of the following *Gemeinden*: Oppenheim, Nierstein	☐	Riesling	●●○○+
Grosslage wines: Niersteiner Gutes Domtal, Oppenheimer Krötenbrunnen	☐	Various	●
Liebfraumilch Rheinhessen	☐	Various	●

Pfalz

KEY WINES		GRAPE VARIETIES	PRICE
QbA and QmP wines from *Einzellagen* of the following *Gemeinden*: Forst, Deidesheim	☐	Riesling	●●○○+
Grosslage wines: Forster Mariengarten	☐	Various	●
Liebfraumilch Pfalz	☐	Various	●

Rheinhessen

This is the largest vinegrowing region of Germany in terms of the area under vines. It is from here that the wines behind many of the labels most commonly seen around the world come. Also here, from a small vineyard, the Liebfrauenstift, in the centre of the city of Worms, Liebfraumilch originated.

Until the mid-twentieth century, nearly all the vineyards of this region faced the Rhine, and its high reputation was built on the excellent wines that were produced there. Since then, as more agricultural land has been converted to vinegrowing, cheaper wines, of lower quality, have succeeded in eroding that reputation. Nowhere has this become more obvious than in the Bereich Nierstein. Here, along the western bank of the Rhine, in a narrow band from just north of Nackenheim to just south of Oppenheim, is found the small proportion of Riesling that remains, planted on slopes of red sandy soil facing the river. The best wines of Rheinhessen, from these sites on the **Rheinterrasse**, are among the very best wines of Germany. They are among the most full-bodied of Germany's Rieslings, with complex, exotic fruit aromas. Unfortunately, the reputation of the wines of Nierstein has been drowned by the seemingly limitless production of the 15 villages that comprise the *Grosslage* Niersteiner Gutes Domtal, where quality is generally of secondary importance. The often sandy soil gives light, easy-drinking wines. No grape variety predominates, though Müller-Thurgau, with its high yields, is the most common, accounting for a quarter of all production. Silvaner is the next most widely planted. Here, co-operative cellars play a major role, producing vast quantities of cheap, bland, sugary wine.

Pfalz

This region stretches north from the French border and is protected by the Haardt Mountains, a continuation of the Vosges of Alsace. In terms of quantity, this is the most important region in Germany for the production of wine. The best wines come from a few villages on the *Deutsche Weinstrasse* (the German wine route): Wachenheim, Forst, Deidesheim and Ruppertsberg. Some 80 kilometres south of the Rheingau, the favourable climate, with mild winters and hot summers, enables the production of many of Germany's finest red wines and white wines with an opulence not found elsewhere in the country. Away from this narrow band of villages, the quality tends to decline as yields increase. The main grape varieties are Müller-Thurgau, Riesling and Kerner, and the soil is largely weathered sandstone.

Terraced vineyards on the slopes of the Kaiserstuhl above Oberbergen, Baden.

Baden

The wines of Baden, Germany's warmest most southerly vineyard region, have been kept a closely guarded secret, though their full body and ripe character makes them most appealing. The region comprises a ragbag of vineyards; the majority stretch along the east bank of the Rhine, from Heidelberg to Basle. There are also odd pockets on the northern shore of Lake Constance and a small enclave, far to the north between the vineyards of Württemberg and Franken.

The two main varieties are Spätburgunder (Pinot Noir) and Müller-Thurgau, closely followed by Grauburgunder (Pinot Gris). The outstanding wines of the region come from **Kaiserstuhl-Tuniberg**, between Freiburg and the Rhein, where the mineral-rich soil in the bowl of an extinct volcano and the suntrap topography work together to impart extra body to both red and white wines. Spätburgunder wines from the Kaiserstuhl are full-bodied and opulently fruity. Many are aged in new oak *barriques*. Because of the high quality and strong demand for German red wines in the local market, these wines are never cheap.

Baden			
KEY WINE		**GRAPE VARIETY**	**PRICE**
Kaiserstuhl Spätburgunder	■	Pinot Noir	●●●○

16 England and Wales

The Romans were the first to plant vines in Britain. By the Middle Ages vineyards were widespread throughout southern England, generally on monastic lands. However, the dissolution of the monasteries under Henry VIII led to a decline that continued until the early 1950s, when Sir Guy Salisbury-Jones planted a commercial vineyard at Hambledon in Hampshire. The area under vines peaked at just over 1000 hectares in the early 1990s. Many vines that were planted in totally unsuitable sites have now been removed, and the current (2004) figure is 812 hectares, spread between 333 properties (317 in England and 16 in Wales).

CLIMATE, SOILS AND VITICULTURE

With the majority of the vineyards lying above 51° N, this would seem to be unlikely territory for the production of wine. However, the UK's maritime climate, tempered by the Gulf Stream and global warming, are giving grounds for increasing confidence as far as the production of wine here is concerned. Spring frosts can be a problem, as can wet and windy weather during the flowering season (mid-June), but a long growing season and mild autumns can compensate for this. Rain during the growing season can lead to problems with disease, but protection can be taken against this. Britain is being considered particularly as a source of quality sparkling wines.

Soils vary considerably. Many of the best sites are south- or south-east-facing, on the rolling hills in southern England. In parts, the subsoil is chalk or limestone from the same geological period as that in Champagne.

Early commercial plantings largely used the traditional Burgundian Double Guyot system of training vines. More modern systems, such as the Geneva Double Curtain, Lyre, Scott Henry and Pendlebogen, have been found to be more suitable for British conditions. They allow large areas of leaf canopy to make as much sugar as possible with the limited sunlight, without shading the fruit, which would inhibit flavour ripeness.

GRAPE VARIETIES, WINEMAKING AND STYLES

Because of the marginal climate, most of the plantings are of early-ripening varieties. Although **Müller-Thürgau** is still the most widely planted variety, its importance is decreasing. Most English still wines are white, unoaked, light in alcohol, high in acidity and made from floral-aromatic varieties such as **Schönburger** and **Madeleine ×
Angevine 7672** (not to be confused with the Loire table grape, Madeleine Angevine). Flavours and aromas are rather like Muscat or Gewurztraminer, though acidity levels are much higher and this is often counterbalanced by a little sugar, generally added as *Süssreserve*, just as in Germany. **Bacchus**, **Huxelrebe** and **Phoenix** produce wines in a similar light, very crisp style, but with a much more nettle-like, herbaceous character which can be reminiscent of Sauvignon Blanc. With all of these aromatic varieties, the low yields give very intense fruit extract, which with the high acidity sometimes allows evolution in the bottle. The rosehip, chamomile and wet leaf flavours that emerge are not to everyone's taste. **Reichensteiner** and **Seyval Blanc** wines are more neutral in character, though still high in acidity. Both varieties are reliable and relatively high yielding with good disease resistance; both are used for still and sparkling wines. Reichensteiner often provides the bulk of blends, toning down the more extreme aromatic character of the other components. Seyval Blanc (a hybrid variety) is often aged in oak, and takes well to techniques such as lees contact, producing medium-bodied wines with peach and yoghurt aromas, and an oaky finish.

For red wines, **Dornfelder** and **Rondo** are most important (most plantings of Pinot Noir are used for sparkling wine). Both release a great deal of colour, resulting in deep black wines with very little tannin. These are generally light in body, with crisp acidity, bramble fruit and a peppery finish. Rondo is one of a small number of hybrid varieties that is permitted for use in quality wines in the EU. Since the late 1990s, planting of red wine grapes has increased by 10 per cent.

Although also used for dry wines, **Ortega**'s high sugar levels and susceptibility to noble rot make it particularly suitable for sweet wines. It has zesty, citrus fruit and moderate acidity.

Of the more than 50 other varieties grown, plantings of **Chardonnay, Pinot Noir** and **Pinot Meunier** have increased by more than 30 per cent since the mid-1990s, largely for the production of sparkling wines.

Very few of the 300+ properties make their own wine; instead, most send their grapes to one of the well-equipped, larger wineries. The wines may then be sold under the name of the property or contribute to one of a growing number of medium-volume brands. These brands are increasing in importance as larger-scale production reduces unit costs, and also enables them to supply the needs of retail outlets. Those that do sell wine under their own label generally sell at the cellar door or through specialist retailers. Half of all vineyards are less than 1 hectare in size, production is small and the costs of labour, land and equipment are high. When these costs are divided between a small output, the unit cost is driven up and prices are generally high. In spite of this, and the uneven quality due to the climate, and winemakers still learning how to make the best wine from the

England and Wales			
KEY WINES		MAIN GRAPE VARIETIES	PRICE
White wines	☐	Various, frequently blends	●●+
Red wines	■	Rondo, Dornfelder, Pinot Noir	●●●+

available grapes, demand for English and Welsh wine is strong. This is almost entirely driven by the local market, though a little is exported.

It is permitted to 'enrich' wine (increase the alcohol content by adding sugar in some form) and, in effect, this takes place nearly every vintage for nearly every wine. Wines can also be sweetened by the use of grape concentrate to balance the high natural acidity of many wines. For table wines this can be imported, but for quality wines it must come from British fruit.

WINE LAWS
With the entry of Britain into the European Community in 1973, its winegrowers became subject to its law concerning both vine-growing and winemaking. This has meant that as soon as certain production figures are achieved, new laws

Picking Pinot Meunier grapes in the rain at Hambledon Vineyard, Hampshire.

are brought into effect. The first of these occurred in 1987, when planting reached 500 hectares and preparations were put under way for the creation of an appellation scheme. This became effective from the 1991 vintage and became known as the Quality Wine Scheme (QWS). Under this scheme, wines that had been approved after testing and tasting, which were made 100 per cent from *vinifera* grapes, and which conformed to certain standards, could be labelled as **English (or Welsh) Vineyards Quality Wine**. The disadvantage of this for many was that no wines that included any of the widely planted Seyval Blanc could be considered. As a result, in 1996, a lower category RWS (Regional Wine Scheme), the equivalent of French *Vin de Pays*, was introduced, permitting wines made from any variety to be assessed. It is anticipated that many wines labelled with either a county source (e.g. Cornish Wine) or a regional source (for example Thames Valley Wine) will appear on the market. Below these two levels, there is UK Table Wine, which is not tested and cannot bear a vintage, a grape variety or a vineyard name on the label.

The quality schemes are administered by the industry body, the United Kingdom Vineyards Association, but the responsibility for the application of EU wine laws is in the hands of the Wine Standards Board, which is jointly sponsored by the Department for Environment, Food and Rural Affairs and the Worshipful Company of Vintners.

A Note on British (and Irish) Wines

Until the beginning of 1996, many of these were sold simply as British Sherry or Irish Sherry, but since then they have had to be labelled as Fortified British Wine and Fortified Irish Wine. By EU law for these two products the country and the word 'wine' cannot be separated on the label, so you can label a product 'Sweet Fortified British Wine', but not 'Fortified British Sweet Wine'. It should be pointed out that these are manufactured from imported concentrated must, not from locally sourced fresh grape juice. Clearly 'British Wine' is a very different kind of product from 'English Wine' or 'Welsh Wine'.

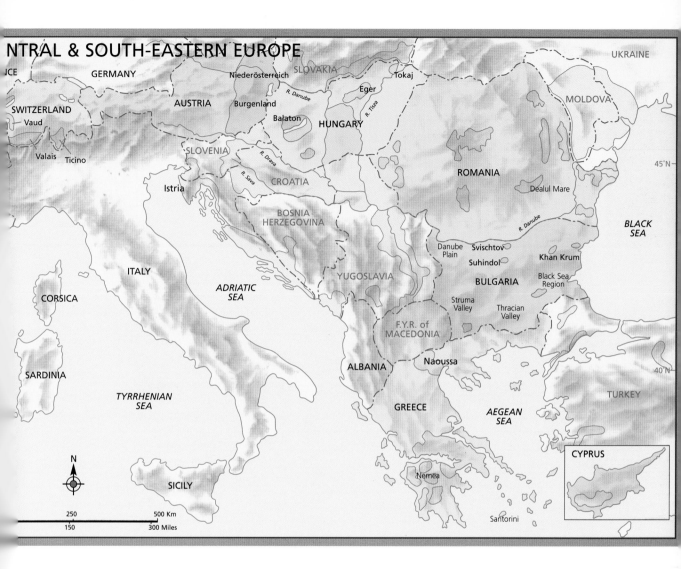

NTRAL & SOUTH-EASTERN EUROPE

UKRAINE

GERMANY   SLOVAKIA

Niederösterreich   Tokaj

AUSTRIA   Eger   MOLDOVA

SWITZERLAND   Burgenland   R. Danube

Vaud   Balaton   HUNGARY

Valais   Ticino   45°N

SLOVENIA

R. Drava   ROMANIA

Istria   R. Sava   CROATIA   Deálul Mare

BOSNIA
HERZEGOVINA   R. Danube

BLACK
SEA

ITALY   Danube   Svischtov
Plain   Khan Krum
ADRIATIC   Suhindol
SEA   YUGOSLAVIA   BULGARIA   Black Sea
Region

CORSICA   Struma   Thracian
Valley   Valley

F.Y.R. of
MACEDONIA

SARDINIA   ALBANIA   Naoussa   40°N

TYRRHENIAN
SEA   TURKEY

GREECE   AEGEAN
SEA

N   CYPRUS

SICILY

Nemea

250   500 Km
150   300 Miles   Santorini

17 Switzerland

In many ways the wine industry of Switzerland is a special case. The demands of the domestic market far outstrip the production of the local vineyards. Until recently local producers received a great deal of protection, with the importation of white wines being strictly limited. Opening up of the market has led to competition, and it is only now that many producers are beginning to consider exporting their wines. Swiss wines are generally expensive to produce; this, together with the strength of the Swiss Franc, means that they are often more expensive on export markets than their intrinsic value. This is a pity, for there are many local wines of individual interest.

With arable land at a premium, vineyards are often planted on steep slopes and everything is done to maximise production; chaptalisation is generally permitted and yields are surprisingly high given the nature of the vineyards.

Swiss wines often reflect the varying styles of the wines from the surrounding countries; this cannot be considered a surprise when one considers its geographical position and its ethnic make-up. Generally, though, white wines have low acidity due to the varieties used, the use of malolactic fermentation and harvesting at high levels of ripeness. Oak, where used, is rarely detectable in these wines. The most influential grape variety is Chasselas, but this travels under a variety of names, according to the region.

REGIONS AND WINES

Three-quarters of the production of Swiss wines comes from the south-facing slopes along the banks of the upper Rhône valley and the northern shores of Lake Geneva, shared by the three cantons of Valais, Vaud and Geneva. The **Valais** is the upper valley of the Rhône. Here, the main grape is Chasselas. Dôle is a red wine made from Pinot Noir and Gamay. There are also a number of local varieties, producing unusual wines.

In **Vaud**, the vineyards slope down to the lake. Here mainly white wines are made from the Chasselas grape. The very finest are aromatically neutral, with low acidity and strong mineral flavours that develop greater richness and complexity as they age. Red and rosé wines are also made, mainly from Gamay.

Ticino lies in the southern area of the Italian-speaking part of Switzerland. Red wines are the speciality, with the best produced from Merlot in a range of styles. Some are light and fruity, like Italian Merlots; others have rich black berry fruit, velvet tannins and toasty oak flavours in youth that are reminiscent of young Pomerol. Some are even vinified as white wines.

Rack and Pinion rail (*crémaillère*) for transporting grapes up the steep vineyards above Lac Léman, Dézaley, Vaud, Switzerland.

Switzerland			
KEY WINES		**MAIN GRAPE VARIETIES**	**PRICE**
Valais	■	Pinot Noir, Gamay	●●○
	□	Chasselas (Fendant)	●●○
Vaud	□	Chasselas (Dorin)	●●●○
Geneva	□	Aligoté, Chasselas (Perlan)	●●
	■	Gamay	●●
Ticino	■	Merlot	●●●○

Austria

No country can have succeeded more in turning around its image as a wine producer than Austria. In 1985 the country was involved in a series of wine scandals that effectively destroyed its reputation. Now its white wines, particularly from its own grape variety, the Grüner Veltliner, are considered to be among the most exciting in the world.

18

WINE LAWS

One important factor in the recovery of Austria's reputation was the new wine law introduced in 1993. Among other things, this severely limits maximum yields for wines carrying a geographical name. Thus Austria, which has approximately half the vineyard area of Germany, produces only a quarter as much wine. The laws bear many resemblances to those of Germany – for example chaptalisation is forbidden for quality wines and many of the terms seen on labels are common to both countries. The various levels of *Prädikatswein* that exist in Germany also apply to Austrian wines, though it has two additional levels of its own. These are *Ausbruch*, which is a classification between *Beerenauslese* (BA) and *Trockenbeerenauslese* (TBA), and *Strohwein* or *Shilfwein*, where bunches of grapes are laid out on beds of straw or reeds during the winter, to take on extra sweetness. It should be stressed that the minimum must weights for the various classifications are higher than their equivalent in Germany. Although sweet wines are a particular speciality of the regions around the Neusiedlersee, in Burgenland, producers in almost every region occasionally produce a TBA or an *Eiswein* when the conditions are right.

Despite the similarity in wine law between Austria and Germany, the wines themselves are different in style. In particular, because of the Central European climate, Austrian wines, which are predominantly dry whites (70 per cent), have more body and alcohol than their German counterparts, but with crisp acidity and primary fruit aromas, which are reflected on the palate.

Vines planted above the Danube benefit from increased air circulation and reflected sunlight, Wachau, Austria.

CLIMATE

The wine-producing regions of Austria, along
with Switzerland and Hungary, have a Central
European climate, with short, cold winters and
long, warm summers. Autumn ripening seasons
are long, making noble rot possible if there is
sufficient humidity. There is much less variation in
annual weather patterns than in northern Europe.

WINEMAKING

A very strong local market, and exports that focus
on luxury wines, result in generally very high prices
for these wines. One benefit is that winemakers
need spare no expense when investing in
winemaking equipment and winemaking education.
The most up-to-date stainless steel equipment will
be found in even quite small wineries, along with
expensive oak *barriques* and, in some of the more
traditional regions, beautifully carved ancient oak
casks. While the experiments of some winemakers
with varieties such as Grüner Veltliner and
Blaufränkisch result in unbalanced oak or excessive
alcohol, there are many successes. Most of the finest
wines, including the small quantities of outstanding
red wine, rarely reach export markets. Most are
consumed by the large, wealthy, local market before
they have a chance to show their full potential.

GRAPE VARIETIES

In all, there are just under 57000 hectares of vines
in Austria, planted overwhelmingly with white
varieties. The importance of red varieties is,
however, increasing.

A third of all plantings are of the **Grüner
Veltliner**, a grape that is capable of giving a broad
variety of flavours: green grapes, salad and white
pepper in youth develop to layers of honey and
toast as the wine ages. It is capable of expressing
quite exaggerated mineral notes when grown with
low yields on appropriate soils. Until recently, it
was mainly sold young, without oak-ageing. It
is said that allowing the wine to 'breathe' a little
in an old neutral cask allows some of the more
assertive primary fruit aromas to mellow and
encourages the more subtle mineral notes to
display themselves. **Riesling** is also grown for
quality wines, especially in the Wachau, Kamptal
and Kremstal. These are usually dry and quite
full-bodied, with ripe, peachy primary fruit. As
with the best Grüner Veltliners, many are bottled
to reflect the characteristics of a single, named
vineyard. Mineral flavours are common, and
these wines can develop great complexity as they
age. Surprisingly good, simple, but sappy quaffing
wines are made from **Welschriesling** in Burgenland
and further south. Particularly in southern
Austria, it has come to be regarded as a quality
variety. It is susceptible to botrytis, and can
produce sensational dessert wines.

For red wines, **Blaufränkisch** produces wines
with moderate tannins, crisp acidity and a peppery,
sour cherry flavour. In the right sites, Blaufränkisch
can express strong mineral flavours. Ageing in
oak results in softer acidity and a sweeter fruit
character. **Zweigelt** (Blaufränkisch × St Laurent)
gives very deep-coloured reds with a soft tannins

and bramble fruit. **St Laurent** is an Austrian speciality that gives wines that are similar in character to Pinot Noir. Many producers are blending these Austrian varieties with international varieties such as Cabernet Sauvignon or Merlot.

REGIONS AND WINES

Under the new legislation, Austria is split into four regions (*Weinbauregion*). These may, in turn, be split into subregions (*Weinbaugebiete*) and districts (*Grosslage*). All are situated to the east of the country, the Alps of western Austria being unsuitable for viticulture. The most important regions for the international market are Lower Austria and Burgenland.

Lower Austria (Niederösterreich)

This is the largest of the regions and the frontrunner in both production and exports. The majority of the vineyards lie on the banks of the Danube and further north towards the Slovak border. Of the eight subregions, the most important for quality exports are the **Wachau**, **Kamptal** and **Kremstal**. Steep, terraced vineyards maximise exposure to the sun, and the long dry autumns allow Grüner Veltliner and Riesling grapes to ripen with immense concentration of flavour compounds in their skins. The wines are sometimes aged for a period in large, neutral, old oak casks before bottling. Expressive varietal fruit and mineral flavours evolve over time to generate complex layers of honey and toast. The best single-vineyard Grüner Veltliners compare in quality, and to some extent in style, with the very finest white Burgundies. The Rieslings are dry and generally more full-bodied than those from the Pfalz or Alsace. Both are highly sought-after and sell for very high prices. Cheaper wines can be sourced in larger quantities from the **Weinviertel**. This region has the first Austrian DAC (equivalent of the French AOC, but with tighter limits on quality and style). A wine labelled as Weinviertel DAC must be a light, fresh, fruity Grüner Veltliner with no discernible oak flavours.

Burgenland

This region lies to the east of Austria, along the border with Hungary, and produces top quality sweet wines. There are four subregions.

Neusiedlersee and **Neusiedlersee-Hügelland** (which includes the well-known village of Rust) surround a vast, shallow lake in the north of the province, the Neusiedlersee. Autumn mists from the lake and from the thousands of small, shallow

Lower Austria (Niederösterreich)

KEY WINES		MAIN GRAPE VARIETIES	PRICE
Wachau/Kamptal/ Kremstal	☐	Grüner Veltliner	●●●○
	☐	Riesling	●●●○
Weinviertel DAC	☐	Grüner Veltliner	●●○

Burgenland

KEY WINES		MAIN GRAPE VARIETIES	PRICE
BA/TBA/*Eiswein*	☐ ▦	Various	●●●○
Burgenland reds	▪	Blaufränkisch, cuvées	●●●○

ponds in the wetland region to the east of the lake are ideal for encouraging noble rot, which occurs almost every year. The vineyards for the most part are on the plain and yields are relatively high for sweet wines. For this reason, and because production of botrytised wines can almost be guaranteed every year, prices tend to be lower than those of equivalent wines from France and Germany. *Beerenauslese* and *Trockenbeerenauslese* wines are generally sold in half-bottles. Other specialities are *Eiswein* and *Schilfwein* or *Strohwein*. High-quality dry reds and whites are also made, from grapes including Zweigelt, St Laurent, Pinot Noir, Pinot Gris, Pinot Blanc and Chardonnay, grown on the slopes that lie away from the lake.

Mittelburgenland and **Südburgenland** lie in the rolling hills to the south-west of the lake. They are the source of Austria's finest red wines, made from Blaufränkisch, or from blends with Blaufränkisch and Bordeaux varieties. These are usually aged in new French oak.

The Neusiedlersee in Burgenland creates ideal misty conditions for botrytis to develop almost every year.

19 Hungary

Vines have been planted in this part of the Danube valley since the fourth century BC, and, as it is one of the great military highways of Europe, it has seen a succession of conquerors. Vineyards have not been cultivated there continuously; from the fall of the Western Roman Emperors until the influx of German settlers in the tenth century, wine production largely fell into abeyance. As on most highways in the Middle Ages, monasteries provided overnight lodging and the monastic orders can be credited with the creation of many of the vineyards that still exist. It was the Benedictines who established the vineyards of Eger and Somló.

The collapse of communism probably had a greater effect on Hungarian wines than on those of any other member of the Eastern Bloc. This is because Hungary had by far the most developed winemaking tradition and the broadest range of native grapes to choose from. Sadly, in a bid to occupy the supermarket shelves of the West, their cousins from Western Europe have replaced many of these varieties. However, a counter-reaction has set in, with investment coming from both outside and within. A new, proud generation of Hungarian winemakers is being created.

WINE LAWS
Hungary has a wine law based on the French *Appellation Contrôlée* system whereby geographical origin determines quality status. In 1997, Hungarian vineyards were reclassified into 22 wine districts, divided into three regions. All wine is classified under one of three headings:

Asztali Bor (Table Wine)

Minőségi Bor (Quality Wine) – a category equivalent to QWPSR

Special Quality Wine – only applicable to botrytised wines. Such bottles must bear the state wine seal.

GRAPE VARIETIES
As well as international varieties, of which **Chardonnay, Pinot Gris, Cabernet Sauvignon** and **Cabernet Franc** are the most important, the following are the main Hungarian specialities:

Furmint makes powerful white wines with flavours of apples when young, developing into nuts and honey as they age. It is used for Tokaji and Somló. **Hárslevelű** (linden leaf) is late ripening and prone to botrytis. It is faintly spicy with pronounced acidity, and is also used for Tokaji.

Sárga Muscotály (Muscat de Lunel) is aromatic, with flavours of orange-blossom. It is best for dessert wines and is the third important variety used for Tokaji. **Olasz Rizling** (Welschriesling) gives crisp, light dry wines, with an aftertaste of bitter almonds and is grown in Balaton. **Irsai Olivér** is an aromatic Muscat cross. Cserszegi Füszeres and Kiralyleányka give similar aromatic, dry wines. Dry whites from these and from international varieties such as Chardonnay tend to be high in acidity, with some balancing residual sugar.

Kadarka is a premium grape that was nearly eliminated under the communists. It ages well in oak. It was once the main component of Szekszárd and Egri Bikaver, but has now been largely replaced by international varieties and **Kékfrankos** (Blaufränkisch), which gives light, purple-coloured wine with high acidity. **Kékoportó** (Portugieser) needs a warm climate. It is best blended due to its soft acids and tannins. When yields are controlled it can benefit from barrel-ageing. It is used for Villany and Szekszárd. **Zweigelt** is the Austrian cross between Kékfrankos and St Laurent. It is widely planted and often gives high yields.

REGIONS AND WINES
Geographically, Hungary can be broadly divided into two as far as its vineyards are concerned. In the south-east lies the Great Plain, where winemaking can be carried out on an industrial scale. The rest of the country is hilly, but rarely rises to over 1000 metres. This is divided into two wine districts, Trans-Danubia and northern Hungary. Within these three broad areas there are 22 wine regions, but few of them have much relevance on foreign markets.

Hungary has a Central European climate with

hort, cold winters and long, warm summers.
Autumn ripening seasons are long, making noble
ot possible if there is sufficient humidity, as in
Tokaji. The average rainfall is approximately
00 mm per year, with a mean annual temperature
of 10.5° C.

Northern Hungary

The best-known and most prestigious of all
Hungary's wine regions is Tokaj-Hegyalja in the
oothills of the northern mountains against the
Slovakian border, and on the banks of the Bodrog
and Tisza rivers. **Tokaji** wine takes its name from
the local town of Tokaj, and is generally called
Tokay in English. The wines can be split into two
distinct groups, the Quality Wines, bottled into
75 cl bottles, and the Special Quality Wines,
bottled into the traditional 50 cl dump bottles.
These latter rank among the world's greatest
sweet wines and are strongly affected by noble
rot. It is the mists from the rivers that create the
conditions in which the *Botrytis cinerea*
flourishes.

The one wine in the Quality group of note is
Tokaji Furmint. It is made entirely from the
Furmint variety, is unaffected by noble rot and is
either medium-dry or dry.

The Special Quality Wines are made almost
exclusively from Furmint and Hárslevelű grapes,
which represent 66 per cent and 33 per cent of the
plantings respectively. The wines come in three
styles.

Tokaji Szamorodni (literally, 'Tokaji as it
comes') describes the vinification process whereby
the wine is produced by putting together all the
grapes as harvested, with no separation of healthy
and botrytised grapes. Consequently, the wine
may be dry (*száraz*) or sweet (*édes*), depending on
the amount of noble rot that is present, but even
the dry wine will show noble rot characters. The
wine is aged in a traditional cask, called a *Gönc*.
The *gönc* for the dry *Szamorodni* is not completely
filled to enable *flor*-like yeast to form naturally on
the wine; the wine develops a character similar to
that of a Fino Sherry.

The word *Aszú* means nobly rotted grapes. In
the production of **Tokaji Aszú**, healthy and
botrytised grapes are separated in the vineyard,
after which the healthy grapes are made into dry
white wine and the rotten grapes are stored. These
can be so rich in sugar that they hardly ferment.
The *Aszú* grapes are then pounded into a paste
before being added to the dry wine to produce the
sweetness required, which varies with the amount
of paste used. In accordance with tradition, the
paste is measured in *puttonyos*. Originally, *Aszú*

Harvesting heavy botrytised (*aszu*) Furmint grapes, Tokaji, Hungary.

grapes were collected at the vintage in a 20 kg
hod or *puttony*. Now the measurement refers to
the residual sugar content in the finished wine and
this qualifies the wine for its designation. On a
label you may see a wine classified as containing
between three and six *puttonyos*. They will have
the following residual sugar contents:

3 *puttonyos*:	60 g/l
4 *puttonyos*:	90 g/l
5 *puttonyos*:	120 g/l
6 *puttonyos*:	150 g/l

The wine is matured for between three and six
years in cask. Over the past decade, there has
been considerable foreign investment in the Tokaji
region. This has brought in new winemakers and
consultants, who have questioned many aspects
of the Tokaji winemaking process. Producers are
still divided over the question as to whether to
allow a certain amount of oxidation at this stage,
and there is a distinct move towards less oxidised
wines. Classic Tokaji is deep amber, with high
acidity and intense aromas and flavours of orange
marmalade, apricots and honey. The best wines
have further complexities which hint at rye bread,
smoke, coffee and caramel, among other things.

Aszú Essencia is made in the same way as Aszú,
but only in the best years and from the best

Hungary			
KEY WINES		**MAIN GRAPE VARIETIES**	**PRICE**
Tokaji	☐	Furmint, Hárslevelű	●●●○+
Bull's Blood	■	Blend (mainly Kékfrankos)	●○
Varietal wines	☐	Chardonnay, Irsai Olivér, Pinot Gris	●○
	■	Cabernet Franc, Cabernet Sauvignon	●○

View of Lake Balaton. The lake stores warmth and creates a mild climate around the shores.

A cellar in the Tokaji region, showing the black cellar mould.

vineyards. The sugar content is in excess of that for six *puttonyos* wine, approximately 200 g/l. Massive concentration of flavour compounds in the wines ensures that they can age for over a century without losing their intense flavours. Tokaji Azsú Essencia is expensive as befits any of the rarest and greatest sweet white wines, on a par with a Château d'Yquem or a top German or Austrian TBA.

The vast majority of Aszú wines have an actual alcohol content between 13.5% abv and 14.5% abv.

South-west of Tokaj, along the same range of hills, lie the vineyards of **Eger**, one source of the historically full-bodied red wine Egri Bikavér, or **Bull's Blood**. It is made from a blend of grapes and aged in large oak casks in miles of cellars cut into the tufa rock beneath the town of Eger itself. Modern Egri Bikavér is usually rather light in tannins and body, and though powerful versions that live up to the name can be found, they tend to be expensive.

Trans-Danubia

The regions surrounding **Lake Balaton** are protected from the dominant north winds by a range of hills. This creates an ideal climate for the production of wine. The soil, which ranges from volcanic to iron-rich, also gives body to the wines. A broad range of varieties is planted here, including Chardonnay, Pinot Gris and Welschriesling. Further south, **Szekszárd** is a region with long warm summers whose red wines, similar in style to those of Eger, may also be known as Bull's Blood.

The Great Plain

Although this sandy, phylloxera-free region accounts for around half of Hungary's vineyards, little of the wine produced here is of sufficient quality to be considered for export.

Romania

With 250 000 hectares of vineyards, Romania is the fifth largest producer of wine in Europe and the eighth largest in the world. However, its wines may not have received the international notice they deserve, for it is also a major consumer of wine, with little being left for export. In recent years, there has been considerable foreign investment in the modernisation of the industry and the wines are now readily available elsewhere. In terms of volume, by far the most important region is Romanian Moldova in the north-east of the country. Here Cotnari is produced. This is a sweet wine made from botrytised native grapes with a reputation that once rivalled Tokaji. Very little of this, or of the dry local wines, is exported; most is absorbed by the large local market.

20

CLIMATE AND TOPOGRAPHY

The country is split in two by the Carpathian Mountains, which lie like the letter L on its back. To the north and west of these the climate is continental. Winters are cold but short, and warm summers extending into long mild autumns allow for a long ripening season and the possibility of noble rot forming in the more humid regions. To the east the Black Sea has a moderating influence: here winters are mild and summers are hot.

REGIONS AND WINES

The vineyards of Romania are split into eight basic regions. The most widely known wines come from the vineyards of **Dealul Mare**. These lie on the south-facing slopes of the Carpathian foothills, north of the capital Bucharest and produce a range of red wines from Pinot Noir, Merlot, Cabernet Sauvignon and local varieties. The wines are generally fruit-driven in style with soft tannins.

Quality wines also come from the coastal vineyards on limestone soils of **Murfatlar**. The better wines are whites made from a range of varieties, including Chardonnay and Pinot Gris, and soft reds from Merlot and Cabernet Sauvignon. Although Welschriesling is omnipresent, most exported Romanian wines are sold as varietals, supporting a broad range of classic European varieties.

Vineyard and church at Dealul Vei in the foothills of the Carpathian Mountains, Romania.

Romania			
KEY GRAPE VARIETIES		**MAIN REGIONS**	**PRICE**
Pinot Noir	■	Dealul Mare	●
Merlot	■	Dealul Mare, Murfatlar	●

21 Bulgaria

The recent history of Bulgarian wine is in some ways a sad one, in others it is exciting. Under the communists the industry was built up to be a major earner of foreign currency. In the late 1980s, the top-selling red wine in Britain was Cabernet Sauvignon from Bulgaria and by 1996 Bulgaria was the second largest exporter of bottled wine in the world. With the collapse of government controls in the industry, the whole infrastructure fell apart, leading to a rapid decline in sales and Bulgarian wines being consigned to the lowest shelves in the supermarkets. A large amount of foreign capital has since been pumped into wineries, but much less has been fed into the vineyards; as a result, yields have fallen dramatically and total production by a third. Many foreign winemakers are now working in the country and there has been a slow increase in the quality. Most of the vineyards are now in independently held smallholdings, with winemaking almost entirely in the hands of large cellars, some co-operatives and some privatised.

WINE LAWS

Since 1946 Bulgaria has built up a system of wine laws, of which the most important is the Wine Act of 1978, which classifies wines into a number of different categories. These are:

Standard wines: basic-level still, light wines, largely consumed on the domestic market.

Special wines: include sparkling, liqueur and fruit wines.

High quality wines without geographical origin: wines from an unspecified region, normally sold under a brand name.

High quality wines with declared geographical origin (DGO): these state the region of production on the label. The grape varieties will also often be mentioned. This status is not declared on the label, which might for example read simply 'Russe Welschriesling', Russe being the producing region in the north of the country.

Controliran: this category is the equivalent of *Appellation Contrôlée* in France. The wines must come from a specified grape variety grown in specified vineyards. The labels must state both the variety and region, and the wine must be passed by a tasting panel. The word *Controliran* will appear on the label. While *Controliran* has a higher status than DGO, it is possible that wines from the same source will be bottled under the two different levels. The word *Controliran* provides an additional guarantee.

Among the other terms which might be found on a Bulgarian wine label is **Reserve**. This is applied to DGO and *Controliran* wines that have been aged for a minimum period in oak. The vessel used is more likely to be a large old oak vat than a small barrel, so that the wine is mellowed rather than picking up oaky flavours. Where they do appear, oaky flavours are most likely to be added through the use of chips.

GRAPE VARIETIES

On the international markets, it was Bulgarian Cabernet Sauvignon that dominated. This has now been joined by Merlot and a number of local varieties including Mavrud, Melnik, Pamid and Gamza. For white wines, the most popular grapes are Chardonnay, together with Aligoté, Dimiat, Rkatsiteli and Muscat Ottonel.

REGIONS AND WINES

Western Bulgaria, including the Thracian and Struma vallays, has an Eastern European climate. This is warmer overall than Central Europe, having milder winters and warmer summers. Much of the wine produced here is red with medium-to-high alcohol, medium acidity, soft tannins and a good fruit character on the nose and palate. Eastern Bulgaria has a Black Sea climate with mild winters and hot summers. Here the main influence is the Black Sea, which tempers what would otherwise be a harsher continental climate.

There are vineyards throughout the country,

xcept in the immediate vicinity of the capital,
ofia. For administrative reasons, the vineyards
ave been split into five regions. As the Cyrillic
ript is used in Bulgaria, variations as to how
lace names are anglicised are often found.

lack Sea Region

his region includes the country's entire coastline
n the Black Sea and stretches up to the River
Danube. The Black Sea moderates the climate,
nabling the accent to be placed on white wines.
hardonnay is the most important export. The
est wines are produced in the hilly region of
humen, which includes the areas of Novi Pasar
nd Khan Krum. The former has *Controliran*
atus for its Chardonnays and the latter for its
Gewurztraminers, though it is better known for
s Special Reserve Chardonnays. Good, unoaked
Controliran Chardonnays are also produced near
Varna on the Black Sea. Inland, where the
mountains reduce the maritime influence, red
wines are made.

Danube Plain Region

This region includes the northern slopes of the
Balkan Mountains and the great Danube plain.
Here there is a moderate continental climate, with
ot summers. The best-known wines of the region
re the Cabernet Sauvignons from Svischtov,
which lies on the Danube itself. Other important
entres of production include Suhindol, where the
country's first co-operative cellar was established
n 1909; Russe, another river port; and Pavlikeni,
lose to Suhindol. All these regions produce
redominantly red wines, though Russe also
roduces white wines.

hracian Valley Region

The **East Thracian Valley Region** comprises part
f the **Thracian Valley** and the hilly region of
akar. Here the climate is continental, though it is
empered by cooling breezes from the mountains.
This is a centre for the growing of Merlot.

The vineyards of the **West Thracian Valley
Region** lie mainly in the valley of the River
Maritsa, and this is the most productive of the
ive regions. The best-known *Controliran* wine is
he Mavrud from Assenovgrad. There are also
mportant plantings of Cabernet Sauvignon around

Bulgaria			
KEY GRAPE VARIETIES		**MAIN REGIONS**	**PRICE**
Cabernet Sauvignon	■	Danube Plain, West and East Thracian Valley	●○
Merlot	■	East Thracian Valley	●
Melnik	■	Struma Valley Region	●○
Chardonnay	□	Black Sea Region	●○

Plovdiv, the country's second city. Oriachovitza,
to the north-east, is best known for its Cabernet
Sauvignon Reserve wine.

Wines from the East and West Thracian Valley
Regions can be blended and sold simply as
Thracian Valley.

Struma Valley Region

Here the vineyards lie in the extreme south-west
of the country, very close to the frontier with
Greece. The speciality grape, perhaps the most
individual in the country, is generally known as
Melnik after the local town. Sadly, little of this is
now grown. It produces full-bodied, highly tannic
wines, which benefit from barrel-ageing. Also
produced is some rather gentler Cabernet
Sauvignon.

**Many Bulgarian vineyards
are trained high and
widely spaced to permit
mechanisation. Here the
oenologist is checking the
ripeness of the grapes in
such a vineyard prior to
harvesting.**

22 Italy

The history of Italian wines is impressive, with early vineyards planted by Greek settlers, possibly as early as 800 BC. The Etruscans produced wine for their own consumption and for trading. Later, the Romans recognised its commercial possibilities. Cato the Censor, in his work *On Agriculture* laid down principles on how to run a vineyard profitably – an important factor was to produce as much wine as possible! The Romans were probably the first to produce wine for keeping; they covered the wine in amphorae, storage jars, with a layer of olive oil, in order to prevent oxidation. So high was the reputation of the classical wines of Italy that the Greeks named the country Oenotria, or land of wine. Despite such a rich history, it is only over the past 40 years or so that Italy has revived its role as a producer of quality wine. The country's wine classification *Denominazione di Origine Controllata* (DOC) was conceived as recently as 1963. Since then, rapid strides have been taken along the road of quality. Italy now battles with France for the title of being the world's largest producer and exporter of wine. Since the mid-1990s the total annual production has slipped from around 55 million hectolitres to around 45 million hectolitres.

As in many other countries, there are contradictory forces at work in the Italian wine world. On the one hand, much of the production is in the hands of smallholders who are part of the rural tradition and are innately conservative. There is often little incentive to produce better wine when the local market is undemanding; wine is part of the daily life in Italy and as such is often taken for granted. The other side of the coin is the native creativity and individuality of the Italian character. In the field of wine, this had led to the creation of numerous idiosyncratic wines of high quality, which are widely discussed, even if their lack of availability might pose problems for the curious consumer.

ITALIAN WINE LAWS

The variety of Italian wines is enormous. Even within the DOC system approximately 1000 different types of wine are being produced in over 300 different geographical locations. This diversity might appear to be an impenetrable maze. The 1992 legislation, the 'Goria Law', is changing a lot, but a number of the country's finest wines still fall outside the quality classifications of DOC and DOCG, usually because they are not produced according to the traditions of the region from which they come. In the past in particular, Italian wine legislators have not been generous to innovators.

Italian wine law recognises four different quality levels. These are, in descending order:

Denominazione di Origine Controllata e Garantita (DOCG): wines must meet all the requirements of DOC and in addition must be bottled in the region of production and be subject to a Ministry of Agriculture tasting, before being awarded the necessary seal of approval. More than 20 wines have achieved this status, and the number is increasing. Among those most regularly found are: Asti and Moscato d'Asti, Barbaresco, Barolo, Brunello di Montalcino, Chianti (including the sub-regions), Gavi, Taurasi, Vernaccia di San Gimignano and Vino Nobile de Montepulciano.

Denominazione di Origine Controllata (DOC): the first designation to be introduced, it is similar to the French *Appellation Contrôlée*, specifying geographical zone, grape varieties, yields and the like. There are now more than 300 geographical entities entitled to their own DOC. For many traditional wines (e.g. Valpolicella, Chianti, Orvieto) the delimited DOC zone extends far beyond the original vineyard area. Some of these regions indicate wines made from the historic sites, which are generally also the best sites, by adding the word **Classico** (e.g. Valpolicella Classico). DOC wines may be further differentiated in a number of ways: still or sparkling, sweet or dry, young or old; by a geographical subregion; or by the grape variety from which they are made.

Indicazione Geografica Tipica (IGT): a recent classification, introduced by the 1992 wine law. It is designed to absorb those *Vini da Tavola* allowed to specify their region or district of origin, such as *Vino da Tavola di Sicilia*. As with the French *Vins de Pays*, of which this is the equivalent, it includes many wines made from grape varieties and techniques not traditional in their area of production, and which are not, therefore, entitled to a higher classification.

Vino da Tavola: a large but a declining segment of the market, partly as a result of EU policies to reduce the so-called wine lake and partly because many of the better wines have been reclassified at a higher level. These wines may not state on the label the geographical source, the grape variety or the vintage. A vast quantity of wine produced in the south and in Sicily is sold as anonymous *Vino da Tavola*.

CLIMATE

Given the location, size and shape of Italy, it is not surprising that there are considerable climatic differences between the country's wine regions. From the Brenner Pass to the south of Sicily there are ten degrees difference in latitude; however, these differences there are lessened by the proximity of the sea and by the mountains. In the north the climate is continental, with cold winters and long, hot summers. However, the Alps and the Dolomites give protection from bitter northerly winds in the winter and stimulate cooling down-draughts in the summer. Here also the major lakes of Como, Garda and Maggiore help create benevolent site-climates by moderating temperatures. Further south, the Apennines form the backbone of Italy from the Po valley to the country's toe. Although the climate is more Mediterranean, with warmer winters and hot, dry summers, the mountain slopes provide sufficient height for cooler growing conditions. In the north, there may be differences between the vintages; these are less marked in the south.

SOILS AND TOPOGRAPHY

There is a broad variety of soils to be found in the vineyard regions of Italy, ranging from volcanic soils on the slopes of Vesuvius and Etna to glacial moraines in the north. Until recently the link between soil type and the grape variety planted had not been the subject of much investigation in Italy. Nevertheless, on hillier ground in particular, the soils tend to be poor, with good drainage, which makes them well suited for vine growing.

GRAPE VARIETIES

The richness of Italy in the world of wine depends on the broad diversity of the wines that it produces. In turn, this is dependent on the diversity of the grape varieties that are planted. It has been calculated that the country is home to more than 1 000 different varieties of *Vitis vinifera*. More importantly, many of these are native to Italy and not found elsewhere in the world. This is surprising when one considers the scale of emigration from Italy during the nineteenth and twentieth centuries. Not all, it must be admitted, produce great wines, but such black varieties as Nebbiolo, Sangiovese and Aglianico are capable of producing world-class wines. The different varieties are discussed more fully below in the section on the individual regions.

Bunches of ripe Barbera grapes in Alba.

VITICULTURE

The diversity of climate, soil and vine inevitably means that there are many different ways of growing vines in Italy. Fortunately, and perhaps simplistically, these can be grouped into two broad headings, which can be traced back to Etruscan and Greek roots.

In central and north-east Italy, vines historically were trained high. The Etruscans used natural supports – olive, fig, walnut and poplar trees, for example. Density of planting was low and, with little pruning of the vines, the yields were high. When grapes were regarded as no more than another crop, this inefficient method of mixed

cultivation was acceptable. Now, as a result of the move towards quality, it has all but disappeared. This Etruscan influence remains, however, in the high-trellis systems still in use in north-east Italy.

The Greeks planted specialist vineyards with low and densely planted vines, giving restricted yields of high-quality fruit. The north-west and south of Italy have favoured this system historically and continue to train their vines on wires, using the cordon (*spalliera*) and the cane (Guyot) systems. When quality is desired, most new vineyards now use one of these two systems, wherever they are in Italy, although in the south, where the hot dry climate lessens the risk of rot, there is a tendency to plant bush vines (*albarello*).

VINIFICATION

The juxtaposition of modern technique and traditional practice is more obvious in the winery than in the vineyards. Especially for red wines old habits die hard, with open vat fermentation and long maceration on the skins. Over the past decade, stainless steel and new oak have replaced potentially unhygienic old oak, and where the latter is still used, many wineries are taking better care to avoid the contamination that can result. With the advent of 'international' grape varieties and the move towards quality, experimentation is well advanced in many directions. Temperature-controlled, stainless steel fermentation vats, control of the malolactic fermentation and ageing in new oak *barriques* are now the tools of the Tuscan, Piedmontese and other winemakers. Advances in the making of white wine have been

High cordon-trained vines in Trentino during the winter; with the Alps in the background.

even more pronounced, with grapes and must protected from contact with oxygen, and temperature-controlled fermentation resulting in clean, fresh wines.

REGIONS AND WINES

Politically, Italy is divided into 20 regions, each of which enjoys a certain degree of autonomy. In every region wine is produced at least of DOC quality. The following are the regions that are most important to the international market.

Piemonte

Piemonte literally means 'at the foot of the mountains'. The whole region is dominated by the Alps, which lie to the north and west, and the Apennines to the south. The local capital is Turin and the vineyards lie in two distinct groups: to the north-east of the city in the direction of Lake

Maggiore, and to the south-east in the Langhe and Monferrato hills, both DOC zones, where we find the towns of Asti and Alba. The climate is severe in winter, but there is a long ripening season in the summer and into the autumn, when fogs are frequent.

Piemonte has the largest area under vines in Italy for the production of DOC and DOCG wines, covering over 40 different appellations. While much noteworthy white wine is made, the reputation of the region is firmly based on its red wines. Four of these have DOCG status, of which the most important are Barolo and Barbaresco. As the status of IGT is not recognised in this province, many wines simply use the catch-all **Piemonte DOC. Langhe DOC** is also an increasingly important name with many leading producers now using it even for their best wines.

Many Italian wine producers, especially those in Tuscany, find the DOC and DOCG regulations too restrictive, and are 'breaking the rules' to produce high quality *Vini da Tavola*, often aged in 225-litre *barriques* alongside the DOCG wines maturing in *botti*.

Piemonte			
KEY WINES		**MAIN GRAPE VARIETIES**	**PRICE**
Barolo DOCG	■	Nebbiolo	●●●○+
Barbaresco DOCG	■	Nebbiolo	●●●○+
Barbera d'Asti DOC	■	Barbera	●●
Barbera d'Alba DOC	■	Barbera	●●○
Dolcetto d'Alba DOC	■	Dolcetto	●●
Gavi DOCG	□	Cortese	●●

These may be of the style of Barolo or Barbaresco, at a lower price, or they can be wines made in a more international style with new oak, sometimes at premium prices. The wines can also include Barbera and Dolcetto, as well as red international varieties in the blend.

Barolo, made solely from the Nebbiolo grape, is considered by many to be the finest of all Italian wines, with premium prices to match. It takes its name from the village of the same name to the south-west of Alba. Traditionally, Barolo is aged for long periods in large oak casks (a minimum of two years, plus a further one in bottle, to have the designation), but certain modernists are now moving towards ageing in *barriques*. The wines have a great concentration of fruit and flavour, with high tannin, acidity and alcohol. Because of this they benefit from further ageing in bottle before they reach their best. When fully mature, these wines show very complex aromas, ranging from floral (rose/violet) through strawberry fruit to notes of mushroom, autumn leaves, tar and leather.

The sister wine, **Barbaresco**, is also made solely from the Nebbiolo grape, though the wines may lack some of the body and concentration of

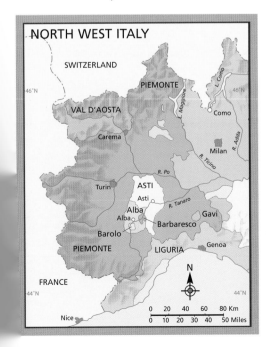

NORTH WEST ITALY

Nebbiolo vines and fog in the Langhe hills.

Barolo. It has lesser minimum ageing requirements. Prices are similar and, as with Barolo, some producers release special bottlings (sometimes specifiying an individual vineyard site). These top bottlings are among the most expensive and most highly sought wines in the world.

From La Morra, overlooking Barolo.

While Nebbiolo is the monarch of the black varieties of Piemonte, a number of others produce good wines. Among these Barbera, with its good acidity levels (**Barbera d'Asti DOC** and **Barbera d'Alba DOC**), has a rapidly improving reputation. Wines from this grape generally fall into two styles: those made to express the exuberant, sour cherry fruit of the Barbera are best consumed while youthful; those that use oak to endow the wine with some tannin and toasty complexity sometimes need some age to show their full potential. Wine from the Dolcetto is generally soft and fruity, although some growers are beginning to make wine of more substance, showing rich, sweet damson fruit, yet still light tannins and low acidity. While the most commonly found is probably the **Dolcetto d'Alba DOC**, the best wine is considered to come from Dogliani. With the exception of the most ambitious, oak-aged Barberas, most of these wines are medium-priced.

The most famous white grape of Piemonte must be the Moscato. This is the base for the **DOCGs Moscato d'Asti** (lightly prickly) and **Asti** (fully sparkling). These highly perfumed, sweet grapey wines should be drunk young and fresh (see Chapter 32).

The most famous still white wine of the region comes from the limestone-rich southern hillside vineyards around the town of Gavi, and is made

from the Cortese grape (**Gavi DOCG**). This has good acidity and is exceptionally dry, with a steeliness uncommon in Italian wines.

Piemonte is also the most important region for the production of vermouth, with major centres in Turin, Canelli and Asti.

Trentino-Alto Adige

Italy's most northerly region is so mountainous that only 15 per cent of the land (in the valley of the River Adige) can be cultivated. Generally, the fertile valley floor is used for other fruit crops; vines are sited on terraces on the lower slopes of the valley wall. Historically, the south of the region (Trentino) around the city of Trento has always been Italian, while the north, the Alto Adige, round the city of Bolzano, once formed part of the Austro-Hungarian Empire. In the latter part of the region, sometimes called the South Tyrol (Südtirol), German is still spoken and used for many of the wine names: the term *Qualitätswein bestimmter Anbaugebiet* may be used as an alternative to DOC for certain wines. Indeed, such is the separation between the two constituent parts of this province that some guides treat them as two separate entities, with the major DOCs of Trentino in the south and Alto Adige (Südtirol) in the north.

While **Alto Adige** is not an important wine region in terms of quantity, it does hold two distinctions. Firstly, it is the region that has the highest proportion of DOC wines, and, secondly, it is the region that exports the highest proportion of its production. This latter distinction comes about because Austria is a keen purchaser of its light, dry, acidic red wines made from the local Schiava and the darker more intense reds made from Lagrein (similar in character to Refosco, in youth and with age). Much of the wine is sold under varietal names. Climatically and commercially, the future would seem to lie in the production of flavoursome white wines. This has led to the planting of quality varieties including Pinot Grigio, Traminer Aromatico (Gewurztraminer), Moscato, Pinot Bianco, Sauvignon Blanc and Riesling.

The less challenging slopes of the **Trentino** are a major source of crisp, light, commercial Pinot Grigio. There is also a local speciality red made from Teroldego, with high acidity, bitter cherry fruit and soft chewy tannins.

Friuli-Venezia Giulia

In the extreme east of the region, on hillsides bordering Slovenia, the vineyards benefit from

Trentino-Alto Adige

KEY DOC WINES		MAIN GRAPE VARIETIES	PRICE
Alto Adige	■	Schiava, Lagrein	●●○
	□	Riesling, Gewurztraminer, others	●●○
Trentino	□	Pinot Grigio	●○
	■	Teroldego	●●

Friuli-Venezia Giulia

KEY DOC WINES		MAIN GRAPE VARIETIES	PRICE
Friuli Grave	■	Refosco, Merlot, Cabernet Franc, Cabernet Sauvignon	●●
	□	Tocai Friulano, Pinot Gris, others	●●
Collio	□	Tocai Friulano, Pinot Gris, others	●●●
Colli Orientali	□	Tocai Friulano, Pinot Gris, others	●●●

contrasting airflows from the Alps and the Adriatic. The most important DOC in terms of quantity is **Friuli Grave**. In this relatively flat plain, most of the wine is red; usually light and fruity blends of Bordeaux varieties. Refosco has a better reputation, giving wines with acidic, red berry flavours and rather harsh tannins that can develop mellow plum and bitter chocolate flavours as they age. It is the whites from the hills that have the highest reputation. Single varietal wines are made, but the best wines are often blends. Increasingly, they are also given some cask-ageing. The climate gives wines that combine a crisp varietal fruitiness with a certain depth of flavour. Even more expressive white wines come from the steeper hillside slopes of the **Colli Orientali** and the **Collio Goriziano** (or simply **Collio**). The accepted white varieties include a mixture of local specialities and celebrated imports. The former includes the widely planted Tocai Friulano (unconnected with the Tokaji of Hungary). This gives a full-bodied, rather neutral wine. Picolit makes prestigious and pricey dessert wines. Also among the more widely planted varieties are Pinot Bianco and Pinot Grigio, Gewurztraminer, Riesling and Chardonnay.

Veneto

The Veneto produces more DOC wine than any other region in Italy, with its climate tempered by the mountains to the north and the sea to the east. The DOC vineyards stretch from the mouth of the Piave east of Venice, to Lake Garda in the west. As far as many export markets are concerned, the three most important wines all come from the west, around the city of Verona. These are Valpolicella, Bardolino and Soave.

Valpolicella DOC is the second most important red DOC of Italy, at least as far as quantity is concerned. The vineyards lie east–west, in a band to the north of Verona. The main grape is the black Corvina, which has a sour cherry or herbal

Shrivelled grapes from Amarone, Valpolicella, Italy.

flavour. A number of other grapes are permitted, including Rondinella and Molinara. Valpolicella comes in a variety of forms. The basic wine is light and fruity, best drunk young, and comes from high-yielding vines grown in hot, fertile, valley floor sites. The very best straight Valpolicellas come from lower-yielding hillside sites, including the **Valpolicella Classico DOC** zone. It is common for a portion of the grapes used to make better Valpolicella wines to have gone through a drying process (*recioto*) to increase fruit concentration, alcohol and viscosity. **Amarone della Valpolicella DOC** is the most distinguished wine of the region. It is produced entirely from semi-dried grapes which, fully fermented, give a wine that is intense and long on the palate. Styles vary widely, depending on the extent of concentration that has taken place during the drying process; whether botrytis has been allowed to affect the grapes; and the degree of oxidation that has occurred during drying, vinification and ageing. Old-fashioned styles are wild, uncompromising port-like wines with high alcohol (14–15% abv) and many strange aromas (chocolate, dark rum, leather). Many producers are now aiming for a purer, cherry fruit style, still with the classic full body, seemingly sweet on the palate yet with a long bitter finish. **Recioto della Valpolicella DOC** is also made entirely from semi-dried grapes; however, the fermentation is stopped early, which gives a full-bodied red wine with a hint of sweetness. This may come as a shock to the unprepared. Finally, for a **Ripasso della Valpolicella DOC** wine, the unpressed skins from an Amarone or Recioto vinification are added to a basic Valpolicella. The re-fermentation that follows will give it additional viscosity and tannins, as well as some of the complex flavours of an Amarone.

Bardolino DOC, from the shores of Lake Garda, which has its own, cooler climate, is typically a light, uncomplicated wine made from the same grape varieties as Valpolicella. It is increasingly found as a rosé. Some growers are now making wines with more concentration and complexity, and **Bardolino Superiore** has been raised to DOCG status.

Soave DOC is the second best-selling DOC wine in Italy, after Chianti. For a long time its main selling point was that it was a wine that would offend nobody. Now, however, the quality has improved considerably and both **Soave Superiore** and **Recioto di Soave** have been promoted to DOCG level. The latter is a sweet wine made

Veneto			
KEY WINES		**MAIN GRAPE VARIETIES**	**PRICE**
Valpolicella DOC	■	Corvina, Rondinella, Molinara	●○
Amarone della Valpolicella DOC	■	Corvina, Rondinella, Molinara	●●●○
Recioto della Valpolicella DOC	■	Corvina, Rondinella, Molinara	●●●○
Soave DOC	□	Garganega	●○
Bardolino DOC	■■	Corvina, Rondinella, Molinara	●
Veneto IGT	■	Corvina, Merlot	●○

using the same drying technique as that for Recioto della Valpolicella. The main grape is Garganega, which has delicate flavours of almonds and some acidity, and when yields are low can display floral notes and grapey fruit. Garganega can be blended with the Trebbiano di Soave (an aristocratic cousin of the more earthy Trebbiano di Toscana) and Chardonnay, though this latter grape may account for no more than 30 per cent of the blend. Some of the best wines come from the Classico region, around the town of Soave itself. Much ordinary Soave is cheap, neutral, quaffing wine.

The **Veneto IGT** is a source of varietally labelled Merlot and some Valpolicella-style wines that are made in non-traditional ways.

Emilia-Romagna

This province lies to the south of the River Po, where the land is relatively fertile and capable of high yields. The region's best-known grape variety is the Lambrusco, which as a *vino da tavola* was once Italy's greatest commercial success on export markets. It has a screw-cap and the fermentation will have been stopped artificially to leave residual sugar, an alcoholic degree of between 7% and 9% abv, and a gentle sparkle. White Lambrusco is made from the same black grapes, with the skins removed immediately after pressing.

There are four DOCs for Lambrusco, and they are excellent examples of a wine style developed to match the local cuisine. The area is rich gastronomically and Bolognese sauces, Parma ham, Parmesan cheese and balsamic vinegar demand wines to refresh the palate. The drier DOC versions of the light sparkling Lambrusco, with their soft fruit, good acidity and low tannins perform this role admirably.

The four DOCs come from around the cities of Modena and Reggio Emilia. The best known are **Lambrusco di Sorbara DOC** and **Lambrusco Grasparossa di Castelvetro DOC**. The vines are trained high on trellises to maintain acidity, and the wine, at its best, is purple, dry, lightly sparkling, low in alcohol, fruity and refreshing. Amongst other things, to qualify for DOC status, the bottle must be closed with a mushroom stopper.

Perhaps the most popular still wine within the region is **Sangiovese di Romagna DOC**. Here clonal selection has a serious effect on the quality, and the better producers offer wines that are way above the rather humble image of the appellation. In the same part of the region, **Trebbiano di Romagna DOC** gives a light, refreshing, still or sparkling white wine.

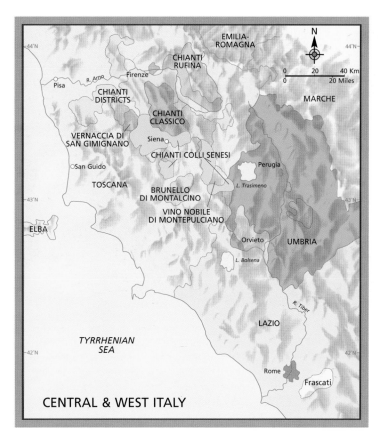

CENTRAL & WEST ITALY

Emilia-Romagna

KEY WINES		MAIN GRAPE VARIETIES	PRICE
Lambrusco Vino da Tavola	■	Lambrusco	●
Lambrusco (di Sorbara/ Grasparossa di Castelvetro) DOC	■	Lambrusco	●●
Sangiovese di Romagna DOC	■	Sangiovese	●○
Trebbiano di Romagna DOC	□	Trebbiano	●

Tuscany

KEY WINES		MAIN GRAPE VARIETIES	PRICE
Chianti Classico/ Ruffina/ Colli Senesi DOCG	■	Sangiovese	●●○○
Brunello di Montalcino DOCG	■	Sangiovese	●●●○
Vino Nobile di Montepulciano DOCG	■	Sangiovese	●●●○
Vernaccia di San Gimignano DOCG	□	Vernaccia	●●
Toscana IGT	■	Sangiovese, Cabernet Sauvignon, Merlot	●○○○

Tuscany

Tuscany is at the forefront of developments in viticulture and winemaking in Italy. Within its boundaries lie six of the country's DOCG areas and it is here that the 'Super-Tuscans' were created, the premium *Vini da Tavola* (as they used to be classified) and IGTs. The region is very hilly

Steam-cleaning of new oak *barriques* prior to their first filling.

This technique was called *governo*. Ageing, too, has been a matter of taste. Some growers believed in using the traditional large oak casks, called *botti*, but small oak *barriques* are now taking over. Normally, two different styles of wine are made: basic Chianti for early drinking, and *riserva*, aged in oak and bottle for over two years before release. The latter generally demands further bottle ageing.

Another quality version of Sangiovese is the **Brunello di Montalcino DOCG**, the best of which vie with the greatest Barolos for the title of the finest, and longest-lived, wines of Italy. Produced solely from the Sangiovese, normally the Sangiovese Grosso, around the town of Montalcino, to the south of Siena, it is an intensely robust wine, which benefits from considerable ageing. The bottle should be opened some time before consumption to let the full complexity of the wine's aroma to develop. By law, the wine must be at least four years old before it can be released on the market; two of these years must have been spent in cask. To give growers more flexibility, a more quickly saleable wine, **Rosso di Montalcino DOC**, has been developed. This is also made from the Sangiovese, but higher yields are permitted and only one year's ageing is required. Some producers use this DOC rather as a top Bordeaux château might have a second label.

Vino Nobile di Montepulciano was the first wine in Italy to be classified as a DOCG. It is made around the town of Montepulciano, under laws similar to those of Chianti Riserva, from another member of the Sangiovese family, the Prugnolo.

There is one white wine DOCG in Tuscany, **Vernaccia di San Gimignano**, produced in an area west of the Chianti Classico zone. This medium-bodied and rather neutral wine is now made for drinking young; traditionally it was made for ageing.

Many Tuscan producers make prestige wines, largely based on Sangiovese, Cabernet Sauvignon or Chardonnay, outside the DOC system. These are the so-called new-wave winemakers who have questioned tradition and whose influence is now extending throughout Italy. The movement originally started as a hobby in 1948, with the planting of Cabernet Sauvignon at the Tenuta San Guido in the Maremma. In 1968, a varietal Cabernet Sauvignon, Sassicaia, was launched, which was unique at that time in the Italian wine

with many sites providing excellent exposure to sunlight. Many of the vineyards are at altitude, and the resulting wide variations in temperature between day and night help the grapes develop aromas and retain their natural acidity. The maritime influence increases towards the west, creating ideal conditions for Bordeaux varieties.

The classic wine of Tuscany, and probably Italy, is Chianti. It is probably the traditional straw flask of Chianti, bought more for decorative use than for what was in the bottle, that has done more to harm the image of Italian wines than anything else. Happily, the quality and reputation of the wines of Tuscany have recovered from this low point. At the heart of the greater Chianti region, between the cities of Florence and Siena, lies the original Chianti, **Chianti Classico DOCG.** Seven satellites, each of which has DOCG status in its own right, surround this. Here the quality can vary considerably, but the constant factor is the Sangiovese grape, which must dominate any blend and is sometimes used on its own. It gives medium-bodied red wines that are high in acidity and tannins; its flavour combines sour cherry notes with a dusty, earthy character. Other black grapes grown include Canaiolo and Colorino and, increasingly, Cabernet, Merlot and even Syrah. The white grape, Trebbiano, traditionally also featured. Chiantis generally have lively acidity, with flavours of sour cherries and tea leaves, developing into earthy notes with age.

Traditionally, many of the better wines of Chianti were given added body by the inducement of a slight secondary fermentation in cask, ideally by the addition of must from semi-dried grapes.

world. This was followed most significantly in 1975 by Antinori's Tignanello, a blend of Sangiovese, with a little Cabernet Sauvignon, aged in *barriques*. The introduction of these two so-called Super-Tuscans may be seen as a turning point for the international image of Italian wines. From here many of the recent changes in Italian viticulture and vinification described in this chapter, began. With these two wines, small in production, but high in profile, Italy reached out to a new level of wine-lovers around the world.

Initially, the legal status of these wines, and the many followers that they inspired, was no more than that of *Vini da Tavola*. They were sold under individual brand names, often designed to catch the eye, or with one of a number of unofficial joint brand names, known as *Predicati*. The 1992 legislation attempted to address the anomaly whereby many of the country's finest wines remained outside the quality system. The introduction of the new category, **Toscana IGT**, allows wines made in non-traditional styles to be awarded Quality Wine status. With its reputation now fully established, the coastal region of **Bolgheri**, the source of many of the original Super-Tuscans, has been elevated to DOC status.

Marche

The most famous wine of this region, which borders the Adriatic, is Verdicchio, traditionally sold in a green, amphora-shaped bottle. This presentation may well have deterred many potential consumers, but this dry white wine can be very good. The use of cold fermentation and stainless steel is common among those producers aiming at the export markets. There are two DOCs incorporating the Verdicchio grape variety in the name; the more readily found is the **Verdicchio dei Castelli di Jesi**. In style it can range from light and fresh to surprisingly full, rich and complex, and the subtle nuances of fennel and other herbs make it an ideal partner for white fish.

The most important red wine DOC in the region is **Rosso Conero**, produced close to the city of Ancona, almost entirely from the Montepulciano grape. This produces wines that are often fuller-bodied, deeper-coloured, though lower in tannin, than those produced from the Sangiovese.

Umbria

Umbria has a topography and climate similar to Tuscany's, but without any maritime influence. Its main wine town is Perugia. Historically, Umbria is known for its white wines from **Orvieto**. These used to be predominantly sweet, but there is now

a tendency for them to be dry. However, there is also some production of *abboccato* wine. Here the *tuffeau* soils are similar to those of Vouvray in the Loire valley, and the best wines too have the flavour of crisp apples. Most, however, are simple, with only a little refreshing acidity and rather neutral. The principal grape is the Trebbiano (locally called Procanico), which may be blended with the more interesting Grechetto, Malvasia and Verdello.

Latium

White wines dominate in Latium and, of these, it is **Frascati DOC** that is best known, having originally built up its reputation on draught in the *trattorie* of Rome. Now its fresh, clean taste and pale colour appeal to many who want to play safe. The basic grapes in the blend are the Malvasia (which develops quickly and shows light, pleasing aromas, full body and low acidity) and the ubiquitous Trebbiano. The best wines, with most character, are those in which the Malvasia del Lazio dominates. With rare exceptions, these wines are simple, low-priced and neutral in style.

Abruzzo

On the leg of Italy, Abruzzo is behind the knee, a region of mountains sliding down through hills to the sea. Whilst most Italian vinegrowers seem to believe that fragmentation in the DOC system generally leads to higher prices, here they have gone for simplicity and, until recently, there were only two: **Montepulciano d'Abruzzo DOC** for the red wines, and **Trebbiano d'Abruzzo DOC** for the white.

The Montepulciano grape is full of colour, with moderate acidity and, in its better wines, quite

Marche			
KEY DOC WINES		**MAIN GRAPE VARIETIES**	**PRICE**
Verdicchio dei Castelli di Jesi	☐	Verdicchio	●
Rosso Conero	■	Montepulciano	●●

Umbria		
KEY DOC WINE	**MAIN GRAPE VARIETIES**	**PRICE**
Orvieto ☐	Trebbiano, Grechetto, Malvasia, Verdello	●

Latium		
KEY DOC WINE	**MAIN GRAPE VARIETIES**	**PRICE**
Frascati ☐	Malvasia, Trebbiano	●

Abruzzo			
KEY DOC WINES		**MAIN GRAPE VARIETIES**	**PRICE**
Montepulciano d'Abruzzo	■	Montepulciano	●○
Trebbiano d'Abruzzo	☐	Trebbiano	●

Campania			
KEY DOCG WINE		**MAIN GRAPE VARIETY**	**PRICE**
Taurasi	■	Aglianico	●●●○

Puglia			
KEY WINES		**MAIN GRAPE VARIETIES**	**PRICE**
Salice Salentino DOC	■	Negroamaro, Malvasia Nera	●○
Copertino DOC	■	Negroamaro, Malvasia Nera	●○
IGT wines	■	Primitivo, Negroamaro, others	●○

tannic. However, the majority of wines are made in the ubiquitous co-operative cellars, seeking to make early drinking, simple wines. (Note: the Montepulciano grape variety grown in Abruzzo should not be confused with the Tuscan town of Montepulciano, which produces wine from the Sangiovese variety.)

Campania

It was in Campania, with the Bay of Naples at its centre, that the finest wines of the classical era were made, with the name of one of the local grapes, the Greco, bearing witness to its origins. The volcanic soils are ideal for the production of fine wines. Sadly, since then, standards have declined and it is only in recent years that a small number of growers have sought to recreate the quality of the past.

Taurasi, a red wine made from the high-quality Aglianico grape, has been promoted to DOCG status. The Aglianico is thick-skinned and retains its acidity, allowing it to be harvested very late, after complex flavours have been allowed to develop. Along with Nebbiolo, this is one of the latest-ripening grapes in Italy and produces full-bodied, tannic wines, with crisp acidity and flavours of dark plum and smoky spice. These wines need ageing. A minimum of three years, with at least one in cask, is required before sale.

Puglia

Lying on the heel of Italy, Puglia has a hot, rather than a warm, climate. Along with Sicily, it has the largest wine production of all Italy and historically it was the source for much of the blending wine that was shipped around the world. Even now, DOC production accounts for less than 5 per cent of the total, though there is a distinct move towards the production of quality wine. On the one side, there is much planting of the best-known French varieties; on the other, there is a drive to make great wines from the best of the local varieties, the Negroamaro, Uva di Troia and Primitivo (Zinfandel). The latter is used for full-bodied reds with high alcohol levels and powerful spiced berry flavours. Nearly all of these appear as **IGT wines**.

Vineyards on the slopes of Monte Vulture, Basilicata.

The two DOCs with more than a local reputation are **Salice Salentino** and **Copertino**; both can be wines of almost port-like medicinal intensity made from the Negroamaro, with a little help from Malvasia Nera.

Basilicata

The instep of Italy is a desolate mountainous region, where the Aglianico grape is king and is responsible for the one DOC wine, **Aglianico del Vulture**, which can appear under a number of guises: young fruit-driven reds, and *vecchio*, aged for a minimum of three years.

Sicily

The largest of Italy's regions also has the largest area under vines, with the vineyards spread widely on the island. The main production, however, comes from the western end. Co-operative cellars have profited considerably from EU financial support. The region has its own quality award, which may be given at any level of wine. This is symbolised by a Q on the label. An increasing amount of good quality wine is appearing as Sicilian IGT. These may be made from indigenous

Basilicata			
KEY DOC WINE		**MAIN GRAPE VARIETY**	**PRICE**
Aglianico del Vulture	■	Aglianico	●●○○

Sicily			
KEY WINES		**MAIN GRAPE VARIETIES**	**PRICE**
Sicilia IGT	☐	Chardonnay, Catarratto, others	●○○○
	■	Nero d'Avola, Cabernet Sauvignon, Syrah, others	●○○○

grapes such as Nero d'Avola, or blends with international varieties for example Catarratto/Chardonnay. Quality varies, with much wine being shipped in bulk to disappear into anonymous blends. The better wines come from the mountainous interior of the island and from the slopes of Mount Etna, where the climate is cooler. A few estates have demonstrated beyond doubt that Sicily is capable of making wines to compete at the very top international level, and the very best wines from both international and Italian varieties can command superpremium prices.

The fortified wine Marsala, produced from vineyards around the port of the same name, is described in Chapter 36.

23 Spain

Spain has a long wine history. Columella, author of the most detailed ancient Roman text about winemaking, came from a family that owned vineyards near what is now Cadiz. At that time the country was a major producer for Rome itself. However, there have probably been more changes in the wine industry since Spain joined the European Union than there have been in all the previous centuries. Modernisation has come in a rush, and this has happened not just in the vineyards and in the wineries, but also in legislation. All is in a state of flux, and to talk of the Spanish wine industry now is to take no more than a snapshot at a particular moment. Spain has a much larger area under vines than either France or Italy, but its annual production is much less than either of them. This is because much of the vineyard area is still planted at very low vine densities, with vines that yield small crops due to the very arid climate and their old age.

WINE LAWS

The wine laws of Spain are continually developing as new regions seek to gain official status for their wines. As in some other countries, there is increasing fragmentation. The current hierarchy is, in decreasing order:

Denominación de Origen Calificada (DOC or DOCa). At present there are two: Rioja and Priorat.

Denominación de Origen – Pago (DO Pago). This is a new category that is just coming into effect. It applies to outstanding single estates, in places outside the DO system, that use only their own grapes to make their wines. In 2004 only two vineyards had qualified.

Denominación de Origen (DO). The number of these has now risen to 60, though many are of only marginal importance. Like French AOC wines, these should be wines of a certain minimum quality, satisfying specifications covering grape varieties, viticulture and location, and should be in a style that is of more than purely local interest.

Vino de la Tierra (VdlT) is the equivalent of the French *Vin de Pays*. While there are currently about 40 of these, only two are of significant, and growing, commercial importance. These are Vino de la Tierra de Castilla and Vino de la Tierra de Castilla y León.

Below this is simple **Vino de Mesa**.

Ageing

Every bottle of DO or DOC wine carries a numbered back-label issued by the local *Consejo Regulador*, or controlling body, guaranteeing the classification of the wine. As well as certifying the region of origin, how long the wine has been aged may be noted. There are minimum requirements for each of the four categories, and generally these apply nationally to all DOs. Some regions – Rioja is an example – may demand additional ageing to qualify.

Vino Joven (literally 'young wine') is a wine that may or may not have spent some time in cask before being bottled in the year following the vintage, for immediate release. **Crianza** red wines must be at least two years old and aged a minimum of six months in small oak casks before release. White and rosé wines must be at least one year old. (There is a move to create a new category that requires some cask-ageing, but lies between *vino joven* and *crianza*.) **Reservas** are generally wines from selected vats of the better vintages. The reds must have been aged in cask and bottle for a minimum of three years, of which a minimum of one year must be in oak cask. The balance between ageing in wood and bottle will be a decision for the individual producer. White and rosé wines must be aged for two years, with a minimum of six months in cask. **Gran Reserva** wines should be produced only in exceptional vintages. Red wine must be at least five years old before release, having spent at least two years in wood and three in bottle. White and rosé wines should be aged for at least four years, with at least six months in oak. Many wines that are labelled Reserva or Gran Reserva have been aged far more than the legal minimum. White and rosé Reserva and Gran Reserva wines are very rare.

GRAPE VARIETIES

Tempranillo takes its name from the Spanish word *temprano*, which means early, and its great advantage is that it is early ripening. Although not Spain's most widely planted variety it is the country's premier grape and appears throughout most of the vineyards of northern Spain, under a variety of names. It likes chalky soil and grows well in a cool climate. Its strawberry-scented wines are quite low in acidity, and it shows its best when blended with other varieties. It ages well. **Garnacha** is the Grenache of southern France and is now the most widely planted black grape in Spain. It gives a big yield of wine high in alcohol, with a tendency to mature early. It is widely used for rosados. Plantings of **Graciano** are now very limited, because of its low yields. It is grown mainly in Rioja, where it is used in the

finest wines. Small quantities are used to add powerful aromas, body and tannins to help the wines age. **Mazuelo** (Rioja) or **Cariñena** (rest of Spain) is the French Carignan. It gives wines that are high in acidity, tannin and colour. A small proportion of this makes an ideal blend with Tempranillo. It should not be confused with the region Cariñena DO, south-east of Rioja and Navarra. **Monastrell** is the Mourvèdre of southern France. It is grown in south-eastern DOs such as Yecla and Jumilla, and gives very dark, powerful spicy wines.

Viura (Rioja) or **Macabéo** (Catalunya) is the same variety as the Macabeo/Maccabeu of the south of France. It gives whites with good fruit and acidity, but to achieve this, yields must be restricted. It is used in Rioja, and appears, usually blended with **Parellada** and **Xarel-lo** in Catalunya. **Malvasia** makes full-bodied heavy whites, and is usually the main component of the very best, traditional-style Riojas, where its richness can balance the frequent lightness of the Viura. In the Basque and Galician parts of the Atlantic coast,

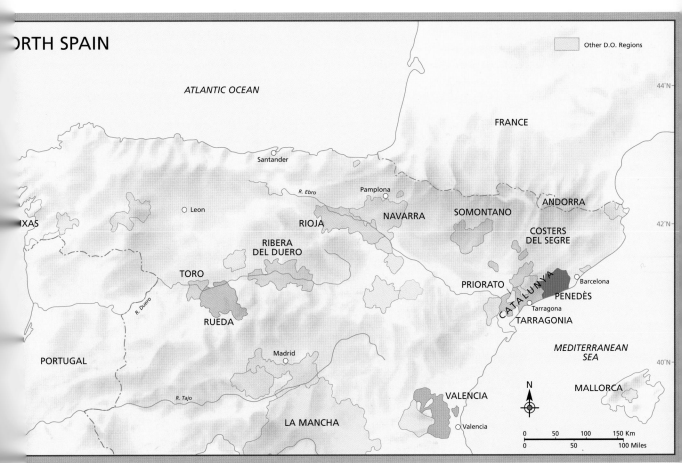

a number of light, crisp, aromatic varieties are grown, of which the most important is **Albariño**.

International varieties are becoming increasingly important. In many parts of Spain, the traditional local varieties have shown little potential for quality wines, and better wines can be more easily made with varieties such as **Cabernet Sauvignon, Merlot** and **Chardonnay**. These and other international varieties are now established and widespread, especially in the north-east. They sometimes appear as blends with local varieties. In this role, they give the consumer a recognisable word on the label, and can add character to the blend, while the local variety component may provide the volume and gives local producers a commercial outlet for grapes that may otherwise struggle to find a market.

REGIONS AND WINES

The principal DO regions of Spain can be grouped together into six geographical regions, each of which has some commonality of climate and grape varieties. The six unofficial groupings are the Upper Ebro, Catalunya, the Duero valley, the north-west (Galicia), the Levant and the Meseta.

The Upper Ebro

There are vineyards along much of the River Ebro, from the Cantabrian mountains to the Mediterranean, but the finest wines, perhaps, of all Spain come from its upper reaches, in the region of **Rioja**, where the mountains give it protection on three sides. The region takes its name from the Río Oja, a tributary of the Ebro. There were vineyards here in Roman times, but the modern history of the region begins when phylloxera destroyed the vineyards of Bordeaux. Many of the Bordeaux merchants, grapegrowers and winemakers moved to northern Spain and established themselves in the region. It is because of this that the trade has been based, until recently, around merchants and their brand names, rather than around vineyards and growers. More recently, the liberation of Spain from the Franco era led to a renaissance of the trade, with a number of new companies being established. This also led to a move away from wines that had spent many years in wood to those that were aged longer still in bottle. In spite of this, the period of ageing still often exceeds the minimum requirements, which in Rioja are greater than for other regions. For example, a *crianza* red wine must spend a minimum of twelve months in cask, rather than the six months stipulated for other DOs. Within the recent past there has also been a decided move towards wines produced by single estate and even from single named vineyards, rather than by blending in the merchants' cellars.

Rioja is a region of small growers, many of whom sell their grapes to merchants or to the co-operative cellars. The vineyards are generally planted with bush vines; wire-training is permitted

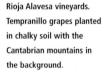

Rioja Alavesa vineyards. Tempranillo grapes planted in chalky soil with the Cantabrian mountains in the background.

for experimental purposes only. Three-quarters of the production of Rioja is of red wine, with 15 per cent rosé and 10 per cent white. The tiny plantings of varieties such as Cabernet Sauvignon in Rioja are generally historical relics. The permitted ones are all traditional varieties. Tempranillo, with smaller components of Graciano and Mazuelo for the more expensive reds, Garnacha for the less expensive *vino joven* wines and rosados, and Viura and Malvasia for whites (Garnacha Blanca is also permitted).

The capital of the province of La Rioja is the city of Logroño, on the River Ebro. This is used as a reference point for the three distinct subregions. Generally speaking, a bottle labelled Rioja will be a blend from more than one of these subregions. The **Rioja Alavesa** is situated to the west of Logroño, on the north bank of the Ebro. The climate is influenced by the Atlantic and is comparatively cool. It has the highest rainfall of the three subregions. The soil is very chalky and the wines are perhaps the lightest of Rioja, but have the most finesse. The predominant grape variety is Tempranillo. The **Rioja Alta** area is also to the west of Logroño, but to the south of the Ebro. The soils are largely of clay, but many are reddish, having a high proportion of iron. The clay soils are better for white wines made from Viura and the iron-rich soils are best for reds from Tempranillo. In the river valley there is some alluvial soil, which suits the Malvasia. The climate is warmer and drier than in the Alavesa, but is still largely maritime. Many of the largest *bodegas* are based in Logroño or the smaller town of Haro. The **Rioja Baja** is situated to the east of Logroño, mainly on the south bank. Here the climate is continental, with hotter summers and more severe winters. The soils are largely heavy clays and the dominant grape variety is the Garnacha. Most of the *vino joven* of Rioja comes from here.

Red wines now range quite widely in style. Traditional Reserva and Gran Reserva reds saw very long periods of oak-aging, resulting in a degree of controlled oxidation and the development of savoury aromas of meat and caramel underpinning the sweet, soft strawberry fruit. These wines were often relatively pale brick-red in colour with distinct browning at the rim. The more modern wines seek to preserve fruit, are generally darker and show more of the tinned strawberry and plum fruit of the Tempranillo. With less extended oxidative ageing to allow the evolution and integration of fruit and oak components, modern Crianzas and Reservas sometimes show obvious oak, and aromas of vanilla, coconut and toast.

The Upper Ebro			
KEY WINES		**MAIN GRAPE VARIETIES**	**PRICE**
Rioja DOC	■ ■	Tempranillo, Garnacha, Mazuelo, Graciano	●●○○+
	□	Viura, Malvasia, Garnacha Blanca	●●○○
Navarra DO	■	Tempranillo, Garnacha, Cabernet Sauvignon, Merlot	●○○
	■	Garnacha	●○
Somontano DO	□	Macabeo, Chardonnay, Chenin Blanc, Gewurztraminer	●●
	■ ■	Local varieties, Cabernet Sauvignon, Merlot, Pinot Noir	●○

Traditionally, the white wines were aged for extended periods in American oak and developed a deep golden colour and savoury, nutty flavours. This deliberately oxidised style is a unique, but rather acquired taste. Modern white wines are often fermented at low temperature, stored in stainless steel and bottled when young to preserve the maximum amount of fruit. Interestingly enough, some of the more modern *bodegas* are also producing oak-aged white wines, but using new French oak rather than the traditional American barrels.

Sample of wine being taken from a new oak cask in Rioja.

Historically **Navarra**'s reputation has been for its rosé wines. These were made from the Garnacha grape, frequently exceeded 15% abv and oxidised early. They were scarcely to the taste of modern wine drinkers! The region understood this and moved rapidly in another direction. This has mainly been the production of quality red wines. Rosés (now made in a lighter, fresher style) are still important, but white wine accounts for no more than 5 per cent of the total production. The 18 000 hectares of Navarra vineyards lie downstream from Rioja and extend from the valley floor to the foothills of the Pyrenées. The

Vineyards in Costers del
Segre.

of the Pyrenées to the north of Zaragoza. It has
a cool climate and plenty of rain. Here a broad
range of imported French varieties is planted,
including Cabernet Sauvignon, Merlot and Pinot
Noir (for reds), and Chardonnay, Chenin Blanc
and Gewurztraminer (for whites). The modern
wines are generally sold under varietal names; the
whites are more widely seen than the reds. These
are replacing the traditional reds and rosados
made from local varieties.

Catalunya

Catalunya, with its long tradition of nationalism,
has fiercely seized upon the Spanish policy of
giving power to the regions. This has traditionally
been the heartland of Cava production and the
'big three' Cava varieties (Parellada, Xarel-lo and
Macabeo) are widely planted here. They are
important for still wines as well as sparkling.

Catalunya is a recently created DO, which covers
the whole province, with a broad range of
climates and wine styles. It came into existence
largely to enable the blending of wines from the
various areas to create the possibility of putting
large quantities of the same wine on the market
under a single name.

Until recently, **Penedés** was the dominant
appellation for the Catalan still wines. The
vineyards lie to the south-west of Barcelona from
the Mediterranean coast up into the hills. As a
result, it has three distinct climatic zones. The
hottest is on the coastal plain where the climate is
Mediterranean, with hot dry summers, producing
mainly full-bodied red wines from Garnacha and
Monastrell. Inland, in the valleys, the climate is
more temperate, with the vineyards supplying
much of the white wine used for the production
of Cava. Further into the hills, vines are grown up
to 800 metres above sea level. Here the climate is
cool and international varieties such as Riesling,
Gewurztraminer and Pinot Noir are grown.
Traditionally, vines have been pruned *en vaso*, a
form of bush-training, but wire-training is now
becoming more common, more particularly for
the French and German varieties.

result is that there are broad variations of both
soil and climate. The vineyards of Navarra have
traditionally been planted with the same varieties
as Rioja, with Garnacha predominating, though a
certain amount of pragmatism has resulted in a
number of other varieties being permitted. These
are Cabernet Sauvignon and Merlot for red wines
and Chardonnay and Moscatel for whites. The
investment in the vineyards has been matched in
the cellars, where small oak barrels are now
being used more widely. Temperature-controlled
fermentation tanks for the white and rosé wines
are now giving much better results. The
traditional wines are similar to Rioja in style,
though many reds gain more colour and aromatic
black berry fruit from the use of Cabernet and/or
Merlot. There are also varietal wines made from
traditional and international varieties.

A loose translation of the name **Somontano** is
'under the mountains' and it lies in the foothills

As well as the diversity of climates, there is also
a wide range of grape varieties grown within the
region. Historically, its reputation has been based
upon white wines made from the local trio of
Parellada, Xarel-lo and Macabeo. In recent years,
the influential Torres company has led the way
in planting many new, international varieties,
including Chardonnay, Riesling, Gewurztraminer
and Sauvignon Blanc. Few of the white wines see

Catalunya			
KEY WINES		**MAIN GRAPE VARIETIES**	**PRICE**
Catalunya DO	☐	Various, including Parellada, Chardonnay	●○○
	■	Various, including Tempranillo, Cabernet Sauvignon	●○○
Penedés DO	☐	Various, including Parellada, Chardonnay	●○○
	■	Various, including Tempranillo, Cabernet Sauvignon	●●○○+
Costers del Segre DO	■	Cabernet Sauvignon, Tempranillo	●○○
	☐	Chardonnay	●○○
Tarragona DO	■	Grenache, Cariñena, Cabernet Sauvignon, Syrah, Pinot Noir	●○○
Priorat DOC	■	Grenache Cariñena, Cabernet Sauvignon, Syrah, Pinot Noir	●●●○+

ageing in cask. The best display very expressive varietal fruit.

Historically, powerful oak-aged wines made from the traditional Garnacha and Monastrell grapes dominated red wine production. Now there are also important plantings of Tempranillo, Cabernet Sauvignon, Cabernet Franc, Merlot and Pinot Noir. There can be little doubt that the broad welcome for French as well as Spanish varieties has enabled the local growers to improve the quality of their wines and enhance the reputation of the region. Because of the broad spectrum of styles and qualities, prices for these wines cover a wide range.

Costers del Segre lies inland close to the town of Lleida. A subsidiary of a Cava company has invested heavily in vineyards and a winery and dominates production here. The climate is continental and rainfall is low, but because the vineyards are classified as 'experimental', irrigation is permitted. The main plantings are of Cabernet Sauvignon, Tempranillo and Chardonnay.

Tarragona comprises a broad range of wines from sweet dessert (and altar) wine produced in the coastal plain, to wines that rival those of Priorat, up in the hills.

Priorat (Priorato) is the new fashionable wine of Spain. This region of craggy hills has a unique soil known as *llicorella*, consisting of layers of red slate, with small particles of mica that sparkle in the sun and reflect heat. Traditional Priorat is a monstrously alcoholic red wine, made from low-yielding old Garnacha and Cariñena vines. Many saw long periods in oak – sometimes in a *solera* – and began to develop *rancio* aromas (well-hung game, mushrooms!). However, it is the modern wines, made from Cabernet Sauvignon, Syrah and Pinot Noir, along with the traditional Garnacha and Cariñena, that raised the profile of this region, with the result that it has gained DOC status. In youth, the modern-style wines show very intense bramble fruit with supporting flavours of new oak. The powerful tannins and massive fruit extract give them a long ageing potential.

The Duero Valley

While the valley of the River Douro is perhaps best known for Port wines, in Spain, under the name of the Duero, it has vineyards producing outstanding wines of worldwide reputation. This part of the country experiences a continental climate, which can be very harsh. Altitude makes for cool nights and there is also an ideal long, dry, ripening season for the grapes.

New vineyards being established in Priorato.

The Duero Valley			
KEY DO WINES		**MAIN GRAPE VARIETIES**	**PRICE**
Toro	■	Tempranillo	●●○
Rueda	□	Verdejo, Sauvignon Blanc	●○
Ribera del Duero	■	Tempranillo	●●●○+

Chalky soils in Ribera del Duero.

Vines supported on low pergolas and farm buildings amidst the pine forest. Fornelos, Galicia (DO Rias Baixas), Spain.

Toro is the first DO region upstream from Portugal. Here the dominant grape is Tempranillo. The extremely hot summers give wines high in alcohol; 14.5% abv is common. The wines are more full-bodied and richer than Riojas, but do not generally have the same ageing potential. In the *vino joven* wines, there is generally a proportion of Grenache; *Reservas* and *Gran Reservas* can be exceptionally full-coloured and tannic when young.

The town of **Rueda** lies to the south of Valladolid. Historically, it has made sherry-style *vinos generosos*, but its image was reborn in 1972 when a Rioja-based company established a winery in the town to make light white wines. The region's chalky soil and continental climate, with cool summer nights, attracted them. The traditional grape of the region, the Verdejo, produces surprisingly elegant wines, as the cool evenings encourage aromatic flavours to develop in the grapes while retaining acidity. Sauvignon Blanc and Viura may now also be used. Modern vinification techniques, such as harvesting at night and fermenting at low temperatures under inert gas to prevent contact with air, preserve the naturally aromatic fruit of these varieties. The resulting wines are crisp and light, with aromas of peaches and melons. They are generally best consumed while young, though some, especially those made from the Sauvignon Blanc, may be barrel-aged. The traditional sherry-style wines are still made, though this is a niche market and is in decline.

Ribera del Duero is a comparatively young DO, which includes some of the country's most prestigious red wines. Its vineyards are found along both banks of the river. Among the reasons for the quality are the high altitude and the limestone-rich soils in the better parts of this region. As in Rueda and Toro, altitude means warm summer days followed by cool summer nights. The result is that Tempranillo from Ribeira del Duero has much thicker, darker skins and higher acidity levels than Tempranillo from Rioja. The resulting wines are darker, with more powerful and astringent tannins, and a much more dark fruit blackberry and plum character. The best wines take well to new French oak, and may be compared in style (and quality) to Classed Growth Médoc. In fact, for more than a century, there have been plantings of Bordeaux varieties such as the Cabernet Sauvignon, Malbec and Merlot alongside the traditional Tempranillo and Garnacha. However, with the exception of Vega Sicilia, most of the best wines are 100 per cent Tempranillo.

Vega Sicilia is aged for many years in small casks, oak vats or concrete tanks before bottling. This formula produces wines of intense complexity. For a long time, these were Spain's most prestigious and most expensive wines. Those titles now have contenders from Priorato and from the growing number of single vineyard, 'high-expression' Riojas. Vega Sicilia was long thought to be a 'one-off', and for over a century, little of its glory reflected on the surrounding region. Starting in the 1980s, modern *bodegas* have shown they are capable of producing wines of similar quality for earlier bottling.

The North-West (Galicia)

The exceptionally damp climate of the northern Atlantic coast of Spain seems scarcely conducive to the production of wine. However, Albariño (the same as the Alvarinho of *vinho verde* over the border in northern Portugal) can give wines of

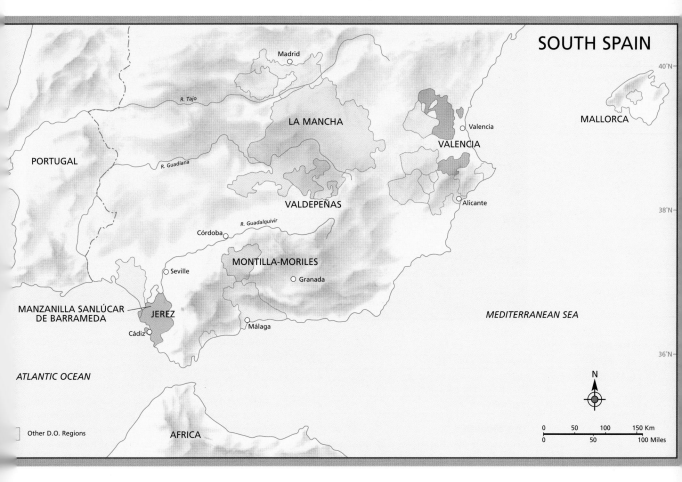

SOUTH SPAIN

Madrid

LA MANCHA

PORTUGAL

R. Tajo

R. Guadiana

VALENCIA

Valencia

MALLORCA

40°N

VALDEPEÑAS

38°N

R. Guadalquivir

Córdoba

MONTILLA-MORILES

Seville

Granada

Alicante

MEDITERRANEAN SEA

MANZANILLA SANLÚCAR
DE BARRAMEDA

JEREZ

Cádiz

Málaga

36°N

ATLANTIC OCEAN

N

Other D.O. Regions

AFRICA

| 0 | 50 | 100 | 150 Km |
| 0 | | 50 | 100 Miles |

---

distinction, which are growing in popularity. The wines of **Rías Baixas** have a distinctive peachy flavour and, with their high acidity and light body, sometimes enlivened with a hint of CO_2, they make an ideal accompaniment for the seafood of the region. Demand is high locally, in the rest of Spain and worldwide. The small production is often disrupted by bad weather, and vintages vary widely in quantity and quality. The result is that this wine, when it can be obtained, is never cheap.

The Levant

The Levant is the region on the Mediterranean coast south of Catalunya.

Historically, **Valencia** was an exporter of bulk wine of little reputation. However, there has been considerable investment in both the vineyards and wineries of the region; as a result it has created its own image as a source of value-for-money, uncomplicated wines. Many are simply red or white table wines made in a style to meet the needs of a particular market.

As recently as the mid-1980s hybrids dominated and low-quality local varieties still account for

most of the plantings. Now, Tempranillo is beginning to take over for red wines, and Macabeo for whites. There are also experimental plantings of international varieties, including Cabernet Sauvignon and Chardonnay, particularly in the inland region of **Utiel-Requena**. A local speciality is Moscatel de Valencia, a highly perfumed sweet wine which may or may not be fortified.

Further south, a number of DO red wines are produced, which are finding placings on international markets: these include **Yecla** and **Jumilla**. Monastrell (Mourvèdre) dominates these deep black wines; they are full-bodied, high in alcohol and have tarry black fruit aromas, sometimes with hints of meat or licorice.

The North-West (Galicia)			
KEY DO WINE		**MAIN GRAPE VARIETY**	**PRICE**
Rías Baixas	☐	Albariño	●●○

The Levant			
KEY WINES		**MAIN GRAPE VARIETIES**	**PRICE**
Valencia	■	Local varieties	●
	☐	Local varieties	●

Widely spaced, low, bush-trained vines in La Mancha, in late spring. Note the vast expanse of flat, arid vineyards.

The Meseta			
KEY WINES		**MAIN GRAPE VARIETIES**	**PRICE**
La Mancha DO	☐	Airén	●
	■	Tempranillo, Cabernet Sauvignon, Syrah	●○
Valdepeñas DO	■	Tempranillo	●

The Meseta

Almost half of Spain's total wine production comes from this vast central plateau. Most vines are grown by smallholders and much of their produce is vinified in co-operative wineries. **La Mancha** is the home of the world's most widely planted white grape variety, the Airén. This may seem bizarre for it is found in few other places in the world and indeed in few other places in Spain. This is a grape without ambition, for most of the wine that it produces is distilled for ultimate appearance as Brandy de Jerez. The climate is hot, dry and extremely continental. The vines are planted far apart and grow so close to the ground that the leaf canopy not only protects the bunches of fruit, but also cools the surrounding ground. This helps preserve whatever moisture there might be in the soil, though irrigation has been permitted since 1996. Traditionally, the wine was stored in enormous clay *tinajas*, like monumental Ali Baba baskets, buried to leave visible no more than the neck. In the days before refrigeration, this was the best that could be done to keep the wine cool.

Now all, or almost all, is changing. Foreign buyers have recognised the potential of the region and have imposed their will upon the cellars. For white wines, the grapes are picked a fortnight or more earlier than in the past. This gives wines with a lower degree of alcohol and fresh acidity. In the cellars, stainless steel is omnipresent and fruity wines are the order of the day. Much of the financing for this has come from the EU. Consequently, a broad range of varieties, including Tempranillo, Cabernet Sauvignon and Syrah, is joining the vast plantings of Airén. In addition, some small estates are producing outstanding wines, most with no higher classification than *Vino de la Tierra*, because they may have chosen to plant 'foreign' grape varieties. While this is primarily a region for cheap, but sound wines, some are excellent – and expensive!

Valdepeñas is an enclave in the south of La Mancha. Its name literally means 'valley of stones'. The wines are mainly red, made from Tempranillo to which a little Airén is sometimes added. The tradition is for them to be aged in old American oak barrels, though some young wines are now made by carbonic maceration.

Portugal

As far as wine production is concerned, Portugal's entry into the EU has come as an unqualified blessing. It has released funds to modernise an industry that had been stagnant under the long dictatorship of António Salazar. At first, the emphasis was on improving the cellars and their equipment; now money is going into the vineyards. Greater respect is being given to the indigenous grape varieties, and these are now being featured more on labels. Another development has been the decline in importance of the co-operative cellar while, at the same time, the single estate, or *quinta*, has come to the fore. As in many other countries, there has been a decline in the quantity of wine that is being produced, but there has been a distinct increase in quality.

Portugal has a profusion of indigenous varieties, which are often known by several different names in different regions. To confuse matters further, the same name may refer to different grape varieties in different regions – a system of nomenclature that appears to have developed in order to frustrate anyone trying to understand Portuguese wines! Alongside the indigenous varieties, the additional flexibility granted in the production of *vinhos regionais* (for example *vinho regional* Alentejano) has led to increased plantings of French varieties such as Syrah and Cabernet Sauvignon. These are often blended with the local varieties.

CLIMATE

Despite the fact that it is only a small country, Portugal has much climatic diversity. The most important influence is the Atlantic Ocean and much of the country has a maritime climate with warm summers and cool, wet winters. However, in some of the inland vineyard areas (Douro, Dão, Alentejo/Alentejano), the climate is continental, hot and dry. The large differences in annual rainfall and average temperature partly account for the diversity of wine styles.

WINE LAWS

As in most of the other wine countries of the European Union, there are four different levels of wines in Portugal. These are:

Denominação de Origem Controlada (DOC), the equivalent of *Appellation Contrôlée*.

Indicação de Proveniencia Regulamentada (IPR), the equivalent of VDQS.

Vinho regional, regional wine, the equivalent of *Vin de Pays*.

Vinho de mesa, table wine.

In 1999 Portugal's quality wine legislation was revised, with the result that most wines that had IPR status have been promoted to DOC. All IPR and DOC wines can be identified by a paper seal (*Selo de Origem*). Originally, this was stuck on the neck of the bottle with a strip under the capsule and over the cork. Now this often takes the form of a back-label.

In addition, there are two terms, Reserva and

PORTUGAL

R. Minho

VINHO VERDE

Oporto

Vila Nova de Gaia   R. Douro

DOURO

42°N

Viseu

BAIRRADA   DÃO

Coimbra   Beiras

ATLANTIC OCEAN

R. Mondego

40°N   40°N

R. Tejo

SPAIN

RIBATEJO

Ribatejano

Estremadura

Lisbon

ALENTEJO

N

Terras do Sado   Alentejano

38°N   38°N

R. Guadiana

0   40   80 Km
0   20   40 Miles

DÃO *(capitals)* = DOC
Estremadura *(lower case)* = VR

Other Wine Producing Regions

Faro

Garrafeira, which indicate potential additional quality. A **Reserva** wine must come from a single vintage, stated on the label, and it must have passed a tasting panel. If it is a wine of DOC status, it must have a higher percentage of natural alcohol than the minimum decreed by law for that DOC. **Garrafeira** can be applied to all wines, not just those at the level of DOC. In addition to

Cruzeta training in Vinho Verde, with two vines planted against each post.

meeting the parameters needed for a Reserva wine, a red wine must also be aged for at least two years in cask and a further year in bottle. White Garrafeira wines must spend at least six months in cask and six months in bottle.

REGIONS AND WINES
Northern Portugal

The **Vinho Verde** region lies mainly north of the River Douro as far as the River Minho, the border with Spain, and up to approximately 90 kilometres inland from the coast. The climate is warm in the summer; however it suffers from extremely high rainfall, mainly during the winter, but also, to a lesser extent during the summer and at vintage time. Because of this, vines have been planted to offer grape bunches exposure to the air. Historically, the vines were often trained up trees and, until the 1974 revolution, it was forbidden to plant fields of vines in the region. Most recently planted vineyards are in the normal double-cordon system, whilst traditional ones use the *cruzeta*, a high-trained cordon system. Vinho Verde literally means 'green wine', but its name has nothing to do with the colour of the wine. Indeed, nearly half the total production is of red wine. Verde refers to its youth or greenness, as traditionally it is the latest vintage that is drunk. A broad range of grapes, varying with the subregions, is used to make the wine, but the most important for white wines are the Loureiro and Padernã. These supply a Riesling-like fresh aroma and crisp acidity. In the north of the region, more expensive white wines, often from single *quintas*, are made from the Alvarinho (= Albariño) grape. These have higher alcohol than other Vinhos Verdes, and have little or no CO_2, though they are still light and express a fresh aromatic green apple fruit character. The grapes, even when fully ripe, tend to be low in sugar and high in acidity. This means that the wines are low in alcohol and cannot by law exceed 11.5%, unless made from the Alvarinho grape. It was the tradition to let the malolactic fermentation take place and bottle the wines during the vintage after the harvest. This gave the wines their characteristic 'prickle'. Nowadays the wines are not permitted to undergo malolactic fermentation and, at the time of bottling, to achieve the same 'prickle', CO_2 is injected into the wine. For export markets the wines are often sweetened by adding some wine whose fermentation has been arrested, and the result may bear little resemblance to those consumed in Portugal.

The light wines of the **Douro** have for long been dependent on the production of the fortified Port wines. By law, for each vintage, the *benefício*

Northern Portugal			
KEY WINES		**MAIN GRAPE VARIETIES**	**PRICE**
Vinho Verde DOC	☐	Loureiro, Padernã	●
	☐	Alvarinho	●●○
Douro DOC	■	Port varieties	●●○○
Dão DOC	■	Jaen, Touriga Nacional, Tinta Roriz	●●
Bairrada DOC	■	Baga	●○

controls the amount of Port that is produced; the grapes that are not needed for the production of Port are then used for the making of the light wine Douro. The vineyards were often the same, though now there are many vineyards where no fortified wine is made. Since the award of DOC status in 1982, the reputation of the light wines has grown and some of them are among the most prestigious, and expensive, in the country. The grapes used traditionally were the same as those used for making Port. However, especially in the upper reaches of the Douro Valley, there have been plantings of varieties such as Cabernet Sauvignon, Sauvignon Blanc and even Gewurztraminer. The best red wines, from vineyards dedicated to light wines, are full-bodied and fruity, sometimes with a recognisably 'Port-like' aroma, with firm tannins and crisp acidity. As with Port, viticulture is labour-intensive and expensive, and the precious fruit can be vinified with great care, resulting in some wines of extremely high quality. The whites, particularly those from high-altitude vineyards, can show fresh varietal fruit and crisp acidity.

The **Dão** region lies south of the Douro some 80 kilometres inland and takes its name from a tributary of the River Mondego. The vineyards lie

Enormous bunches of Loureiro grapes used for Vinho Verde.

Terraced vineyards in the Douro Valley.

between 200 and 400 metres above sea level on a plateau with granitic soil. They are sheltered on all sides by mountains, making the area much drier than on the coast. Since the mid-1990s, the wines have changed from being generally dull and heavy to having much more fruit character. The potential of individual grape varieties such as Jaen for early maturing, fruity wines and the Touriga Nacional for wines to age is now being exploited. When made from Jaen, the wines are mainly red, deeply coloured, fruity and lighter in tannins and

Portugal is the major supplier of cork for wine bottles. These trees have recently had their corky bark removed.

Southern Portugal

KEY WINES		MAIN GRAPE VARIETIES	PRICE
Ribatejo DOC	■	Castelão Frances, international varieties	●
Alentejo DOC	■	Trincadeira, Aragonez	●○○
	□	Roupeiro, Antão Vaz, Arinto	●○
VR Alentejano	■	As Alentejo DOC + other Portuguese and international varieties	●○
	□	As Alentejo DOC + other Portuguese and international varieties	●○

acidity than most Portuguese reds. Touriga National and Tinta Roriz (Tempranillo) are used to supply tannins, acids and more concentrated fruit to blends. The best white wines are full-bodied and rather nutty, being made with the Encruzado grape.

The name **Bairrada** owes its origins to the Portuguese word for clay (*bairro*) and here the soils are mainly heavy clays with high limestone content. This damp, rainy region lies between Dão and the sea, north of the university town of Coimbra. Most of the wine is red, made from the local Baga grape, whose individual style has been compared to Nebbiolo in Piemonte. Traditionally, these wines were fermented with the stalks, took decades to reach their peak and needed decanting before being served. Modern-style wines still have plenty of tannin and acidity, but express more peppery berry fruit. About 15 per cent of the total production is white wine. This is mainly made from the highly acidic Bical grape. When made from fully ripe grapes, these wines can have a wonderfully exotic, peachy perfume, which becomes toasty as the wine ages.

Southern Portugal

Ribatejo DOC, or 'banks of the Tagus', is a recently created DO, which includes most of the vineyards in the alluvial river plains of that river and often gives high yields. Heavy crops of Fernão Pires give large quantities of neutral, dry white wines for the local market. The exported wines are mainly red, made from traditional Portuguese grapes, such as Castelão Frances, and a selection of international varieties. With restricted yields, Castelão Frances can make wines with crisp acidity, raspberryish fruit and firm tannins; as yields are increased, the wines become thin and harsh.

Alentejo DOC, or 'beyond the Tagus', is an important wine region, south-east of Lisbon, stretching to the Spanish frontier. In fact, it is a major region of cork oaks as much as it is of vineyards. The climate is continental, with very low rainfall and hot summers. The soils are predominantly loam, mixed with granite and schist. Trincadeira is the most important quality grape here, producing dark, plummy wines with hints of chocolate and coffee, further enhanced when aged in oak. Aragonez also contributes to blends, or may be bottled separately.

Roupeiro and Antão Vaz make full-bodied, honeyed white wines with low acidity, sometimes lifted by blending in some crisp, aromatic Arinto

the same as the Padernã of Vinho Verde). Some
more ambitious wines are fermented or aged in
oak to provide extra depth and complexity.

Vinhos Regionais and Vinhos de Mesa

There has been much expansion of the **Vinho
Regional** category, particularly in the **Alentejano**,
though Vinho Regional wines are exported from
Terras do Sado, south of Lisbon, and **Beiras**,
which includes the Bairrada and Dão DOC zones
in the north. Growers in these regions are
experimenting with 'foreign' grape varieties such
as Cabernet Sauvignon and Syrah into blends.

Over the years, Portugal has had considerable
success on international markets with rosé wines,
generally slightly sweet and with a light prickle on
the tongue. In the United States, these have been
called 'crackling rosés'. These are simple **vinhos
de mesa**. The style (sparkling/still, sweet/dry) is
chosen to meet the needs of the particular target
export market.

25 Greece and Cyprus, The Eastern Mediterranean and North Africa

Greece, probably more than any other country, has benefited from its entry into the EU, for this has enabled it to modernise its wine industry, while looking to both the past and future. Fashionable grapes have been introduced from Western Europe, but the plantings of the historical varieties, probably grown since classical times, have also been extended. A small number of large merchants dominate the industry, though an ever-increasing number of boutique wineries with foreign-trained winemakers are producing excellent wines.

GREECE

In the mountainous mainland and the islands of Greece, vineyard space is at a premium. Even so, only half the grapes grown are used for the production of wine, with the balance being used for table grapes and raisins. Many Greek wines, particularly for the domestic market, remain very traditional in style. One example of this is the classic Retsina, a wine flavoured with pine resin which was mentioned by writers as early as the third century BC. True Retsina is a white wine, made from Savatiano and Rhoditis grapes. (A little rosé is also made.) Pine resin, drawn from local trees, is added to the wine when it is young and removed at the first racking, by which time the wine has acquired its distinctive character. The term *Traditional Appellation (TA)* is used as a designation for Retsina in Greek wine law and this has been incorporated into EU law, though it is a method of production rather than a geographical description. Other wine laws have been harmonised with the EU regime, with French being adopted as the international language.

There are two terms for Quality Wines:

Appellation d'Origine de Qualité Supérieure (AOQS) applies to light wines. There are 20 regions with this classification.

Appellation d'Origine Contrôlée (AOC) applies to liqueur wines. There are eight different regions with this classification. These are mainly made from dried Muscat grapes, or the red Mavrodaphne.

Outside these, the **Vin de Pays** category is especially important for international varieties and wines made in non-traditional styles. As a proportion of overall production, that of Quality Wine and Vins de Pays both remain small, though they are increasing. The overwhelming majority of wine is table wine.

Northern Greece

In the Macedonian regions, the climate is distinctly cool, with many of the vineyards planted at altitude. This is a region for the production of red wines, with the major appellation being **Naoussa**. The Xinomavro grape, at its best here, is capable of giving wines with powerful tannins, high acidity and complex aromas and flavours reminiscent of Barolo. It is also blended with international varieties for local Vins de Pays. Many interesting Vins de Pays are also being made in the Côtes de Meliton region, on the western flank of the next peninsula to Mount Athos. Here red, white and rosé wines are made from a mixture of international and Greek varieties.

The Peloponnese Peninsular

The Peloponnese region accounts for a third of the production of Greek wine and the vineyards are free of phylloxera. **Nemea** produces red wine exclusively from the Agiorgitiko grape, from vineyards above 250 metres. The Mediterranean climate is one of short, mild winters, but generally hot summers, so many of the better vineyards are

Greece			
KEY AOQS WINES		**MAIN GRAPE VARIETIES**	**PRICE**
Naoussa (Macedonia)	■	Xinomavro	●●
Nemea (Peloponnese)	■	Agiorgitiko	●●
Santorini (Island)	□	Assyrtiko	●●
KEY *VIN DE PAYS*	■	Various local + international	●○
	□	Various local + international	●○

Looking across to the town of Naoussa and Mount Vermio. View from Ktima Kyr-Yianni, Yanakohori, Naoussa, Macedonia, Greece.

BELOW LEFT
Close-up of a very old Assyrtico vine in Santorini, the basket-like training system helps to secure the vine against high winds.

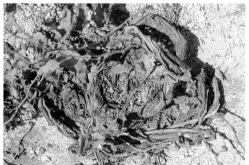

north-facing and at altitude, to make for cooler growing conditions. Rainfall is generally limited to autumn and spring, with a little in the winter; summers are dry. Even with high-altitude vineyards, the wines are soft, plummy and low in acidity, though they can have very rich, spicy fruit.

The Islands

The island wines with the highest reputation for quality are the powerful dry white **Santorini**, made from the Assyrtiko grape. This variety retains its acidity well even when very ripe, and produces wines with an exquisite Viognier-like perfume, and mineral flavours from the volcanic soils. Many of the vineyards are very old, with the vines coiled like ropes to resist the strong winds. Yields are low, and the efforts involved in tending the vines are seldom rewarded in the prices that

can be charged. Sadly, pressure from the local tourist industry is resulting in the destruction of the vineyards to make way for holiday complexes.

In terms of volume, **Crete** is by far the most important of the islands, and its wine industry is in the process of a much-needed renaissance. At present its Vins de Pays appear to be the only wines to reach export markets. **Cephalonia** also produces wines of international standing, from the **Robola** variety. These are medium-bodied, with crisp acidity and citrus fruit.

Old vineyards in Santorini.

CYPRUS

The one wine with any international, or historical, reputation is **Commandaria**. This liqueur wine takes its name from the Grande Commanderie, established by the Knights Templar, who are credited with having popularised it at the time of the Crusades. Once rated as one of the great dessert wines of the world, Commandaria, was, in January 1963, the first Cypriot wine to be granted Quality Wine status in the EU. It is made from sun-dried bunches of grapes. Spirit is added to the must before fermentation has finished and it is then aged in a *solera* system.

Cyprus, along with Chile, claims to be a country whose vineyards are entirely phylloxera-free, but this has led to a fear of experimentation with imported grape varieties. Plantings are dominated by the local black Mavro and white Xynisteri varieties, which account for 90 per cent of the acreage and produce drab wines. Whether it is cause or effect is uncertain, but much of the production is turned into concentrated musts (largely for the British wine industry), liqueur wines or brandy. Basic wines are also sold to the markets of Eastern Europe.

Fortunately, the government has become aware of the cul-de-sac down which its wine industry could be heading and plantings have been made of more interesting varieties, such as the Grenache and Carignan. Most of the vineyards are of bush vines planted on the southern slopes of the Troodos Mountains, with the grapes being sold to one of four major wineries.

Many vineyards in Cyprus are planted high in the Troodos mountains and benefit from cooler temperatures. The Mavro vines are usually bush-trained.

LEBANON

Wine production in Lebanon is concentrated in the Beka'a Valley, where the vineyards are at an altitude of about 1 000 metres. Here the grape varieties come mainly from southern France, though there are also important plantings of Cabernet Sauvignon. An increasing number of producers are making high-quality red wines that are inspired by Bordeaux, but show extra ripeness and exotic spice. The wines can range from very classical, cedary and cassis-flavoured Cabernet Sauvignon-led blends through to powerful, full-bodied wines with challenging balsamic and leather aromas, depending on the producer and the vintage. White wines are also made, varying in style from wines with gentle varietal fruit to some that are deliberately oxidised, golden in colour and richly nutty.

ISRAEL

Israel's modern industry dates from the latter part of the nineteenth century, when many Jews returned to the country and Baron Rothschild donated a vast sum of money for the planting of vineyards as part of an agricultural resettlement programme. Of the five defined regions, Samaria, which includes Mount Carmel, is the most important for the export of quality wines. Eighty per cent of production is in the hands of just three wineries, but there are now more than 90 other wineries, mainly of small size.

Kosher wines must satisfy the following requirements:

- The vine must be in its fourth year before its grapes are used to make wine.
- The vineyard must be left fallow every seven years. (This applies only to vineyards in the biblical lands.)

Vines planted in the
Beka'a Valley, Lebanon.

- Vines may not share the vineyards with any other crop.
- From the moment that the harvested grapes arrive at the winery, they may be handled only by Sabbath-observing Jews, and all the equipment used in winemaking, ageing and bottling must consist of kosher materials. (For Kosher wines made in the US, France, South Africa and elsewhere, this is the only rule that must be strictly observed.)

In order to be described as **Kosher for Passover**, it must not have contact with any bread or dough (leavened or unleavened). **Meshuval** is wine that has been boiled or subjected to pasteurisation in order to become sufficiently altered that there would be no danger of it being used for non-Jewish religious rites.

NORTH AFRICA

When North Africa was under French rule, the region made two-thirds of all the wine produced in the world. With Independence the wine industries of Morocco, Algeria and Tunisia went into a period of hibernation from which they are only just beginning to emerge. Of the three countries, **Morocco** would appear to have the brightest future. The vineyards lie at an altitude of over 500 metres and are cooled by winds from the Atlantic. Many of the vineyards have plantings of old vines and there is an appellation system in place with 14 classified regions. The traditional Carignan and Cinsault grapes are now being joined by varieties from Bordeaux and the Rhône. In **Tunisia**, too, there has been recent investment in winery equipment. The best wines come from the coastal vineyards near Tunis itself. Here powerful reds and Muscats, both sweet and dry, are produced. **Algeria**, once by far the most important of the three countries in terms of production, appears to have lagged behind, with production now a shadow of what it used to be. The state monopoly, which controls the industry, claims to have established substantial new plantings of international grape varieties.

26 South Africa

When we talk of New World vineyards, it is easy to overlook the fact that wine has been made continually in South Africa for some 350 years. The first vines were planted in 1654 in the Cape, which was an essential supply station for the Dutch East India Company. In 1688, some 150 Huguenots, fleeing persecution in France, arrived in South Africa. Many of them had winemaking skills and they established a settlement at what is now called Franschoek. At the same time, Governor Simon van der Stel was planting his own vineyard at Constantia, in the shadow of Table Mountain. Historically, most of the grapes grown in South Africa were used for the production of brandy and fortified wines. Currently, there are about 108 000 hectares under vine, with only a ninth of that area specifically planted with grapes for distillation, though many of the other plantings could be considered dual-purpose. As well as grapes used for wine and brandy production, a considerable proportion are used for grape juice and grape concentrate.

WINE LAWS

The wine legislation in South Africa dates back to 1973, and is known as Wine of Origin. A Certification Seal on each bottle is awarded only after tasting by an independent panel, and guarantees the accuracy of the information on the label. If a vintage is stated, 75 per cent of the wine must come from that particular year. If a variety (which is known locally as a cultivar) is specified, it must comprise 75 per cent of the total. The stated variety and vintage must constitute 85 per cent of the wine for those sold in the EU, but 100 per cent of the grapes must come from any stated production area. The smallest production area recognised in the Wine of Origin legislation is the **Estate** (see Producers, below). Groups of estates constitute **Wards** (such as Franschoek, Constantia), which are grouped into **Districts** (such as Paarl, Stellenbosch, Overberg). The largest recognised production area is the **Region**. Not all districts are part of a region, and not all Wards are part of a District. As a result, production area boundaries can be quite untidy. For example, the almost-all-embracing 'Coastal Region' creates many blending options as it includes wards in the districts of Paarl and Stellenbosch, as well as the ward of Constantia (which is not part of any district).

PRODUCERS

Historically, the South African wine trade was controlled by a master co-operative, the **KWV**, which was set up in 1918 to create stability at a time of chronic over-production. Its powers grew to such an extent that it came to oversee all sales of wine at all levels. Recently, it has been privatised and is having to compete with other producers. This seems to have brought a breath of fresh air to the trade, though it does mean that the growers no longer have a guaranteed price for their grapes. Ultimately, this should lead to improved quality.

There are now three main types of wine producer in South Africa. First come the **co-operative**

SOUTH AFRICA

CAPE PROVINCE

- COASTAL REGION
- BREEDE RIVER VALLEY REGION
- Other Vine Growing Districts

TULBAGH
WORCESTER
PAARL
KLEIN KAROO
Cape Town
Paarl Franschoek
CONSTANTIA
ROBERTSON Swellandam
Stellenbosch
SWELLENDAM
STELLENBOSCH OVERBERG
Walker Bay

N

0   50   100 Km
0   50 Miles

32'S
34'S

cellars, who are responsible for the majority of all the wine made. They have invested considerably in equipment in recent years. Some of them market their own wines, while others sell their wines in bulk to the major merchants. Recent developments have led to a rapid expansion in the number of **estate wineries**. These must make wine from grapes grown only on their own land, and many of them have built up considerable individual reputations. Finally, there is a small number of independent wholesale **merchants** and cellars, who buy in both grapes and wines to sell mainly under their own labels. They might also distribute the wines of a certain number of estate wineries on an exclusive basis.

CLIMATE

Overall, the climate is Mediterranean in character and well suited to the production of wine. The cold Benguela ocean current has a significant cooling effect which extends far inland. Irrigation is needed in regions of low rainfall. Over the past few years, vineyard plantings have expanded into entirely new regions. These include cooler zones close to the coast, on both sides of the Cape of Good Hope.

GRAPE VARIETIES

Recently, demand for red wines has outstripped supply with the result that the local wine industry is now concentrating more on noble red grape

varieties that have global appeal. **Cabernet Sauvignon** and **Merlot** are used for varietal wines and also for elegant, Bordeaux-style blends. Where there are iron-rich clay soils, Merlot is capable of creating very dark, plummy wines that are

Stainless steel fermentation tanks at Vergelegen.

Irrigation is forbidden in EU vineyards, but is common in many New World vineyards, as here at Franschoek, South Africa.

Klein Constantia with False Bay in the background.

reminiscent of Pomerol. Syrah is also successfully cultivated, and is used both for rich, dark-berry scented, full-bodied reds, and for more elegant, peppery wines. There are large plantings of **Cinsaut** (spelt without an 'l' in South Africa), which is often used to contribute savoury flavours to blends, though it can appear on its own. **Pinotage** (Pinot Noir × Cinsault) creates wines in a range of styles. It is sometimes blended with international varieties, as part of a 'Cape Blend'. On its own, typical Pinotage has a red berry fruit

character, and wines from old bush vine wines can be very full-bodied, with rich, spiced, berry fruit. Some wines can show hints of meat, rubber, banana and even nail varnish. These rather wild flavours can make the wine attractively complex when they do not dominate. Pinotage is certainly a variety whose limits are still being explored.

White wine still accounts for well over half of all production, with a fifth of the vineyards being planted with **Chenin Blanc**, known locally as Steen. While the importance of this variety has declined, growers are now making better use of its versatility, producing, as in the Loire Valley, great wines, in both sweet and dry styles. Barrel fermentation and barrel ageing contributes extra body and toasty oak flavours to some of these wines. **Chardonnay** has shown the potential to make wines of exceptional quality, particularly in the cool sites. Burgundian techniques such as

South Africa			
KEY GRAPE VARIETIES		**MAIN REGIONS**	**PRICE**
Cabernet Sauvignon	■	Stellenbosch	●●○○
Pinotage	■	Coastal	●○○○
Chenin Blanc	□	Coastal	●○○
Chardonnay	□	Walker Bay, Coastal	●●○○
Sauvignon Blanc	□	Constantia, Coastal	●●○

barrique fermentation and lees-stirring may contribute to the character of these wines. **Sauvignon Blanc** is also grown with great success, showing a range of possible styles. Some are light, crisp and full of the grassy varietal character. Others take advantage of oak to supply structure and complexity, and are able to develop nutty and vegetal flavours in the bottle. Muscat of Alexandria (here called Hanepoot) is capable of producing stunning dessert wines, including the recently revived Vin de Constance.

REGIONS AND WINES

South Africa's vineyards are divided into what are called, in descending order of size, regions, districts and wards. In all, there are five regions (of which three are in the Cape), 16 districts and almost 50 wards. In addition, there is the term Western Cape, which covers all the vineyards of the Cape and is a catch-all appellation allowing single varietal wines to be blended from the different regions and sold in the EU.

Coastal Region

For fine wines, the Coastal Region is the heartland of production. The oldest district, **Constantia**, has a small number of prestigious vineyards and lies in the outer suburbs of Cape Town. In the other direction are the rolling hills of Durbanville district. Both are influenced by the nearby sea and offer ideal conditions for Sauvignon Blanc wines that display the full spectrum of aromatic varietal characteristics. Further inland lies the district of **Stellenbosch**, at the heart of the quality wine production area. Here the climate is somewhat warmer and the soils are of granite and sandstone. Good examples of a range of international varieties may be found here, though it is most famous for reds made from Bordeaux varieties and Pinotage. It is also the site of the national Viticultural Research Institute. **Paarl** is slightly warmer still, and houses the cellars and offices of the KWV as well as a number of important estates. Some miles to the east of Cape Town, in the district of Overberg, the ward of **Walker Bay** includes the Hemel-en-Aarde Valley, where many of the country's best Pinot Noirs and Chardonnays are produced.

Breede River Valley Region

Over the Bain's Kloof Pass lies the Breede River Valley, which has a distinctly warmer climate and the two important wine districts of **Worcester** and **Robertson**.

27 Australia

The first Governor of New South Wales recognised the potential for winemaking on his arrival in 1788. From the first plantings, vineyards have now spread to every state in the Commonwealth, even, though only nominally, the Northern Territory. The transformation in the image of Australian wines has been rapid. It is many years since it was seen as a producer of Port- and Sherry-style wines. It is now recognised in many markets as a significant producer of quality wines. This progress has taken place as the result of heavy investment, from within Australia and from outside, in the planting of vineyards and the construction of wineries with the most modern equipment. This expansion has occurred with exhilarating speed, but rapid growth has come at a cost. Australia is yet another country suffering from periodic wine gluts in an over-supplied world market. Yet competitiveness in the international market is more important for Australia than for any other major wine-producing nation, because the domestic market is comparatively small and static. In 1984, export sales accounted for no more than 4 per cent of production, now they are more than half. A combination of keen pricing, consistent quality and supplying styles of wine that the market sought has led to successful creation and expansion of new markets. However, selling wines at over-aggressive prices threatens the long-term viability of the Australian wine industry: Australia's largest wine producer was almost brought to its knees by ill-conceived pricing policies on European markets; they were producing too much wine and had to sell it at discounted prices.

The success of Australian wines, as well as wines from other New World countries, is due to a combination of factors that can probably be best summed up by the one word 'certitude'. It is not by chance that their expansion has been largely on the back of varietally labelled wines. By selling a grape variety rather than a region, this gives the inexperienced wine drinker a clear idea of what they can expect. As they advance along the path of knowledge, they can begin to learn about the other factors that go to create the taste of a wine. Most New World producers have eagerly taken on board also that, in this age of supermarkets, a bottle has to sell itself. Packaging is all-important: the product must be eye-catching to the hurried supermarket shopper. Informative back-labels have also supported the appeal of many New World wines. It is not that they are intrinsically better than what the consumer has known for generations: they offer something that is different and exciting.

What advantages do New World winemakers have over their Old World colleagues? Firstly, in many cases land is cheap. Indeed, in parts of Australia (and Argentina too), it is there for the planting. However, while the land may be cheap, water also must be readily available in sufficient quantities to grow grapes. If there is sufficient rainfall, then it is unlikely that the land will be at a bargain price! It would be naïve, however, to think that land in the New World is always cheap. There are other parts of Australia where premium vineyard land is as expensive as most places in France. In many cases the vineyards have been so planted as to make the most of the sophisticated machinery that has been developed. Economies of scale are very important in most New World wine production.

The main niggle that Old World winemakers have about their New World colleagues is that they claim that the wine legislation is too liberal. The real problem, however, is that the wine industry of Europe has bound itself up in a web of regulations, often designed to restrict production to keep prices high. Take one simple case: irrigation. Until recently, this was forbidden within the EU, except for establishing young vines. The fact is that in many parts of Europe it is difficult to make quality wine without irrigation. Now, with strict limitations, it is permitted. In EU regions, the only permitted method of adding oak flavours to a wine was by ageing it in cask. In the New World, this can be achieved much more cheaply by the use of oak chips or by inner-staves. Should new techniques for producing more acceptable wines at lower prices be rejected just because they are new? It would be a shame if such techniques were used for the great wines of Bordeaux and Burgundy, but there are few reasons why they shouldn't become everyday practice for *Vins de Pays*. On the other hand, chaptalisation is widely used in Europe; in the New World it is generally forbidden (though it might be said that this is because it is rarely needed).

Finally, there is the question of mind-set. For many European winemakers, tradition is all-important. The New World winemaker approaches winemaking with fewer preconceptions and less baggage; they can make the wine in the way that they think best. This aspect of the upsurge in Australian wine production can be seen in the vast number of Australian 'flying winemakers' roaming the vineyards of the world seeking broader experience and spreading the gospel of Australian wines: 'quality control'.

CLIMATE, TOPOGRAPHY AND SOIL

Comparatively little of the Australian landmass is suitable for the production of wine. Most of the vineyards that have been planted are either comparatively close to the coast or are in the extended valleys of the Murray–Darling, where water is available for irrigation. However, as in other countries, the boundaries are being extended particularly for cool climate vineyards and there are increased plantings in such areas as Tasmania and high-altitude sites on the mainland.

It is very easy, and dangerous, to make generalisations about Australia, but overall the climate may be described as Mediterranean. There is little difference between the vintages for a wine coming from 'South-Eastern Australia' (the most common geographical source on Australian wine labels), because the area from which the wines may be blended is so huge. However, there may be major differences between the zones. Each one might be able to construct its own vintage chart. The vintage generally takes place from February to the beginning of April, though it can be as late as May in cooler regions.

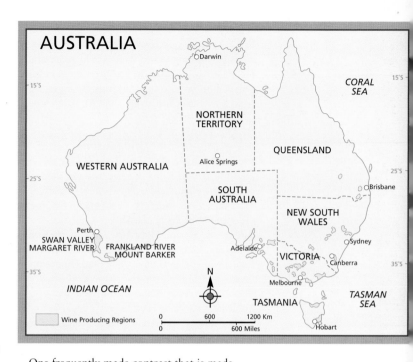

One frequently made contrast that is made between European winemaking and New World, particularly Australian, winemaking is that European quality wine is said to be led by *terroir*, or the desire to express origin, whereas winemaking in the New World uses technology to create quality, irrespective of origin. This is a misleading simplification for both. It is true that to the extent that we understand the reasons why some of the traditional sites make the great wines they do, much of the explanation is to be found in physical characteristics such as the availability of sufficient but not excessive water, heat, sunlight and nutrients. It is also true that techniques such as sophisticated irrigation regimes and management of the leaf canopy (to create cool and shade for the ripening grapes) can replicate some of the advantages of the great traditional sites. Also, adjustments such as adding acid or tannins to musts can further correct many remaining deficiencies in the raw materials for winemaking. The ultimate limits to what science can do to improve the quality of wines are still not known. In spite of all of this, to claim that *terroir* is unimportant in Australia would be wrong. Many wines are made from special sites, or regions, that do display clearly recognisable regional characteristics. Some of these characteristics will be described under the regional sections that follow. Even without these, it should be recognised that many 'South-Eastern Australia' blends are exactly that: they carefully combine elements from many regions, each offering different characteristics, and each contributing to the balance and complexity of the whole. If *terroir* were truly unimportant, there would be no need for multi-regional blends, and there would be no premium to be paid for fruit from prestigious regions such as Coonawarra and McLaren Vale.

GRAPE VARIETIES

Approximately 90 different grape varieties are planted commercially in Australia. In all, there are over 150 000 hectares of vineyards and there are eight red varieties and eight white varieties with more than 1 000 hectares. These are, in descending order of importance, red: **Shiraz**, **Cabernet Sauvignon**, **Merlot**, **Pinot Noir**, Ruby Cabernet, **Grenache**, **Mataro** (Mourvèdre) and **Cabernet Franc**; white: **Chardonnay**, Sultana (Thompson Seedless), **Semillon**, **Riesling**, Muscat Gordo Blanco, **Sauvignon Blanc**, Colombard and **Verdelho**. (Those marked in bold appear as quality varietal wines and quality blends; the rest are used for bulk wine production.)

For red wines, the classic Australian variety is **Shiraz**. For many years it was unfashionable, and there was excess supply. Sadly, many ancient, low-yielding vineyards were destroyed during the vine-pull scheme of the 1980s. Those old vines that remain are now highly valued, as vine age is thought to be a major contributory factor to quality in Shiraz wines. Hot regions such as the Hunter and Barossa Valleys produce a soft earthy spicy style that develops leather and caramel notes as it ages. A leaner, more peppery style is made in cooler regions such as Margaret River, Western Victoria and the Central Ranges Zone in New South Wales. These qualities may be combined in a multi-regional blended wine. Shiraz is also used to give softness and body to blends with Cabernet Sauvignon, performing a similar role to Merlot in Bordeaux. Historically, this allowed a wine with much of the character of a Cabernet Sauvignon to be produced in larger quantities at a lower price. Now, this blend survives on its own merits. (It might be observed that in the nineteenth century, the very best Bordeaux wines were given extra body and flavour by blending in some Syrah from Hermitage.) Shiraz–Viognier blends, following the example of Côte-Rôtie, are becoming more common. It is found that the Viognier contributes to the aromatic complexity and the texture of the blend. This has inspired experimental blends of Shiraz with other white varieties.

Australian **Cabernet Sauvignon** is generally darker, with firmer tannins and higher acidity than Australian Shiraz. It may appear as a blended wine, either with Shiraz or, increasingly, with Merlot. Both add complementary flavours and result in a softer wine. Australian Cabernet Sauvignon usually displays ripe black fruit characters (blackcurrant, black cherry), often underpinned by toasty, meaty oak notes. Classic regions include Coonawarra and Margaret River.

Ten years ago, **Chardonnay** was the most popular grape in Australia. It is planted widely

'Potter Fermenter Tanks.' Enormous fermentation vessels in the McLaren Vale.

throughout the vineyard regions, and is made in a wide range of styles. Much Australian Chardonnay is blended from these regions, and will include components that give different aromas (peach, melon, fig, banana), and different degrees of oak, lees and malolactic flavours. Most Australian Chardonnay sees some degree of oak treatment, whether through the use of chips, inner-staves or cask fermentation and ageing. However, it is becoming more common to see unoaked Chardonnays. It is also very common to blend Chardonnay with Semillon. There are sound commercial reasons for this (a wine with many characteristics of Chardonnay can be stretched with cheaper Semillon, and the wine can be made in larger quantities). Semillon can also add crisp acidity and refreshing herbaceous notes to the blend.

Many of Australia's finest white wines are made with **Riesling**. These typically have bold citrus fruit (lime, lemon, grapefruit) in youth, that develops into toast, honey and petrol notes as the wines age. The wines are unoaked, and are usually dry or slightly off-dry, though some sweet wines are also made. Classic regions include the Eden and Clare Valleys in South Australia.

Important, but rather under-appreciated dry wines are made, with **Semillon**. It is planted widely, but the classic region is the lower Hunter Valley, whose dry Semillons are light-bodied, with crisp acidity and flavours that are initially rather neutral but evolve into a complex spectrum of toast, nut and honey flavours with bottle age. In Western Australia, a much more herbaceous style is made, which could be mistaken for Sauvignon Blanc.

Fashion has a more important role to play perhaps in Australia's vineyards than anywhere else in the world. Areas under the individual varieties may change because of new planting, but in Australia head-grafting is particularly popular as a way of achieving a more rapid changeover. Most vineyards are still very young and are wire-trained for efficient machine-tending and harvesting. However, for a surprisingly large number of varieties, the oldest living vines are to be found in Australia. Many of these ancient, ungrafted bush-vines are a century or more old. Most are to be found in phylloxera-free South Australia.

WINE LAWS AND THE LABEL INTEGRITY PROGRAM

While there is a long tradition within Australia of the use of terms such as Burgundy, Claret, Chablis and Hock in labelling their wines on the domestic

Australia			
KEY GRAPE VARIETIES		**MAIN REGIONS**	**PRICE**
Shiraz–Cabernet blends	■	South-Eastern Australia	●○○
Shiraz	■	Barassa Valley, Hunter Valley, McLaren Vale, Coonawarra	●●○○
Cabernet Sauvignon	■	Margaret River, Coonawarra	●●○○
Bordeaux blends	■	Margaret River, Yarra Valley	●●○○
Pinot Noir	■	Yarra Valley, Mornington Peninsular	●●●○
Chardonnay–Semillon blends	☐	South-Eastern Australia	●○
Chardonnay	☐	Adelaide Hills, Hunter Valley	●●○○
Riesling	☐	Eden Valley, Clare Valley	●●○○
Semillon (dry)	☐	Hunter Valley	●●○○
Semillon (botrytised)	☐	Hunter Valley	●●○○

market, agreement has been reached with the EU that the few that remain are being phased out.

A Geographical Indications (GI) Committee was created at the end of 1993 'to make determinations of geographical indications for wine in relation to regions and localities in Australia'. **Australian GI**s are not appellations in the strictest sense, as they do not specify grape varieties, viticultural methods and yields, or wine styles in the manner of European appellations. It is thought that such stipulations would limit experimentation and progress, especially given the relatively short period that Australian grape growers have had to trial different varieties. The GI legislation is part of the Label Integrity Program, ensuring the validity of the information on the bottle label. If regions, varieties or vintages are stated, then 85 per cent of the wine in the bottle must come from those regions, varieties or vintages. Matters of quality and style are then left to the consumer, who is unlikely to buy a second bottle of a wine if they have not enjoyed the first; and the producer, who would have to face the financial consequences of not being able to sell an inferior product. While vintages and varieties are easy to define, the drawing of the regional boundaries has led to more controversy. A hierarchy has been created with zones and regions, which can be used on wine labels to indicate the geographical source.

Within the EU, wines that are blended from several regions may not be sold as quality wines and so are not entitled to state a vintage or varietal composition. Clearly, grape variety is an important marketing tool for many Australian wines. The South-Eastern Australia super-zone covers approximately 95 per cent of the total production of Australian wine and was designed to enable blending across most of Australia for varietally labelled wines sold in the EU.

Below that, each of the states is a zone, and

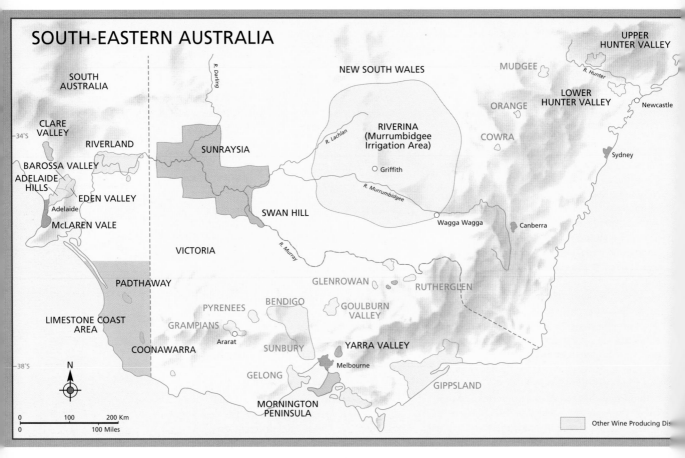

SOUTH-EASTERN AUSTRALIA

within each state, there will be further zones. In turn, these may contain a number of regions. For example, Coonawarra is a region within the Limestone Coast zone, which is within South Australia, which is within South-Eastern Australia. So a wine from Coonawarra, could be blended with a wine from Padthaway and described as Limestone Coast, with one from the Barossa Valley and be described as South Australia, or with one from the Hunter Valley and described as South-Eastern Australia.

One effect of this is the dominance of wines labelled with the origin South-Eastern Australia among the large-volume brands, and the virtual disappearance on export markets of sources such as Hunter Valley. It should also be noted that some longstanding areas of production such as Sunraysia, in New South Wales, are not accepted as names for zones or regions.

SOUTH-EASTERN AUSTRALIA
Riverland in South Australia, Murray–Darling in Victoria and Riverina in New South Wales are the major sources of fruit for Australia's big brands. Blending in components of wine from regions such

as Barossa, Adelaide Hills or McLaren Vale may enhance these wines. The choice of components in the blend will depend on the grape variety, the style sought and the price point that is to be met. A few of Australia's most prestigious, and most expensive, wines take advantage of the blending opportunities provided by this appellation.

SOUTH AUSTRALIA
Producing almost 43 per cent of Australia's total, South Australia is a phylloxera-free state and there are strict quarantine regulations as to the movement of plant material. The vineyards are concentrated in the south-east of the state.

Lower Murray Zone
Fruit from vast irrigated vineyards in the **Riverland Region** supply large quantities of fruit for bulk wine production. Riverland fruit is almost without exception healthy and can be of good quality, as in the dry conditions there are few problems with rot or mildew. This creates ideal conditions for organic viticulture, but the hot conditions also mean that the grapes tend to reach sugar ripeness before they have had a chance to develop much flavour.

Barossa Zone

To the north of the state capital Adelaide lies the **Barossa Valley**, the 30-kilometre long heartland of fine wine production. German immigrants from Silesia settled here in the middle of the nineteenth century, and the little vineyard towns still maintain a distinctly German character. Here the soils in the valley bottom are mainly ironstone and limestone. In the hot climate, old bush vines produce outstanding Shiraz, Grenache, Mataro and Cabernet Sauvignon. Classic Barossa Shiraz is full-bodied, soft, earthy and spicy, and develops aromas of leather as it ages. In the cooler vineyards of the surrounding hills, particularly in the **Eden Valley Region**, outstanding Rieslings are made. These are medium-bodied and dry or slightly off-dry, with high acidity. Their clean, lime-citrus fruit in youth develops into petrol, honey and toast notes as the wine ages.

Mount Lofty Ranges Zone

Riesling is also the speciality of the **Clare Valley Region**, which lies to the north of Barossa. These tend to be lighter in body and more austere in style than the Rieslings of the Eden Valley, due to the cooler climate and especially cool nights. They also age extremely well. Just to the east of Adelaide lie the **Adelaide Hills Region**, a cool climate region that specialises in making elegant Chardonnays. These have high levels of natural acids and a very perfumed fruit character of nectarines and lemons. This region also has a growing reputation for its Sauvignon Blanc.

Fleurieu Peninsular Zone

To the south is the **McLaren Vale Region**, where breezes from the nearby ocean temper the climate. Red wines from Cabernet Sauvignon, Shiraz and, more recently, Merlot dominate. In all three cases the style emphasises soft, very juicy fruit, in the bold aromas and on the palate. Nearby **Langhorne Creek Region** is a source of earthy, mouth-filling Shiraz.

Limestone Coast Zone

Far to the south-east of Adelaide, almost 400 kilometres away, not far from the border with Victoria, lies what is now known as the Limestone Coast. Under the influence of cold currents from the Antarctic, the climate is distinctly cool. Here the most renowned vineyard area is that of the **Coonawarra Region**. This is a narrow strip of land 1.5 km by 15 km, with a distinctive red, *terra rossa*, soil over limestone subsoil. Here Cabernet Sauvignon is king. Similar soils are found, and wine made, in the nearby **Padthaway Region**.

VICTORIA

Historically, the vineyards of Victoria were the most important in all Australia, but most of them were destroyed by phylloxera and were never replanted. However, it has now overtaken New South Wales and is responsible for more than a quarter of the total production. What is interesting about Victoria is the broad diversity of the wines it offers.

North-West Victoria Zone

In the north-west of the state lie the bulk-producing vineyards of the **Murray–Darling Region**. Along with Riverland in South Australia and Riverina in New South Wales, this irrigated, inland region provides large quantities of healthy fruit to provide the bulk of most South-Eastern Australia blends.

Lush green vineyards in the cool climate Adelaide Hills.

View of a section through soils at Coonawarra. Iron-rich soil lies over free-draining limestone. The structures in the background are fermentation tanks.

North-East Victoria Zone

Further up the Murray River is the **Rutherglen Region**, renowned worldwide for its Liqueur Muscats and Tokays. These are covered in Chapter 36.

Port Phillip Zone

The city of Melbourne lies on Port Phillip Bay, and Port Phillip is the name of the zone that encircles the bay, with a number of individual areas. Of these, perhaps the best known is the **Yarra Valley Region**, which stretches out from the north-eastern suburbs of the city. Here the climate is quite cool with more than 1 000 mm of rain a year. The soils range from a mixture of loams to exceptionally fertile, red, volcanic earth. Pinot Noir is the speciality here, though there is also much Chardonnay and Cabernet Sauvignon, not to mention some excellent sparkling wine. Pinot Noirs from this region are generally full-bodied and rich in fruit, but avoid the jammy, baked flavours that Pinot Noir acquires when grown in warm regions. Chardonnays show citrus fruit character and crisp acidity. Cabernet Sauvignon and its blends have firm tannins and noticeable acidity. Pinot Noir and Chardonnay are also a speciality of the **Mornington Peninsula Region**, to the south of the city. This is primarily a region of small estates, with the sea on three sides to give an extremely maritime climate.

Central Victoria Zone

As well as being a source of sturdy Shiraz and Cabernet wines, the **Goulburn Valley Region** is a source of distinctive white wines from Rhône varieties such as Marsanne, Roussanne and Viognier, as well as delicate, age-worthy Rieslings.

Western Victoria Zone

This includes the **Pyrenees** and **Grampians** regions. These are sources of powerful, tannic Shiraz. Altitude leads to cooler temperatures, with the result that the wines have higher acidity levels, and more peppery spice than most other Australian Shiraz wines. There is also a long tradition of making sparkling wines here.

NEW SOUTH WALES

In terms of production, New South Wales, now comes a close third, after Victoria. The main glory of the state is the wine of the Hunter Valley, which lies some 160 kilometres to the north of Sydney, inland from the city of Newcastle.

Hunter Valley Zone

The valley is split into two, with the majority of the production being in the **Lower Hunter Valley**. Here vineyards might vie for space with coalmines. The best soils are a form of volcanic basalt. This is a region with a difficult climate, for with more than 750 mm of rain, which falls throughout the year, including harvest-time, rot can be a major problem. Phylloxera is also present. Despite this, a large number of major wineries are based in the Lower Hunter. One suspects that they owe their success to the proximity of Sydney and a thriving tourist business. Also, much wine is imported from elsewhere to counter the unreliability in the quality of Hunter Valley wines from year to year. The outstanding grapes of the Lower Hunter are Semillon and Shiraz. Semillons are harvested early, with low sugar levels and high acidity. The wines are light in alcohol and almost neutral in flavour when first bottled, yet they develop extraordinary flavours of honey and toast as they age in the bottle. Shiraz from the Hunter Valley is usually very soft and earthy in style. Some 60 kilometres further north are the vineyards of the **Upper Hunter Valley**. Here the climate is drier and the vineyards are generally irrigated. One company dominates, as does one grape variety, Chardonnay.

Central Ranges Zone

Inland from Sydney, on the western slopes of the Great Dividing Range, lie the three Regions of **Mudgee**, **Orange** and **Cowra**. In all three, the cooler climate gives some very concentrated Chardonnays and Cabernet Sauvignons.

Big Rivers Zone

Here, inland from the central ranges, lie the bulk production regions of the **Murray–Darling Region**, where those two rivers join, and the **Riverina Region**, in the irrigated valley of the Murrumbidgee. Botrytised wines made from Semillon are a speciality of the region around the town of Griffith, in Riverina. Most are very reasonably priced, and the best are extremely high in quality.

WESTERN AUSTRALIA

Every winemaker in Western Australia will tell you that although they make no more than 3 per cent of the country's wine, they win 30 per cent of the medals. Given the fact that they are excluded from providing wine for South-Eastern Australia, except perhaps as a minor constituent of the blend, the local producers have succeeded in ploughing their own, lonely furrow. The success has come about despite the fact that the wines of Western Australia have regularly sold at prices well above those sought by their eastern rivals.

Western Australia has lived more happily with the image of boutique wineries creating quality wines, rather than that of providers to the mass market.

Greater Perth Zone

The historic wineries of Western Australia lie in the **Swan Valley Subregion**, just to the north of Perth, which has a very hot climate.

South-West Australia Zone

The real success of the state is centred on the **Margaret River Region**, some 200 kilometres to the south of Perth. Here, with the cold sea nearby, the maritime climate is cooler, though it includes a broad range of site climates. Some of these are warm enough to make outstanding Cabernets and Bordeaux blends, and others cool enough to give elegant Chardonnays and grassy Semillons that are similar in style to New Zealand Sauvignon Blancs. The rainfall is comparatively high at 1 150 mm per year, but it falls mainly in the winter. The main hazard appears to be ravenous flocks of birds. Over time, the area to the south has also been opened up. The **Great Southern Region** includes the subregion of **Mount Barker** and **Frankland River**, known for deeply coloured Cabernet Sauvignon; tannic, peppery Shiraz; and elegant, pure-fruited Riesling. The **Pemberton** region is gaining a reputation for Pinot Noir and Chardonnay.

TASMANIA

Producing only three bottles in 1 000 of Australia's wine, the hundred or so growers in Tasmania, which has the coolest climate in the country, will benefit from global warming. Originally they saw their role as providers of excellent base wine for sparkling wines; now they are in the process of creating a reputation for fine Pinot Noirs and aromatic whites from Alsatian varieties.

28 New Zealand

It is often difficult to comprehend how small a player New Zealand is in the world of wine. If one considers the area it has under vines, it only just manages to make the top 50 countries in the world, and in terms of production, it has only just made the top 30. Non-New Zealanders control more than 85 per cent of this and half the total production is in the hands of one international company. Because the domestic market for New Zealand wines is so small, the wine industry has to rely on exporting. Britain is by far the most important export market, but great inroads are now being made in North America and, perhaps surprisingly, in Australia. What has to be realised is the dynamism of the New Zealand wine industry. It must also be understood that, as far as fine wine production is concerned, all has been achieved within the lifetime of one generation. The first vines were planted in Marlborough, now the most important wine region in the country, as recently as 1973. The potential for expansion of the area under vines is great, with new areas being developed each vintage.

Although there has been a recent explosion in wine production, vineyards were first planted as long ago as 1833 by James Busby, who had been a pioneer of the wine industry in Australia. In the second half of the nineteenth century, many settlers from Dalmatia came to work the gum-fields of North Island and, in due course, they planted vineyards. They were the true wine pioneers, and one only has to look at the surnames of those families that own many of the leading wineries today to see that their influence lives on. Initially, most of the production was of fortified wines, so-called 'sherries' and 'ports'; then the Müller-Thurgau grape ruled. It was not until the early 1970s that quality varieties such as Chardonnay and Cabernet Sauvignon were first planted.

LOCATION AND CLIMATE

Because it consists of two relatively long narrow islands, the climate is predominantly maritime, though in the northern vineyards around Auckland it is subtropical. The sunniest vineyard region in the country is Marlborough in the north-east of the South Island. The driest and most continental is Central Otago, which is the most southerly vineyard area in the world, though to put things in perspective, it lies only as far south as Montélimar in the Rhône valley lies north. Excessive rainfall is perceived to be the most important climatic problem and, for this reason, most vineyard areas are on the eastern seaboard, where they are protected from the prevailing west wind by the mountainous spine of the country.

VITICULTURE AND WINEMAKING

Coming late in the field has given New Zealand certain advantages as far as wine technology is concerned. Being a leader in the dairy industry has also helped, as there was considerable familiarity with the benefits of stainless steel and temperature control. High standards of hygiene and careful handling of fermenting wines results in very pure, intense varietal expression in the wines. This has been most dramatic with Sauvignon Blanc, with which New Zealand has created a new classic style.

It is in the vineyard, however, that New Zealand has led the field, being the pioneer in canopy management and trellising techniques, to make the best use of the available heat and sunlight to create sugars and flavours in the grapes. Peculiarly, many growers still plant ungrafted vines, even though phylloxera is widespread in the country. The reason for this is that, while the government has not made grants available for the planting of vineyards, they have been available for the replanting of vineyards destroyed by the disease!

GRAPE VARIETIES

New Zealand as a quality wine producer owes much to **Sauvignon Blanc**, as the distinctive herbaceous wines of Marlborough conquered the

world. Marlborough Sauvignon Blanc is now widely regarded as a world benchmark for that variety. Intense aromas centre on capsicum, cut grass and elderflower, but may include passion fruit, stony mineral notes and hints of creamy oak. The better wines, with their intense fruit concentration and high acid levels, are capable of developing vegetal, asparagus notes with bottle age. The most widely planted grape is **Chardonnay**. As with other New World countries, all the winemaking options (oak, malolactic, lees-ageing and so on) are explored with this variety, leading to a wide range of styles. Those from Gisborne tend to show riper, more exotic fruit than the leaner wines from Marlborough and Central Otago. All tend to have a pure, clean fruit character and crisp acidity.

Until recently it had been perceived that because of its climate, New Zealand was a country for white wines only. Now **Pinot Noirs** are being favourably compared with those from Burgundy. Exceptional examples can be found from Martinborough (rich, cherry-fruited and velvet-textured), Marlborough (usually a little lighter and more vegetal), and Central Otago (complex and powerful, yet elegant). Combined, Chardonnay, Sauvignon Blanc and Pinot Noir account for more than three-quarters of all plantings in New Zealand. There is then a substantial drop, with **Merlot, Cabernet Sauvignon** and **Riesling** each having between 5 and 10 per cent of the plantings. Müller-Thurgau leads the

rest of the field, but is in rapid decline, while varieties such as Pinot Gris and Syrah are increasing.

North Island			
KEY GRAPE VARIETIES		**MAIN REGIONS**	**PRICE**
Chardonnay	☐	Gisborne	●●○
Cabernet Sauvignon, Merlot	■	Hawkes Bay	●●○○
Pinot Noir	■	Martinborough	●●●○

Mechanical harvester used in Gisborne.

REGIONS AND WINES
North Island

The **Auckland** region extends north of the city of the same name, producing mainly red wines from grapes grown on heavy clay soils. This and the minor region of Northland are the warmest vineyard areas in the country. On the East Coast, around Poverty Bay, is the region of **Gisborne**. This claims to be the Chardonnay capital of the country and has exceptionally fertile soils. Further south, along the East Coast, is the area of **Hawkes Bay**, around the twin towns of Hastings and Napier. Although Chardonnay is again the most important variety, this is probably the best region

Vines covered in netting to protect them from birds, Auckland.

South Island			
KEY GRAPE VARIETIES		**MAIN REGIONS**	**PRICE**
Sauvignon Blanc	☐	Marlborough	●●○
Chardonnay	☐	Marlborough	●●○○
Pinot Noir	■	Central Otago, Marlborough	●●●○

Aerial view of
Marlborough, showing
the scale of viticulture in
the region.

in New Zealand for Cabernet Sauvignon and
Merlot, particularly on the gravelly soils of
Gimblett Road. In Wairarapa, north of the
capital, Wellington, lies the small provincial town
of **Martinborough**, where a number of boutique
wineries have established a solid reputation for
their wines, particularly rich, full-bodied, cherry-
scented Pinot Noir.

South Island

On the north-east corner of the South Island,
centred on the town of Blenheim, is the region
of **Marlborough**. This is the sunniest part of the
country and because of this, the area under vines
is expanding rapidly. The best vineyards are on
the stony soils of the Wairau Valley, but many of
the new plantings are prone to frost. This might
be termed the Sauvignon Blanc capital of the
world as the wines here have an unmatched

capacity to concentrate their natural herbaceous
character. There are also important plantings of
Chardonnay and Pinot Noir, both of which are
also used for sparkling wines. At the extreme
north-west corner of the island is the region of
Nelson, which is perhaps best known for its fruit
orchards. However, there are wineries in the
Moutere Hills and the long fine autumns make
this potentially the best place in New Zealand for
late-harvest wines, especially those made with
Riesling. It is probably in **Canterbury** that the
greatest possibilities for expanding the country's
vineyards can be found. At present most of them
are concentrated in Waipara, but they are also
outside the city of Christchurch. The vineyards
of **Central Otago** lie way to the south in the
middle of the Southern Alps. Here the climate is
Continental, with warm days and cold nights.
These extreme differences in temperature make
for concentration of fruit flavours. Many of the
vineyards are planted in desert conditions, but
there is plenty of river water for irrigation. Pinot
Noir, Riesling and Pinot Gris appear to be the
most successful varieties. There is rapid expansion
here of the area under vines.

The United States, Canada and Mexico

When the Norsemen arrived in North America, they marvelled at the profusion of vines growing wild there to such an extent that they called the newly discovered land Vinland. Much later, successive waves of British, Dutch and French immigrants tried to plant vineyards on the eastern seaboard, but met with little success. It was not until the first half of the nineteenth century that a thriving grape industry, dependent upon native American vines, was built up, largely by German immigrants in Ohio. Now there are vineyards, of greater or lesser importance, in all the 50 states of the United States. Some of these will be dependent on European vines planted on American rootstocks, some will be producing wine from American varieties, descendants of the original wild vines, and some will rely on hybrids. The main centres of the wine industry are California, the Pacific north-west (Washington, Oregon and, to a lesser extent, Idaho) and New York State. Canada and Mexico also produce wine, with the main vineyard centres being in the province of Ontario, on the Niagara peninsula, and southern British Columbia, in the Okanagan Valley for Canada, and Baja California for Mexico.

29

THE UNITED STATES: WINE LAWS

The first thing that must be realised about the United States and its wine laws is that there is legislation at two distinct levels: the Federal Law and the State Law.

As far as Federal Law is concerned, this used to be in the hands of the Bureau of Alcohol, Tobacco and Firearms (BATF). In 1978, this instituted the system of American Viticultural Areas (AVAs) to supplement an existing appellation system; the combined scheme is still evolving. An AVA is a guarantee of source but is not related to quality or production. In addition, anyone can petition for an AVA, of any size. This has come to mean, in effect, that some AVAs have just one winery within their boundary. If an AVA is mentioned on the label, at least 85 per cent of the wine must be grapes grown within that area. Recently, certain aspects of the business of the BATF have been transferred to the Alcohol and Tobacco Tax and Trade Bureau.

State Laws vary considerably from state to state. For example, Oregon requires most of its varietal wines to contain 95 per cent of the variety mentioned on the label, Washington 85 per cent and California, and most other states, 75 per cent. At the other end of the spectrum, largely for climatic reasons, New York State allows its producers to label as local wine something that might have 35 per cent sugar and water added, in addition to 25 per cent of wine from elsewhere! Historically, much American wine was labelled with generic names such as Burgundy or Chablis, however the rise of varietal wines, and the glut of wine on the market, have all but destroyed these, even on the domestic market.

CALIFORNIA

Sometimes it is difficult to appreciate just how young the wine industry in California is. Spanish missionaries planted the first vines at La Paz in Baja, California, but it was not until 1769 that they founded their first mission on what is now US soil at San Diego. The furthest north that they ventured was Sonoma, where the Franciscans built a mission in 1823. They brought the Mission grape, which, while it does not produce fine wine, can survive in difficult climates and needs minimal tending. It is still grown in parts of California, particularly for the production of fortified wines. California's first commercial wine was produced in 1824, with the first vineyard of any size being planted by J. J. Warner in Los Angeles in 1831. The Gold Rush of 1849 led to a boom in the wine

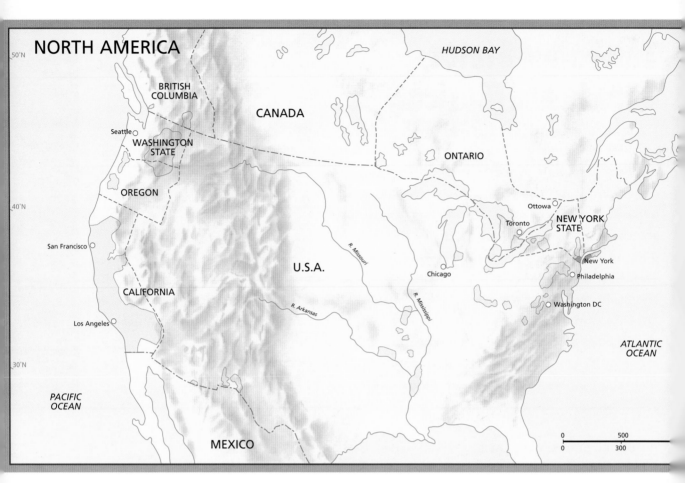

industry, with plantings in the Sierra foothills, close to the potential consumers. In 1851, a Hungarian, Agoston Haraszthy, introduced a number of grape varieties from Europe and after a return visit ten years later, brought with him 300 different varieties. This might be said to be the foundation of the modern California wine industry. From 1920, Prohibition led to a serious decline in winemaking, as it could be used for medicinal and sacramental purposes only, though an increasing demand for grapes for the production of 'grape juice' at home kept many vineyards in business. From Repeal in 1933 until the mid-1960s, winemaking was concentrated in the Central (or San Joaquín) Valley and was mainly of liqueur and jug wines.

Since the 1960s, the area under vine has more than trebled and there has been a proliferation of boutique wineries often specialising in varietal wines or 'Meritage' (Bordeaux-style) blends. At the other end of the scale a small number of enormous wineries are producing millions of cases a year.

This polarisation does not exist in just the size of the wineries. The range of prices is also huge. The surfeit of grapes once led to one major California retailer selling the 'two buck chuck', a varietal wine at $2 a bottle. At the other end of the scale, there is no shortage of wines retailing at $150 a bottle, or more. The move towards quality wine has been noteworthy, with even the largest commercial wineries investing heavily in the production of better and, no doubt, more profitable wines. While the smaller wineries will concentrate on wines from their particular AVA, most Californian wine is sold as just that, having been blended from wines across the state.

CLIMATE

The state of California extends for some 1 100 kilometres from north to south, and there are vineyards throughout most of its length. The range of climates varies largely, but there is one common factor: a lack of rain during the ripening season. To counter this, drip or sprinkler irrigation is widely practised; unirrigated vineyards are rare.

During research into the matching of vines to micro-climates, this climatic variation led the oenological faculty at the Davis Campus of the University of California to create a classification system based upon 'degree days'. In this, regional climates are ranged on a scale of I (the coolest) to V (the hottest). Using this system, all potential vineyard areas in California have been classified into one of these five zones and grape varieties most suited to each zone identified. Zones I–III are considered to be the most suitable for the production of premium wines.

The currents of the Pacific Ocean have a major role to play in the climate, for they create cooling mists and fogs which roll in during the morning and provide not only temperature contrasts, but also much needed humidity. These fogs are particularly prevalent during late May and early summer as the landmass warms and creates breezes which bring the fogs in off the sea. This helps in adding finesse to the final wine. Where there is no such influence inland, summer temperatures regularly reach 40° C or more.

GRAPE VARIETIES

You can be sure that somewhere in California there will be someone growing almost every wine grape that you will ever have heard of!

For cheaper blends, Colombard, Chenin Blanc, Thompson Seedless, Carignan, Ruby Cabernet and Barbera are the main constituents. These will mainly come from the hot Central Valley, where the soil is very fertile and irrigation used heavily to produce industrial crops of even the finest

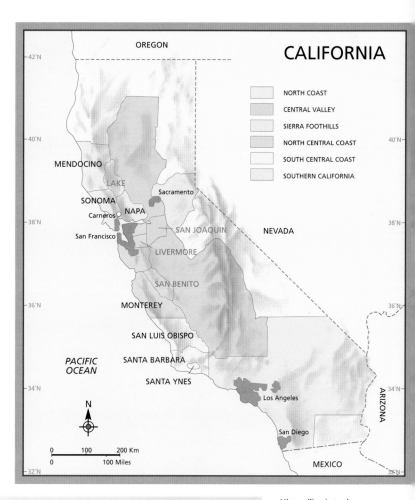

CALIFORNIA

NORTH COAST

CENTRAL VALLEY

SIERRA FOOTHILLS

NORTH CENTRAL COAST

SOUTH CENTRAL COAST

SOUTHERN CALIFORNIA

Mists rolling in to the Ridge vineyards at Santa Cruz.

California			
KEY GRAPE VARIETIES		**MAIN REGIONS**	**PRICE**
White Zinfandel	▪	Central Valley	●
Zinfandel	■	Sonoma, Sierra Foothills, Santa Cruz	●●○○+
Cabernet Sauvignon	■	Napa, Sonoma	●●○○+
Merlot	■	Napa, Sonoma, Monterey	●●○○+
Pinot Noir	■	Carneros, Sonoma	●●●○+
Chardonnay	□	Carneros, Sonoma, Monterey	●●○○+
Sauvignon Blanc	□	Napa	●●○○+

varieties. This leads to weak fruit flavours and rather dilute wines. The major problem in California as far as quality is concerned is the size of the yield. This is exacerbated by the demands of the domestic market, which is largely fashion-driven. One year everybody may be crying for White Zinfandel, the next for Chardonnay or Merlot, with the result that producers push their vines to the maximum with excessive irrigation. Yields are often frighteningly high, particularly in the Central Valley. Any shortfall is satisfied by blending in other grapes. Not surprisingly this leads to wines of doubtful quality and the vagaries in demand have led to over-production of some varieties. The jug wines of the past have largely been replaced by today's 'two buck chuck' – varietal wines at very low prices.

Zinfandel is regarded as California's 'own' grape variety and is widely planted for blends, for varietal wines and for the sweet, faintly pink or 'blush' **White Zinfandel**. For a long time its origins were unknown, but it is now recognised as the Primitivo of Italy. There are many old vineyards consisting of Zinfandel, often appearing as a 'field blend' with other varieties. These, and younger vineyards in prime sites, can be sources of rich, full-bodied red wines. This variety has a tendency to ripen unevenly, with the result that by the time full ripeness has been achieved for the whole bunch, some of the grapes will have started to raisin. The resulting concentration leads to intense red berry flavours and extreme alcohol levels, often with small amounts of residual sugar.

Many varietal **Cabernet Sauvignons** are simple, soft, juicy wines with light tannins and a little black cherry varietal fruit, sourced from the Central Valley. Prime sites, of which the most famous are in the Napa Valley, can produce extremely expressive wines that rival the quality of the best produced anywhere. Apart from the site and the variety, there are two main influences on the style of these, and other premium Californian wines: the long hang-time of the fruit, which results in an opulent, complex spectrum of ripe flavours in the grapes, though it can lead to

unbalanced, high alcohol; and no expense spared winemaking, including strict selection of grapes, high-tech equipment and temperature-controlled barrel cellars, which result in wines that are very well crafted, often with powerful, toasty flavours from new French oak.

As **Merlot** has been very fashionable, many cheap examples are available that have very soft tannins and little varietal character. Many of these wines exist to meet the demand that was created following the discovery of the beneficial effects of red wine on health. (It is ironic that some are so soft and light that some Hungarian *white* wines were recently found to have more of the beneficial compounds!) Better Merlots come from cooler sites such as Monterey and the North Coast regions, especially Napa. These deeply coloured wines have soft, velvety tannins, full body, high alcohol and classic varietal flavours of blackberry and plum.

In the past, much **Pinot Noir** was planted in sites that were too hot, resulting in rather baked, jammy wines, and wines that had little flavour as sugar ripeness was reached before flavours were able to develop properly. Many of the early Pinot Noirs were planted for sparkling wines. When this market failed to develop as rapidly as anticipated, they were used for still wines. Unfortunately, they were the wrong clones, and many wines lacked varietal fruit. There are now some very fine wines from cooler regions such as Russian River Valley and Carneros. Styles range widely, according to

Zinfandel grapes on 100-year-old vine in Lytton Springs Vineyard of Ridge, Healdsburg, Sonoma Co., California. Some grapes are starting to shrivel, resulting in a concentration of flavours and sugars.

the potential of the location and the aims of the winemaker. Some are light in colour, with classic gamey and vegetal notes, though most show rich layers of ripe red fruit flavours (red cherry, strawberry). There are very few cheap Californian Pinot Noirs.

All of the winemaking options that **Chardonnay** offers are explored in California. Classic California Chardonnay is very full-bodied (almost liqueurish), high in alcohol, low in acidity and has obvious flavours of oak, hazelnut and butter underpinning the exotic peach and banana fruit flavours. There are plenty of more restrained examples too, from cooler regions such as Carneros and Russian River Valley.

Most of California is too warm to make **Sauvignon Blancs** in the modern, clean, vegetal aromatic style, and winemaking usually follows the model of Bordeaux. Fermentation and/or ageing in oak results in full-bodied, spicy wines (often with hints of licorice), with just a little green pepper vegetality. Many Sauvignon Blancs that have received this treatment are sold as Fumé Blanc. Many cheap versions come from unsuitably warm sites and show little recognisable varietal fruit.

The current fashion for Rhône-style wines has also led many growers to plant varieties such as Syrah, Mondeuse, Viognier and Marsanne. The American market is very susceptible to fashion

and this has led to problems when, for example, the latest diet has suggested that Merlot is good for your heart. Wineries have not always been able to satisfy instant demand, and this has led to problems of quality and veracity.

MAIN VITICULTURAL AREAS
The principal vineyards are grouped into six regions, three of which, by virtue of their more northern coastal position, are important for the production of premium wines and contain the majority of the well-known counties and AVAs.

North Coast Region
This comprises the vineyards to the north of San Francisco Bay. Perhaps the best-known area of all is the **Napa Valley AVA**. This has the most expensive vineyard land and some of the most prestigious wineries of California. Morning mist rolling in from the Bay ensures the climate is milder to the south, which is in Davis Zone I. Here the area of **Carneros AVA**, which also extends into Sonoma County, specialises in producing Pinot Noir and Chardonnay, much of it used for making sparkling wine. Further up the valley, where the soils are volcanic, the climate is almost Mediterranean, and the northern end is in Zone III. Spring frosts can be a problem in the valley bottom. To the west, the wines of **Sonoma County** have a burgeoning reputation, with the prestigious areas of Russian River Valley best known for Pinot Noirs, and Dry Creek Valley for Zinfandel. To the north, the large and very diverse region of **Mendocino County** includes the very cool Anderson Valley, a supreme source of grapes for aromatic white wines such as Riesling and Gewurztraminer, as well as sparkling wines.

Air-conditioned barrel cellar at Arrowood, Sonoma.

Carneros, overlooking the Bay.

Huge fan used to disperse frost pockets, Oakville, Napa.

North Central Coast

This includes the fertile valley floor of the Salinas Valley in **Monterey County**, where the cool, dry climate gives Chardonnay wines of unusually high acidity and crisp, citrus flavours, as well as Merlots with grippy tannins and rich dark berry fruit. The diverse region the **Santa Cruz Mountains** includes cool locations with poor, inhospitable soils where some of California's greatest wines are produced, including pioneering wines from Rhône varieties. Here the climate is Zone I. Throughout the region, the best wines come from hillside vineyards.

South Central Coast

In the region of the South Central Coast, the mountains lie east–west, rather than north–south, thus encouraging the flow of cool ocean breezes. Here there has been much planting by major wineries, as climatic research showed this to have great potential for the production of quality grapes. Further inland the climate changes from Zone I to Zone II or III. The best known subregions here are the varied Santa Ynez Valley in **Santa Barbara County** and **San Luis Obispo County**, which includes Paso Robles AVA, a source of very fine Zinfandels.

Central Valley

This is where 80 per cent of Californian wine is produced. It stretches for some 600 kilometres south from Sacramento and quantity is the password, not only for grapes but also for vegetables. The climate is mostly hot (Zone V), and a whole range of new varieties have been created at Davis to make the most of the conditions. Among the more successful are Ruby Cabernet and Emerald Riesling. The towns of the valley host the major wineries, which are continually looking for new ways to use the surplus production. 'Pop' wine, wine coolers and brandies all play a role. At the north end of the Valley, in the delta of the Sacramento river, is the AVA of **Lodi**, where the climate is cooler and better wines are made.

Sierra Foothills AVA

These vineyards lie at the foot of the Rockies, where the original vineyards were planted during the Gold Rush. Hot days and cool nights (Zones III and IV) give good fruit concentration. Here the specialities are often old vine Zinfandels and Italian varieties.

Southern California

Finally, we have the vineyards between Los Angeles and San Diego. Here there have been the pressures of urban sprawl and Pierce's Disease.

FUTURE DEVELOPMENTS

California is fortunate that it has at its door what is potentially the largest wine market in the world. Like many other producing regions, it is finding it difficult to match production to demand. In addition, it has two individual and particular problems. The first of these is phylloxera; sloppy research at Davis Campus led to extensive use of the rootstock AXR-1, which subsequently proved not to be resistant to phylloxera, with the consequence that over half the vineyards of the Napa Valley had to be replanted. More recently, Pierce's Disease has spread from the orange groves of southern California. This is carried by insects called sharpshooters and is, for the vine, both incurable and fatal. While it is possible to create a *cordon sanitaire* to avoid the problem, this is no more than a stop-gap solution.

THE PACIFIC NORTH-WEST

The vineyards of the north-west are divided between the states of Washington, Oregon and, to a much smaller extent, Idaho. Climatically again, they can be divided by the influence of the Pacific Ocean. The coastal vineyards of Oregon and Washington have a maritime climate, and benefit from the influence of the warm currents of the North Pacific Drift. The other vineyards of Washington and those of Idaho are definitely continental, with bitterly cold winters and hot summers.

Oregon

In Oregon, the vineyards stretch south from the city of Portland. Those of the **Willamette Valley** are almost at its gates. Here the winters are mild and the summers warm and cloudy. The most successful grape is Pinot Noir, followed by Pinot Gris and Chardonnay. The quality of the wines is already very high, and with better clonal selection is improving rapidly. South of the Willamette Valley come the Umpqua and Rogue River Valleys, almost on the California state border. Here the warmer climate allows the growing of Cabernet Sauvignon and Merlot.

Washington State

In Washington State, there are vineyards around Puget Sound, but most are planted well inland in the infertile valleys of the Columbia and its tributary, the Yakima, with a further AVA, Walla Walla, much further to the east. This is virtual desert with wine-growing made possible only by irrigation with river water. Phylloxera is not a problem, but severe winter frosts occur approximately once every six years, sometimes reducing the subsequent crop by a half or more. Washington now follows California as the second most important state for grape-growing. Sales are dominated by one major winery group with a high proportion of the grapes coming from independent growers. Chardonnay, Merlot and Cabernet Sauvignon are the most important grapes, though Syrah is showing a great deal of promise.

NEW YORK STATE

This is the third most important state for grape growing in the United States, though two-thirds of its acreage is of *Vitis labrusca* grapes for jams and jellies. The introduction of the Farm Wineries Act in 1976 has led to an enormous increase in the number of wineries, most of them planting *vinifera* grapes, rather than the American varieties and hybrids that had previously dominated production.

There are three major vineyard areas for the production of wine in the state. The first of these is the Finger Lakes, where the lakes each have individual local climates. The Hudson Valley, to the north of New York City, is a long-established but minor vineyard area. Of more interest are the vineyards on Long Island where a broad range of European varieties thrives. Water on three sides creates a mild, maritime climate.

CANADA

In Canada, the Provincial Liquor Boards control production, including the local **Vintners Quality Alliance (VQA)** regulations that cover the delimitation of appellations, as well as viticultural and winemaking standards. *Labrusca* wines, which used to account for the majority of the production,

Pacific North-West USA			
KEY GRAPE VARIETIES		**MAIN REGIONS**	**PRICE**
Pinot Noir	■	Oregon	●●●○
Chardonnay	□	Washington	●●○○
Cabernet Sauvignon, Merlot	■	Washington	●●○○

Canada			
KEY WINE		**MAIN GRAPE VARIETIES**	**PRICE**
Ice-Wine	□	Riesling, Vidal	●●●●+

do not qualify, though certain other hybrid and American varieties are permitted for VQA. Wines also have to be submitted to an independent jury for assessment.

The most important quality wine production area in Canada is the **Niagara Peninsular** on the southern shore of Lake Ontario. Here the local site climate offers mild conditions, with a large body of water to the north and the Niagara escarpment, causing down-currents of air, to the west and south. A particular speciality is **Ice-Wine**, which has been a great commercial success in the Far East.

The second most important area for the production of wine in Canada is the **Okanagan Valley**, close to the city of Kelowna, 320 kilometres east of Vancouver. Here there are approximately 2 000 hectares of *vinifera* grapes planted in desert conditions. The most successful are the Sauvignon Blanc, Pinot Gris, Riesling and Gewurztraminer.

Harvesting Vidal grapes for Ice-Wine, Niagara-on-the-Lake, Ontario, Canada.

MEXICO

Mexico has approximately 50 000 hectares of vineyards, the fourth largest area in Latin America, and the longest-established winery in the Americas was established in what is now the town of Parras in the sixteenth century, yet it is only a minor producer of wine. Most of its production goes for distillation into brandy, with table grapes and raisins also being more important outlets for fruit than wine.

The blending of imported wine is not unknown, though recent legislation means that a wine bearing the words *Hecho en Mexico* on the label must be made entirely from Mexican-grown grapes.

Almost all (90 per cent) of the quality wine production of the country comes from vineyards in northern Baja California, the 1 300 km long peninsula along the Pacific Coast. Here the vineyards are concentrated in three valleys running in from the Pacific Coast. Of these, the most important is the most northerly, the Guadelupe Valley, just north of the resort of Ensenada. The coastal influences are similar to those in California, with the cold Alaska current causing morning fogs, giving welcome humidity to the vines. The vineyards are drip-irrigated with water drawn from subterranean aquifers. Salination is a problem. Although the soil is sandy, most vines are grafted.

The most successful wines are full-bodied reds and a broad range of European varieties is grown. Petite Sirah and Zinfandel are particularly successful. As well as three major producers, there is a small number of boutique wineries, largely producing Bordeaux-style blends.

SOUTH AMERICA

The history of wine throughout Latin America begins with the arrival of the Spanish and the Portuguese from the end of the fifteenth century. With every boatload of *conquistadors* came a priest and he brought with him the Bible and vine shoots to plant vineyards for wine for the Mass. The first vines were planted in what is now the Dominican Republic as early as 1493 and this invasion can be said to have come to an end with the building of the Mission in Sonoma in California as late as 1823. The importance of production in the New World can be judged by the fact that the governments of both Spain and Portugal forbade the making of wine, except for the Mass, in their American colonies in order to protect domestic growers. The further away these colonies were from their mother country, the more difficult it was to apply the law and Peru became the dominant wine-producing centre of the Americas, with an area under vines three times larger than it is now. Two factors at the beginning of the nineteenth century led to the development of the current wine industry of South America: the first was the collapse of the Spanish Empire, and the second was social unrest in Europe which led to thousands emigrating to the New World. The Portuguese, Italians and Spaniards who settled in South America took with them their need for wine as an essential part of their daily diet and, around their new homes, they planted the vines to give them this wine.

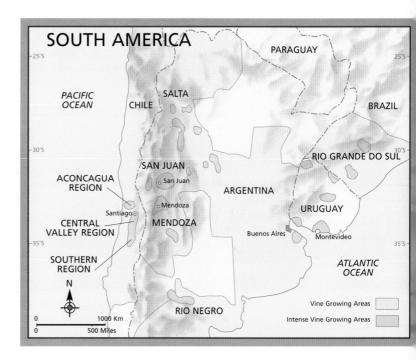

30 Chile

The most important provider of South American wines to the export markets of the world is Chile. It arrived at this position by rather a different route from other countries. The modern wine trade began in the middle of the nineteenth century when two factors contributed to the creation of a very wealthy middle class. These were the exploitation of the country's mineral resources and its key geographical position as a supply centre for boats furnishing California's Gold Rush. All things French became fashionable and much of the newly earned wealth was invested in Bordeaux-style châteaux and vineyards in the suburbs of Santiago. As a result, production was concentrated on four varieties: Cabernet Sauvignon and Merlot for red wines and Sémillon and Sauvignon Blanc for white. Since the fall of the dictator General Pinochet in 1989, the wine industry has boomed and there has been much foreign investment in vineyard planting and modern wineries. Stainless steel and oak casks are now commonplace. Sales particularly to the United States and Europe have soared.

Chile has many advantages for the production of good wine. The climate is near-perfect, with the prevailing winds blowing onshore from the Pacific. There is a long ripening season and the lack of rainfall is compensated by unlimited quantities of snowmelt from the Andes. This is channelled to the vines through an extensive irrigation system, attached to rights for the individual growers. Dry farming can be carried out effectively only in the south of the country.

Phylloxera is not present in the country and this means that most vines are ungrafted. However, with the extension of drip irrigation, nematodes can be a problem and grafted vines are becoming more common. The biggest problem as far as production of quality wine is concerned is successfully restricting the vigour of the vines. High yields are commonplace.

GRAPE VARIETIES AND WINES

The Chilean domestic market is small, so internationally demanded varieties now dominate production. **Cabernet Sauvignon** and **Merlot** are used for varietal wines, and for Bordeaux-style blends. Typically the wines show strong varietal flavours, with intense berry fruit and capsicum character. It should be noted that much of what has been sold as Merlot is in fact the historic Bordeaux variety **Carmenère**. It gives elegant, velvet-textured reds, and is being built up as the speciality wine of Chile. **Chardonnay** wines show great fruit purity, due to the ripeness and health

A modern winery at Colchagua.

of the grapes. Casablanca is emerging as a region of great potential, with crisp grapefruit and banana-scented wines that may have some oak treatment. With **Sauvignon Blanc** the picture is more complicated. Much of what had been sold as Sauvignon Blanc came from the variety Sauvignonasse, which produces wines of much less distinction. As new vineyards are planted and old ones are grafted over to the true Sauvignon, the quality of Chilean Sauvignons is improving rapidly.

During the past few years there have been efforts to widen the range of grapes being grown and there are now wide plantings of Carignan, Malbec, Pinot Noir and Syrah for red wines. The local red wine grape, País, thought to be the same as the Mission of California, is in rapid decline. Overplanting of Cabernet Sauvignon has led to that grape being used for the local bulk wine

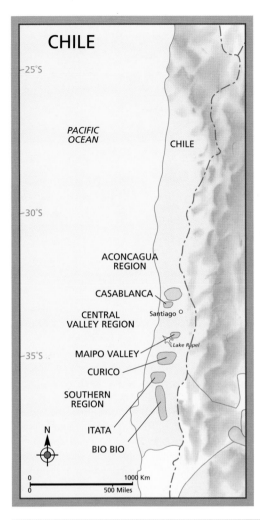

CHILE

25°S

PACIFIC OCEAN

CHILE

30°S

ACONCAGUA REGION

CASABLANCA

CENTRAL VALLEY REGION

Santiago

35°S

MAIPO VALLEY

CURICO

Lake Rapel

SOUTHERN REGION

ITATA

BIO BIO

N

0   1000 Km
0   500 Miles

market. Muscat of Alexandria is widely planted, particularly in the more northerly vineyards bordering the Atacama Desert, for distillation into the local brandy, *pisco*.

While many producers use the term *reserva* to denote that the wine has received some oak treatment, it has no legal significance, and, due particularly to pressure from the Spanish, is scheduled to be forbidden.

REGIONS AND CLIMATES

The classification system of the vineyard regions is based on four tiers: regions, subregions, zones and areas. A wine may name as its source any of these four levels. Thus a wine from around the town Santa Cruz can state that it comes from Santa Cruz (the area), Colchagua Valley (the zone), Rapel Valley (the subregion) or Central Valley (the region).

Aconcagua Region

The best Chilean white wines from Chardonnay and Sauvignon Blanc, and the best Chilean reds from Pinot Noir, are considered to come from the **Casablanca Valley**. It lies close to the sea, at a

Chile			
KEY GRAPE VARIETIES		**MAIN REGIONS**	**PRICE**
Chardonnay	☐	Casablanca, Central Valley	●●○○
Sauvignon Blanc	☐	Casablanca, Central Valley	●○
Pinot Noir	■	Casablanca	●●○○
Cabernet Sauvignon	■	Maipo, Rapel	●○○○
Merlot	■	Maipo, Rapel	●○○○

Vineyards planted on the valley floor in the cool climate Aconcagua Valley.

Grapes being sorted to
ensure only healthy, ripe
grapes are used for
winemaking, Colchagua.

point where the coastal *cordillera* of the Andes
almost dies away, allowing the maritime influence
of the cold Humboldt Current to create a cool
climate. The morning fogs have the same effect as
those that occur in Carneros (California), slowing
ripening, but allowing complex flavours to
develop due to the longer hang-time.

Central Valley Region

By far the most important of the five viticultural
regions is the Central Valley south of Santiago. It
lies between two *cordilleras* of the Andes that run
parallel to each other, north to south. The nearby
Pacific, with its cold Humboldt Current, helps
create a moderate, maritime climate, with
temperatures somewhere between those in Napa
and those in Bordeaux. These are perfect
conditions for Bordeaux varieties. Over 90 per
cent of all the wine that Chile exports is produced
here. Within this region, there are important
subregions, such as the **Maipo Valley**, surrounding
the capital, Santiago. This is a centre for fine red
wine production and is the site of many old
Cabernet Sauvignon vines, some of which have an
unusual, warm site-climate now they have been
engulfed by the expanding suburbs of Santiago.
(One is reminded of the position of Haut Brion, in
the outskirts of Bordeaux.) The Colchagua Valley,
a zone within the **Rapel Valley** sub-region, is an
outstanding zone for Cabernet Sauvignon, Merlot
and Carmenère, which appear as single varieties
and as Bordeaux-style blends. This zone has seen
considerable foreign investment, from the United
States and France. The best wines are made with
the same care as classed-growth Bordeaux, and
show great promise. They sell for very high prices.
Further south, in the **Curicó** sub-region, the
conditions are cooler, due to the effects of latitude
and cloud cover. A wide selection of international
varieties is grown there.

Southern Valley Region

There is a never-ending search for new, and better,
vineyard areas within the country. This has led to
the planting of more hillside vineyards, vineyards
closer to the sea, for example in the cool southerly
subregions of **Bío-Bío** and **Itata**, where irrigation
is unnecessary. These are suitable for aromatic
whites such as Riesling and Gewurztraminer.

Argentina, Uruguay and Brazil

The wine industry of Argentina is firmly rooted in the mass immigration from Europe during the second half of the nineteenth century. Argentina received many Italians, Spanish (mainly Basques and Catalans) and Swiss, and they planted vineyards in the lee of the Andes, particularly around the cities of Mendoza and San Juan. Initially, consumption was largely local, but with the opening of the Buenos Aires al Pacífico railway to Mendoza in 1885 (with a line to San Juan, a year later) the much larger markets of Buenos Aires and the world were opened up. At its peak in 1977, the country had more than 350 000 hectares of vineyards, now the figure is just over 200 000 hectares. Similarly per capita wine consumption has more than halved from its 1970 peak of 91.75 litres per year. As an open economy did not arrive until 1990, no money was available for investment in wineries or vineyards. However, since then there has been considerable investment, led by the Chileans. The collapse of the peso in 2001 led to a brief decline in sales, but also offered incentives for further investment from abroad.

31

ARGENTINA

The vineyards for the most part lie close to the Andes, in a series of irrigated oases in what is otherwise desert. These green patches are spread over more than 1 000 kilometres, from the province of Salta in the subtropical north, to Río Negro in the south on the frontiers of Patagonia.

CLIMATE, WEATHER AND VITICULTURE

With the exception of those of Río Negro, most of the vineyards lie 500 metres or more above sea level, and in Salta, close to the town of Cafayate, they regularly extend to 2 000 metres or more, allowing suitably cool sites to be found close to the equator. Historically, because of the heat, most vineyards were planted in the *parral*, or pergola, system. This lifted the grapes away from the searing heat close to the ground. New, quality-focused vineyards more commonly use a lower-yielding cordon training system.

In the rain-shadow of the Andes, rainfall is extremely low, but water can be drawn from rivers flowing down from the mountains or from subterranean aquifers. Flood irrigation is used in 90 per cent of the vineyards. Where drip-irrigation has been introduced, the vines tend to be grafted because of the increased risk of damage from nematodes. (Phylloxera, though present, is not regarded as a serious problem.)

Spring frosts are an occasional problem, but summer hail is a regular hazard. It has been calculated that this has the potential to destroy 10 per cent of the crop in an average year, so netting of the vines as a protection is widespread. Because of its dry climate, there are few problems with rot or mildew, and Argentina is an important producer of organic wines.

WINEMAKING

A combination of high-yielding vineyards, low labour costs and dry sunny conditions makes it possible to select large quantities of fully ripe, healthy fruit at low costs. Many modern wineries

Flood irrigation in Mendoza.

Argentina			
KEY GRAPE VARIETIES		**MAIN REGIONS**	**PRICE**
Malbec	■	Mendoza, Río Negro	●○○
Cabernet Sauvignon	■	Cafayate, Mendoza	●○○
Chardonnay	☐	Mendoza	●○○
Torrontés	☐	Cafayate	●○

Vines held in a netting frame to protect them against hail, Mendoza.

have invested in the most up-to-date equipment, enabling temperature-controlled fermentations to take place in hygienic stainless steel. A few estates are using oak *barriques* for premium wines, though some of Argentina's best red wines are still made in the old-fashioned way, with long periods of ageing in large old oak casks before bottling.

GRAPE VARIETIES

For marketing purposes, Argentina promotes two particular specialities: **Malbec** is used for full-bodied, brambly red wines. **Torrontés** gives full-bodied, dry white wines with Muscat-like aromas. However, there are many other varieties introduced by the immigrants, such as Bonarda, Barbera and Sangiovese from Italy and Tempranillo from Spain, which give distinctive wines either as mono-varietals or as blends. **Cabernet Sauvignon**, **Merlot** and **Syrah** are widely planted for red wines and **Chardonnay** and, increasingly, Viognier for white wines.

Nearly half the vineyard area is planted with low-quality historic varieties such as Criolla and Cereza, but these are used for basic, local market table wine, or for turning into grape concentrate. Their importance is declining as they are replaced by international varieties.

REGIONS

The heartland of wine production in the country is in the two provinces of Mendoza and San Juan, which together account for more than 90 per cent of production. It is only in **Mendoza** that there is a hierarchy of appellations. These are divided into five regions and a larger number of departments and then subdivisions. A wine may give as its origin any one of these. Of these regions the Upper Mendoza River (*Región Zona Alta del Río Mendoza*) is considered to be best for red wines, whilst the cooler Uco Valley (*Región del Valle de Uco*) is best for white wines and cooler climate grapes such as the Pinot Noir. Argentina was the first country in South America to have a DOC (*Denominación de Origen Controlada*) system. This was introduced for the 1992 vintage and applies to just two *departmentos*, San Rafael and Luján de Cuyo, both in Mendoza. For San Rafael any one of six grape varieties may be used, but for Luján only the Malbec is permitted. Sadly, few wines are sold bearing a DOC label and there appears to be no clear idea as to what it means.

The vast majority of Argentina's large volume, varietally labelled wines come from this region, along with many blends of international varieties (e.g. Bonarda-Tempranillo). Although very good examples of Chardonnay and Cabernet Sauvignon exist, arguably the best wines are made with Malbec. The wines are very different in style from those of Cahors, showing richer, riper damson fruit and softer tannins, often with peppery, spicy flavours in the finish. They share with Cahors their dark purple colour, rich tannins and full body.

The second most important province in terms of production is **San Juan**. Here the climate is distinctly hotter and there is, as well as light wines, large production of vermouths and grape concentrate.

Further north, and hotter still, is the province of La Rioja, where 80 per cent of the production comes from one group of co-operative cellars. To avoid disputes with Spain, the wine for export markets is labelled as coming from the **Famatina Valley**.

In the far north, **Cafayate**, in Salta province, is the home of the Torrontés grape. The high-altitude vineyards have large differences between day and night temperatures, allowing aromas and flavours to develop, while preserving acidity levels. Cabernet Sauvignon also does well here, showing strong black cherry varietal character.

Finally, in the far south, we have the relatively cool **Río Negro** region. The majority of production is of red wine made with Malbec grapes, though there is great potential for high-quality white wines. Malbec from Río Negro has much higher acidity levels, and drier, more chewy tannins than the Malbec from the warmer vineyards in Mendoza. It is much more elegant and 'Old World' in style, and the tannins, acidity and rich fruit allow it to develop smoky, tobacco-like notes with bottle age.

URUGUAY

Uruguay is a small player in the world of wine, having an annual production similar to that of New Zealand. The climate is temperate, with maritime influences that are reminiscent of Bordeaux. There are four distinct seasons a year, with an average annual temperature of 18° C and rainfall of 1 000 mm. Rain falls throughout the year and mildew and black spot are common. In a bid to minimise the effect of the damp climate, vines are widely trained on the lyre system.

Uruguay's winemaking history starts with the immigration of Basque settlers in the 1870s, who brought with them a range of Basque grape varieties. The most important of these is Tannat, which has become something of a Uruguayan speciality. It is used for everything from fortified wines and sweet rosés to elegant, Bordeaux-style, tannic reds. The latter are the most important wines for export markets, and for many of these, a component of Merlot is used to soften the powerful tannins. Most vineyards are planted around the capital, Montevideo, and are planted on gently undulating hills. The soils range from heavy clay to sand.

With a shortage of red wine in Brazil, this country has proved a convenient, near-at-hand outlet for much of Uruguay's production.

BRAZIL

Despite the fact that it has a landmass approaching that of China, Brazil has nowhere within its borders a climate suitable for the production of fine wine. Most regions are too hot and lack the defined seasons needed to guide the annual growth cycle of the vines. Because of the hot, damp climate, nearly 80 per cent of the grapes grown are either American varieties or hybrids. Per capita wine consumption is very low as cane

Vines trained on high cordons to lift them away from the ground's reflected heat, Mendoza.

spirit has a preferential tax regime. Despite this, it does have an important wine industry and is the third largest wine producing country in South America.

Production of the better wines is centred in the *Serra Gaucho* (the cowboy hills) in the state of Río Grande do Sul. The vineyards in this hilly region benefit from the cooling effects of altitude and the relatively southerly location, though damp conditions mean that rot and mildew are a problem. Here, mainly Italian immigrants produce wines and grape juice, and much of the wine is sparkling, aromatic and sweet, following the Asti model. This region accounts for more than 80 per cent of the country's wine. There is even a nascent *Appellation Contrôlée* Vale dos Vinhedos, though this is no more than a geographical qualification.

There are two other regions of lesser importance. In the south of the country along the border with Uruguay, vineyards have been planted on free-draining, sandy soils. In the tropical north of the country, there have been extensive recent plantings in the Middle Valley of the Río São Francisco. Here the river water is available to irrigate what would otherwise be a desert, and two vintages a year are produced. Syrah proves to be a surprising success.

32 Sparkling Wines

It is not surprising that Champagne and folklore should go hand in hand and this starts with its creation as a sparkling wine. Legend would have us believe that sparkling Champagne was invented by Dom Pérignon, a monk who became cellar master at Hautvillers in 1668. However, six years earlier, Dr Christopher Merret had described how English coopers added sugar to still wines to make them sparkle. In the mid-1660s there was a strong demand in London for 'brisk and sparkling wines'. At the same time, the refugee Marquis de Saint Evremont had made the still wines of Champagne popular at court. Fashion dictated that the two should come together and it was only in London that the two necessities for the sale of sparkling wines – solid glass bottles and cork stoppers – were available. These did not reach France for another 25 years or so. With the bubbles being induced in a separate process, almost any wine can be made to sparkle. Indeed, during the nineteenth century, you could find such products as Clos de Vougeot Mousseux and sparkling Sauternes.

Today there are three basic ways of producing bubbles in a wine: a secondary fermentation in bottle; a second fermentation in tank; and carbonation.

FERMENTATION IN BOTTLE
The Traditional Method

This is the classic method of producing Champagne and the best sparkling wines around the world, where they are sold under a variety of names. These include *Crémant* in France and Luxembourg, *Cava* in Spain, *Cap Classique* in South Africa and *traditional method*. The historical description was *méthode champenoise*, or champagne method, but the EU forbade this in 1994 as it was thought to be confusing.

The winemaker's aim at **first fermentation** is to produce a still wine, usually with crisp to high acidity and moderate alcohol. A few producers ferment some or all of their base wines in old oak casks, though temperature-controlled stainless steel is more common. Some wines may be allowed to undergo malolactic fermentation, while in others it will be prevented. These decisions depend on the style of wine that the producer is seeking to make.

It is then time for the blender to practise the art of **blending** (*assemblage*). For a producer's standard non-vintage wine, the aim is to produce, consistently over the years, a wine of chosen quality to a defined style. The blender may have a range of wines from different grape varieties, different vineyards and even different years. To help achieve consistency as well as to benefit from the extra depth of flavour provided by aged wines, each year a proportion of the production may be stored in bulk as reserve wine for use in future blends. With many New World sparkling wines a vintage may be stated, but a small percentage of reserve wines may still legally be used. Storage of reserve wines is expensive, however, and in regions where reliable vintage conditions make their use unnecessary, reserve wines are rarely used. Where a vintage is stated on a bottle of Champagne, 100 per cent of the base wines must come from that year. Given that, in the larger Champagne companies, over 100 different wines from just one vintage might be available, it is easy to see that the number of different permutations can be astronomical. Laboratory analysis of the wines may be of some assistance, but the blend has ultimately to be achieved by tasting. It is essential that each company have an experienced head blender, for it is upon the quality of the blend that the reputation of the company rests or falls.

For rosé wine, all producers outside Champagne will make their base wine by the *saignée* method, removing the must after a very short period of skin contact. Most champagne producers, however, make their wine by blending red and white base wines, which is permitted at any stage of the process up to and including the time of the addition of *liqueur de tirage* described below. Pink Champagne is the only quality rosé wine produced in this way within the EU.

Other terms that can be found on a sparkling wine label include **Blanc de Blancs**, a wine made just from white grapes. In Champagne, this has to be Chardonnay, and the style is usually very crisp and light in body, with fresh citrus and apple fruit. **Blanc de Noirs** wines are also seen. This indicates a white wine made just from black grapes, though in the United States it can indicate a distinct pinkish tinge to the wine. Champagnes and other sparkling wines made exclusively from Pinot Noir and Pinot Meunier tend to be full-bodied, with rich fruit and a long finish. The term *crémant* used to be applied to wines with a little less than full sparkling wine pressure, and hence a more 'creamy' mousse. It has not been permitted for Champagne since 1994, when the Champenois agreed to leave the term for other sparkling wines from France and Luxembourg in return for their forfeiting the right to say that they were made by the *méthode champenoise*.

Before bottling, a small proportion of *liqueur de tirage* will be added. This is a cocktail of wine, sugar, yeast nutrients and a clarifying agent. It is this that will set off the **second fermentation** in the bottle and create the sparkle. The bottle is then closed with a temporary seal. This is usually a crown cork, with a plastic cup sometimes inserted to collect the dead yeast cells. The bottles are then laid to rest horizontally in stacks in the producer's cellars. The temperature at which the wine is stored is yet another factor that affects its ultimate quality. At lower temperatures, the second fermentation and subsequent yeast autolysis are slowed down, but more complex flavours can develop. When the yeasts get to work on the sugar, causing the second fermentation, they create three things: alcohol, CO_2, and when they die, having completed their first task, a deposit on the side of the bottle. As the wine slowly ferments, the gas, being unable to escape, is slowly dissolved into the wine.

During the subsequent **maturation** in the bottle, the dead yeast cells eventually break down and their enzymes interact with the wine. This process is known as **yeast autolysis** ('self-digestion') and it is an essential part of the process for traditional and transfer method sparkling wines. This process releases compounds that contribute to the flavour of the wine, especially the yeast, bread, biscuit and toast notes that are characteristic of sparkling wines made this way. Autolysis typically lasts for between four and five years, but has been known

to continue for as long as ten years. The time that a wine spends on its lees contributes much to its final quality. For non-vintage Champagne it has to be a minimum of 15 months, and for vintage Champagne, at least three years. For other quality sparkling wines such as Cava and New World quality sparkling wines, nine months is required. These minimum periods are regularly exceeded.

The next two stages in the traditional method are designed to facilitate the removal of the sediment in the bottle. At this stage the bottle is binned, lying horizontally (*sur latte*), with the deposit on the side of the bottle. Riddling (*remuage*) moves this deposit into the neck of the bottle, against the cork. This is followed by disgorgement (*dégorgement*), the removal of the sediment.

Riddling is achieved over a period of time by altering the position of the bottle from the horizontal plane, on which it has lain for some time, to the upside-down vertical. The result will be that the deposit slides gently down from the side of the neck and finally into the plastic cup in the neck of the bottle. The traditional technique was developed at the beginning of the nineteenth century, by the widow 'Veuve' Clicquot herself and her *chef de cave* Antoine Müller. The neck of the bottle is put in an angled hole in a rack known as a *pupitre*. This consists of two hinged boards; 60 bottles can be held on each side. The holes are at an angle of 45° so that the bottles can be held at any angle between the horizontal and the vertical. The bottle starts off horizontal, and then each day is given a gentle shake and a twist and inclined more towards the inverted vertical. The work is done by hand. A skilled *remueur* can manipulate up to 30 000 bottles a day. Gradually, the more solid yeast particles move down towards

The traditional Champagne press holds four tonnes of grapes, which will yield 2 550 litres of juice. The shallow press reduces damage to the grapes.

Remuage

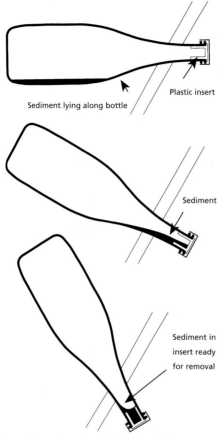

Sediment lying along bottle

Plastic insert

Sediment

Sediment in insert ready for removal

the neck, pushing the lighter ones before them. Ultimately, the bottle will be taken away to be binned with the crown caps downward. This is a labour-intensive and very costly process. Consequently, over the years a number of mechanical and semi-mechanical systems have been developed so that the work can be carried out in bulk. Not only is there a considerable saving in labour, but also in time. Perhaps the most effective tool is the *gyropalette*, a cage holding 504 bottles on a hydraulic arm. Whole banks of these can be controlled by a computer to rotate and incline, thus simulating the action of the *remueurs*. Most producers now use these, though they normally keep a few *pupitres* for the tourists to admire, and for bottles of unusual shape or size.

Whichever method is used, bottles that have completed the process often receive a further period of ageing standing on their necks. This is described as being *sur pointe*. With only a small surface area in contact with the wine and autolysis complete, the lees in the bottle do not contribute further to the flavour of the wine. Indeed, the wine

is in something like a state of suspended animation, though the presence of the lees can keep the wine fresh for years, even decades. The longer the wine spends on its lees, however, the quicker it will age when disgorged. A balance then has to be struck to achieve the ideal period that wine spends on its lees. Certain vintage Champagnes are described as *dégorgement tardive* or R.D. (*récemment dégorgé*; a proprietary term). These are old wines that have been disgorged just before shipment to retain their freshness.

As the sediment is now lying on the inside of the crown cork, the pressure inside the bottle will drive it out once it is opened. To make the process of **disgorgement** less messy, the neck of the bottle is frozen in a brine solution. When the bottles are then moved into an upright position and placed on a conveyor belt, the ice holds the now solid sediment in place, so keeping the wine clear. The crown cork is then removed and the plug of ice is ejected under pressure, sediment and all, together with its retaining plastic cup. The whole process from here to inserting the final cork is fully automated and takes a short time to avoid pressure loss and the possibility of oxidation.

Inevitably, during disgorgement a small amount of wine is lost. The bottle is therefore topped up to the correct level and then a mixture of wine and cane sugar solution, known as *liqueur d'expedition*, is added. The amount of sugar used will depend on the ultimate sweetness that is required for the wine. This part of the traditional method is called **dosage**. An important feature of each producer's style is the sweetness, or probably more accurately today dryness, of the wine. This element of house style is determined by the composition of the dosage, which will vary from company to company. Most sparkling wines are naturally very dry; nevertheless, as in any wine, even the driest will contain a very little unfermented, or residual, sugar. The list below describes the total sugar content of the finished wine, rather than the quantity added as dosage. These are the terms widely used to describe the sweetness, or dryness, of sparkling wines.

Brut Nature/Brut Zero/Ultra Brut = bone dry 0–2 g/l

Extra Brut = very dry 0–6 g/l

Brut = very dry to dry 0–15 g/l

Extra-Sec/Extra Dry = off-dry to medium-dry 12–20 g/l

Sec/Dry/Secco/Seco/Trocken = medium-dry 17–35 g/l

Demi-Sec/Riche/Halbtrocken/Semi-Dulce/Abbocato = sweet 33–50 g/l

Doux/Sweet/Dolce/Doce/Dulce = luscious 50+ g/l

It will be noted that the grades overlap, so the winemakers (or marketeers perhaps) have some flexibility in how they choose to describe their product. The Brut of one producer, for example, may be the Extra-Sec of another.

In order to maintain a perfect seal, a sparkling wine cork has to be compressed considerably before it is inserted into the neck of the bottle. In its original shape, it takes the form of a cylinder with an area on its face about three times that of the neck of the bottle; the familiar mushroom shape is acquired after corking. Even with this degree of compression, a wire muzzle is added for complete security. The cork is made up of two sections, the combination of which has been shown to give the most effective seal. The end that is in contact with the wine consists of two or three horizontal slices of whole cork; the balance is made up of composition cork. Quality-conscious producers will then age the wine for a further period of a few months to allow the *liqueur d'expedition* to integrate into the wine, and the wine to recover from the violent process of disgorgement.

Finally, before dispatch to the customer, the bottle will be dressed. The very deep foil around the neck of many bottles of sparkling wine is there because in former times, when the wines were not topped up after disgorgement, the foil was used to hide the large gap between the wine and the cork!

It is a matter of taste whether the wine sees further ageing. The best traditional method sparkling wines are certainly able to evolve in the bottle: the bubbles become creamier and less aggressive, and sugars from the *liqueur d'expedition* allow honey and toast notes to develop. Compounds remaining from autolysis can develop into aromas of bread, biscuit and toast; and the fruit can develop alongside these, sometimes resulting in a fabulously complex interplay of flavours.

The Transfer Method

This method attempts to gain the advantages of a second fermentation in the bottle without the disadvantages and expense of the complicated process of sediment removal required by the full traditional method. Up to the stage of riddling, the process is the same as in the traditional method. In particular, as with that method, yeast autolysis occurs during the maturation in the bottle, as long as the wine is matured for a sufficient time. In this case, though, the entire contents of the bottle are disgorged into a tank under pressure, filtered in bulk and rebottled into a fresh bottle.

This can give good sparkling wines at a cheaper

Gyropalettes are far more efficient for *remuage* but represent a considerable investment on the part of the producer.

Sediment in the neck of a Champagne bottle prior to *dégorgement*. This bottle is sealed with a cork and staple; most houses use crown-corks.

price than the traditional method. With large batches that can easily be tested, it is easier to ensure consistent quality. It is accepted, however, that the quality of the bubbles can be affected, particularly with manual and semi-automatic methods. These might slightly reduce the pressure or increase oxidation, though fully within acceptable limits. A distinction can be drawn between the two processes on the label; one using the transfer method may state that the wine is 'bottle-fermented' while traditional method wines might say 'fermented in *this* bottle', though it is more likely to state traditional method or *méthode traditionelle*.

The transfer method is mainly used in the New World, particularly Australia, where it accounts for 80 per cent of the sparkling wine production. Although it is certainly not unknown in Europe, no one makes a speciality of it. It might be pointed out, however, that in Champagne only half-bottles, bottles, magnums and, rarely, jeroboams go through the full Champagne process, all other sizes are decanted and thus might be said to have undergone the transfer method.

CHAMPAGNE
The Champagne Region

The most northern vineyard area of France, the Champagne region lies north-east of Paris, its heart in the form of a double fish-hook, with the valley of the River Marne as its shank. The three main vineyard concentrations are the Vallée de la Marne, the Montagne de Reims and the Côte des Blancs. In the Marne Valley, many of the most important companies are based in the town of Epernay. To the north is the Montagne de Reims, with beyond it the cathedral city of Reims, the other important centre of the trade. To the south runs the Côte des Blancs. All these vineyards are in the *département* of the Marne. Some 90 kilometres south of the Côte des Blancs, but still part of the appellation, are three detached areas: around Sézanne in the Marne and Bar-sur-Seine and Bar-sur-Aube, in the Aube *département*. More recently, in order to cater for increased demand, there has been an extension of vineyards into the more northerly *département* of the Aisne.

Climate and Soils

Because these are among the most northerly vineyards in Europe, it is by no means easy to make a wine that is better than drinkable. The winters are cold and the summers warm, rather than hot. The average temperature during the growing season is 16° C. In such a climate, it is difficult for the grapes to achieve full ripeness, and they might have no more than 8.5% abv of natural potential alcohol. For a vintage wine, 9.5% abv is needed. In the New World, grapes would never achieve flavour ripeness with such low degrees of potential alcohol. The typical product, then, is a light, crisp wine, high in acidity and low in alcohol. It is ideal as a base for sparkling wine, the high acidity particularly playing a very important part in seeing that the final wine is well balanced. A little wine is sold in its still form, though it may not be called Champagne. It has the separate appellation Côteaux Champenois.

The sub-soil in the Champagne region is mainly chalk, except in the Aube, where it is Kimmeridgean marl. The chalk has an important role to play, because it retains water well. The average rainfall is only 650 mm (as opposed to over 800 mm in Bordeaux) but the chalk ensures that there is always water there when it is needed. The soil characteristics of the different villages contribute to the characteristics of the fruit that they produce. Each village in Champagne is rated for quality on a percentage scale, under a system known as the **echelle des crus**. Seventeen villages have the top rating 100 per cent and are known as **Grands Crus**; 43 villages are **Premier Crus** with a rating of 90–99 per cent; the lowest rating of all is 80 per cent and applies to some villages outside the Marne *département*. Unlike Burgundy or Alsace, it is the whole village that is rated. Inevitably, there will be some outstanding sites

CHAMPAGNE

SOISSONS
R. Aisne
R. Suippe
R. Vesle
REIMS
R. Ourcq
Verzenay
Mailly-Champagne
Verzy
MONTAGNE
DE REIMS
Hautvillers
R. Marne
Bouzy
Ay-Champagne
VALLÉE DE LA MARNE
Tours-sur-Marne
EPERNAY
Chouilly
Cramant
Avize
Oger
CHÂLONS-
SUR-MARNE
Le Mesnil-sur-Oger
Vertus
R. Marne
R. Saulx
CÔTE DES
BLANCS
Sézanne
CÔTE DE
SÉZANNE
R. Aube
R. Seine
R. Voire

•   Grand Crus villages
○   Pemier Crus villages
---   Champagne Region

N

0   10   20   30 Km
0   10   20 Miles

TROYES
R. Seine
BAR-SUR-
AUBE
BAR-SUR-
SEINE
CÔTES DÈS BAR

within villages that have lower ratings. Equally, not every plot within a village rated as 100 per cent will offer the same top level of potential. The vine grower and annual weather conditions also have a part to play in this marginal climate. A skilful or lucky grower may produce outstanding grapes from a lesser site, while grapes from top sites may be ruined by incompetence or freak weather. For the very top level, however, everything must work together: a site of great potential, skilful viticulture and a great vintage.

In the past the price paid to the growers was based upon the *echelle des crus*. A base price per kilogram of grapes was agreed for the harvest and then the grower would receive the percentage of the base price dependent on the rating of the village where they grew their grapes. Thus a grower in a *Grand Cru* village would receive the full price, while one in a lesser village might receive four-fifths of the base price. Since the EU now forbids such price-fixing, individual contracts are negotiated between the growers and the merchants.

Viticulture and Grape Varieties

Three main grape varieties are used in the making of Champagne: Chardonnay, Pinot Noir and the rather humbler Pinot Meunier. In the Marne Valley, all three varieties are found, though **Pinot Meunier** is favoured, its late budding and early ripening making it better suited to this northern climate with spring frosts and summer rains. It gives an easy-to-drink fruitiness, and is especially important for wines that are to be enjoyed while

Champagne			
KEY STYLES		**MAIN GRAPE VARIETIES**	**PRICE**
Non-vintage (NV)	☐ ■	Pinot Noir, Pinot Meunier, Chardonnay	●●●○
Vintage	☐ ■	Pinot Noir, Chardonnay, Pinot Meunier	●●●●
Prestige Cuvée	☐ ■	Pinot Noir, Chardonnay	●●●●+
Rosé	■	Pinot Noir, Pinot Meunier, Chardonnay	●●●○+
Blanc de Noirs	☐ ■	Pinot Noir, Pinot Meunier	●●●○+
Blanc de Blancs	☐	Chardonnay	●●●○+

Champagne cellar cut out of chalky subsoil.

The bleak scenery of Champagne.

young. The Montagne de Reims is largely planted with the black varieties, particularly **Pinot Noir**. This variety produces wines of great body and length, and provides the backbone to most blends. **Chardonnay** is most common in the Côte des Blancs. It gives much lighter wine than in Burgundy and is relied upon to impart acidity, floral and citrus fruit character, lighter body and fine-textured bubbles.

Vineyards are laid out with rows a maximum of 1.5 metres apart, with the individual vines being planted 0.9–1.5 metres apart. A number of pruning methods are authorised, though the best vineyards either use the *Taille Chablis* (for Chardonnay) or the *Cordon de Royat* (for Pinot Noir and Pinot Meunier). Both methods leave large amounts of old wood, which improves frost resistance, and makes it easier to grow a second crop in years when frost has destroyed the first buds. In both cases, the vines are trained low on wires and are spur-pruned.

Vinification

In Champagne, mechanical harvesters are forbidden so all the grapes are picked by hand and placed in small plastic cases to minimise any damage to them. Particular care has to be taken with the black grapes. Immediately after picking, the grapes are taken to the press-house and weighed. They are then pressed quickly to avoid oxidation, or the juice from the black grapes being tinted by the colouring matter in their skins. (It may appear strange that while most Champagne is white, it is mainly made from black grapes.) Each village will generally have at least one press-house to make sure that the grapes are pressed as rapidly as possible.

The harder the grapes are pressed, the more undesirable attributes, such as harsh tannins, are likely to be found in the wine, whereas the first gentle pressings are rich in both sugars and desirable acids. Dom Pérignon was the first to record this. He went on to design a large diameter vertical press specifically for making white wine from black grapes. This type of press, known as a *Coquard Press*, traditionally takes a single charge of four tonnes of grapes, though the size can vary considerably. Now more modern horizontal pneumatic presses are being installed, which apply more gentle and controlled pressure. Whichever press is used, the amount of juice that can be extracted is strictly controlled. The law states that from 160 kg of grapes no more than 102 litres of juice must be extracted. As the fruit is pressed, the juice is separated into two classes – the first 80 litres of any 100 will be classified as *cuvée* and

the balance as *taille*. The finest Champagnes will be made solely from *cuvée* juice. Any juice drawn off after the *taille* must be sent for distillation.

The *cuvée* and *taille* juice from each grape variety and from each village should be stored and fermented separately. Generally, this will take place in temperature-controlled stainless steel vats, but more producers are returning to the tradition of the first fermentation of at least part of their wine, taking place in often new oak barrels. Winemaking then follows the stages of the traditional method. Storage during second fermentation, autolysis, *sur pointe*- and post-disgorgement ageing takes place in cellars that are generally dug out of chalk, many of which stretch for kilometres under Reims and Epernay. The advantage that they all have is a constant, cool temperature of 10–12° C.

The fact that the climate is marginal encourages the production of **non-vintage** blends to even out the differences between wines made in different years. Born out of pragmatism, but refined over the years, this practice now permits the winemaker to create, and thereafter to maintain consistently, the individual house style. It is often said that the ideal wine from Champagne is non-vintage, but in most years there will be some houses producing **vintage** wines. These will have individual characteristics and will vary in style from year to year. Even in the very best years, no more than a maximum of 80 per cent of the crop can be sold as vintage wine. This leaves the balance as reserve wine for future blending. Overall, vintage wine remains the exception rather than the rule. In style, vintage wines should be fuller in body with greater intensity of fruit than non-vintage wines, and show more toast or biscuit character due to their longer period of autolysis. Many producers will also offer a **Prestige Cuvée**. Most, though not all, are vintage wines; all are produced from the highest quality base wines and are blended with great care. Often they will be aged longer before release and will be designed to support further ageing.

The Champagne Trade

Despite the fact that the process of making Champagne requires considerable investment of money and time, approximately 3 750 growers, particularly in the most highly rated villages, sell their own Champagne, though in many cases it will have been vinified at a co-operative cellar. As their fruit is likely to come from one locality only, the terms *Grand Cru* and *Premier Cru* frequently appear on their labels (though some of the major houses are also beginning to stress the classification of their base wines). The majority of the growers, though, sell their grapes to a co-operative cellar or to one of the Champagne-producing houses.

The co-operative cellars play an important role in Champagne, processing, at one stage or another, over half the wine that is produced. Only 7 per cent of the total sales, however, is under the label of a co-operative; the rest is sold on, either as base wine to one of the *négociant* houses, or as 'buyers' own brands' (BOBs) for supermarkets and similar outlets. Of all wine that appears on the markets of the world, 70 per cent bear the label of one of the 264 *négociant* 'houses'. However, between them they only own 12 per cent of the vineyard area. This shows the extent to which they rely on the growers and co-operatives for their raw material. They will collaborate closely with them throughout the year, especially in the press-house at vintage time. Within the ranks of the Champagne houses, there was once an inner group called the *Syndicat de Grandes Marques de Champagne*. Although this no longer exists, top brands are still often referred to as *Grande Marque Champagnes*. The small number at the base of a Champagne label may indicate whether it has been made by a grower (RM), a co-operative cellar (CM) or a Champagne house (NM), or if it is a brand name not owned by the producer (MA).

By law the word Champagne must be branded on that part of the cork that enters the bottle. Champagne is also the only AC wine in France that does have to bear the words *Appellation Contrôlée* on the label.

OTHER BOTTLE-FERMENTED SPARKLING WINES

While the climate and the soil of Champagne provide a unique parentage for the wine, there are many other regions in the world that have adopted the method of secondary fermentation and maturation in the bottle to produce sparkling wine. Indeed the Champagne houses themselves have not been slow to establish wineries in places as diverse as the Loire Valley, Brazil, India, Australia, New Zealand, California and even Korea. The reasons for this are twofold: first, because of the geographically constrained vineyards, production of Champagne is limited and, particularly in boom years, the price can rise rapidly. Secondly, the whole image of Champagne is that of a luxury product (on a major brand more than 10 per cent of the retail cost is accounted for by the promotional spend). As a result of this, many governments strictly limit its importation, particularly if there is a local wine industry to protect.

Other Bottle-Fermented Sparkling Wines

KEY WINES		MAIN GRAPE VARIETIES	PRICE
Crémant d'Alsace AC	☐	Pinot Blanc, Riesling, Chardonnay	●●
Crémant de Bourgogne AC	☐	Chardonnay, Pinot Noir	●●
Crémant de Limoux AC	☐	Mauzac, Chardonnay, Chenin Blanc	●●
Crémant de Loire AC	☐	Chenin Blanc, Chardonnay, Cabernet Franc	●●
Saumur AC	☐■	Chenin Blanc, Cabernet Franc	●●
Vouvray AC	☐	Chenin Blanc	●●○
Cava DO	☐■	Macabeu, Xarel-lo, Parellada, Chardonnay	●●○
Australia	☐■	Pinot Noir, Chardonnnay, others	●●●●○
	■	Shiraz	●●○
California	☐■	Pinot Noir, Chardonnay, others	●●○○+
New Zealand	☐■	Pinot Noir, Chardonnay, others	●●●●
South Africa Cap Classique	☐■	Pinot Noir, Chardonnay, others	●●○

France

Not surprisingly, there are a number of other French sparkling wines made by what must be known now as the traditional method. One such group, the **Crémant** wines, gave an upgraded status to a small number of long-standing AC sparkling wines. The name and the tighter controls were introduced in 1975. The controls include such matters as the proportion of the grape varieties in the blend, the yields of juice and the time the wine spends on the lees (minimum nine months). The wines in this group include Crémant d'Alsace, Crémant de Bourgogne, Crémant de Limoux and Crémant de Loire. Generally speaking, each of these wines will be made from the grapes used for making the best still white wines of the region. However, a proportion of lesser varieties, such as the Aligoté in Burgundy, is permitted. Crémant d'Alsace relies mainly on Pinot Blanc and Riesling, though the aromatic varieties such as Gewurztraminer and Muscat are forbidden and Chardonnay is permitted.

There is also a further number of traditional method AC sparkling wines in France. These include the Chenin Blanc-based wines of **Saumur** and **Vouvray** on the Loire.

Spain

The second major European producer of traditional method sparkling wine is Spain, where it is known as **Cava**. The term Cava is a DO (currently in the process of promotion to DOC status), and covers the method and the area of production. The trade centres on the town of Sant Sadurni d'Anoia, where the cellars rival those of Champagne. While by far the majority of the wine is produced in the Catalan vineyards of Penedés, it

Tank Method Sparkling Wines			
KEY WINES		**MAIN GRAPE VARIETIES**	**PRICE**
Asti DOCG	☐	Muscat Blanc à Petits Grains	●○
Deutscher Sekt	☐	Müller-Thurgau, Riesling	●●○
Sekt	☐	Various	●○

can also be produced in a number of other DO regions. These include Rioja, Navarra and Utiel-Requena. The wines must be made by the full traditional method and must spend a minimum of nine months in bottle before disgorgement. The cork must bear a four-pointed star on its base.

Most Cava is dry and low in acidity, with some character from yeast autolysis. The flavour will vary considerably with the grapes that have been used. In Penedés, the main grape varieties used are those traditionally grown locally for white wine. Maccabeo (the Viura of Rioja) gives rather neutral wines. Xarel-lo can be strongly flavoured and earthy. Parellada imparts a hint of apples. More producers are now using Chardonnay, which can supply much needed fruit and acidity. Unlike Champagne, few wines are made for ageing.

The New World

It is principally to the countries of the New World that the Champagne houses have turned in order to diversify. In a number of solo and joint ventures, some fine quality sparkling wines are being produced using not only the traditional method. Most of the better New World sparkling wines are based upon Pinot Noir and Chardonnay and thus rely on cooler climate vineyards, in regions such as Tasmania and the Yarra Valley in Australia, Marlborough in New Zealand, Carneros in California, and Oregon. Although Champagne varieties and methods are used, the wines tend to have richer, riper fruit. However, the wide variety of vineyard locations, and differences of winemaking philosophies and commercial goals, result in a great diversity of styles when it comes to such matters as degree of autolysis, fruit character and the balance between fruit and oxidative flavours and/or acidity. There is often considerable financial investment in the vineyards and in the winemaking facilities, and quality can be outstanding. Many large brands are produced using labour-saving production techniques, such as the transfer method, which reduces costs and increases value for money and/or profitability.

Sparkling reds are made from a range of grape varieties in Australia, though Shiraz is by far the most important. Some use a proportion of reserve wines and/or barrel ageing to add depth and complexity.

There are also large quantities of very cheap sparkling wines made in New World regions from non-Champagne varieties, using the tank method.

THE TANK METHOD

It is probable that most of the sparkling wine consumed in the world is made by this method. In French, this method is called *cuve close*, or the Charmat method, after the Frenchman who developed it at the beginning of the twentieth century. In this method, the second fermentation takes place in a sealed tank rather than in a bottle. Dry base wine is placed, together with sugar, yeast nutrients and a clarifying agent, in the tank and following the second fermentation the resulting sediment is removed by filtration under pressure, before the wine is bottled.

The chief advantage of the tank method is that it considerably reduces production costs. It does, however, tend to produce larger, more uneven bubbles, that do not last as long as those from bottle-fermented wines. It is also true that the majority of tank method wines show none of the subtlety of flavour imparted by yeast autolysis, because this does not normally occur. For the production of sparkling wines that show the character of the base wines, without the alteration and masking that occurs with autolysis, this can be the ideal method. This is particularly useful with aromatic varieties such as Muscat and Riesling, and fruity styles of sparkling wine such as Prosecco from north-east Italy. Recent research has demonstrated that autolysis can be induced by, for example, using paddles to stir up the sediment and bring it more into contact with the wine during the second fermentation. The quality of the base wine and care in production count for much, and it may be that when trying to meet a low price point, the best wine is produced by compromising on the production method and investing in the base wines. Nevertheless, under French law, no tank method sparkling wine can be of AC status.

Sekt

Sekt from Germany is virtually all tank-fermented, though a few of the most expensive brands are fermented in bottle. Germany is an enormous market for sparkling wine and has the highest per capita consumption in the world. Most of this is Sekt.

In legal terms, Sekt is not necessarily a German wine, but is a wine that has been made sparkling in Germany. The base wines come generally from France or Italy. On the other hand, **Deutscher Sekt**, in addition to being made sparkling in

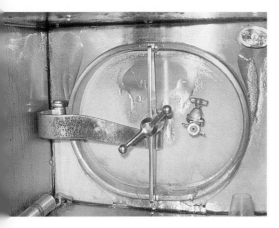

Ice building up on the
outside of tanks used for
Asti fermentation.

Germany, must also use only German-grown grapes. The best is made from Riesling, though the higher-yielding Müller-Thurgau is more commonly used. Recently, there has also been an increase in varieties such as the Chardonnay, Auxerrois, Pinot Blanc and, most successfully, Pinot Noir. If all the grapes for the wine come from one of the 13 *Anbaugebiete*, then the wine can bear the superior appellation of **Deutscher Sekt bA**. Some of the top estates will produce such wines from individual *Einzellage*, though these premium Sekts are most likely to be produced using the traditional method.

Asti

The Asti method is often considered a variation of the tank method, but is different in that it does not involve the original production of a still *dry* wine. In the Asti method, the sweet juice from pressed grapes is fermented to about 6% abv and is then chilled and filtered to stop the fermentation. At this stage the partially fermented must is still, not sparkling. Sugar and selected yeasts are then added and the must is put into sealed tanks to continue its fermentation. When the required alcoholic degree is achieved, the wine is chilled, membrane-filtered to remove the live yeast, and bottled under pressure. This leaves a sparkling wine, quite low in alcohol, typically only 7–7.5% abv, but with a high residual sugar content. For the Asti DOCG itself, the grape used is Muscat, with its distinct grapey aroma and taste. In the finest wines, the wines have much more length and a distinct flavour of peaches and tangerines. Asti is best drunk very young and is usually fermented only when required. The unfermented must, in the meantime, is stored under refrigeration. If it spends too long in storage before being consumed, it loses its attractive fruitiness, and develops unattractive vegetal flavours, reminiscent of geraniums.

CARBONATION

The third major way of making a wine sparkle is by carbonation. This is the one method that does not use the CO_2 produced as part of an alcoholic fermentation, but takes it from a cylinder. It puts bubbles in, but does not otherwise alter the wine. This is the cheapest method of all, and it shows. The bubbles are large and disappear quickly. For this reason this method is not used for any wines with claims to quality. In France, a wine so made has to state on the label *vin gazéifié*; such wines seem to find their natural market as prizes on fairgrounds. In the UK, such wines are only seen as Sparkling Light British Wines.

33 | Port

There can be no wine that is more British than Port, for it was created by the British for the British. While, for preference, the British have generally preferred to drink French wines, on occasion, mainly for political expedience, they have had to look elsewhere and their eyes have turned to Spain and Portugal, largely for ease of shipment. For eight years, from 1678, the import of wines from France to Britain was prohibited, and in 1703, the Methuen Treaty was signed with Portugal, which immediately increased trade between the two countries. At that time, the red wines of Portugal were thin and acidic, largely incapable of standing up to the rigours of the voyage across the Bay of Biscay and unappealing to the consumer. However, two English merchants on a wine-buying trip had noted a possible answer to these problems as early as 1678. At the monastery of Lamego, some 90 kilometres up the Douro Valley, they had tasted a soft, slightly sweet red wine, which they felt would be very attractive for their customers. The Abbot told them that his secret was that he added some brandy to the wine before it finished fermenting. If this story is true, it was more than 50 years before such wines were commercially shipped to London. While Port is considered a typically British drink, the most important export market is France, where the lighter wines are used overwhelmingly as an aperitif. In Britain, current sales are well below their peak, but a renaissance is being led by demand for the finer wines, both there and in the United States.

Port is the classic example of a liqueur wine made by adding alcohol to halt the fermentation before it has finished naturally. The wines all have some residual sugar. Most are sweet; some are very sweet indeed.

SOILS AND TOPOGRAPHY

Over the millennia, the Douro has carved a deep-sided ravine through the rock of schist and granite. When vines were first planted hundreds of years ago, there was not even soil, just precarious flaking slopes of slate and granite, and the baking sun. This may sound like rather improbable conditions for any sort of farming, yet it became the first wine region in the world to be officially delimited, in 1756. The delimited region stretches some 60 kilometres from the Spanish frontier to just downstream of the town of Régua. However, the heartland of the region is around the town of Pinhão, some 20 kilometres upstream from Régua. It is round here that many of the finest estates, or *quintas*, are found. The vineyards are planted on terraces cut into the schistous rock on the steep hillsides. European Union funds have led to much modernisation in the vineyards.

The trade in Port is centred on Porto, at the mouth of the River Douro. This is Portugal's second city and it lies approximately 70 kilometres downstream from the nearest Port vineyards. The offices of the trade organisations are there, though the cellars, or lodges, of the various shippers are just across the river in the town of Vila Nova da Gaia.

CLIMATE

The Douro vineyards are protected from the rain-bearing winds by the 1 400 metre-high Serra do Marão. The climate here is dry and continental with temperatures reaching 40° C during the height of the summer and 30° C at vintage time. In the winter, there can be severe frosts. There is a dramatic decrease in rainfall as you move upriver. While Porto is the second wettest city in Europe, with an annual rainfall of 1 200 mm, in Régua it is 900 mm per year, in Pinhão 700 mm and at Barca d'Alva on the Spanish frontier it is only

400 mm. What rain there is falls mainly in the spring and the autumn, often in violent downpours.

VITICULTURE

Originally, the vines were planted on narrow terraces (*socalcos*), which might be no more than three rows of vines wide. For planting, explosives had to be used to break up the schist. Fortunately, this generally appeared in vertical strata, which allowed the roots of the vines to penetrate more easily. For the most part these have been replaced by *patamares*, broader terraces, which permit denser plantation and the use of machinery. Erosion is limited by the construction of earth embankments. On the less steep slopes, vines are trained along wires, but on the steeper ones, this proves to be impracticable.

VINEYARD CLASSIFICATION

The production of Port is very tightly controlled and, each year, every *quinta* is given a quota as to the volume it may produce. (Any extra wine can be sold as Douro DO light wine and as this is becoming increasingly popular, the quota system is becoming less of a problem for the producers, though the ultimate price that can be expected for the grapes is significantly less.) The theory behind this is to ensure that more wine is not produced than can be sold profitably. In calculating the quota for each vineyard, a number of factors are taken into consideration. The grower can control some, but not all. In descending order of importance these are:

- low yield
- altitude
- soil composition
- location
- training of vines
- grape varieties planted
- degree of slope
- exposure to sun
- spacing of vines
- shelter from prevailing winds
- age of vines.

Having considered these factors, the vineyards are rated from A to E, with three-quarters falling into the C and D levels. Not only does the classification affect the quantity of Port that might be produced; it also affects the price that it will ultimately fetch on the open market, and the style of port for which it will be used.

VINIFICATION

Traditionally, the rapid **extraction** of colour and

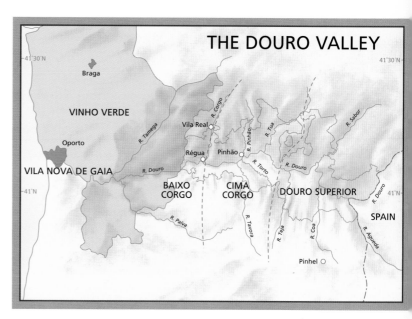

THE DOURO VALLEY

tannins from the grapes was achieved by treading the grapes in granite troughs, or *lagares*. The grapes, either crushed or uncrushed, would be emptied into these, and then trodden for up to 12 hours by teams of workers. Periods of regimented marching up and down in the troughs may be alternated with activities such as dancing. The fermenting must would then be put into open top vats and the cap regularly immersed to extract more colour. All this may still happen in the more traditional *quintas*, whose wine can be sold at high prices and labour costs absorbed, but robotic *lagares* and mechanical punching down are becoming more common. For less prestigious wines, *autovinifiers* may be used. In this method

Terraced vineyards at Quinta do Seixo.

the crushed grapes are put into sealed vats and the pressure of the CO_2 given off by the fermentation is used to force the juice up through pipes so that it continually sprays over the cap of skins, pips and stalks. As can be imagined, this is a much more economical process. One disadvantage is that there are substantial capital costs involved in installing the special vats. An alternative is the traditional pumping over, common to most vineyard regions, though this leads to a less vigorous extraction of colours, flavours, and tannins from the skins.

FORTIFICATION

When sugar in the fermenting wines has been converted to between 6% and 9% abv, spirit at 77% abv is added in the proportion of one part of spirit to four parts of wine. This kills the yeasts and stops fermentation. The spirit must have a grape base, though it is more likely to come from France, Italy or Spain than Portugal. The moment at which the fortification takes place depends on what degree of sweetness is required in the resultant wine. As soon as fortification has taken place, the wine is drawn off into casks, as there is a danger that the increased alcohol might release further, harsh tannins.

Autovinification

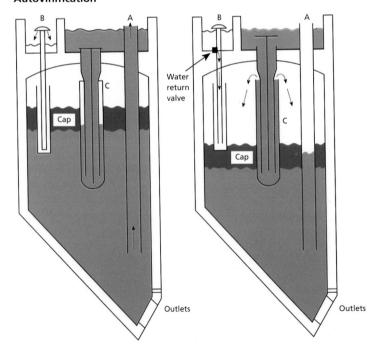

Grapes are crushed and loaded into the sealable, lower section of the autovinifier. As fermentation occurs, pressure builds up and forces must up the column, A, into the open trough at the top. When a pre-determined pressure is reached the water valve, B, releases the gas pressure and the weight of the must forces it down the central column, C, and over the cap, submerging it and extracting both colour and tannin. The cycle is repeated every twenty minutes for the whole of the fermentation period, one and a half to two days.

GRAPE VARIETIES

Over 80 grape varieties are permitted for the production of Port, and there may be even more in the vineyards. Traditionally, in the older vineyards, a number of different species were planted together and the growers are unaware of what they have. However, with the modernisation of the vineyards, the larger producers are tending to plant blocks of individual varieties, most suited to the soil and site climate. Port is almost without exception a blend, and varietal character is seldom identifiable, so it could be argued that grape varieties simply do not matter. Currently five black varieties are preferred:

- **Tinta Roriz** (Tempranillo) has low yields, but adds finesse to the blend. By Portuguese standards, this is a lightweight grape.

- **Touriga Nacional** is considered the finest grape of the Douro. It gives an exceptionally low yield of small berries. The wines are full-bodied and concentrated. Due to its rarity, cost and quality, this will be used only for the very best wines.

- **Touriga Franca** (formerly *Touriga Francesa*) is also a premium grape, though not at the level of the Touriga Nacional. Its wines are robust and have an excellent perfume.

- **Tinta Cão** had all but disappeared, but with EU funding has enjoyed a renaissance. Its bunches are small and the grapes tiny; it adds tannin to wines.

- **Tinta Barroca** is a thick-skinned variety, giving soft, fruity wines. It is an early ripener.

The comparatively small quantities of white Port that are made use white grape varieties.

MATURATION AND WINE STYLES

In the spring following the vintage, wine is transferred to the shippers' warehouses or lodges. Road tankers have replaced the picturesque sailing boats, the *barcos rabelos*, that used to bring the wines downstream. The boats are still used, however, for publicity purposes and can be seen tied up at riverside quays. Most of the lodges are in the narrow streets of Vila Nova da Gaia, which lies on the opposite bank of the Douro to Porto. Here the milder, damper climate is better suited for maturation. Little wine is stored up the Douro, where the fierce summer temperatures tend to result in harsher wines. In the Port wine trade, the traditional cask used for storage in the lodges is the 'pipe' containing 550 litres. A variety of styles is available on the market and a number of factors contribute to these. They may include the quality of the base wine; whether it comes from a single year or is a blend of years; how long it has spent in cask; and whether it is filtered before bottling.

White Port is made from white grapes. It is generally golden in colour, low in acidity, with some of the honey and nut aromas of deliberate oxidation. They can range from off-dry to sweet (the style should be mentioned on the label). They are non-vintage, wood-matured and generally sold at two to three years old.

Ruby Port is a style that has traditionally been most popular on the UK market. It is young, non-vintage, full-bodied, deeply coloured wine, generally sold at less than three years old. Many are sweet, simple wines with rather harsh alcohol. The better ones are labelled as **Reserve Ruby** Ports. These are a blend of higher quality wine, from one or more vintages, that are cask-matured for up to five years before bottling. They are full-bodied, with richer fruit and better integrated alcohol and, like all wood-matured, filtered ports, they are ready for drinking when bottled.

Tawny Port is a style much favoured by the French. Broadly speaking there are two styles. Blending ruby and white Ports will produce the cheaper wines. Such wines can be recognised by their pink rim. On the other hand, **Reserve Tawny Port** is the result of at least seven years maturation in cask. They are very soft and smooth and can be recognised by their more russet, or tawny, rim. They are a blend of different years. **Tawny Port with an Indication of Age** can be labelled only as 10, 20, 30 or **over 40 years old**. To qualify for such a label, the shipper must show that they have stock of sufficient wine of that age in their lodge and that the wine must be consistent with the characteristics typical of a wine of that age. The age stated may therefore be an average, rather than a minimum. The label must state the year of bottling, which is important as these wines lose their freshness after bottling. They are the finest of all Tawny Ports and the best are exceptionally complex and concentrated. They do not throw any sediment after bottling and therefore do not need decanting. After opening, they should last in the bottle for a few weeks. The oxidative ageing in cask results in browning and a loss of colour, and the development of aromas and flavours of walnuts, coffee, chocolate and caramel, to accompany faded and developed versions of the berry fruit notes of younger Port.

Crusted Port is a British speciality and until recently occurred only with wines bottled in England. As English bottling of Port is now forbidden, some Portuguese shippers have taken it up. These are high-quality ruby wines of one

Port			
KEY PORT STYLES		**MAIN GRAPE VARIETIES**	**PRICE**
White	☐	Various, blended	●●○
Ruby	■	Various, blended	●○
Reserve Ruby	■	Various, blended	●●
Tawny	■	Various, blended	●●
Reserve Tawny	■	Various, blended	●●○
Tawny with an Indication of Age	■	Various, blended	●●●○
Crusted	■	Various, blended	●●●●
Late Bottled Vintage	■	Various, blended	●●●○
Colheita	■	Various, blended	●●●●+
Vintage	■	Various, blended	●●●●+
Single Quinta Vintage	■	Various, blended	●●●●+

or more vintages, bottled young and unfiltered. As they throw a heavy sediment, or crust, they need decanting.

Late Bottled Vintage Port (LBV) is a wine from a specific, but not necessarily a 'Declared Year' (see Vintage Port below), that has been aged in cask for between four and six years before bottling. The **traditional style** of LBV is bottled, unfiltered, after four years and continues to improve in the bottle. This style needs to be decanted. Most LBVs are in the more **modern style**. These are matured in cask for six years and filtered before bottling, after which they are ready for consumption and do not need decanting. These generally have richer, more complex fruit flavours than ordinary Ruby Ports, and may have detectable tannic 'grip'. In the past, LBV Ports never came from the same year as a Vintage Port, but some companies now produce both styles in the same year. The label of a LBV wine must include not only the vintage year, but also the year of bottling. Irrespective of style, a

Touriga Nacional vines, overlooking the Douro at Quinta dos Canais.

View down the River Douro with the Port lodges of Vila Nova de Gaia on the left and the waterfront area of Oporto, Cais da Ribeira, on the right.

bottle of LBV Port can be kept for up to two weeks after opening.

Colheita Ports are particularly popular in Portugal itself. They are wines of a single vintage that have been aged in cask until just before sale. The minimum period is eight years, though with most wines it is considerably longer. Effectively, they are very fine old Tawny Ports and, as such, do not need decanting. As well as giving the vintage, the label must state that the wine was aged in cask and when it was bottled.

Vintage Ports are among the longest-lived wines produced anywhere. They are exceptional products of one particular year, typically, from the best vineyards only, which are bottled when they are two years old. Full, rich and tannic when young, Vintage Ports mature slowly and may not reach their peak until 20 years or more old. They will throw a heavy deposit, and should be decanted and consumed within a few days. Each company can decide whether it wishes to 'declare'

a vintage. There is not always common consent as to which is a 'vintage' year. For example some houses declared 1991 as a vintage year, some 1992 and some both. However, there was general unanimity, for example, as to the 2000 vintage.

Single Quinta Vintage Ports are full Vintage Ports that are the product of a single estate, the flagship of the shipper's vineyard holdings. Like Vintage Port they are not made every year, but they fall into two main groups. On the one hand, there are those vineyards which will declare a vintage in all the great years and have built up an individual reputation. On the other hand, there are some shippers who, in the best years, will use the wines as important constituents in their own blend. They will then declare a vintage for their *quinta* wine in the 'not quite so good' years when they have not declared a vintage for the shipper's brand. Single *quinta* vintage ports are often aged in Porto by the shippers and released when they are mature.

Madeira

34

The island of Madeira lies in the north Atlantic Ocean some 500 kilometres west of the Moroccan port of Casablanca and 1100 kilometres from Lisbon. It is an autonomous region within Portugal and as such is within the EU. The island is extremely fertile, partly because the soils are of volcanic origin, but also because, during the fifteenth century, the dense forests that covered it were burnt down to clear land for grazing. This gave exceptionally high potash content to the soil. Its geographical position made the island a very important supply station for voyages from Europe to the Americas, South Africa and the Indies. As a result its wines became widely known and their sales were largely in the hands of British companies. Historically too, wines were often sent on long voyages as part of their ageing process. Nowadays France is the most important export market, though much of the wine sold there is used only for culinary purposes.

CLIMATE, SOILS AND VITICULTURE

The island is very mountainous and the vineyards are mainly found on the slopes on the northern and southern coasts. The vines are generally planted on pergolas, allowing other crops to be grown underneath. Rain falls mainly on the high ground and irrigation is carried out through a network of small channels called *levadas*. The climate of the island is warm and damp, with an annual rainfall of 640 mm. Fungal diseases are a major problem.

GRAPE VARIETIES AND WINE STYLES

During the second half of the nineteenth century, powdery mildew and phylloxera all but destroyed the island's wine trade. American hybrid varieties dominated the new plantings, replacing the four traditional varieties, Sercial, Verdelho, Bual and Malvasía (Malmsey). Now well over 80 per cent of the plantings of *vinifera* vines are of the lesser Tinta Negra Mole. Entry into the EU has meant a dramatic upheaval in the way that the wines of Madeira are produced and labelled. First, the use of hybrid varieties in the production of the wine is totally forbidden. Secondly, the names of specific grapes, such as Verdelho and Bual, can be used only for wines made with a minimum of 85 per cent of the grape concerned. As such names had been used to describe the style of the wine, rather than the provenance, and as noble grapes account for less than 10 per cent of those used in Madeira, this altered the labels on the market almost overnight.

Tinta Negra Mole accounts for the vast majority of plantings of grapes used for Madeira. It gives a high yield of sweet, pale red wine. This colour gives even the youngest wines something of the appearance of age. It is credited with having the chameleon-like ability of adapting itself to a variety of required styles, but is not used for higher quality wines such as Special Reserve or Vintage. **Sercial** is grown mainly on the highest vineyards of the island on north-facing slopes. It gives the driest, palest wines, with very high acidity. **Verdelho** is planted on lower slopes on the north side of the island, giving wines with medium-dry style and stone fruit aromas. **Boal** (often anglicised to **Bual**) grows mainly around Camara de Lobos on the south side of the island and gives a medium-sweet wine with a dry finish. **Malvasía** (generally sold under the name of **Malmsey**) provides the sweetest of all the wines of Madeira. The two characteristics that mark out all of these wines are their high acidity, and their smoky, burnt sugar aromas.

With the restriction on the use of the traditional grape names, Madeiras are now generally described in two ways: by the degree of sweetness, and/or by their age. A wine that was, until quite

Madeira		
KEY MADEIRA STYLES	**MAIN GRAPE VARIETIES**	**PRICE**
Finest / 3 year old ☐	Tinta Negra Mole	●●
Reserve / 5 year old ☐	Tinta Negra Mole, Noble varieties	●●
Special Reserve / 10 year old ☐	Noble varieties	●●●
Extra Reserve / 15 year old ☐	Noble varieties	●●●○
Vintage ☐	Noble varieties	●●●●+

Cliffside terraced
vineyards near Funchal.
Irrigation is achieved
through a system of small
aquaducts, called
'levadas'.

recently, sold as *Sercial* would now be labelled
'**Dry**' if not actually made from Sercial and,
similarly, former Verdelhos, Buals and Malmseys
are now sold respectively as '**Medium Dry**',
'**Medium Sweet**' and '**Rich**', if not made from
noble varieties.

VINIFICATION AND AGEING

One benefit that membership of the EU has
brought is access to grants for the modernisation
of wineries. This means that for fermentation
stainless steel and temperature controls are almost
universally used. The fermentation may be allowed
to run its full course and then the final degree of
sweetness of the wine achieved by the addition of
vinho surdo (intensely sweet grape juice fortified
to 20% abv). Alternatively, the fermentation can

be arrested without all the sugar having been
fermented out by the addition of grape spirit.
This depends on the producer and the style of
wine that they are seeking to make.

In order to replicate the accelerated ageing of
the wine that used to be achieved by sending it in
cask as ballast on long sea voyages, two techniques
have been developed. The highest quality wines
are left in cask on racks (**canteiros**) in the lofts of
the merchants' lodges. More commonly the wine
will spend a minimum of three months in an
estufa, or heating chamber. These take two forms.
The more industrial system is a large concrete
tank with a hot water coil, which heats the wine
to a temperature between 40° and 50° C. The
alternative is for the casks of the wine to be put
in a room maintained at a temperature of about
40° C. The latter method is considered to be
better for the wine, though it is more expensive
in both space and time.

With regard to age, the regulations permit the
labelling of wines as 3, 5, 10 or 15 years old.
Alternatively, a wine labelled '**Finest**' must be 3
years old, '**Reserve**' 5 years old, '**Special Reserve**'
10 years old and '**Extra Reserve**' 15 years old.
A wine bearing a specific **vintage** must be made
from just one of the noble grape varieties, from
a single year, and must have been aged in oak for
a minimum of 20 years. Some older wines might
bear a *solera* date, though the *solera* system (see
Chapter 35) no longer exists on the island.

Great Madeira is a wine that has no upper limit
on ageing. It is virtually indestructible, and
opened bottles may be left open indefinitely with
no deterioration of the wine occurring.

Sherry and Montilla-Moriles

Sherry takes its name from the town of Jerez, which lies in the south of Spain, in the province of Cádiz in Andalucia. The wine was popular in Britain from Tudor times and the English merchants were well established in the region from that period. By the 1850s, it accounted for 40 per cent of the imports of wine into Britain. While Sherry, like all fortified wines, has lost some of its popularity, the United Kingdom remains the most important export market. After a period of declining sales in Britain, the Sherry market appears to have stabilised. It is dominated by sweet wines, Cream and Pale Cream, selling mainly at Christmas time. However, there is a slow increase in the sales of quality wines including Finos and Manzanillas, as well as the premium age-dated wines. Sales of dry Amontillados, Olorosos and Palo Cortados are minimal.

SHERRY

The worldwide image of the wine suffered seriously in the 1970s and early 1980s with the flooding of the market with low-quality wine as a result of overproduction. Consequently, with the financial support of the EU, a considerable area of vines has been uprooted in order to achieve a better balance of supply and demand. There has also been a move to increase the production of white table wine to mop up further grapes. Three further steps have been taken to raise the image of Sherry. The first is a decree restricting the amount of stock that a company is permitted to sell on the market in any one year. This normally is in the region of one third, effectively meaning that most Sherry is at least a three-year-old wine. Secondly, there was a voluntary move by all Sherry companies to forbid the export of Sherry in bulk. The two exceptions to this rule are state monopolies and the food industry, e.g. Sherry used in sauces, chocolates, etc. The third, and most recent development, is the introduction of age-dated Sherries, which has given a boost to the premium end of the market.

The Sherry Trade

The Sherry trade is dominated by brands owned by the major Sherry 'houses'. These companies have their *bodegas*, or ageing warehouses, in Jerez itself, or the two smaller seaside towns of Sanlucar de Barrameda and Puerto de Santa María. Most own vineyards, but they will also buy grapes and must from the large number of vineyard owners, many of whom have grouped themselves into co-operative cellars. They might also buy wine from the small group of *almacenistas*, vineyard owners who make and age their own wines, but who do not bottle or market them themselves. Usually, these *almacenista* Sherries are used to contribute to the flavour spectrum of blends, but they can also be bottled in their pure form, and are among the most classical and characterful of all sherries.

Soils and Vineyards

The soils of the area are divided into three distinct types, *albariza*, *arena* and *barro*, though the reduction in the area under vines has drastically lessened the importance of the last two. **Albariza** now dominates the vineyards of Jerez. This is a very compact soil with a high chalk content, which gives good drainage, whilst retaining moisture. Muddy and slippery when wet, it dries to a hard crust which inhibits evaporation. There are a number of locally recognised subtypes of this soil, depending on the proportion of limestone, which may be as much as 80 per cent or as little as 30 per cent. In the sunshine, the vineyards are a dazzling white, due to the reflection off the chalk. *Albariza* is mainly found in the heartland of the Sherry region, in the rolling hills between Jerez and the Guadalquivir River. It is here that the finest grapes are grown.

The second soil is **arena**, or sand (compacted sand accounts for 70 per cent of the composition, with the limestone 10 per cent or less). *Arena* contains a proportion of iron oxide, which gives it

Contrasting brilliant
white albariza soil in the
background with browner
soil in front.

a russet-brown colour, though its subsoil is often
chalky. Productive and easy to work, its wines
generally lack subtlety. This soil is now mainly
planted with Moscatel grapes, and much of what
used to be vineyard land here has been given over
to the growing of vegetables and flowers in
polythene tents.

The third soil type is **barro**, or dark clay. This is
the richest soil, lying on the lower land, mainly in
the south-east of the region. It gives high yields of
wine with more body but less quality than those
of *albariza* soils. Much of what was vineyard land
here now produces wheat.

Climate

The climate here may be described as subtropical,
with the mean winter temperature being 10.7° C
and summer 23.7° C. The sun shines on almost
300 days in the year. The average rainfall is
650 mm, which is high for Spain, but most of
this falls between October and May. During the
summer, therefore, water is a precious commodity
and must be carefully managed. For this purpose,
collection troughs, known as *aserpias*, are dug
between the rows of vines. On the plus side, all
this gives a very long ripening season, though
drought may be a problem.

Grape Varieties

Palomino accounts for more than 90 per cent of
the area planted. This is one of those varieties that
seems to come into its own with just one wine –
in this case, Sherry. Elsewhere it seems to be
incapable of giving a wine of distinction. The
albariza soil of Jerez, where it is planted, must be
its lifeblood, for here it is the base of almost every
wine. The grape is very thin-skinned and this can
lead to the fruit splitting, causing rot in the period
leading up to the vintage. There is always a
conflict as to when it should be picked: early so
as to retain acidity, or late to give alcohol and
reduce the need for fortification alcohol on which
a higher tax is payable. In either event, it is picked
by hand because of its delicate nature and
susceptibility to damage, and workers can be seen
placing the cut bunches carefully in plastic boxes,
containing 15–17 kg of grapes.

Pedro Ximénez (PX) is generally planted on the
lower-lying vineyards on *arena* and *barro* soils
and, after picking, the grapes are generally left to
dry in the sun on grass mats. This concentrates
the sugar levels. The resultant wine is often used
for sweetening purposes. In recent years, the area
under Pedro Ximénez has decreased considerably
within the Sherry region, and the grapes and wine

have been brought in from either Montilla or Málaga. This is permitted by the Sherry DO regulations.

Viticulture

Yields in Jerez, as elsewhere, vary considerably and are directly related to the rainfall during the previous autumn and winter. The average is somewhere around 65 hl/ha, with a maximum of 80 hl/ha permitted in the better vineyards and 100 hl/ha in the more peripheral ones. Soils are fertilised with manure every three to five years in order to maintain, but not increase, the yields.

The traditional planting space in the vineyards is 1.5 m × 1.5 m. Now, however, to enable more effective use of tractors, the vines are planted 1 metre apart, with 2 metres between the rows. The vines used to be freestanding bush vines with props to support the branches, but wire-training is becoming more common. The training used in Jerez is an adaptation of the single-Guyot system, called *vara y pulgar*. The main problems in the vineyards are rot and mildew due to early summer rains, and chlorosis due to the high limestone content of the soil.

Vinification

The **vintage** normally begins during the first week of September. When the grapes are picked, the Pedro Ximénez bunches are laid out in the sun to increase their sugar content. In order to speed up this process, plastic tunnels are now replacing the traditional grass mats. The Palomino grapes, however, are pressed immediately. As the temperature at vintage time can be very high, there is a real danger of oxidation, so press-houses are often established in the vineyards. Pressing is now generally carried out by horizontal (Vaslin or Willmes) presses. The first 70 per cent, mainly free-run, juice is used for Finos and the light Sherry styles, with the next 20 per cent (up to a maximum of 72.5 litres per 100 kg of grapes) for Olorosos and other less fine wines. Anything above this must be sent for distillation.

After pressing, acidification with tartaric acid now generally takes place. The juice is then held with SO_2 for 24 hours, so that it can clear. It is then normally pumped into stainless steel vats where **fermentation** takes place under temperature control. Natural yeasts are generally adequate for this. Some traditionalists still ferment their wines in 600-litre oak butts. Generally, the wines are fermented at between 25° and 30° C, much higher than is usually considered suitable for white wines. However, at lower temperatures, the aldehydes and other constituents that give Sherry

A *capataz* using a *venencia* to fill *copitas* with samples of Sherry.

its particular style do not develop. It is important to realise that all Sherries, with the exception of Pedro Ximénez and Moscatel, are fermented dry. Any sweetness is added later in the production process.

There are two basic styles of Sherry: Fino and Oloroso. The development of these used to owe as much to nature as to the art of the winemaker. However, they now are in a better position to control the future of a wine. The controls that can be applied at the time of fermentation play a major role in this. The future of a wine can be recognised when it is still very young. The first **classification** takes place soon after the first fermentation has finished. In December or January following the vintage, each tank or cask is tasted and the *capataz*, or head cellarman, will take samples to determine each wine's future. The more delicate wines are destined to become Finos, and will be marked with one stroke (*una raya*, /). Richer, heavier wines will become Olorosos and are marked with two strokes (*dos rayas*, //). At this early stage, natural yeast, known as *flor*, will be growing on the surface of a wine. So as not to disturb this layer, the *capataz* collects the sample, in the case of butts, using their traditional and distinctive *venencia*. (In Sanlucar, the *capataz* uses a less flexible tool made of bamboo.)

Flor has an important effect on the wines as they age beneath its surface. To exist it feeds on

The *solera* system

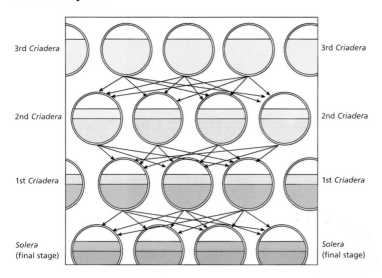

3rd *Criadera*

2nd *Criadera*

1st *Criadera*

Solera
(final stage)

3rd *Criadera*

2nd *Criadera*

1st *Criadera*

Solera
(final stage)

The *solera* system is a method of fractional blending in which old wine is constantly refreshed with younger wine. To ensure consistency, wine is taken from each butt in one *criadera* to be blended in to each butt of the next.

Fino Sherry butt, showing blanket of *flor* yeast on the surface.

and winter. In Sanlucar de Barrameda, on the other hand, where the Atlantic gives a more balanced climate, *flor* is active all the year round. Its sensitivity to ambience is such that the temperature and humidity of individual *bodegas* will influence the styles of the maturing Sherry. For optimum effect, *flor* needs to be refreshed periodically and this is achieved naturally by the replenishment of maturing wine in the *solera* system described below.

Once the selection of styles has been made, **fortification** is carried out using *mitad y mitad* (half and half), a mixture of high-strength alcohol and old wine, with the recipe varying from company to company. Until this fortification, both must and young wines are referred to as *mosta*. Finos are fortified to between 14.5 and 15.5 per cent, the optimum strength for the growth of *flor*, and Olorosos to 18 per cent, which prevents its existence.

As Sherry is rarely sold as a vintage wine, but rather as a style and a brand, continuity of style and quality over the years is important. Jerez has developed this by its own form of fractional blending, known as the **solera system**. Following their initial fortification, the wines are drawn from the tanks into clean butts until the latter are about 5/6th full. For Finos, *flor* will naturally come with the wine. All wines enter the preliminary stage of the *solera* unblended, in what is known as the *añada* (the term is also used to describe the young wine before maturation and blending). After a further six months, the Finos will be split again into potential Finos and the more full-bodied Amontillados. These latter have a less thick *flor*. Temperature control is important throughout the *solera* cycle. *Bodegas* are designed with high roofs to keep the temperature as cool as possible, and will often be aligned to make the most of any prevailing breezes. The soil floors are often watered to increase the humidity. On the other hand, the young Olorosos may be stored outside so that the heat from the sun can naturally increase the oxidation.

Each style of wine will have its individual *solera*, which comprises a number of different *criaderas*, or parcels of the same wine at a particular stage in its ageing. The oldest *criadera* is known as the *solera* itself. When a quantity of a given wine is required for bottling, an equal amount is drawn from each of the butts in the *solera*. This is replaced with an equal amount from each butt in the next oldest *criadera*, and so on, with the youngest being topped up from the *añada*. This operation is called 'running the scales'. This was originally done by hand with

oxygen, alcohol and glycerine and, in the process, reduces the overall acidity of the wine. As it provides a protective blanket on the surface of the wine it also prevents oxidation, which, by contrast, is necessary for Oloroso Sherries. In addition it increases the level of acetaldehyde, which gives Sherry its individual flavour. The optimum alcoholic level for *flor* is between 14.5% abv and 15.5% abv. The heat of summer and the coldness of winter also affect the action of *flor*, which works best at temperatures between 15° and 20° C. Therefore, in Jerez it is active in the spring and autumn and quiescent in the summer

Running the scales in a *solera*.

buckets, but now pumps are generally used. It can be complex and time-consuming, as care must be taken to blend horizontally as well as vertically. That is to say, each butt must not be replenished from just one butt, but from a number of younger butts. In this way, consistency is maintained.

Not more than a third can be drawn out at any one time, and if one draws out the maximum, this can be done only three times in any year. Effectively, for Olorosos and Amontillados, this might happen three times a year, whereas for Finos and Manzanillas, in order to have optimum freshness, less may be drawn out, more frequently. This all means that in any one *solera* there should remain an amount, albeit perpetually diminishing, of the original wine. In the older Sherry houses, the original *soleras* may well have been laid down more than 200 years ago. Because of this system of fractional blending, very few sherries are vintage dated, though a number are dated from the laying down of the *solera*.

Once the wine has finished ageing in the *solera* – an average of three to five years for a quality Fino, up to ten years for Amontillados and Olorosos, and 25 years or more for the finest wines – it will undergo a variety of treatments to prepare it for **bottling** and sale. Traditionally, much wine was fortified once more just before shipment. This was largely because each market expected its Sherries at different strengths. Now, particularly within the EU, it is becoming the

norm to ship wines at the *solera* strength. Thus, for Britain most Finos and Manzanillas are now being shipped at 15 per cent, giving duty benefits. It is also at this stage that wine may be sweetened or coloured, though the latter process has now all but disappeared with the decline in demand for 'Brown' Sherries. For Cream Sherries and Sweet Olorosos, the sweetening is generally achieved with Pedro Ximénez wine; for Pale Cream Sherries, concentrated grape juice is added. Sherry naturally has a high tartrate content and is liable to throw crystalline deposits. To minimise the risk of this almost all Sherries are now chilled in bulk to $-8°$ C and kept at that temperature for eight days in order to precipitate the tartrates. They are then normally fined and filtered to leave the wine star-bright. Finos and Manzanillas will generally undergo micro-filtration in order to remove any traces of *flor* that might lurk in the wine.

Sherry			
KEY SHERRY STYLES		**MAIN GRAPE VARIETIES**	**PRICE**
Fino	☐	Palomino	●●
Manzanilla	☐	Palomino	●●
Amontillado	☐	Palomino	●●○○
Palo Cortado	☐	Palomino	●●●○
Oloroso	☐	Palomino	●●●○
Pedro Ximénez (PX)	☐	Pedro Ximénez	●●●○
Cream	☐	Palomino	●●
Pale Cream	☐	Palomino	●●

Sherry Styles

Over the years, a broad range of Sherries has been made available to the trade. These have evolved from the two basic styles, Fino and Oloroso, plus the in-between Palo Cortado.

Finos are pale in colour and should be light, dry and clean on the palate. They are, for a Sherry, low in alcohol and should be consumed young, since they tend to lose their freshness once bottled. The essential influence on the style is the presence of *flor* in all layers of the solera. A Fino that has been aged in a *bodega* in the seaside town of Sanlucar is known as a **Manzanilla**. Because of the cooler climate, the *flor* remains active throughout the year; this gives the wine an individual character, generally with a delicate, salty tang. In Spain, this is the most fashionable Sherry to drink, with sales far surpassing those of Fino. When young it is known as *Manzanilla Fina*. Manzanilla now has a separate DO (Manzanilla de Sanlucar de Barrameda).

A true **Amontillado** is an aged Fino or Manzanilla from which the *flor* has died away. This happens naturally after a period of about seven years of ageing as a Fino, since by this stage all the nutrients needed to support the *flor* culture will have been consumed. Amontillados are fortified to be slightly higher in alcohol than a classic Fino. They are browny-yellow in colour and dry, with intense nutty flavours from the oxidative ageing that follows the period under *flor*. The name comes from the neighbouring vineyard area of Montilla; literally suggesting that the wine has been 'Montilla-ised'. Because of the laborious double-ageing process, true Amontillados are never cheap. **Commercial Amontillados** are generally a blend of pure Amontillados, with some components of younger Finos and/or Olorosos, and are sweetened to become medium or medium-dry. This latter style is most common on the British market.

Palo Cortado is a very rare style of Sherry and occurs when an elegant wine, that has been selected to become a Fino fails to sustain its culture of *flor*. The resulting wine has similar aromas and flavours to an Amontillado, but, on the palate, has the full body of a dry Oloroso.

A pure **Oloroso** (literally 'fragrant') is a full-bodied, russet-coloured dry wine, which has oxidised from the beginning. It will have robust aromas and flavours that can be very savoury, meaty and nutty. Many Olorosos are sweetened with an element of PX, which even in tiny quantities can add detectable notes of raisin and prune. Some Olorosos that are sweetened with PX (or other sweetening agents such as mixes of grape juice and grape spirit) are labelled **Cream**. Some Cream Sherries may also have components of Fino, Manzanilla and/or Amontillado Sherries in the blend.

Pedro Ximénez (**PX**) is the finest dessert wine of Jerez, produced from sun-dried grapes. It has a concentrated flavour of grapes, raisins and dried figs. Very dark, almost black, and extremely sweet, it can achieve a sugar content as high as 400 g/l.

With the exceptions of Fino, Manzanilla and PX Sherries, all of these wines may be sweetened with a small amount of PX in order, it is said, to improve the balance of what are otherwise extremely dry wines. This sweetening may not be mentioned on the label, but the very powerful influence of PX can be felt on the nose and the palate. The latest addition to the Sherry family is a Fino that has been sweetened by the addition of concentrated grape juice, known as **Pale Cream**. These commercially very successful wines are light in colour and medium-bodied, with sweet, grapey flavours.

AGE-DATED SHERRIES

As a non-vintage product, in the past it was difficult to indicate the difference between the very old, complex Sherries, and those that are blended to create a certain style at the lowest possible price. To help consumers recognise the difference, the categories **VOS** (Vinum Optimum Signatum/ Very Old Rare Sherry) and **VORS** (Vinum Optimum Rare Signatum/ Very Old Rare Sherry) were created to indicate solera wines where the bottled product has a minimum average age of 20 years and 30 years respectively. More recently, age-dated categories for **15-year-old** and **12-year-old** wines were created. These apply to Amontillado, Palo Cortado, Oloroso, and PX styles.

MONTILLA-MORILES

In Spain, liqueur wines are known as *vinos generosos* and some are produced in regions other than Jerez. These include neighbouring Huelva, Gandia in Valencia and Rueda near Valladolid. As far as international markets are concerned, however, the only one of any importance is Montilla, in the Province of Cordoba, to the north-east of the Sherry-producing area. Indeed, Montilla for a long time was considered part of the Sherry region and is still the major supplier of PX to the Sherry houses. In addition, it gave rise to the word Amontillado. Commercially, Montilla found its niche on the shelves of British supermarkets, because the wines fell into the duty band of wines not exceeding 15 per cent alcohol. This, therefore, gave them a price advantage over Sherry; an advantage that has now been partly lost with Sherry Finos and Manzanillas now being shipped at 15 per cent. A regrettable side-effect of this is that the wines of Montilla have come to be looked upon as nothing more than cheap substitutes for sherry, when, in fact, many of them can claim greatness in their own right.

Many of the larger *bodegas* are in the town of Montilla, which lies at the centre of the vineyard region. Being inland, the climate has more extremes than that of Jerez, with summer temperatures frequently exceeding 40° C. Rainfall is rather higher, though it falls mainly during the winter. The soils are of two types: chalky *alberos*, similar to the *albarizas* of Jerez, and the reddish, compact loam *ruedos*, which are found more to the centre and the west of the region.

At the vintage, there are three qualities of juice: the free-run juice is reserved for Finos, the first pressing is used for Olorosos and second pressing is distilled. Fermentation generally takes place in the traditional concrete *tinajas*. Subsequently *flor* occurs in some casks and **Fino**-style wines will be produced. **Oloroso** styles are kept in butts with no ullage to prevent the growth of *flor*. Ageing is as in the Sherry region, in butts in *bodegas*,

Montilla-Moriles			
KEY WINES		**GRAPE VARIETY**	**PRICE**
Finos, Amontillados and Olorosos	☐	Pedro Ximénez	●
Dry, medium and cream	☐	Pedro Ximénez	●
Pedro Ximénez (PX)	☐	Pedro Ximénez	●●●

following the *solera* system. As far as their production is concerned, the main difference is that the wines naturally achieve higher degrees of alcohol than Sherry, so fortification is the exception rather than the rule. They are included in this chapter however, because they are much closer in style to Sherry than any light wine. Most of the same styles as Sherry are found: Finos, Amontillados and Olorosos. Laws concerning minimum alcohol levels restrict use of these terms: 15 per cent for Fino and 16 per cent for Amontillados and Olorosos. Because of this, the British market rarely sees these terms on Montilla labels, but rather the blander terms such as **dry**, **medium** and **cream**. The most prestigious wines are the exceptionally fine **PX**s. These are made in the same way as the PX wines of the Jerez, but the hot, dry summer conditions in Montilla-Moriles are particularly favourable to this thin-skinned variety, and it is there that it finds its most glorious expression.

36   Other Fortified Wines

Fortified wines are made throughout the world. Their robustness gave them a wide appeal, to producers and shippers as well as consumers. The category includes ancient wines such a Malaga, Commandaria and the recently revived Vin de Constance. Classic styles such as Port and Sherry have been imitated in many regions, with some success. There is also a profusion of fortified Muscats such as those made in Australia, California, Spain, Portugal, Italy, Greece and southern France.

VINS DOUX NATURELS (VDNS)

High-strength (95% abv) grape spirit is added to a partially fermented must to make a strong (15–20 per cent), sweet wine, the Vins Doux Naturels (VDNs). Most are bottled young, for immediate consumption, and are full of flavours that derive directly from the grapes. Muscat particularly lends itself to this style, resulting in boldly perfumed, intensely sweet wines. Appellations include **Muscat de Beaumes de Venise** in the Rhône, and **Muscat de Saint Jean de Minervois, Muscat de Frontignan, Muscat de Mireval, Muscat de Lunel** and **Muscat de Rivesaltes** in the Languedoc. The last of these is the only one to permit the inferior Muscat of Alexandria. As this variety is easier to grow, it dominates the wines of Muscat de Rivesaltes, with the result that they are generally the cheapest Muscat VDNs, but they are also less perfumed and characterful.

Grenache is also used for VDNs, in **Rasteau** in the Rhône, and **Banyuls, Maury** and **Rivesaltes** in the Languedoc. Some are bottled young and fresh; others see some oak-ageing, which in some cases leads to deliberately oxidised wines with flavours of caramel, coffee and walnut. The word *rancio* may appear on the label to indicate this kind of wine.

NEW WORLD FORTIFIED WINES

In new vineyard areas, liqueur wines have often dominated early production, largely because they are easier to make, to keep and to ship to foreign markets. It is not surprising, therefore, that such countries as Australia, New Zealand and South Africa have had wine industries that were long dominated by the production of liqueur wines, in the style of both Sherry and Port. In all of these markets, the importance of these wines has been overtaken by the increasing demand for 'light' wines.

Sherry- and Port-style wines are still made in South Africa, California and Australia. Some are of exceptional quality. Although the names 'Sherry' and 'Port' are now protected, the terms Fino, Oloroso, Amontillado and Tawny are still used in Australia for those styles. Where *flor* had not occurred naturally, it was cultivated and injected for the making of Fino-style wines.

Australia's most unusual contributions to the world of fortified wines are its Liqueur Muscats and Liqueur Tokays, made respectively with Muscat Blanc à Petits Grains and Muscadelle. The most celebrated of these come from the extremely hot region of **Rutherglen** in north-east Victoria. Rich, sweet juice is gently extracted from grapes that have begun to raisin on the vine. (The breezy, dry conditions mean botrytis is avoided.) As with VDNs, alcohol is added before fermentation is complete. The sweet wines are then aged in a version of a *solera* system, in hot sheds. Oxidative ageing occurs, and evaporation leads to the wine becoming ever more concentrated. The final product is an intense, full-bodied, sticky-sweet wine, with an array of flavours that encompasses dried fruit (raisins, citrus peel, apricots, prunes), cooked fruit (marmalade), caramel, toffee, nuts and coffee.

MARSALA

Marsala, which takes its name from the town of the same name on the westernmost promontory

Vins Doux Naturels			
KEY WINES		**GRAPE VARIETIES**	**PRICE**
Muscat VDNs	☐	Muscat Blanc à Petits Grains (Muscat of Alexandria for Muscat de Rivesaltes)	●●○
Grenache VDNs	■	Grenache	●●○○

New World Fortified Wines			
KEY WINE		**GRAPE VARIETY**	**PRICE**
Rutherglen Muscat	☐	Muscat Blanc à Petits Grains	●●●○

of Sicily, is a liqueur wine that owes its creation to a Liverpool merchant John Woodhouse in 1773. Twenty years or so later, it came to the attention of Lord Nelson and as a result gained wide fame, Nelson's victuallers bought it as an alternative to rum before the Battle of the Nile in 1798. More recently, the reputation of Marsala has suffered as a result of poor winemaking practices, which have included the addition of such items as egg-yolks or coffee. The DOC has been revised to exclude such practices. Such products are still made by a number of firms, though the word Marsala cannot appear on the label.

Marsala is made from fermented wine, the produce of Cataratto (bulk wines), Grillo (quality wines) and Inzolia grapes, fortified with grape spirit and sweetened, either with boiled down must (*mosto cotto*), or with grape juice whose fermentation has been stopped with spirit (*mistela*). The older wines are then aged in a form of *solera* system. The DOC allows the following qualities:

Fine: One year's ageing (the vast majority falls under this category).
Superiore: Two years' ageing.
Superiore Riserva: Four years' ageing.
Vergine or *Solera:* Five years' ageing.
Vergine Stravecchio or *Vergine Riserva:* Over ten years' ageing.

Marsala can also be classified by colour:

Ambra: The amber colour may give the impression of age, but is achieved with boiled grape must.
Oro: Gold (no mosto cotto permitted).
Rubino: Ruby wine, made from red grapes. A recently created style.

At its very best, Marsala is an agreeable, complex wine; most finds its place in the kitchen.

VERMOUTHS AND AROMATISED WINES

The history of vermouth is similar to that of many liqueurs. It dates back to medieval times when the goodness of wild herbs was preserved by steeping them in either wine in the case of vermouth, or spirit in the case of liqueurs. Monasteries often prepared both for medicinal purposes. There is no reason why vermouths should not be made anywhere where there is a plentiful supply of base white wine and the herbs to infuse in it. The main centres of production have traditionally included Turin in Italy and Chambéry in the Savoy region of France.

Vermouth takes its name from the German word *Wermut*, which means wormwood (the herb that gives absinthe its characteristics). This was originally an important ingredient of cures for intestinal worms, though many other herbs now contribute to the various products on the market. Each producer will have their own formula for each of the styles. These may include roots, spices and fruits, as well as herbs. They are macerated in wine, which is then sweetened with sugar or mistelle, and fortified. If necessary, caramel is added to achieve a consistent colour.

For the best French vermouths, the wine may be aged for up to two years, with one year being spent outside in casks exposed to the sun. Chambéry vermouth is generally more delicate in flavour than other French vermouths. The base wine can come from anywhere (in practice, generally the south of Italy) but the process of converting into vermouth has to take place in the town of Chambéry itself in order for the wine to have this appellation.

Once opened, bottles of vermouth begin to oxidise and rapidly lose their freshness.

Brown muscat grapes (muscat blanc à petits grains) beginning to raisin. Ideally, they are picked when about a quarter shrivelled, to make Rutherglen liqueur Muscat.

37 Distillation

Spirits are drinks that have been produced by the concentration of alcohol present in a fermented liquid by distillation. They are normally sold at a strength of 37–43% abv compared with 7–15% abv for wines and, generally 3–8% abv for beers, though some liqueurs and cask-strength spirits may be much stronger, and some liqueurs may be much less. Distillation was used as early as 3500 BC in Mesopotamia for the creation of perfumes, but it was not until about 1100 AD that wine was first distilled to make spirit. It was considered to have magical properties and was known as the water of life, *aqua vitae* in Latin, *eau de vie* in French and *uisge beatha* in Gaelic, which developed to the whisky we know today.

THE PRINCIPLES OF DISTILLATION

The concentration of the alcohol is achieved by separating the various components or fractions that make up the fermented liquid, called the alcoholic wash. This separation is possible because each of those fractions boils, and turns to vapour, at a different temperature. It is possible, therefore, to heat the liquid to a particular temperature, collect the vapours given off and turn them back to liquid by cooling, or condensing, them.

As far as spirits for human consumption are concerned, the relevant factor is that ethanol, or potable alcohol, boils at 78.5° C and water at 100° C. Thus, if the base liquid with alcohol is heated to 78.5° C, the alcohol itself is vaporised leaving behind the other constituents, of which the major part will be water. The broader the range of vapours that is condensed, the more flavour the spirit will have, but the greater the danger of harmful constituents in the condensed liquid.

THE STILLS

There are two basic types of still, the pot still and the continuous still. A **pot still** looks like a large copper kettle and is heated by direct heat. The vapours collect in the head and are led off through a narrow tube at the top, called the swan's neck, from where they go to the condenser. Here they are liquefied. Such a still is not very heat-efficient, but it produces spirits with character. Pot still distillation is a batch process. That is to say, the still has to be refilled each occasion. This is both time- and labour-intensive. Most spirits made with a pot still are double-distilled; they go through the process of distillation twice.

The most commonly used **continuous still** is the patent still, sometimes called a Coffey still, after Aeneas Coffey, its inventor. This consists of two vertical columns, the analyser and the rectifier. Steam enters the bottom of the analyser, rises and meets the wash, which has been heated in the rectifier, descending the column. The alcohol in the wash is vaporised as it encounters the hot steam. It rises and is passed to the bottom of the rectifier. As the hot vapour rises it is cooled by the pipe carrying the cold wash and will condense. This distillation is a continuous process, with the various vapours being condensed and drawn off

Patent continuous still

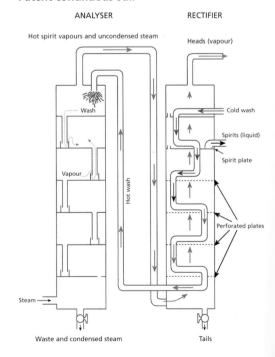

ANALYSER   RECTIFIER

Hot spirit vapours and uncondensed steam

Heads (vapour)

Wash

Cold wash

Spirits (liquid)

Vapour

Spirit plate

Hot wash

Perforated plates

Steam

Waste and condensed steam   Tails

from the still at different alcoholic strengths, according to where in the still the individual spirit plate is placed. The spirit can have a high degree of alcohol and purity, so only one distillation is needed. The result is a more neutral spirit than that obtained from a pot still. If the spirit plate is placed to remove a lower-strength spirit, it will have more flavour and character, but will be much harsher.

In all cases where a potable spirit is being sought, the distillate will be divided into three distinct parts. These are the heads, containing the most volatile compounds (including any methanol, which must be disposed of), the heart, or potable fraction (mainly ethanol, and some flavour components), and the tails (undesirable higher alcohols, plus an increasing quantity of water). The first and last of these will not be included in the final spirit as they contain toxic compounds.

All spirit when it comes off the still is colourless. Any colour in the final product is obtained in the ageing process, or by the addition of colouring material at the time of blending and bottling.

RAW MATERIALS
Anything that can be fermented can be used as a raw material for spirit – whether fruit, grain or vegetable. Where sugar is present in the primary material, as in molasses or fruit, the fermentation can be started directly. With grain spirits, the initial fermentation can take place only after the starch that is naturally present has been converted into sugar. Some spirits can be made from one particular material only, such as brandy from grapes. Others, such as vodka, can be made from a broad range of raw materials, including various grains, potatoes, and even sugar cane and grapes.

38 Brandy and Other Fruit Spirits

The spirit distilled from wine made from grapes is generically known as brandy and is made widely around the world. The two most prestigious regional brandies are made in France. These are Cognac and Armagnac and both have AC status. Spirit can also be distilled from the *marc*, or pomace, the residue after the grape skins have been pressed, such as Italy's *grappa*. It can also be distilled from the lees, the residue left in a wine barrel after bright wine is drawn off.

COGNAC

The Cognac region lies in the *départements* of Charente and Charente-Maritime, just north of, and contiguous to, the vineyards of Bordeaux. Because of the proximity of the vineyards to navigable rivers and the sea, the wines of the Charentes found ready customers in England and the Low Countries. The lightness, however, made them poor travellers and they found a more ready market when they were distilled. The first mention of *eau de vie* in the region dates back to 1549, though distillation did not become commonplace until the seventeenth century. It was not until the eighteenth century that a number of families came to settle in the region and to control the trade: the Martells from Jersey, the Hennessys and the Hardys from Ireland, the Hines from Dorset and the Otards from Scotland.

Ugni Blanc, the white grape variety used for the majority of Cognac, is neutral in character and high in acidity, making it suitable for distillation.

Viticulture and Vinification

Cognac is the third largest vineyard area in France and the vines are cultivated by a number of small growers, who sell their produce to the distilling firms. The ideal wine for distillation should be high in acidity, so the majority of grapes grown in the region produce wines that would not normally be considered undrinkable. They are also low in alcohol, being between 8% abv and 10% abv. Chaptalisation is forbidden if the wine is destined for distillation. Eight grape varieties are permitted, but the most important by far is Ugni Blanc (Trebbiano), accounting for over 90 per cent of plantings. After phylloxera, Folle Blanche (historically the most important) was found to be unsuitable for grafting.

Districts and Soils

The region is divided into six districts: **Grande Champagne, Petite Champagne, Borderies, Fins Bois, Bons Bois** and **Bois Ordinaires/Bois Communs**. The term Champagne here has nothing to do with the Champagne region. What they do have in common are soils with a high chalk content. It is believed that the chalkier the soil, the better the wine for distillation into Cognac. The two Champagne districts and the Borderies lie around the town of Cognac. They produce the best spirits. The Fins Bois is the largest area, accounting for approximately 40 per cent of the total production. The Bois Ordinaires are of lesser importance, with the vineyards mainly being on the sandy soils of the Altantic coast. Sometimes the area appears on the label, in which case the Cognac will have been distilled solely from wine coming from that area. The term **Fine Champagne** is used for a blend from the two best areas, the

Grande and Petite Champagnes, with the former accounting for at least half the blend.

Distillation

The distillation season in Cognac runs from the November following the vintage, through to the following March. Cognac is a double-distilled spirit and the only still permitted is the copper Charentais pot still. This has a capacity of 30 hl, but only 25 hl is distilled at any one time to allow for expansion when boiling. The wine is heated to 80° C by direct heat; traditionally this was coal-fired, but now gas is used. The vapours collect in the top of the still and then enter the swan's neck by a pipe which may pass through a vessel (wine-heater) where it warms the next batch of wine due for distillation before reaching the condenser. The result of this first distillation, the *brouillis*, has a strength of between 26 and 30% abv and will be about a third the volume of the original wine.

For the second distillation, the *brouillis* from three batches of first distillation are combined and redistilled to produce a spirit of up to 72% abv. On this occasion, the heads and the tails of the distillation are removed. However, because this form of distillation is not precise, they still contain usable ethanol, so they are collected and returned to the still with the next batch of *brouillis*. The style and quality of the spirit are affected by the characteristics of the original wine; the shape of the still, particularly the still-head; whether or not a wine-heater is used; the proportion of heart collected; and the subsequent maturation.

Maturation

The spirit is aged in casks made of Tronçais or Limousin oak, for a minimum of two years, but generally for very much longer. During this process, the strength of the spirit will reduce naturally, generally to somewhere around 60% abv. At the same time it will mellow and soften, taking on colour and flavour from the wood. What evaporates is known as the 'angels' share'. This causes a black fungal growth on the outside of the buildings, which gives them a sooty industrial look. Before shipping, a final blending of the house style will be carried out and the spirit will be broken down to 40% abv with distilled water. The colour can be adjusted at this stage by the addition of caramel. The authorities guarantee the age of a Cognac only for the first six years of its life and the following definitions are backed by that guarantee, though in practice spirits labelled as such will generally be much older.

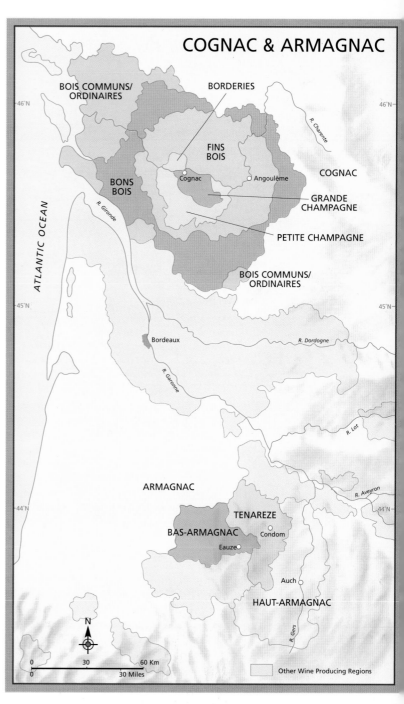

*** or **VS**	two years old (*compte 2*)
VSOP	four years old (*compte 4*)
XO	six years old (*compte 6*)

Within the Cognac industry, there is a system of certificates of age, known as **comptes**, and each parcel of spirit must have the relevant documentation. The certificates are based on the length of time that the spirit has spent in oak.

Cognac pot still

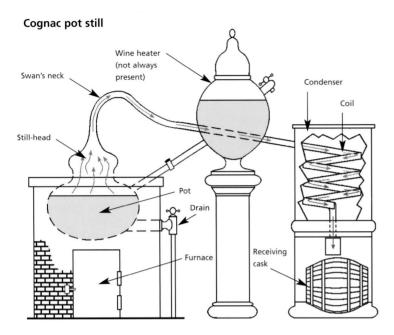

When the spirit comes off the still it is classified as *compte* 00, a classification it retains until the distilling season finishes on 31 March in the year following the vintage. During the first full year in oak it is *compte* 0, changing on 31 March, when it becomes *compte* 1. At the end of the second year it becomes *compte* 2, and so on, up to a maximum of *compte* 6, when it can be sold as XO.

At a certain stage, it is deemed that the spirit will no longer benefit from ageing in cask. At this point it is transferred to glass carboys for storage. The oldest Cognacs are generally stored in a separate warehouse, known as the *paradis*, or 'paradise'.

In Cognac, because of the climate, the cellars are comparatively warm and the spirits develop rapidly. For this reason Cognac is sometimes shipped to Britain when young and aged there more slowly, in cool, damp cellars. Over the years, this produces a smoother spirit, known as **early-landed Cognac**. The label should state the date of distillation, of shipment and of bottling, for it is the ageing in cask in Britain that is important. At present, vintage Cognac is not permitted on the French market, but it may be shipped young in cask to Britain, for ageing under government supervision in bonded warehouses. In such circumstances, as long as the distillation is of a single year, it may bear a vintage date.

ARMAGNAC

The second great AC grape spirit of France is Armagnac. This is also produced in the south-west of France, but to the south-east of Bordeaux,

to the west of the River Gers. Lying further inland than Cognac, it does not have the maritime influence, but enjoys a drier climate and warmer summers. Armagnac claims a longer history than Cognac, probably having been first produced by the Moors in the twelfth century. However, for a long time it was little consumed outside its area of production, due to difficulties with distribution. This is not a region of major brands, but rather more of individual producers.

Districts and Soils

This is an area of mixed agriculture, with vines playing only a comparatively minor role in the local economy. The vineyards are split into three areas, of which the one with the highest reputation for its spirits is Bas Armagnac, in the west of the region. Here there is a rich topsoil covering a subsoil of sand and clay. The wines from here, which are low in alcohol and high in acidity, give the best spirit, which is often distilled and sold under the name of a single domaine and with a vintage.

The area of Ténarèze has a mixture of rich topsoil and chalk which ultimately give a spirit with a fuller flavour. The final area, the Haut-Armagnac, has chalky soil, but unlike Cognac, this gives the poorest wines for distillation. Ironically, this is because the wines are of better quality and can be sold as wine, generally Vin de Pays des Côtes de Gascogne, rather than being distilled.

Grape Varieties

The grape varieties that are planted for making Armagnac are Ugni Blanc and a few others including the ancient Folle Blanche, and the hybrid Baco Blanc 22A. This last was created because it proved difficult to graft Folle Blanche onto American rootstock. It is the only hybrid grape variety approved within the French AC system, but replanting of it is forbidden. Ugni Blanc is by far the most important, but it is not quite as dominant as it is in Cognac.

Distillation

This is on a much more artisanal scale than in Cognac, and is generally carried out in the single-distillation Armagnac still, a rather primitive form of patent still. The wine is heated by the steam in the condensing tube and then enters the top of a second column, where it meets hot air rising from the furnace. The alcohol vaporises and passes into the condenser to be liquefied. Heads and tails are removed during the single distillation, with the former coming off as vapour and the latter as a

Armagnac still

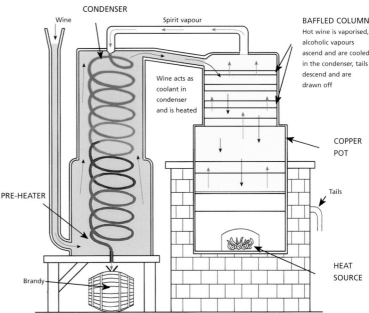

Wine

CONDENSER

Spirit vapour

BAFFLED COLUMN
Hot wine is vaporised, alcoholic vapours ascend and are cooled in the condenser, tails descend and are drawn off

Wine acts as coolant in condenser and is heated

COPPER POT

PRE-HEATER

Tails

HEAT SOURCE

Brandy

liquid residue. The spirit comes off the still at a lower strength than in a pot still (about 60% abv) and retains a higher proportion of flavours. Since 1972, the use of pot stills has been permitted, though these give a less pungent, stronger spirit.

Maturation

The other big factor that contributes to the individual style of Armagnac is the wood used to create the casks in which it is aged. Mostly this is the 'sappy' Monlezun oak, from local forests in the Bas Armagnac, though the use of Tronçais oak is also permitted. As with Cognac, the wood imparts most of the colour, though this may be adjusted by adding caramel. Because of its more primitive distillation and the different oak in which it is aged, Armagnac is generally described as a more rustic spirit than Cognac. Cognacs may be more floral, grapey and fragrant, yet retain their alcohol 'bite'; Armagnacs are fuller-bodied and rounder, with a more pruney, dried fruit character.

Armagnac classifications have lower minimum age requirements than Cognac. They are:

***	one year old (*compte* 1)
VSOP	four years old (*compte* 4)
XO	five years old (*compte* 5)

Many producers age individual casks of Armagnac from a single distillation. These are often sold with a vintage date.

OTHER GRAPE SPIRITS

Apart from the method of distillation, by pot or patent still, two other types of grape spirit are produced around the world. As we have seen, Cognac and Armagnac are distilled from wine and, almost without exception, where wine is made brandy is distilled. French grape brandy, which holds an important place on the British market, is produced in a small number of government-controlled distilleries, situated around the country. The raw material does not necessarily come from France, and is distilled in a patent still. Although it will often be labelled with terms similar to those used in Cognac, such as VSOP or Napoleon, these have little legal significance on these non-AC products.

Spanish Brandy

In Spain there are two regions with DO-controlled brandy production, Jerez and Penedés. Here the base wines generally come from La Mancha. To qualify for the DO, the spirit must be aged in the Jerez or the Penedés region. In Jerez, ageing is through the *solera* system. A Gran Reserva brandy guarantees that the youngest spirit in the blend is three years old, though it is much more likely to be ten or 15 years old. These brandies are often deep in colour and very soft and sweet, though styles and quality can vary widely.

Pisco

This is a grape spirit, often made from Muscat wines. The two major producing countries are

Armagnac is distilled in both pot stills as in Cognac and, as here, in the traditional Armagnac still, a continuous still consisting of two copper columns.

Peru and Chile. In the former it is almost a peasant product, being produced mainly by smallholders with primitive pot stills. In Chile, there are two major producers making it on an industrial scale. It is usually white, unaged and has distinct aromas of the Muscat base material.

Italian brandies are generally distilled from Trebbiano (Ugni Blanc) wine in patent stills. Generally they are light in character, but are rather harsh. Other major brandy-producing countries include South Africa and Australia. It should be recognised that brandy is produced industrially in many countries in the world, with the lower qualities being generally made with patent stills and the better with pot stills. (The largest pot still brandy distillery in the world is in South Africa.) Often the base wine used for distillation does not originate in the country of distillation, but is commodity wine bought on the open market. With excess production around the world, this is currently easy to obtain. For example, the world's biggest selling brandy, Presidente, comes from Mexico. Currently, the Mexican vineyards are incapable of producing wine at a low enough price, so Mexican brandies are being largely distilled from surplus Australian wine. Similarly, most German brandy is produced from imported wine, mainly Italian.

Marc, Grappa and Pomace Brandies

A second type of grape spirit is distilled from the pomace, or the residue of skins, pips and juice, left after pressing. Generally this is sealed off in casks or pits, and left to ferment before distillation. Perhaps the most famous spirit of this family is the Italian *grappa*, which is often distilled from single grape varieties. Similar spirits are produced in Galicia, in Spain, and in Portugal. In France, they are known generically as *eaux de vie de marc* and are produced in most vineyard regions. Marc de Bourgogne is particularly well known. While this is aged in oak barrels, most members of this family are not aged at all, or are stored in glass carboys. They are colourless spirits

and often sold at quite high strengths, sometimes over 50% abv.

CALVADOS

This is the best known of the world's apple spirits. It comes from Normandy and Brittany in north-west France, and forms part of the AC system. In all, there are eleven distinct producing regions within the appellation Calvados, but the best comes from the **Pays d'Auge**, just east of the city of Caen. This has the AC Calvados du Pays d'Auge and has to be distilled twice in copper pot stills and aged for at least two years. The lower quality Eau-de-Vie de Cidre de Normandie can be made in patent stills and has much less flavour and character. Apple spirits are also made in North America, where they are generically known as applejack.

FRUIT EAUX-DE-VIE

These are the result of the distillation of fermented fruit, which is then aged, generally in glass carboys. Consequently, they take on no colour and are usually served very cold to accentuate the pure fruit flavour. While these are distilled widely in Europe (and in other parts of the world), the finest are considered to come from both sides of the Rhine: Alsace and the Vosges in France, the Black Forest in Germany and northern Switzerland. In Germany such spirits are described as *Wasser*. Amongst the most popular fruits for distillation are cherries (eau-de-vie de kirsch/ Kirschwasser), pears (poire Williams), raspberries (eau-de-vie de framboise), damsons (eau-de-vie de quetsch) and yellow plums (eau-de-vie de mirabelle). However, even such unlikely materials as holly berries may be used. The quantity of fruit needed to produce just one bottle of such a spirit is considered to be around 3 kg, so prices are never low.

A cheaper alternative is called *Geist* in German; in this some of the original fruit is macerated in the distillate. Such spirits are also widely made in the Balkans, where slivović is the best-known example.

Whiskies

An essential stage in the production of any spirit is the fermentation of the raw material to form an alcoholic wash that can be distilled. For fruits this is a simple process, as fruit contains sugar. For grain spirits, the starch in the grain must be converted into sugar before fermentation can take place. By far the most important of the grain spirits is whisk(e)y, which was probably distilled by Irish monks as early as the fifteenth century. What purports to be the oldest operating distillery, in County Antrim, in Northern Ireland, received its grant in 1608. Note that while in Scotland and Canada whisky is spelt without an 'e', in Ireland and the United States it usually gains an 'e' before the 'y'. There is no rule, however.

39

SCOTCH WHISKY

The main difference between Scotch and other whiskies is that while the majority of whiskies are the product of a single distillery, Scotch whisky, for more than 150 years, has generally been the result of blending the product of a number of distilleries together. To complicate matters further, there are two distinct styles of whisky within that blend: malt and grain. Malt whisky is the product of a pot still distillation, with malted barley as the raw material; grain whisky comes from the distillation of mainly maize in a patent still. Malt whisky contributes most of the flavour, though it may account for less than half of the blend; grain whisky fills out the blend as well as making a subtle contribution to the flavour. It is possible to buy single whiskies – generally malt, though occasionally grain – unblended.

Malt Whisky

The original Scotch whisky was malt whisky, produced from barley in a pot still. The first stage of its production is the **conversion** of the starch in the barley to sugar. This, in effect, comes about through a controlled germination. The barley grains are seeds that would, under the right conditions, grow into new plants. The grain is first soaked in regularly changed water for 48 hours in the 'steeps'. This releases the enzymes, which convert the stored energy in the form of starch into sugar, which the seed needs in order to grow. The damp barley is then spread out on the malting floor and turned regularly. Alternatively, it is put into temperature-controlled, rotating Saladin boxes. Here germination starts and the barley becomes 'green malt'. Once the conversion has started, but before leaves and roots are formed, the growth is arrested in kilns. The heat

of the kiln dries the grain and if peat is used, the smoke (or 'reek') gives added flavour to the barley which is now called malt.

The malt is then ground in a mill to form 'grist' and this is mixed with hot water in a large vat, known as a mash-tun. Here it is regularly stirred with large paddles. This completes the conversion process and extracts the sugar. The resulting sweet liquid is known as **wort**. This is drawn off into large **fermentation** vats, called 'wash-backs'. It is here that the raw material for distillation, a beer-like liquid called 'wash', is produced.

All Scotch malt whisky is produced in a pot still, generally with a double **distillation**, occasionally with a triple distillation. Two separate stills are used. The first, the 'wash still', converts the wash, at about 13% abv, to 'low-wines' of about 30% abv. The low-wines are

Scotch whisky stills are generally much larger than their equivalents in Cognac.

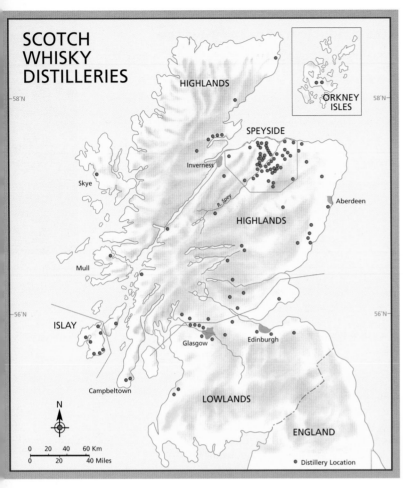

SCOTCH
WHISKY
DISTILLERIES

HIGHLANDS

ORKNEY
ISLES

SPEYSIDE

Inverness

Skye

R. Spey

Aberdeen

HIGHLANDS

Mull

ISLAY

Glasgow   Edinburgh

Campbeltown

N

LOWLANDS

ENGLAND

0   20   40   60 Km
0   20   40 Miles

● Distillery Location

Traditionally, the casks of choice for the maturation of Scotch whisky were freshly emptied sherry butts. However as Sherry is now almost entirely bottled in the area of production, these are no longer easily available. This has led to experimentation with all sorts of wine, and even beer casks. Because the legislation concerning the production of Bourbon whisky insists on new barrels, used Bourbon casks are now very widely used, particularly for the ageing of grain whisky. First-fill Sherry casks can give strong raisin and cake aromas to the whisky, and can quickly mask the character of the original distillate. First-fill Bourbon casks tend to have a more subtle effect. Second-fill casks result in a slower maturation, and fewer flavours being absorbed from the cask.

While each individual malt whisky distillery will have its individual style, geographically they are grouped into four **regional styles**. Within these regions the malt whiskies tend to share certain common characteristics. **Highland and Island** distilleries are situated north of a line from Greenock to Dundee. They produce the many intensely flavoured malts, with distinct peatiness, but also floral and honey characteristics. Within the Scottish Highlands, the distilleries in the **Speyside** area produce particularly elegant whiskies that are highly sought after, either as components of blends or as single malts. The distilleries on the island of **Islay**, off the west coast of Scotland, produce the most fully flavoured and peatiest whiskies, with aromas and flavours of smoke, seaweed, iodine and tar. These are imparted by the local peat used for the malting, which was originally created from decayed marine, vegetable matter. **Lowland** malts come from south of the line from Greenock to Dundee; these produce the lightest style of malt whisky, which is generally used for blending.

Grain Whisky

This is industrially produced in a patent still, rather than batch-produced in pot stills. The basic raw material is imported maize, which is ground to form a flour and then cooked under steam pressure to release the starch. A small amount of malted barley is then added and the enzymes this contains convert the starch to sugar. The wort produced from this is of a lower strength than that for malt whisky. Grain whisky is distilled to a higher degree than malt whisky, but not as high as gin or vodka, though these may also be made using the same stills. New-make grain spirit is white and quite pungent, with aromas of licorice spice. It is much smoother than new-make malt spirit, and could be consumed straight away.

collected and redistilled in the smaller spirit still, to produce raw whisky, known as 'British Plain Spirits' at about 70% abv. This comes from the middle part of the distillate; the **heads** (**foreshots**) and the **tails** (**feints**) are removed. As in Cognac these contain noxious substances, as well as ethanol, so are blended with the next lot of low-wines for redistillation. It is up to the individual distiller to decide which proportions are rejected as foreshots and feints; the ultimate flavour of the spirit will depend upon this decision. Where the spirit leaves the second still, it passes through the spirit safe, which is under the control of the government authorities, the Customs and Excise. From this point onwards, it remains under their supervision until duty is paid, or it is exported.

A number of factors affect the style of the individual malt whisky. These include the barley and the way it is malted, the yeast, the water, the design and height of the still and, most importantly, the **maturation**. The distillate can be described only as British Plain Spirits until it has been aged in oak cask for three years.

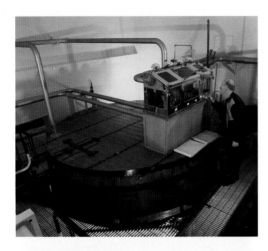

The spirit safe at
Dalwhinnie.

have an age statement such as 8 years old,
12 years old or 17 years old. Again, this means
that all the spirit within the blend has at least the
age stated. In practice this means that the grains
will often be of the minimum age, while the malts
may be considerably older.

Malt Whisky

A **single malt** is the product of one distillery,
often aged for a considerable time before release.
Generally, the whisky will be a blend of different
casks and ages in order to provide some
consistency, but all the whiskies will be from the
same distillery. Occasionally, particularly with
exceptionally old whiskies, there may be single-
cask bottlings. Each malt has a distinctive flavour
and style, which the expert can recognise 'blind'.
Malt whiskies are increasingly appreciated in
some export markets, such as Italy and Spain.
Vatted, or **blended malts** are blend of whiskies
from a number of different malt whisky
distilleries. It may have a tighter geographical
description, such as Speyside or Islay. Own-label
malt whiskies, by their nature, are usually vatted.

IRISH WHISKEY

There are currently three distilleries remaining in
Ireland. Bushmills in Northern Ireland makes malt
whiskies, as well as blends using grain whiskies
from Middleton in the Republic of Ireland. Most
of the Irish whiskey brands are produced at the
Middleton site. Interlinked pot stills and
continuous stills, a choice of malted or unmalted
grains, and a choice of different barrels results in a
vast range of whiskey styles, from which a range
of brands may be blended. The key characteristics
of whiskies from both Bushmills and Middleton
are that the malt is entirely unpeated, and triple
distillation occurs (though, as a result of the system
of interlinked stills at Middleton, it is possible that
a spirit will emerge having been distilled four, five
or more times). The result is a very smooth, soft,
mellow whiskey. Cooley distillery makes a number
of brands in the same soft, smooth styles. But it
also sometimes uses peat, and one of its brands is
similar in style to Islay Single Malt.

AMERICAN WHISKIES

A **straight whiskey** must have a minimum of 51
per cent and a maximum of 80 per cent of one
grain in its mash bill. It must be distilled to a
maximum of 80% abv, and it must be aged for a
minimum of two years in new charred oak barrels;
whiskies that are less than four years old must
state the age on the label. A **blended whiskey**
must be at least 20 per cent straight whiskey.

By law, Scotch whisky
must be matured in
Scotland in oak casks for
a minimum of three years.

However, it falls under the same laws as all Scotch
whisky and so must be aged for a minimum of
three years. It benefits considerably from the
softening effects of oak. This spirit matures
quickly. Almost all is used in blended whiskies,
but single and vatted grain whiskies can be found.

Blended Whisky

Both malt and grain whiskies are available as
'single' whiskies, that is, the product of one
distillery only. Most whisky, however, is sold as
blended whisky, a mixture of any number of
whiskies from different grain and malt distilleries.
Standard blends will rarely state an age on the
label, though the youngest spirit in the blend must
be a minimum of three years old. The quality
of the blend will owe a lot to the nature of the
malt whiskies that it contains. Malt whisky
imparts more flavour – and is a more expensive
constituent. **Deluxe blends** will contain grain and
malt whiskies, but generally receive more
character from the latter. Most deluxe blends will

The rest will be bulked up with cheap, neutral, grain spirit. **Sour mash** is a method of ensuring consistency from one fermentation batch to the next, and avoiding microbial spoilage of the fermenting beer. A portion of the acidic residue from one distillation will be added to the mash about to be fermented for a later batch. Most American whiskies are produced using various versions of a patent still. However, because they are distilled to a much lower strength than gins, vodkas or even grain whiskies, they emerge from the stills with many characterful flavour compounds, but rather harsh alcohol. The hot ageing environment and the use of active new casks means that drinkable spirit can emerge after only a couple of years, though most whiskies are aged for much longer than this.

Bourbon

Bourbon is a straight whiskey that must be at least 51 per cent maize. Although it takes its name from Bourbon County in Kentucky, where most is produced, it can be made anywhere in the United States. The whiskies are stored in very hot warehouses, which results in an accelerated ageing process and a rapid extraction of tannins, sugars, colours and coconut and vanilla flavours from the wood. Although a few premium brands use pot stills, most use continuous stills. Unlike Scotch whiskies, which may use caramel to adjust colour, all of the colour in a Bourbon must come from the ageing process.

Within the huge warehouses, different locations result in different styles of ageing. A producer may introduce a barrel rotation regime to ensure consistency across the barrels; alternatively, consistency may be achieved by blending barrels with different characters. Barrels at the centre of a warehouse tend to age more slowly as they are exposed to fewer extremes of temperature. Ultimately, they give whiskies with more complexity and finesse. Barrels that have particular desirable characteristics may be bottled separately as **Small Batch Bourbons**. Other Small Batch Bourbons are, literally, Bourbons that have been distilled and aged in small batches. There is no legal definition of small.

Rye Whiskey

Rye whiskey in the United States is a straight whiskey that must be made with a mash bill of not less than 51 per cent rye. This gives whiskies with a particularly firey, spicy character.

Tennessee Whiskey

A Tennessee whiskey must satisfy all the regulations of a straight whiskey, except that in addition it must be distilled in Tennessee and the spirit must be filtered through maple wood charcoal before ageing. This latter process, also known as the **Lincoln County Process**, was probably introduced by Russian or Polish settlers who had experience of vodka production. Although charcoal used for filtering vodka is of a very high standard of purity, and strips colour and flavour from the spirit as well as making it less harsh, the charcoal used in the Lincoln County Process is much less pure and gives a very smoky character to the whiskey.

Canadian Whisky

In Canada, there is no restriction as to the proportion of grains in the mash. The distillation industry in Canada received an important boost from Prohibition in the United States, which established an important, though clandestine, market for its whiskies. Although it is sometimes labelled as Canadian Rye, Canadian whiskies do not have the spicy character of true Rye whiskies. Canadian legislation states that 'Canadian Whisky (Canadian Rye Whisky, Rye Whisky) shall be whisky distilled in Canada, and shall possess the aroma, taste, and character generally attributed to Canadian Whisky'. This opens the opportunity to include significant proportions of neutral grain spirit, and even sherry and other fruit-based wines.

Other Whiskies

Whisky is produced in a number of other countries around the world, though a distinction should be made between those whiskies that are no more than a blend of locally produced spirit and vatted Scotch malts and those countries that genuinely distil both grain and malt spirits. Among these latter countries are India and Japan – the largest malt whisky distillery in the world is in the latter country. In both countries, however, much Scotch whisky is imported for blending. As far as international sales are concerned, these locally blended whiskies have little relevance outside their domestic markets.

Rum

40

Sugar cane originated in the monsoon areas of Asia, but had reached Spain by the fourteenth century. Christopher Columbus took the plant to Hispaniola, and subsequent Spanish expeditions spread it throughout the West Indies. Although Puerto Rico became the first country to produce rum on a commercial basis as late as the mid-nineteenth century, records show that a product had been made from distilled, fermented sugar cane for 300 years before this.

FERMENTATION AND DISTILLATION

Most rum is made from molasses and is a by-product of the sugar industry. Where molasses is used, it is diluted with water before fermentation. Distillation may take place in a pot still, though almost all rums are distilled in continuous stills. The strength to which they are distilled dictates a large part of the final character. Lower distillation strength brings complexity, but results in a loss of smoothness. A few rums are made directly from fermented cane juice, and these have a very different, rather fresh, grassy character. Rums flavoured with spices or lemon are becoming more widely available.

AGEING

Colour is a poor indication of age. White rums may be bottled directly after distillation, or may have been aged in oak for a number of years to generate more mellow flavours, and then had the colour (and some flavours) stripped by charcoal filtration. Dark rums may have developed their sweet character and deep colour due to extended oak ageing, or they may simply have had caramel and sugar added. For this reason, it is rather meaningless to characterise rums as '**white**', '**golden**' or '**dark**'. Rums aged in tropical climates tend to age very quickly, as the heat accelerates the ageing process. Oak is usually used, and the process may be classical static ageing or a *solera* system.

STYLES OF RUM

The main influences on style are the base product (molasses or cane sugar juice), the manner of distillation (pot still or continuous; the higher the strength, the purer the product, but the result is a loss of character), and ageing and sweetening. Although many of the larger rum brands are blends, it is important to realise that, as with malt whisky, different styles traditionally emerge from the different Caribbean islands.

Cuba

This is the original home of white rums, distilled to be nearly neutral. Some are aged in oak casks to soften the alcohol, and are then charcoal-filtered to remove colour. This style, which differs only subtly in flavour from vodka, is much copied and most 'Cuban-style' rum is produced in Puerto Rico, the Bahamas or Brazil.

Jamaica

The colour of Jamaican rums runs from white through to deep gold. Because of the fermentation process and relatively low-strength distillation, even the seemingly innocuous white rums are bursting with estery aromas and flavours. These very pungent rums typically have a strong, exotic fruit (banana, mango) character, which in the aged, golden rums can be accompanied by roasted, nutty notes.

Sugar cane fields, the raw material for Rum.

The continuous still of Bacardi produces light, white Rums.

Rum maturing in oak barrels in the tropics will mature quicker than those matured in cooler northern countries.

Barbados

Barbados produces white, golden and dark rums, all of which are generally characterised by a fruity, elegant style.

Guyana

These are also known as Demerara rums. The tropical climate results in rapid ageing, and the rums quickly gain complex, sweet, spicy flavours. Most are golden in colour, a result of the use of caramel as much as the effects of age. Guyana is the major exporter of molasses for distillation elsewhere.

Martinique and Guadeloupe

These islands specialise in rums distilled from fermented cane juice. Many of the resulting rums are white and full of fresh apple and grass aromas from the sugar cane base. Aged versions are also made. These have softer alcohol and some oak flavours, though the sugar cane notes begin to disappear. While the sugar cane rums are labelled *Rhum Agricole*, there are some rums distilled from, usually imported, molasses. These are unromantically labelled *Rhum Industriel*.

Brazil

Cachaça is a colourless spirit distilled mainly from sugar cane in Brazil, where, largely because of its low price, it is very popular. Indeed, its success in just that one country makes it one of the largest volume spirits in the world.

Other Regions

Large quantities of rum, in a variety of styles, are also made in Trinidad, Tobago, Venezuela and Puerto Rico. One of the few regulations for the production of rum is that the country must grow some sugar cane. Consequently, rums are also made in the Philippines, Australia, South Africa, Central and South America, and the Indian and Pacific Ocean Islands.

Tequila and Mezcal

In pre-Columbian times, Native Americans fermented the sap of various agave species to produce *pulque*. **The Spanish** *Conquistadores* **brought the technology to distil** this *pulque* **to produce the first** *mezcal*. **Production was refined from the seventeenth century onwards, around the town of Tequila in Mexico. The Blue Agave was identified as the species of agave that gave the finest** *mezcals***; and processes of converting the starch to sugar, as well as fermentation, distillation and ageing were improved. It was not until the late nineteenth century that significant quantities were exported, to the United States, which remains the most important export market by far.**

41

PRODUCTION

The base material for **Tequila** is the Blue Agave. This is not a cactus, but a spiky succulent that is related to the yucca. It takes at least eight years before it is ready to harvest, with the result that it is very difficult for the tequila industry to adapt to short-term changes in demand. The long ripening time also adds costs to the production process. After the long, sharp, spiky leaves have been removed from the heart (*piña*) of the harvested agave, it is cooked slowly to convert the starch into fermentable sugars. The sweet juice is then extracted, and other fermentable sugars, usually cane sugar, may be added before fermentation. After distillation, the spirit is reduced in strength and may be aged for a period in oak barrels before bottling.

Note that **mezcal** is a generic term for this category of spirit. Any species of agave may be used for this, the growing area includes a number of regions outside the delimited Tequila region, and the methods of converting the starch in the *piñas* to sugar vary widely. Those that use the traditional underground smoke-pits often retain strong smoky flavours.

TEQUILA STYLES

Plata (silver), **Blanco** (white) and **Joven** (young) tequilas are not usually aged. If they are, any colour they have picked up is removed by charcoal filtering. Some are very harsh but, for purists, these tequilas express the character of the base material in its most authentic form. They can be very pungent, with vegetal and peppery, spicy notes.

Joven Abocado tequilas are not aged, but caramel is used to alter the colour and flavour.

Reposado ('rested') tequilas require a minimum of two months in oak barrels. In the hot climate, the spirit is noticeably mellowed in this time, though some of the characterful pungency may also be lost. Colour often comes from caramel, rather than age.

Añejo ('aged') tequilas are aged in oak barrels for at least a year. New or old oak may be used. Considerable complexity can develop, and the greatest Añejo tequilas approach very fine Cognacs in style (and price). However, over time, the characteristic flavours of the agave are lost, and whether the complexities that develop with age compensate for this is a debatable point.

By law, at least 51 per cent of the alcohol in a tequila must come from the distillation of blue agave juice. The rest may come from any other sugar distillate, and these tequilas can be labelled **mixto**. Tequilas that are made entirely from agave will generally state '100% agave' on the label.

42 Gin and Other Flavoured Spirits

The origins of these products lie in attempts to disguise the harsh flavours of raw spirits by flavouring them with pungent herbs and spices. Those that used juniper, which was thought to be good for the kidneys, developed into Gin; those that mainly used caraway became Aquavit; and those that used aniseed or licorice became Arrack/Raki, Ouzo or Absinthe and Pastis.

GIN

Gin is made from almost neutral spirit that has been flavoured with a range of botanicals, of which the most important is juniper. The origin of the spirit may vary; it may be molasses- or sugar beet-based, or, more commonly, grain spirit.

Botanicals

Although juniper is always the dominant flavour, followed by coriander, a range of botanicals is used, including citrus peel, licorice, orris root, angelica and star anise. With the exception of a few Dutch Gins, these do not see any ageing before bottling. They are reduced to bottling strength with demineralised or spring water.

Cold-Compounded Gins

The very cheapest gins use **cold compounding** to flavour the spirit. This involves simply adding the flavours to the spirit in the form of essential oils. The resultant product may be quite pungent at first, but as the flavours are not very well 'fixed', the aromas disappear quickly and the flavours are weak.

Distilled Gins

Gins labelled as **London Gin, Distilled Gin** or **Plymouth Gin** use a superior range of distillation techniques to extract the flavours from the botanicals. Either the botanicals are added to the neutral spirit to macerate for a period before a further distillation, or the vapour is passed through the botanicals during distillation.

Juniper is the most important of the many botanicals used to flavour Gin.

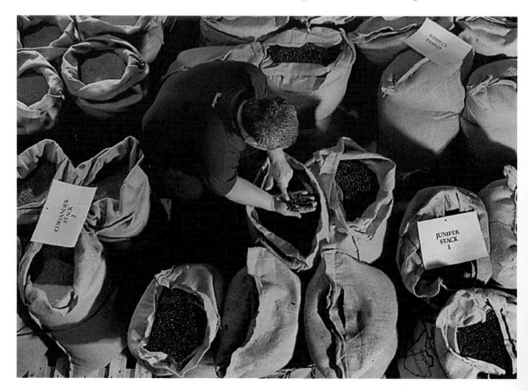

AQUAVIT

This is the national spirit of many Scandinavian countries. It can be distilled from grain or potatoes and is then flavoured with caraway, citrus peel, aniseed and/or other herbs and spices. Some are aged in oak casks before bottling.

ANIS, ARRACK/RAKI, OUZO, ABSINTHE AND PASTIS

Flavoured spirits are widely produced around the world; each country will have its favourites. Aniseed is popular in France and many other Mediterranean countries. In France and Spain these drinks are called **anis**, in Greece **ouzo**, and in Turkey and the Middle East **raki** or **arrack**. **Absinthe**, which has undergone a recent revival, is a member of the same family. This is flavoured with wormwood and aniseed. French absinthes tend to be sweeter, with dominant aniseed flavours. Eastern European absinthes tend to be more bitter, with a balance of component flavours. French **pastis** is flavoured with a combination of herbs, of which the dominant one is licorice. Its traditional centre of production is the port of Marseilles. All of these unsweetened spirits are generally consumed as aperitifs with water and, sometimes, sugar. They all turn cloudy when the water is added.

The rectified base spirit for London Dry Gin is re-distilled in a pot still in the presence of botanicals.

43 Vodka

The name originates in Slavic words that translate as 'little water'. This is probably the world's oldest spirit, with documents showing production in Russia in the ninth century, and similar distillates produced from wine in Poland in the eighth century. Early vodkas were flavoured with fruit, spices and herbs to mask the harsh flavours. The techniques of charcoal filtration for mellowing and purification were not developed until the eighteenth century.

Vodka is a white, more or less neutral-tasting spirit. It will have been distilled to a high strength (usually using continuous stills), and then filtered through charcoal to remove impurities before bottling. Because it is distilled to such a high strength, very little of the character of the base material appears in the spirit. A wide range of base materials can be used, including cereal grains, potatoes, and even grapes. It would be wrong to say that vodkas are totally neutral, however. Some trace of the base material flavours always remains, and may be an important part of the character of the spirit, particularly with eastern-style and some premium western vodkas. As well as differing subtly in their flavour, vodkas also differ in the quality and texture of the spirit. Some are very soft, creamy and smooth; others can be quite harsh, with a noticeable spirit 'bite', which can be part of the character of the vodka and does not always indicate a poor quality spirit. Broadly speaking, there are three styles.

EASTERN-STYLE VODKAS

Eastern-style vodkas, such as those from Russia and Poland, tend to retain more of the character of the base material. They have characterful flavours, but the alcohol may seem harsher. Potato-based vodkas have a particularly creamy, luxurious texture, though they are expensive to produce. Rye-based vodkas have a subtle, but noticeably spicy flavour. Barley and wheat are also used.

WESTERN-STYLE VODKAS

In contrast, western-style vodkas aim for smoothness and neutrality, often at the expense of character. The best have a soft creamy texture. They are the ultimate innocuous spirit, and their mixability makes them ideal for cocktails where the main flavours do not come from the base spirit.

FLAVOURED VODKAS

The third style is flavoured vodkas. These may be made with modern flavourings such as orange, cranberry or vanilla, or they may follow traditional recipes that use cherries, bison grass, plums or honey.

Liqueurs

The origins of liqueurs are medicinal. In the Middle Ages the monastic orders were centres of learning and healing. Most monasteries would have their own herb garden in which they would grow the plants they needed for their remedies and which they could not find growing wild in the immediate countryside. These remedies often took the form of infusions. Although it was possible to dry many of the herbs, it was discovered that their benefits were better preserved if they were macerated in alcohol. The treatment would then be available throughout the year. Like many medicines, the taste was often most unpalatable. Sugar had been known in Europe since the time of the Crusades, though it was not widely affordable until the end of the sixteenth century. A spoonful of this helped the medicine go down! Even today many liqueurs maintain their monastic association (Chartreuse for example) or are produced in ports where the ingredients, most importantly the common element sugar, were most widely available. Bordeaux and Amsterdam, for example, remain important centres for the production of liqueurs.

A liqueur is a spirit that has been sweetened and flavoured. The role of many liqueurs appears to be little more than that of bricks to be used in the construction of cocktails and will be based on neutral spirit. Many traditional liqueurs are intended to be consumed on their own. These are generally based on specific, aged spirits, such as Grand Marnier, which has a Cognac base, and Drambuie, based on Scotch whisky. Many others are simply made by infusing or macerating the flavouring ingredients in the spirit and adding sugar. Ideally, if the flavour is of fruit, fresh fruit will be used. As this might restrict the period of production, in order to maintain year-round freshness of their product, the manufacturer might hold stocks of the fruit in a cold store. Inferior, cheaper liqueurs are made by mixing flavouring essences and artificial colourings with the spirit and sugar.

It is important to distinguish between a liqueur, such as cherry brandy, and its distilled fruit spirit equivalent. The former is sweeter, usually has a lower alcohol content and is coloured. It should be considerably cheaper, not only because of the lower duty, because it has less alcohol, but also the quantity of fruit needed for its production is much less. The flavourings of liqueurs can be divided into four different categories:

FRUIT
Blackcurrant – Crème de Cassis
Sloe – Sloe Gin
Apricot – Apricot Brandy
Cherry – Cherry Brandy, Heering Cherry Liqueur, Maraschino
Orange – Curaçao, Cointreau, Grand Marnier, Mandarine Napoléon
Peach – Southern Comfort

HERB
Multi-herb – Galliano, Bénédictine, Chartreuse, Drambuie, Glayva
Seed – Kummel
Mint – Crème de Menthe

BEAN, KERNEL, NUT
Coffee – Kahlua, Tia Maria
Chocolate – Crème de Cacao
Nuts – Amaretto, Malibu

FARMYARD
Egg – Advocaat
Cream – Bailey's Irish Cream

Appendix 1: Service and Storage

STORAGE OF WINE

If a wine is incorrectly stored it can affect the flavour and in severe cases the wine will become faulty.

The following general points should be followed when storing wine:

- For long-term storage, the temperature for all wines should be cool and constant, preferably between 10° and 15°C, as extremes of cold and heat can cause damage.
- Store wine on its side to ensure the cork remains in contact with the wine, if the cork dries out it can let in air, and the air will oxidise the wine.
- Keep wines away from strong light. Natural sunshine or artificial light will heat the wine and it will become stale and old before its time.
- Keep wine away from vibrations, in order for it to lie undisturbed.

SERVICE TEMPERATURES
White, Rosé and Sparkling Wines

STYLE OF WINE	EXAMPLE OF STYLE OF WINE	SERVICE TEMPERATURE
Medium/full-bodied, oaked white	White Burgundy, Fumé Blanc	Lightly chilled 12° C
Light/medium-bodied white	Muscadet, Pinot Grigio, New Zealand Sauvignon Blanc, Fino Sherry	Chilled 10° C
Sweet wines	Sauternes, Sweet Muscats	Well chilled 6–8° C
Sparkling wines	Champagne, Cava, Asti	Well chilled 6–8° C

Note that over-chilling can mask the flavours in white wines.

Red Wines

STYLE OF WINE	EXAMPLE OF STYLE OF WINE	SERVICE TEMPERATURE
Light-bodied red	Beaujolais, Bardolino, Valpolicella	Lightly chilled 12° C
Medium/full-bodied red	Claret, Red Burgundy, Rioja, Australian Shiraz, Châteauneuf-du-Pape, Barolo, Amarone della Valpolicella, Vintage Port	Room temperature 17–18° C

Note that the average room temperature will vary with the time of year and/or heating or air conditioning. Take care that red wines do not become too warm or too cold.

Ice buckets or wine coolers are often used to keep white, rosé and sparkling wines cold. An ice bucket will be filled three-quarters full with equal quantities of ice and water so that the bottle is fully surrounded by iced water.

GLASSWARE

An enormous range of glass shapes and sizes are used for the service of wine, each designed to emphasise a particular wine's characteristics. The use of the correct glass will enhance the drinking experience.

Red Wines

Red wines are best served in larger-sized glasses. This will allow air to come into contact with a large wine surface and develop the aromas and flavours.

White and Rosé Wines

White wines require medium-sized glasses so that the fresh, fruit characteristics are gathered and directed towards the top of the glass.

Sparkling Wine

Sparkling wines are served in flute glasses. This shape enhances the effect of the bubbles (and thus the wine's aroma) allowing them to travel through larger areas of the wine before bursting at the top of the glass. For this reason the old-style, saucer-shaped glasses are completely inappropriate, as the bubbles are very quickly lost.

Fortified Wine

Liqueur wines should be served in small glasses to emphasise the fruit characteristics rather than the alcohol. However, the glass should be large enough to allow swirling and nosing.

Preparing Glasses

Clean glassware is of the utmost importance, as even the slightest taint can ruin the flavour of the wine. This can also apply to 'clean' glasses from a dishwashing machine; it is worth checking the glasses to make sure no detergent or salt residue remains in the glass as this can give strange flavours to wines and, in the case of sparkling wine, make it lose its sparkle more quickly. When polishing glasses it is best to use a linen cloth, as this will not leave bits of fluff in the glass.

OPENING A BOTTLE OF WINE

- Remove the top of the capsule, by cutting round below the lip of the bottle. This can be done with a capsule remover or knife.

- Clean the neck of the bottle with a clean cloth.
- Draw the cork as gently and cleanly as possible using your selected corkscrew.
- Give the neck of the bottle a final clean inside and out.
- Pour a sample into the host's glass for approval.

OPENING A BOTTLE OF SPARKLING WINE

It is important to remember that there is considerable pressure in a bottle of sparkling wine. Chilling to the correct temperature helps to reduce this. Even when the wine is chilled, it is possible for the cork to spring violently from the bottle and injure someone.

- Remove the foil and then the wire muzzle.
- The cork must be held in place by the hand from the moment the wire is removed.
- Tilt the bottle at an angle of about 30 degrees, gripping the cork, and use the other hand to grip the base of the bottle.
- Turn the bottle, not the cork.
- Hold the cork steady, resisting its tendency to fly out, and ease it slowly out of the bottle.
- The gas pressure should be released with a quiet 'phut' not an explosion and flying corks.

DECANTING WINE

Wines with a heavy deposit need to be decanted. This deposit is quite natural and is formed during the ageing process of many good red wines.

- First remove the bottle horizontally from its rack and place in a decanting basket. Alternatively, hold carefully, making sure the deposit is not agitated.
- Remove the top of the capsule and clean the shoulder and neck of the bottle.
- Very gently remove the top of the capsule and clean the shoulder and neck of the bottle.
- Remove the bottle from the basket, being careful not to disturb the deposit. Holding the bottle in front of a light, pour the wine carefully into the decanter until the deposit can be seen near the neck. At this point stop pouring.

ORDERING WINE

It is useful to know how many measures you can get from a standard 75 cl bottle. This will help you work out how many bottles you would need for an order.

6 × 125 ml glasses

4 × 175 ml glasses

3 × 250 ml glasses

THE RESPONSIBLE APPRECIATION OF ALCOHOL

The drinks industry places increasing emphasis on the responsible appreciation of alcoholic beverages.

Dangers exist in two principal ways. Mild intoxication can impair the ability to perform potentially dangerous tasks, such as driving a motor vehicle or operating factory machinery. Regular excessive drinking can lead to permanent ill health, as well as behavioural, emotional and financial problems.

Assessing Intake of Alcohol

In order to guard against these problems, consumers need to assess reliably how much alcohol they have taken. There is a simple relationship between different drinks in terms of the amount of alcohol they contain. In standard measures each type of drink contains a similar amount of alcohol known as one unit.

One unit =
10 ml of pure alcohol
a half pint of ordinary beer or lager at 3.5% abv;
or a single 25 ml measure of spirits (e.g. whisky, gin, brandy) at 40% abv;
or a 125 ml glass of wine at 8% abv (a 175 ml glass of wine at 12% abv is 2.1 units);
or a 50 ml glass of Port at 20% abv.

The accumulative effects of regular alcoholic consumption are difficult to chart precisely. Few would dispute, however, the strong correlation between excessive drinking and the onset of liver cirrhosis.

The UK Health Education Authority has advised that damage to health is almost unknown in:

- men who consume no more than 21 units per week;
- women who consume no more than 14 units per week.

Regularly drinking moderate amounts is less harmful than drinking a large quantity at once. The Health Education Authority recommends limits of 3 to 4 units daily for men and 2 to 3 for women. The lower figure for women is because, in most women, a lower percentage of their body weight is made up of water, so alcohol becomes more concentrated in their body tissue and because they have lower levels of the stomach enzyme that metabolises alcohol.

Although excessive consumption of alcohol is likely to cause health problems, recent research has indicated that moderate consumption of alcohol can be beneficial to health.

Appendix 2: Principles of Food and Wine Matching

Most wines are produced as an accompaniment to food, and there are many established guidelines for matching food with wine successfully. Originally wine styles evolved to complement the cuisine of a region, so this is often a good starting point for finding a good wine and food combination.

There is no single choice of wine that must be drunk with a certain dish, but some are definitely a better match than others. To achieve the best match it is necessary to analyse the basic components in both the wine and the food. The principle is to try to balance these, so that neither the food nor the wine overpowers the other.

THE BASIC CONSIDERATIONS

The main elements to consider are:

Food flavours and textures
- weight/richness of food
- flavour intensity
- key flavours in food

Wine flavours and textures
- weight/body of wine
- flavour intensity and characteristics
- acidity
- tannin
- sweetness

Weight

The first and most important element to consider should be to match the weight of the food with that of the wine.

Rich heavyweight foods, like game, roast meats and red meat casseroles, need a full-bodied wine. Powerful red wines are often the favoured choice, although it is the weight of the wine which is the most important consideration rather than its colour or flavour. Often a rich full-bodied white wine is a better match for meat than a lighter red wine.

Lighter food, such as plain white meat or fish, is complemented by more delicate wine. Although white wines are the normal choice, light-bodied, low-tannin red wines can also be successful.

Flavour Intensity and Character

After weight, the next most important element to consider is flavour and how intense that flavour is. Flavour intensity, although similar to weight, is not the same. Think of a food that has a lot of weight but is low in flavour, say a plate of plain boiled potatoes or plain boiled rice, both are heavy in weight but light in flavour. At the other end of the scale think of a plate of raw, thinly sliced red or green peppers; these are high in flavour but light in weight. Wines can be the same. Riesling for example makes a lightweight wine that is intensely flavoured; while Chardonnay makes full-bodied, heavyweight wines that can be low in flavour. Delicate wines and strong flavoured foods do not match.

Isolating the dominant flavour in a dish is not as simple as it sounds, often the dominant flavour is in the sauce. Take a chicken curry for example; it is not the flavour of chicken that dominates. So think weight and then flavour intensity when selecting a suitable wine. A rich creamy sauce will need a wine of sufficient weight to match the food and one that will complement the smooth creamy, buttery flavours of the sauce.

It is also worth considering the way the food has been cooked. If a food is cooked by a moist, gentle method such as steaming, it will require a lighter-bodied wine than a food that is roasted, which will require a wine that is fuller and more robust in body as the method of cooking adds intensity of flavours to the food. Foods that have been cooked by frying will need lighter wines with good acidity, as the method of cooking increases the fat content. A slow-cooked dish that has been braised or stewed will be weightier and need fuller-bodied wines, as the flavours are intensified by the method of cooking.

The flavour character of a wine can sometimes be matched with food. For example:

- grapey or floral characteristics like wines from the Muscat variety with fruit

- spicy flavours like Gewurztraminer with spicy dishes (the term spice when describing a wine can mean a number of different aromas and flavours such as white pepper, black pepper, cloves, cinnamon, nutmeg and ginger)

- oaked wines with smoked foods – the stronger the smoke the greater the oak can be

- more neutral wines, such as Muscadet or Soave complement delicate flavoured food like seafood, and would be overpowered by stronger flavours.

Acidity

The acidity found in food must be matched by the acidity in the accompanying wines. Acidity is something we rarely think about in food. Tomatoes, an everyday ingredient in many foods, are extremely high in acidity. One of the characteristics of Italian red wines are their noticeable acidity. This is because Italian cuisine is dominated by two ingredients – tomatoes and olive oil – hence wines that go with Italian food need good acidity in them. Vinaigrette is a good example of acidity being added to a dish. The oil needs to be cut by the sharpness of acidity. So when making a vinaigrette you blend olive oil and vinegar together.

Dishes dominated by tart acidic flavours, like lemon, lime or vinegar, can be difficult and require care when matching as they will overpower most wines.

Tannin

Tannin in red wine reacts with protein molecules. Foods with a high protein content, particularly red meat, will soften the effect of the tannin on the palate. This is why wines from tannic grape varieties, such as Cabernet Sauvignon or Syrah/Shiraz, go well with roast meat and stews.

Light, fruity red wines with low levels of tannin like Beaujolais and Bardolino, will complement white meats as these are low in proteins and lighter than meats such as lamb and beef.

Tannin in combination with oily fish can result in an unpleasant metallic taste, so the general recommendation is to avoid red wines with fish. However, low tannin reds are fine with meaty fish. Wines with a high tannin content can also taste bitter with salty foods.

Sweetness

Dry wines can seem tart and over-acidic when drunk with any food with a degree of sweetness. Sweet food is best with wine which has a similar or greater degree of sweetness; the sweeter the food the sweeter the wine needs to be. Late-harvest wines, especially botrytis-affected wines, and sweet Muscat-based wines are the ideal choice for puddings.

Fat and Oiliness

Wines with a good level of acidity can be superb with rich, oily foods, such as pâté. For example, Sauternes works well with *foie gras*. Here the weight of both wine and food are similar, and the acidity in the wine helps it cut through the fattiness of the food. This is also an example of matching a sweet wine to a savoury food. Crisp wines such as Riesling and unoaked Barberas can make a good match with fatty meats such as duck and goose.

Spice

Hot spices like chilli reduce the sweetness in wine and can make dry red wines seem more astringent. Spices can also accentuate the flavours of oak. A good match for spicy food are wines that are made from really ripe, juicy fruit, either unoaked or lightly oaked. Wines such as New Zealand Sauvignon Blanc can work well with spiced foods, as can ripe Chilean Merlot.

Smoke

Smoked foods need wines with enough character to cope with the strength of the smoking. Lightly smoked salmon is a classic partner for Brut Champagne; smoked meats like pork can benefit from some slight sweetness in the wine like that found in some German Rieslings; smoky barbecued flavours suit powerful oaked wines like Australian Shiraz.

Salt

Salty foods are enhanced by a touch of sweetness. Think of classic combinations like prosciutto and figs. The same works with wine. Roquefort cheese and Sauternes and Port and Stilton are famous matches. Salty foods also benefit from a little acidity. Avoid tannic wines as the salt seems to bring out the bitterness of the tannin. Salty foods such as olives, oysters and other shellfish go best with crisp, dry, light-bodied white wines. Manzanilla or Fino Sherry are classic partners for olives and nuts.

These guidelines and recommendations should avoid disastrous combinations, but individual taste is the final consideration. Experimentation can yield surprising results.

Appendix 3: The Label

From the earliest times, wines have been known by their geographical origins. In the Bible, specific wines are mentioned by name, and the classical Greeks and Romans had classifications for their wines based upon their perceived qualities. Early wine labels show the minimum of detail – perhaps no more than the name of the village from which the wine came. Over the past few years there have been two distinct moves which have led to more information appearing on the label: one led by the consumers and the other by the authorities. The rapid growth in wine consumption, particularly in those countries where it has not been a tradition, has led to the consumer wanting to know more about what they are drinking. In the United States, for example, many back-labels will have a miniature essay on the origin of the wine, how it was made and with what it should be drunk. In parallel with this, the increasing complexity of the trade has meant that the authorities have sought greater protection for the consumer. As far as wine is concerned, this means that every bottle brings with it certain guarantees. These may be on the cork, the bottle, the capsule, the label or the back-label.

This chapter is concerned with the legal aspects of labelling, and focuses on EU legislation. This is because a large proportion of the world's wine is made in the EU, or is consumed there and must satisfy its legal requirements. EU law comes in many forms. The provisions governing labelling are mostly contained in the EU Regulations, which are translated into all the principal EU languages and published in EU Official Journals. The Regulations are legally binding and override any individual national rules covering the same areas. Ultimately EU law will apply to all alcoholic beverages in all EU countries. EU Regulations covering spirits and liqueur wines have been published, but at present these do no more than outline the general principles. Until the detail has been published in the form of Regulations, national laws apply, but they have been amended in order to comply with current EU Directives. Note that *Liqueur wines* is the legally correct term to what are generally referred to as fortified wines, wines to which alcohol in the form of grape spirit has been added, either before, during or after fermentation.

As the definition of wine in the EU requires that it has a minimum of 8.5% abv (with the exception of Germany where it is 6.5% abv), the term **alcohol-free wine** is forbidden. **De-alcoholised wine** is permitted if the product is obtained from a base wine that conforms to the EU definition of wine. It is essential to differentiate between the categories. Should a customer ask for an alcohol-free drink, he must not be offered a low-alcohol one.

EU WINE LABELLING REGULATIONS
Still Wines Produced in the EU
All still wines offered for sale in the EU must be labelled in accordance with EU Regulations, even if produced outside the EU. Anything that is not expressly permitted is forbidden. These Regulations allow for five different categories of still wines:

1. Quality Wine Produced in a Specified Region (QWPSR)
This is a category for wine made from grapes grown within a specified region in the EU and does not, therefore, apply to wines made outside the EU. The region concerned must be registered with the EU, and legislation in each member country will implement the EU criteria for the category. Such legislation will cover:

- grape varieties, authorised or recommended
- viticultural practices, particularly pruning systems
- maximum yields per hectare
- controls on winemaking, acidification, enrichment, ageing and so on
- minimum (and sometimes maximum) alcohol content
- analysis, and sometimes tasting, tests of the finished wine

QWPSR label

Brand name

QWPSR region, as registered with EC. Grapes will have been grown within the region and wine made according to the rules set for the wine.

QWPSR category in Spanish wine law.

Name and address of producer and bottler.

Vintage 1997 Crianza indicates that the wine will have been aged in cask and bottle for certain minimum periods, set by Spanish law.

Country of origin.

Alcohol content (by volume at 20° C).

Volume contents and 'e' mark.

Many countries have two categories of QWPSR. France has *Appellation Contrôlée* (AC) and the lesser category of *vin de qualité supérieure* (VDQS). Similarly, Italian Quality Wine is divided into DOC and the higher DOCG and German into QbA and the higher QmP. Details of these different classifications are found in the country chapters.

2. Table Wine with Geographical Description

This is a wine, other than a quality wine, from an EU country, which mentions a specific source within, and is produced under the laws of, that country. No confusion should exist between the geographical description of a table wine and any QWPSR region. Examples of these wines include *Vino de la Tierra* (Spain), and *Vin de Pays* (France). The label may show a vintage and up to two grape varieties.

Still Wines Produced within the EU

3. Table Wine

The term table wine can be expressed on the label in any of the principal EU languages, e.g. *Vin de Table, Vino da Tavola, tafelwein, vino de mesa*. As an expression it may be applied only to wines produced within the EU, thus a wine within the EU cannot be described on the label as 'Australian Table Wine'. Such wines may be blended from various countries within the EU, but the fact must be mentioned on the label in the language of the country of consumption, with a phrase such as 'Blend of wines from different countries of the European Union'. Only very general rules apply to table wine production, the most important being that the finished wine must have a minimum of 8.5% abv and a maximum of 15% abv, except in Greece, where wines up to 17% abv are allowed. Chaptalisation is not permitted. Table wine labels may mention neither a vintage nor a grape variety.

Still Wines Produced in Non-EU Countries

1. Wine with Geographical Description

This is a wine produced outside the EU, known officially as a 'third country wine', which names the specific producing region in the country. Such wines might be Marlborough Sauvignon Blanc from New Zealand or Suhindol Cabernet Sauvignon from Bulgaria. The region must be on a list approved by the EU authorities and must not be confusable with a Quality Wine name. Thus, for example, the province of La Rioja in Argentina cannot sell its wines in the EU under that name, but rather as Famatina Valley. The region may be small, such as Gimblett Gravels, or very large, such as South-Eastern Australia, which potentially includes well over 90 per cent of the production of that country. A vintage may be mentioned on the label and (normally) up to two grape varieties. Many countries outside the EU have their own, legally defined statements of quality or source (such as AVAs in the United States) and these may appear on bottles sold in the EU. Such statements do not, however, have any legal significance within the EU. Where vintages, grape varieties and regions are stated,

KEY EU COUNTRY	QWPSR	TABLE WINE WITH GEOGRAPHICAL DESCRIPTION	TABLE WINE
France	AC/AOC VDQS	Vin de Pays	Vin de Table
Germany	QmP QbA	Landwein	Deutscher Tafelwein
Italy	DOC, DOCG	IGT	Vino da Tavola
Spain	DO, DOC	Vino de la Tierra	Vino de Mesa
Portugal	DOC	IPR	Vinho de Mesa

most countries have arranged derogations that allow the wine to be made with a minimum of 85 per cent (75 per cent for California) of grapes from the stated vintages, varieties and regions. Otherwise, 100 per cent is required.

2. Wine

This is a non-EU wine that does not fall into the previous category. Grape varieties and vintages may not be mentioned. The blending of wines from two non-EU countries is forbidden, as is the blending of EU and non-EU wines.

For each category, the Regulations specify what must be on the label and what is permitted to be on the label. Anything not specified on either list is forbidden. For example, the style of the wine may be described (for example sweet); on the other hand, health warnings, which are compulsory in the United States, are forbidden in the EU.

Sparkling Wines

There are four different categories of sparkling wine laid down, which, with the exception of the first, have no still wine equivalent. As with light still wines, only those items specifically permitted may appear on the label: more information being mandatory in the higher categories.

1. Quality Sparkling Wine Produced in a Specified Region

This can be produced only from within the EU, at AC or comparative level. Such examples are Crémant de Bourgogne, Moscato d'Asti and Cava. They must be made sparkling by a secondary fermentation, either in tank or in bottle, which is in accordance with the local regulations.

2. Quality Sparkling Wine

This must be produced by fermentation in bottle or tank. A minimum of nine months must elapse from the time that the fermentation began until the wine is put on the market for bottle-fermented wines and six months for tank-fermented wines. During this time, bottle-fermented wines must spend a minimum of 60 days on their lees, whilst tank-fermented wines must spend a minimum of 80, unless made in a vat equipped with rousing paddles, for which the period is reduced to 30 days. Whilst this category is mainly for EU wines, it has been extended to a number of wines from other countries.

For these first two categories the word 'aromatic' may appear on the label if the wine is made from a grape variety such as Muscat or Gewurztraminer.

Table wine label

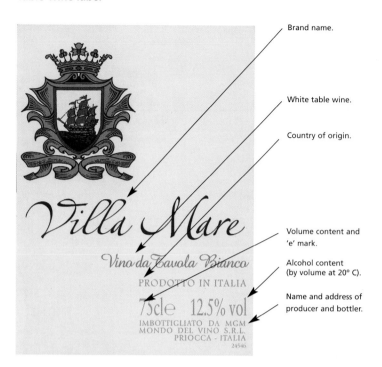

Brand name.

White table wine.

Country of origin.

Volume content and 'e' mark.

Alcohol content (by volume at 20° C).

Name and address of producer and bottler.

3. Sparkling Wine

This can come from within or outside the EU. The one stipulation is that the sparkle must come from fermentation. No geographical source smaller than the country of origin may be mentioned.

4. Aerated Sparkling Wine

This is used on carbonated wines and the production method must be clearly mentioned on the label with such a mention as 'Obtained by Addition of Carbon Dioxide'. No geographical description more precise than the country of origin may be mentioned.

GENERAL EU LABELLING REGULATIONS
Varietal Labelling

Any wine produced in the EU that mentions a grape variety on the label must contain at least 85 per cent of that variety. For most non-EU countries (and indeed for some within it) the wine must contain 100 per cent of that variety, though there are derogations for some countries including Australia, New Zealand, Argentina and Chile, where it is 85 per cent, and the United States where it is 75 per cent. A limited number of countries outside the EU, may name two or three varieties on the label, and exceptionally, and peculiarly, Australia may name up to five, as long

Third country wine label

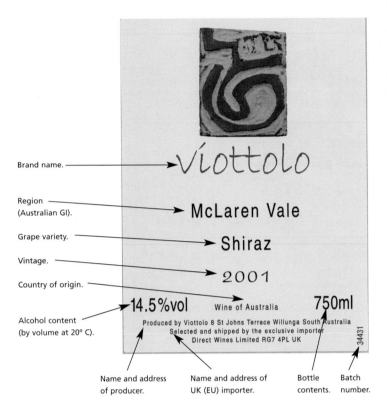

Brand name.

Region (Australian GI).

Grape variety.

Vintage.

Country of origin.

Alcohol content (by volume at 20° C).

Viottolo

McLaren Vale

Shiraz

2001

14.5%vol   Wine of Australia   750ml

Produced by Viottolo 8 St Johns Terrace Willunga South Australia
Selected and shipped by the exclusive importer
Direct Wines Limited RG7 4PL UK

34431

Name and address of producer.

Name and address of UK (EU) importer.

Bottle contents.

Batch number.

as they each represent a minimum of 5 per cent of the blend. For EU wines any number of grapes can be mentioned as part of a 'descriptive text', but a maximum of two can appear as stand-alone information.

Vintages

Statement of a vintage is optional for EU QWPSRs, EU Table Wines with a Geographical Description, and non-EU wines with a Geographical Description. For most wines, particularly large-scale brands that take advantage of blending across regions and varieties, the vintage is not important; it is simply an indication of age. It allows us to follow the evolution of the wine in the bottle, or make a judgement of how fresh or stale it is likely to be. Some wines are not labelled with a vintage, either because it is forbidden (as for EU Table Wines, and non-EU wines that fall outside the Geographical Description designation), or because they are made from a blend of vintages (such as most Champagnes and Sherries). This can be a problem, as even the longest-lived Champagnes do evolve within the bottle, and it can be impossible for the consumer to guess how long a wine has been waiting on a shelf or in a warehouse. Some conscientious producers add a disgorgement or bottling date to the back-label. For wines such as Fino Sherries, which lose their freshness very quickly after bottling, this can be a very useful guide to the retailer (aiding stock rotation) and to the purchaser.

Lot Marking

Finally, under EU regulations, in case of complaint, a consumer must be able to look at a label and recognise a distinctive reference by which the producer can check back to the bottling batch and, if necessary, recall the total parcel. Often this is a coded series of figures or letters. Such historical systems as Codedge, by which the edge of the label was nicked to a certain pattern, are no longer permitted. A batch number is not needed if the total parcel of wine was bottled at one time. This might well be the case for such wines as domaine-bottled Burgundies. Nor is it needed for wines bottled before 1 July 1992.

Glossary

Abbreviations   **F** = French   **G** = German   **I** = Italian   **P** = Portuguese   **S** = Spanish

Abboccato	**I**	Medium-sweet and full-bodied.
Accolage	**F**	The viticultural procedure of tying the vine branches to the horizontal wires.
Acetic acid		The acid component of vinegar. The product of oxidation of ethanol by the action of acetobacter in the presence of oxygen. A volatile acid present in small quantities in all wines. Excessive amounts result in a vinegary nose and taste.
Adamado	**P**	Sweet.
Adega	**P**	Winery.
Aerobic		Requiring oxygen to operate.
Alcohol		Potable alcohol, as contained in alcoholic drinks, is ethanol, sometimes called ethyl alcohol. **Actual alcohol** is the amount of ethanol present in a wine, measured as a percentage of the total volume at 20° C as shown on the label. **Total alcohol** is the sum of the actual and potential (from unfermented sugars) alcohol.
Almacenista	**S**	A producer of Sherry who ages it and then sells it in bulk to a merchant.
Alte Reben	**G**	Old vines.
Amabile	**I**	Medium-sweet.
Anaerobic		Able to operate without oxygen.
Analyser		That part of a patent, or Coffey, still in which the alcohol present in the pre-heated wash (q.v.) is vaporised by steam.
Anbaugebiet	**G**	Designated quality wine region.
Annata	**I**	Vintage.
Anreicherung	**G**	Must enrichment (q.v.).
Ascorbic acid		Vitamin C. Used in winemaking, along with sulphur dioxide to prevent oxidation.
Aspersion		Method of protection against spring frosts whereby the vine are sprayed with water, which freezes, coating the buds with ice. The buds are not damaged because of the latent heat of the ice.
Assemblage	**F**	Blending of a number of different parcels of wine, particularly in Bordeaux or Champagne.
Ausbruch	**G**	An Austrian quality category for sweet wines, the minimum must weight required is higher than that for *Beerenauslese*, but lower than that for *Trockenbeerenauslese*.

Auslese	**G**	German quality wine category, indicating an unchaptalised wine made from selected bunches of exceptionally ripe grapes.
Azienda (or Casa)	**I**	An estate that makes wine from both its own and bought-in grapes.
Azienda (or Casa) Agricola	**I**	An estate that uses only its own grapes in the production of its wine.
Azienda (or Casa) Vinicola	**I**	A producer who buys in and vinifies grapes.
Barrique	**F**	Cask (q.v.) with a capacity of 225 litres. Traditional to Bordeaux, but now used throughout the world.
Battonnage	**F**	Lees stirring (q.v.).
Baumé	**F**	French scale used in measurement of must weight (q.v.).
Beerenauslese	**G**	German quality wine category, indicating an unchaptalised wine made from individually selected, super-ripe grapes. These will usually be affected by botrytis, and will have exceptionally high sugar levels.
Bentonite		Clay like material used for fining (q.v.).
Bereich	**G**	A group of communes (*Gemeinde*).
Bianco	**I**	White.
Biodynamic		A form of organic viticulture (q.v.) that follows the teachings of Rudolf Steiner. Vine treatments are timed to match astronomical cycles.
Biologique	**F**	Organic.
Black rot		Fungal disease of the vine prevalent in warm, wet weather, which causes black stains on the leaves.
Blanc	**F**	White.
Blanco	**S**	White.
Blended whisk(e)y		Scotland: a blend of grain and malt whisky. US: A blend of straight whiskey and neutral corn spirit.
Blue fining		Removal of iron or copper casse (q.v.) from a wine by the addition of potassium ferrocyanide.
Bodega	**S**	Winery.
Bonne chauffe	**F**	The second distillation used in Cognac to convert the *brouillis* to eau de vie.
Bordeaux mixture		Solution of copper sulphate and lime in water, used to spray vines as protection against fungal diseases.

Botanicals		Flavourings used in gin production.
Botrytis cinerea		Fungus which attacks the grape berry. In certain circumstances it will form unwanted grey rot, in others, desirable noble rot.
Botte	I	Traditional large barrels used in Italy in various sizes up to 160 hl. (Plural *botti*.)
Bottiglia	I	Bottle.
Branco	P	White.
Brix/Balling		A system of measuring must weight (q.v.), and thereby potential alcohol.
Brouillis	F	The product of the first distillation in Cognac.
Brut	F, S	Dry (of a sparkling wine).
Bush training		Training of vines as free-standing plants, not needing the support of a trellis (q.v.).
Butt		Traditional barrel used in Sherry production, holding about 600 litres.
Buttage	F	The process of earthing up the bases of the vines to protect them against frost.
Cane		Partially lignified one-year-old wood on a vine, pruned to between eight and 15 buds. If pruned to just two or three buds, it is referred to as a spur (q.v.).
Cane pruning		System of vine pruning in which one or more long canes of one-year-old wood, remain to produce new shoots.
Cantina sociale	I	Co-operative cellar.
Cap		Floating mass of grape skins, stalks etc. on the surface of red must when fermenting.
Carbonic maceration		Fermentation of whole bunches of black grapes with the berries initially intact. The intracellular fermentation results in well-coloured, fruity red wines, with little tannin.
Cascina	I	Farmhouse (has come to mean estate).
Cask		Wooden barrel, usually made of oak, used for fermentation, maturation and storage of wines. Traditional names and sizes vary from region to region.
Casse	F	Unwanted haze in wine caused by instability.
Casta	P	Grape variety.
Cava	S	DO traditional method sparkling wine.
Cave	F	Cellar (often underground) or winemaking establishment.
Cave co-operative	F	Co-operative cellar.
Cépage	F	Grape variety.

Cerasuolo	I	Cherry pink.
Chai	F	Above-ground warehouse for storing wine, usually in barrel.
Chalk		A kind of limestone (q.v.) that is almost pure calcium carbonate.
Chaptalisation		Must enrichment (q.v.), specifically using beet or cane, named after Comte Chaptal, the Napoleonic minister who advocated its use.
Charmat method		Sparkling wine production process in which the secondary fermentation takes place under pressure in a sealed tank. Also called tank method or *cuve close*.
Château	F	Vineyard in Bordeaux, generally, but not always, with accompanying house.
Chauffe-vin	F	Wine heater. Part of a Cognac still, used to heat the wine before it enters the pot still.
Chiaretto	I	Light or pale rosé.
Classic	G	A German category for dry quality wines.
Classico	I	The original centre of a DOC region, making the most typical wines.
Clay		An extremely fine-grained, soft rock. Clay soils often retain large amounts of water, which keep the soil cool, and may drown the vine roots.
Climat	F	A vineyard site.
Clonal selection		Selection of plants from a particular variety for specific desirable features (which may include early ripening, good fruit, high, or low, yields and resistance to diseases).
Clone		One of a population of plants that are the descendants of a single individual and have been propagated by vegetative means. Unlike descendants by sexual propagation, each clone will have features identical to the parent plant.
Clos	F	Historically, a walled vineyard, though the walls may no longer exist.
Col de Cygne	F	Swan's neck. The part of a Cognac still that transports the vapours from the pot to the condenser.
Colheita	P	Harvest.
Commune		A small wine-growing region, usually surrounding one village.
Compte	F	Age classification system used in Cognac and Armagnac, starting with *compte* 00 for freshly distilled spirit.
Congeners		Organic compounds giving flavouring and aromas in alcoholic beverages. Products of the fermentation, distillation and maturation processes, they include such compounds as ketones, esters and aldehydes.

Consorzio	I	Producers' trade association, whose members' wine are identified by an individually designed neck-label.
Continentality		The difference between summer and winter temperatures.
Co-operative cellar		Winemaking (and sometimes bottling and marking) facilities that are jointly owned by a number of growers.
Cordon		Horizontal extension of a vine trunk.
Côte	F	Hillside.
Côteau(x)	F	Slope(s).
Courbe de fermentation	F	Record of temperature and density of a particular vat of must or wine during fermentation, plotted as a graph, used by the winemaker to monitor the wine's progress.
Crianza	S	Spanish DOC wine that has satisfied certain minimum age requirements for ageing in cask and bottle.
Crossing		Breeding of new vine varieties by cross-pollination of two different varieties of the same species. For wine production, this is usually two varieties of *V. vinifera*.
Cru	F	A single 'growth', generally of quality. It might be a village or a vineyard.
Cru artisan	F	A rank of Bordeaux châteaux, below *cru bourgeois* (q.v.).
Cru bourgeois	F	A rank of Bordeaux châteaux, below *Cru Classé* (q.v.).
Cru Classé	F	A classified growth, normally in Bordeaux.
Cuve	F	Vat or tank.
Cuvée	F	1. The juice resulting from the first pressing in Champagne. 2. A blend.
Debuttage	F	Removing the protective earth that has been placed around the base of the vine during buttage (q.v.).
Dégorgement	F	Removal of the sediment from a bottle in traditional method sparkling wine production.
Dégorgement tardive	F	A Champagne that has been disgorged after an exceptionally long period of yeast autolysis, or ageing *sur pointe* (q.v.).
Degree-day		A method of classifying climatic zones based on the sum of the average daily temperatures above 10° C (the temperature at which the vine starts to grow) during the growing season.
Demi-Sec	F	Medium-dry.
Density of planting		The number of vine plants per area of land, usually expressed as vines per hectare, and will vary from 3000 to 10000 or more per hectare. Low plant density has the advantage of lower establishment costs, but higher density will generally give better quality wines, given a fixed yield per hectare. Factors such as mechanisation will affect the choice of plant density.
Département	F	French political region.
Diurnal range		The difference between daytime and night-time temperatures. A wide diurnal range encourages fruit aromas and acid retention; warm nights encourage sugar build-up.
Doce	P	Sweet.
Dolce	I	Sweet.
Domaine	F	Estate.
Dosage	F	Adjustment of the sugar level in sparkling wines by the addition of *liqueur d'expedition* (q.v.) after *dégorgement* (q.v.).
Doux	F	Sweet.
Downy mildew		Fungus appearing as downy patches on the vine leaves, reducing photosynthesis. Also called peronospera.
Dulce	S	Sweet.
Eau-de-vie	F	Distilled spirit; literally, 'water of life'.
Edelfaule	G	Noble rot.
Edes (Hungary)		Sweet.
Einzellage	G	Individual vineyard.
Eiswein	G	Sweet wine made from frozen grapes.
Elaborado (por)	S	Produced (by).
Elevé en fûts de chêne	F	Aged in oak barrels.
Embotellado (por)	S	Bottled (by).
En Primeur	F	Wines, especially from Bordeaux, that are sold before they are bottled.
Erzeugerabfullung	G	Estate-bottled.
Estate		A producer who makes wine from grapes grown on their property only.
Estufagem	P	Heating process used in the production of Madeira, to caramelise the sugars in the wines.
Ethanol		*See* Alcohol.
Extra-Sec	F	Off-dry (sparkling wines).
Fattoria	I	Estate.
Federspiel	G	In the Wachau, a category lying in between Steinfeder and Smaragd (q.v.).

Feints		The tails (q.v.). Fraction of the second distillation of Scotch malt whisky.
Fermentation		The conversion, by the action of yeast enzymes of sugar to alcohol.
Fermentazione naturale	I	A naturally produced sparkle in a wine.
Fining		Removal of matter in suspension in a wine by the addition of a fining agent such as bentonite (q.v.), which acts as a coagulant.
Fixed acidity		The acidity in wine detectable only on the palate (cf. volatile acidity [q.v.]), composed of tartaric, malic and lactic acids.
Flor	S	Yeast growth which forms particularly on the surface of Fino and Manzanilla Sherries, giving them a distinctive taste and protecting them from oxidation.
Foreshots		The heads (q.v.) fraction of the second distillation of Scotch malt whisky.
Frizzante	I	Slightly sparkling.
Fusel oils		Toxic by-products of distillation, containing long-chain hydrocarbons, removed as part of the tails (q.v.).
Garrafeira	P	A superior wine with additional ageing.
Gemeind	G	A commune.
Gônc		Traditional cask, used in Hungary for ageing Tokaji.
Governo	I	Vinification technique, occasionally used in the production of Chianti, in which a small quantity of semi-dried grapes or concentrated must is added to the wine after fermentation to induce a slight secondary fermentation, increasing the glycerine content of the wine.
Graft		The union of a small piece of one plant, including a bud (the scion [q.v.]) on to a supporting rootstock (q.v.). In viticulture the most important use is the grafting of a *V. vinifera* scion on to a rootstock having some American parentage and thus tolerant of phylloxera.
Grains Nobles (Sélection de...),	F	Botrytis-affected grapes (wine made using a selection of nobly rotten grapes). This is a legal description in Alsace, but the phrase may occasionally be seen on wines from other regions, such as Condrieu, Mâcon, and Côteaux du Layon.
Gran Reserva	S	A wine that has seen long ageing in cask and bottle. Minimum periods are set by law and vary from one region to another.
Granvas	S	Tank-fermented sparkling wine.
Green malt		Grains of barley which have been soaked and which have started to germinate, converting the stored starch into sugar. When dried in a kiln, green malt becomes malt (q.v.).

Grey rot		Malevolent form of *Botrytis cinerea* (q.v.), affecting unripe berries or black grapes, causing off-flavours and lack of colour.
Grist		Ground grains, such as barley.
Grosslage	G	A group of adjoining vineyards. Not to be confused with *Einzellage*.
Gyropalette	F	Hydraulically operated, computer-controlled racks for mechanical *remuage* (q.v.).
Habillage	F	The dressing (foil etc.) that a bottle of sparkling wine receives before it is dispatched from the winery.
Halbtrocken	G	Off-dry.
Head grafting		A process that allows an established vineyard of one variety to be grafted over to another, more profitable variety, without having to grub up and replant.
Heads		The first 'fraction' to be vaporised during distillation: containing, in addition to ethanol, volatile and toxic compounds such as methanol.
Hybrid		A vine variety resulting from the cross-pollination of two vines of different species, usually one *V. vinifera* and one of American origin to breed in tolerance of phylloxera. Also called interspecific crossing.
Imbottigliato all'origine	I	Estate-bottled.
Invecchiato	I	Aged.
Irrigation		The supply of water to the vine by means of artificial canals, flooding, overhead sprays or drip systems on individual vines. Until recently, this was forbidden in EU vineyards except for young vines not in production, and experimental vineyards. It is used widely elsewhere.
Kabinett	G	German QmP category, indicating wine made without chaptalisation from grapes harvested at ordinary ripeness.
Lagar	P, S	Trough, generally made of stone or concrete, used for treading grapes. Superseded in most regions by more modern methods, but still occasionally used in the Douro.
Lees		The sediment of dead yeast cells that gathers at the bottom of the tank or cask once fermentation is completed.
Lees stirring		A process of mixing the lees (q.v.) with the wine, usually in cask, to help extract components that will give the wine extra flavour and body.
Lieu Dit	F	A named vineyard site not of *Premier Cru* or *Grand Cru* status.
Limestone		A sedimentary rock consisting mainly of calcium carbonate. Its drainage, and water-retention properties make it particularly suitable for

viticulture. The calcium content inhibits the uptake of acid-neutralising potassium, thereby helping grapes retain their acid.

Liqueur d'expédition   **F**   Final adjustment to the sweetness of sparkling wine prior to corking. Also called *dosage*.

Liqueur de tirage   **F**   Mixture of wine, sugar and yeast added to still wine to promote a secondary fermentation in sparkling wine production.

Liquoreux   **F**   Very sweet, especially botrytis-affected wines.

Liquoroso   **I**   Strong, often fortified, wine.

Loess   Literally, 'loose'. A very fine, wind-blown deposit of silt, or sand and silt. Like clay soils (q.v.), they have a high capacity for retaining water.

Low-wines   The water-white liquid with an alcoholic content of around 30% abv which results from the first distillation of Scotch malt whisky. Cf. *brouillis* (q.v.).

Lutte raisonnée   **F**   A form of viticulture that, although not organic, attempts to avoid unnecessary systematic use of synthetic chemicals.

Maceration   Period of time when the skins are in contact with the fermenting must during red wine vinification.

Malolactic fermentation   Conversion of harsh malic acid into softer lactic acid by the action of lactic bacteria.

Malt   Barley which has undergone the malting process of soaking, germination and kilning to convert the starch present in the original grain into fermentable sugar.

Manipulant   **F**   A grape-grower who also makes wine, especially in Champagne.

Marc   **F**   1. The residue of skins pips and stalks left in a press after the extraction of juice or wine. In English, this is called pomace.
2. The name given to one charge of a traditional vertical press, especially in Champagne.

Mash bill   The mix of grains in a whisky.

Maso, Masseria   **I**   Estate.

Merchant   1. A company that buys grapes or finished wine for vinification, maturation and blending before sale.
2. A wine dealer.

Mesoclimate   Site climate (q.v.).

Metodo charmat   **I**   Tank-method sparkling wine.

Metodo classico, metodo tradizionale   **I**   Traditional method, bottle-fermented sparkling wine.

Micro-climate   1. The climate within the canopy of the vine.
2. Used informally to refer to the site climate, or mesoclimate (q.v.).

Millésime   **F**   Vintage date.

Mise en bouteille (par)   **F**   Bottled (by)

Mise en bouteille au château/domaine   **F**   Château/domain-bottled.

Mise sur lie   **F**   Bottled on its lees.

Mistelle, Mistela   **F, S**   A mixture of unfermented grape juice and alcohol.

Moelleux   **F**   Medium-sweet.

Monopole   **F**   A vineyard, especially in Burgundy, that has only one owner.

Mosto Cotto   **I**   Reduced, concentrated grape must, used as a sweetening agent.

Mousseux   **F**   Sparkling.

Muffa nobile   **I**   Noble rot (q.v.).

Must   Unfermented grape juice, destined to become wine.

Must enrichment   The addition of sugar or rectified concentrated must to grape juice prior to fermentation to increase the final alcoholic content of the wine. Strict controls govern its use (cf. *chaptalisation*).

Must weight   Density, or specific gravity, of grape juice prior to fermentation. Measurement of the must weight enables the winemaker to estimate the final alcoholic content of the wine.

Négociant   **F**   Merchant (q.v.).

Noble rot   Benevolent form of *Botrytis cinerea* (q.v.) which concentrates the sugars of ripe grapes, facilitating the production of the finest sweet wines.

Non-Filtré   **F**   Unfiltered.

Oechsle   German scale for measuring must weight (q.v.).

Oidium   Powdery mildew (q.v.).

Organic   A wine made from organically farmed grapes that is one where synthetic pesticides, herbicides, fungicides and fertilisers have not been used.

Passérillee   **F**   Grapes that have begun to shrivel on the vine, resulting in a concentration of sugars.

Passito   **I**   A generally strong, sweet wine made from partially dried grapes.

Peronospera   Downy mildew (q.v.).

Pétillant   **F**   Lightly sparkling.

Petit château   **F**   In Bordeaux, one of the many château brands that fall outside the classifications.

Photosynthesis		The conversion of carbon dioxide and water to usable organic compounds, especially carbohydrates, by plants, using light energy absorbed by the green chlorophyll in the leaves.
Phylloxera vastatrix		The most serious insect pest of the vine. It feeds on its roots and, in the case of European *V. vinifera*, will kill it. There is no known way of eradicating the louse, but its effect can be stopped by grafting the *V. vinifera* scion (q.v.) on to American rootstock.
Pipe		Traditional cask (q.v.) used in the Douro for Port production. Two sizes are recognised, the 550-litre production, or Douro, pipe and the 534-litre shipping pipe.
Podere	**I**	A small estate.
Powdery mildew		Fungus which attacks the vine, initially appearing as floury white dust on the leaves and grapes, eventually causing the grapes to split. Also known as *Oidium*.
Prädikat	**G**	The various subcategories of German Quality wines (*Kabinett*, *Spätlese*, *Auslese*, *Beerenauslese*, *Trockenbeerenauslese*, as well as *Eiswein*). Austria adds the category *Ausbruch*, but does not include *Kabinett*.
Primary aromas		Aromas in a wine that arise directly from the fruit (q.v. secondary, tertiary).
Produttore	**I**	Producer.
Propriétaire	**F**	Owner.
Pruning		Removal of unwanted parts of the vine, mostly wood that is one year old, or less, in order to regulate the yield and control the vine's shape. The main pruning, usually carried out by hand, is during the vine's dormant period in the winter.
Pupitre	**F**	Rack consisting of two hinged boards through which holes have been bored to hold the necks of sparkling wine bottles during *remuage* (q.v.).
Puttunyos		Measure of sweetness in a Tokaji wine.
Quinta	**P**	Farm or estate.
Racking		Drawing off clear wine from a cask or vat and moving it to another, leaving the sediment behind.
Raisin	**F**	Grape.
Recioto	**I**	Similar to passito (q.v.), made with part-dried grapes.
Récoltant	**F**	Someone who harvests their own grapes.
Récolte	**F**	Vintage or harvest.
Rectifier		The second column of a Coffey or patent still, in which the alcohol rich vapour from the analyser (q.v.) is condensed to form spirit, while heating the cold wash. Heads and tails are removed here.

Refractometer		Hand-held instrument consisting of a prism and a series of lenses used for gauging the must weight (q.v.) of grape juice to assess the ripeness of the fruit.
Remuage	**F**	'Riddling'. Moving the sediment to the neck of the bottle prior to *dégorgement* (q.v.) in traditional method sparkling wine production.
Reserva	**P, S**	For Spanish DO and DOC wines this indicates ageing in cask and bottle for legally defined minimum periods. For other wines, such as those of Chile, it has no legal meaning.
Reserve		May indicate a superior quality wine, or wines that have seen a period of ageing. Or it may indicate very little. This word has no legal meaning.
Residual sugar		Unfermented sugar remaining in the wine after bottling. Even dry wines will contain a small amount.
Rich	**F**	Sweet (sparkling wines).
Riserva	**I**	Reserve, for DOC wines, one that has been aged in cask and/or bottle for a particular length of time.
Rootstock		Phylloxera-resistant or tolerant vine, usually with some American parentage, on to which a *V. vinifera* scion is usually grafted. (Rootstocks may be selected to achieve other effects, such as lime-, or nematode-resistance, or to increase or decrease yields.)
Rosado	**S**	Rosé.
Rosato	**I**	Rosé.
Rosso	**I**	Red.
Rouge	**F**	Red.
Scion		Section of plant material grafted on to a rootstock. For wine making, this will be *V. vinifera* grafted on to American rootstock (q.v.).
Sec	**F**	Dry.
Secco	**I**	Dry.
Seco	**P, S**	Dry.
Secondary aromas		Aromas in a wine that arise from the fermentation (q.v. primary, tertiary aromas).
Selection	**G**	A German category for quality dry wines from single vineyard sites.
Semisecco	**I**	Medium-dry.
Semi-seco	**S**	Medium-dry.
Site climate		The climate of a plot of vines, perhaps a vineyard, or part of a vineyard. See also *Mesoclimate*, *Micro-climate*.
Smaragd	**G**	In the Wachau (Austria), rich, full-bodied dry wines from late-harvested grapes.

Solera		System of fractional blending used in the production of Sherry, wherein older wine is refreshed by the addition of younger wine.
Spätlese	**G**	German quality wine category, indicating a wine made without chaptalisation from late-harvested grapes.
Spumante	**I**	Sparkling wine made by any method.
Spur		A short cane (q.v.) of one-year-old wood with two or three buds.
Steinfeder	**G**	In the Wachau (Austria), the lightest bodied wine category for dry wines.
Straight Whiskey		US. A whiskey made from at least 51 per cent of one grain, distilled to no more than 80% abv, and aged for a minimum of two years in new oak casks.
Stravecchio	**I**	Very old, particularly of Marsala and spirits.
Strohwein, Schilfwein	**G**	Sweet wine made from grapes that have been dried on straw or reed mats.
Sulphur dioxide (SO$_2$)		Highly reactive and pungent gas which is used in winemaking as an anti-oxidant and antiseptic. May be added to wines and musts as gas in the form of metabisulphite (solid) or produced in an empty cask by burning a sulphur candle (additive E220).
Super Second		Bordeaux Châteaux that were second (or third) growths in the 1855 Classification, but which sometimes produce wines that rival the first growths for quality. Which châteaux qualify is a matter of debate.
Supérieur	**F**	Indicates a higher degree of alcohol.
Superiore	**I**	Superior. For DOC wines this may mean that it came from the best vineyards within the region, had been aged longer or had a higher degree of alcohol.
Sur lie	**F**	A wine that is aged on its lees (q.v.).
Sur Pointe	**F**	Ageing of a bottle of sparkling wine, neck down, after yeast autolysis is complete, but before disgorgement.
Süss	**G**	Sweet.
Süssreserve	**G**	Unfermented, sterile grape must added to dry wine prior to bottling to increase sweetness and balance excess acidity. Not to be confused with must enrichment (q.v.).
Systemic fungicides		Chemicals used to combat fungal diseases of the vine by being absorbed into its tissues, rather than remaining on the surface.
Szamorodni (Hungary)		'As it comes'. Wine made from grapes that have not been sorted according to their degree of botrytis.
Száraz (Hungary)		Dry.
Taille	**F**	1. Pruning. 2. The juice resulting from the second pressing of grapes in Champagne.

Tails		The third fraction collected during distillation, containing ethanol and a number of less volatile compounds, many of which are toxic.
Tannin		Chemical compound present in the skins, stalks and pips of grapes which is extracted during red wine vinification. Tannin is a preservative in red wine, giving a dry sensation on the gums when present.
Tartaric acid		The acid responsible for most of a wine's acidity. Detectable only on the palate. May be added to wines lacking acidity in warm vineyard regions.
Tenuta	**I**	Estate.
Terroir	**F**	A sense of place expressed in a wine, which may include the effects of climate, site climate, soils, aspect, slope, and even local grape varieties, yeast cultures and winemaking practices.
Tertiary aromas		Aromas in a wine that are due to the effects of ageing (q.v. primary, secondary aromas).
Tinto	**P, S**	Red.
Tonneau	**F**	900 litres. A unit of volume used in the Bordeaux trade, equal to 100 cases of twelve 75 cl bottles of wine.
Trellis		Any manmade system of support for the vine, usually consisting of posts and wires.
Tri (pl. Tries)	**F**	A selection of grapes, especially those grapes picked during one passage through a vineyard, selected at the perfect level of ripeness for sweet wines.
Triage	**F**	Process of sorting grapes according to quality before winemaking.
Trocken	**G**	Dry.
Trockenbeerenauslese	**G**	The sweetest category of German quality wine.
Uva	**I**	Grape.
Uvaggio	**I**	Blend of grapes.
Vara y Pulgar	**S**	A system of vine pruning used in Jerez.
Vecchio	**I**	Old. For DOC wines there are controls as to how this word may be used.
Vendange	**F**	The wine harvest.
Vendangé à la main	**F**	Hand-harvested.
Vendange Tardive, VT	**F**	Late-harvest. A wine made with exceptionally ripe grapes.
Vendemmia	**I**	Vintage.
Vendimia	**S**	Vintage.
Véraison	**F**	The moment when a grape begins to change colour.
Vieilles vignes	**F**	Old vines. Not a legally defined term.

Viejo	**S**	Old.
Vigna, vigneto	**I**	Vineyard.
Vignoble	**F**	Vineyard.
Vin	**F**	Wine.
Vin de paille	**F**	Wine made from grapes that have been dried.
Vin de rebéche	**F**	Any juice remaining in the grapes after the extraction of the *taille* (q.v.) in Champagne. It must be distilled and cannot be made into wine.
Viña	**S**	Vineyard.
Vine/grape variety		One of a number of recognisable members of a particular vine species. They may result from natural mutation or deliberate crossing (q.v.).
Vine species		Any of the members of the genus *Vitis*. Most wine is made from European species, *Vitis vinifera*, but using American rootstocks from the species *V. rupestris* or *V. riparia*.
Vinha	**P**	A plot of vines.
Vinho	**P**	Wine.
Vinification		Winemaking.
Vino	**S, I**	Wine.
Vino generoso	**S**	Fortified wine.
Vino novello	**I**	New wine, bottled shortly after the harvest.

Viticoltore, Vignaiolo	**I**	Grower.
Viticulture		Grape growing.
Vitigno	**I**	Grape variety.
Vivace	**I**	'Lively'. Slightly sparkling.
Volatile acidity		Acetic acid (q.v.) in a wine. A small amount exists in all wines and is an important part of the aroma or bouquet. Excessive amounts indicate a faulty wine.
Wash		Any alcoholic liquid resulting from fermentation which is destined to be distilled.
Winzergenossenschaft	**G**	Co-operative cellar.
Wort		The sweet liquid resulting from the extraction of sugar from malt, which is fermented to give wash (q.v.) in whisky production.
Yeast		Generic term for a number of single-celled micro-organisms which produce zymase, the enzyme responsible for converting sugar into alcohol. The most important wine yeast is *Saccharomyces cerevisiae*.
Yeast autolysis		Breakdown of dead yeast cells after the secondary fermentation in sparkling wine production. Among other things, it gives the wine a yeasty, or biscuity, nose.

Index

Numbers in **bold** type indicate significant references.